WORDS ON WORDS

John B. Bremner

MJF BOOKS
NEW YORK

Published by MJF Books
Fine Communications
Two Lincoln Square
60 West 66th Street
New York, NY 10023

Words on Words
ISBN 1-56731-282-9
Library of Congress Card Catalog No. 98-66477

Manufactured in the United States of America on acid-free paper

MJF Books and the MJF colophon are trademarks of Fine Creative Media, Inc.

10   9   8   7   6   5   4   3   2   1

To Mary, whom words cannot describe

INTRODUCTION

WORDS are my professional life. It was nurtured by the study of classical and modern languages, which was part of the characteristic education of my generation, at least in my native Australia. Unfortunately, such education has become uncharacteristic, especially in the United States. I have witnessed the steady growth of literary ignorance during a career of more than a third of a century as a professional journalist, a professor of journalism and a newspaper consultant.

Many of my students arrive in my writing and editing classes as college juniors with an almost total ignorance of English grammar and usage and only a smattering of any foreign language. And these are prospective journalists whom one would expect to be less illiterate. But the blame is hardly theirs. It belongs mostly to their teachers, many of whom either blame their students' previous teachers or pass the buck to later ones. Worse, many teachers of English don't know the grammar of their own language. You can't give what you don't have. Worse yet, many young teachers are being taught not to teach grammar. What used to be the first art of the trivium has become trivial.

Much of the American press and many of the learned journals have been deploring this tragedy for years. But ours is becoming a no-fault society and not much is being done to stay the surge of literary barbarism.

To love anything, you must first know it. To love words, you must first know what they are. Yes, words are symbols of ideas. But many words have lives of their own. They have their own historical and etymological associations, their own romantic and environmental dalliances, their own sonic and visual delights. To teach words and to foster a love of them, I have tried to teach that one must know not only what a word signifies, how it is spelled, how it is pronounced and what part of speech it is, but especially why it is called what it is called. These are the purposes of a dictionary. These, along with discussion of good and bad writing, some verbal gamesmanship and excursions into mythology and literary allusion, are the purposes of this book.

INTRODUCTION

The book stresses the parts of speech, the grammatic sol-fa whose harmony produces the polyphony of syntax. Never, however, is grammar stressed for the sake of "rules." The criteria are order, logic and common sense.

Also stressed is the etymology of our beautiful bastard language, bred from so many other languages, ancient and modern. I do not apologize for this emphasis. I am not a member of what Theodore M. Bernstein, in *Miss Thistlebottom's Hobgoblins*, calls "the OMIOM academy (Original Meaning Is the Only Meaning)." Words do grow from their roots. Some do change their meaning. Words, as Harry G. Nickles says in *The Dictionary of Do's and Don'ts*, are "like hair and toenails"; they "cannot be denied their normal growth, but reason and good taste suggest that they be trimmed before they turn unruly." Knowledge of the etymology of a word will introduce one to the meanings of many similar words, apply reason and good taste to change in meaning, expand vocabulary and develop a command of words to organize and beautify the logic and rhetoric of ideas.

The book is intended not only for journalism students and professional journalists, but also for all others who seek to intensify their love affair with the English language.

My thanks go to my former teachers. I especially thank: Sister Mary Philomena, my elementary school teacher fifty years ago in Brisbane, Australia, who drilled me in grammar and etymology; John Hohenberg, prolific author and former professor in the Graduate School of Journalism, Columbia University, who painstakingly tried to transform a propagandist into a reporter; Lewis Jordan, former news editor of the *New York Times*, who launched me into a career in editing; and Arthur M. Barnes, my doctoral chairman in the School of Journalism, University of Iowa, who introduced me to sane professional research.

I thank my colleagues at the University of Kansas, particularly Edward P. Bassett, former dean, Del Brinkman, present dean, and Professor Calder M. Pickett, all of whom encouraged me to undertake this work, part of the research for which was done during a sabbatical leave from the university.

I am most grateful to Oscar S. Stauffer, chairman of Stauffer Communications, Inc., whose generous endowment of the Stauffer Chair has enabled me to continue as a professor at Kansas.

I thank Joan McQuary, managing editor of Columbia University Press, who loves editing professors and at least one Editing professor.

I thank all others who have helped me, especially my students, who have been my crown and my cross, my joy and my sometimes tender torment.

Works quoted more than once in the book are usually referred to by an abbreviated title or name. They are:

American Heritage	William Morris, ed., *The American Heritage Dictionary of the English Language.* New York: American Heritage and Houghton Mifflin, 1969.
AP	Howard Angione, ed., *The Associated Press Stylebook and Libel Manual.* New York: The Associated Press, 1977.
Barzun	Jacques Barzun, *Simple & Direct.* New York: Harper & Row, 1975.
Bernstein	Theodore M. Bernstein, *The Careful Writer.* New York: Atheneum, 1965.
Dictionary of Proper Names	Geoffrey Payton, ed., *The Merriam-Webster Pocket Dictionary of Proper Names.* New York: Pocket Books, 1972.
Espy	Willard R. Espy, *An Almanac of Words at Play.* New York: Clarkson N. Potter, 1975.
Evans	Bergen Evans and Cornelia Evans, *A Dictionary of Contemporary American Usage.* New York: Random House, 1957.
Fowler	H. W. Fowler, *A Dictionary of Modern English Usage.* New

York: Oxford University Press, 1965.

Hohenberg — John Hohenberg, *The Professional Journalist*. 4th ed. New York: Holt, Rinehart and Winston, 1978.

HTK — John B. Bremner, *HTK: A Study in News Headlines*. Topeka, Kan.: Palindrome Press, Mainline Printing, 1975.

Jacobs — Noah Jonathan Jacobs, *Naming-Day in Eden*. New York: Macmillan, 1958.

Macdonald — Dwight Macdonald, *The String Untuned*. Washington: Council for Basic Education, 1962.

Mencken — H. L. Mencken, *The American Language*. New York: Knopf, 1937, 1945, 1962.

Moore — John Moore, *You English Words*. London: Collins, 1961.

Morris — William Morris and Mary Morris, *Morris Dictionary of Word and Phrase Origins*. New York: Harper & Row, 1977.

Morsberger — Robert E. Morsberger, *Commonsense Grammar and Style*. New York: Crowell, 1972.

Newman — Edwin Newman, *Strictly Speaking*. Indianapolis: Bobbs-Merrill, 1974.

Nickles — Harry G. Nickles, *The Dictionary of Do's and Don'ts*. New York: McGraw-Hill, 1974.

Nurnberg — Maxwell Nurnberg, *Punctuation Pointers*. New York: Scholastic Book Services, 1968.

O'London — John O'London, *Is It Good English?* London: George Newnes, 1924.

Opdycke	John B. Opdycke, *Harper's English Grammar*. New York: Harper & Row, 1966.
Partridge	Eric Partridge, *A Dictionary of Slang and Unconventional English*. New York: Macmillan, 1970.
Shaw	Harry Shaw, *Dictionary of Problem Words and Expressions*. New York: McGraw-Hill, 1975.
Shipley	Joseph T. Shipley, *Dictionary of Word Origins*. New York: Philosophical Library, 1945.
Strunk	William Strunk, Jr., and E. B. White, *The Elements of Style*. 3d ed. New York: Macmillan, 1979.
Webster	*Webster's New International Dictionary*. 2d ed. Springfield, Mass.: G. & C. Merriam, 1959.

Other works mentioned are: W. H. Auden, *Academic Graffiti* (London: Faber, 1971); Jacques Barzun, *On Writing, Editing, and Publishing* (Chicago: University of Chicago Press, 1971); Floyd K. Baskette and Jack Z. Sissors, *The Art of Editing* (New York: Macmillan, 1977); Edmund Clerihew Bentley, *Biography for Beginners* (London: T. W. Laurie, 1925); Edmund Clerihew Bentley, *Clerihews Complete* (London: T. W. Laurie, 1951); Theodore M. Bernstein, *Miss Thistlebottom's Hobgoblins* (New York: Farrar, Straus and Giroux, 1971); Theodore M. Bernstein, *Watch Your Language* (Great Neck, N.Y.: Channel Press, 1958); Ambrose Bierce, *The Devil's Dictionary* (New York: Dover, 1958); William F. Buckley, Jr., *Inveighing We Will Go* (New York: Putnam, 1972); G. K. Chesterton, *The Thing* (New York: Dodd, Mead, 1930); John Ciardi, *Someone Could Win a Polar Bear* (Philadelphia: Lippincott, 1970); Robert E. Garst and Theodore M. Bernstein, *Headlines and Deadlines* (New York: Columbia University Press, 1961); Stella Gibbons, *Cold Comfort Farm* (London: Longmans, Green, 1934); James D. Koerner, *The Miseducation of American Teachers* (Boston: Houghton, 1963); Ring Lardner,

INTRODUCTION

The Young Immigrunts (Indianapolis: Bobbs-Merrill, 1920); Afferbeck Lauder, *Let Stalk Strine* (Sydney: Ure Smith, 1965); A. J. Liebling, *The Press* (New York: Ballantine Books, 1961); James Lipton, *An Exaltation of Larks* (New York: Grossman, 1968); Don Marquis, *archy and mehitabel* (Garden City, N.Y.: Doubleday, Doran, 1928); Margaret Nicholson, *A Dictionary of American-English Usage* (New York: New American Library, 1958); Richard O'Connor, *Heywood Broun* (New York: Putnam, 1975); George Orwell, *Politics and the English Language* (Evansville, Ind.: Herbert W. Simpson, 1947); Mario Pei, *Words in Sheep's Clothing* (New York: Hawthorn Books, 1969); Laurence J. Peter and Raymond Hull, *The Peter Principle* (New York: Bantam Books, 1970); Earle Tempel, *Humor in the Headlines* (New York: Pocket Books, 1969); Kate L. Turabian, *A Manual for Writers of Term Papers, Theses, and Dissertations* (Chicago: University of Chicago Press, 1955); Bill Vaughan, *Bird Thou Never Wert* (New York: Simon and Schuster, 1962); Bill Vaughan, *Half the Battle* (New York: Simon and Schuster, 1967); Bill Vaughan, *Sorry I Stirred It* (New York: Simon and Schuster, 1964); Evelyn Waugh, *The Loved One* (London: Chapman and Hall, 1948); *Winners & Sinners*, New York Times.

John B. Bremner

Lawrence, Kansas, January 1980

A/AN, *see* **ARTICLE: A; AN; THE**

ABBREVIATION
Political and educational institutions and other bureaucracies tend to spawn shoals of organizations and agencies and boards and commissions and committees and task forces, and each has an abbreviation or acronym (see ACRO-), leaving readers up to their gills in a sea of alphabet soup.

AP has good advice about the use of abbreviations: "Do not follow an organization's full name with an abbreviation or acronym in parentheses or set off by dashes. If an abbreviation or acronym would not be clear on second reference without this arrangement, do not use it. Names not commonly before the public should not be reduced to acronyms solely to save a few words."

So use only those abbreviations you can reasonably expect will be well known to your readers.

The same principles apply to headlines, which are supposed to be clear. As clear as calculus in kindergarten is this kind of acronymic jabberwock: "ARD Asks KUEPC / To OK SUA, UDK." Similarly, readers of a headline calling for the foundation of an SPSD were forced to get into the story to find out about the Society for the Prevention of Senile Delinquency. But here's a beautiful abbreviation in a head over a World War II story: "Grapes of RAF in Berlin."

ABDOMEN
Except in a clinical context, *abdomen* is a nice-nelly word for BELLY.

ABECEDARIAN
A felicitous word. It comes from the first four letters of the alphabet. By extension, *abecedarian* has come to mean one who is either learning or teaching the elements of any subject. Originally, it was used of one who was either learning or teaching the alphabet.

ABJURE / ADJURE
From Latin *ab* + *jurare*, to swear from, *abjure* means to renounce, to repudiate, as in "He abjured his boyhood beliefs." From *ad* + *jurare*, to swear to, *adjure* means to appeal to solemnly, to entreat earnestly, as in "I adjure you, O daughters of Jerusalem, if you find my beloved, that you tell him that I languish with love" (Song of Solomon).

ABLATIVE ABSOLUTE
A term from Latin grammar. Another term for it is absolute construction. It refers to a phrase that contains a noun (or a pronoun) that governs a participle and is grammatically independent of the rest of the sentence: "The course being wet, officials stopped play."

Distinguish this from the barbarous construction called the dangling participle: "Swimming in strong surf, her bikini fell off." Here the phrase *swimming in strong surf* is not grammatically independent of the rest of the sentence; the participle belongs to the subject of the clause, *bikini*. The sentence says that her bikini, not she, was swimming.

The ablative absolute is grammatical; the dangling participle isn't. The ablative absolute, however, is a weak construction because participles often are wishy-washy words. Try to use finite verbs: "Because the course was wet, officials stopped play."

ABNORMAL
From Latin *ab* + *norma*, away from the norm or rule, *abnormal* embraces both *subnormal*, below the norm, and *supernormal*, above the norm.

ABOLISHMENT
An affectation due for abolition.

ABOUT
A handy word in the adverbial sense of *approximately*. It's shorter than *approximately*, it's Anglo-Saxon and it's grammatically purer than *some*, which has crept into newspaper jargon as an adverb. Say "about three hundred people," not "some three hundred people." But watch redundancy: "I'll see you at about 3 or 4 o'clock" (*3 or 4* is already an approximation); "The attendance was estimated at about 50,000" (*about* is already an estimate; so is a round number). And because *about* signifies approximation, don't use it with an exact figure.

About, in the prepositional sense of *concerning*, is again a handy word. It's preferable to the tag Latin of *re* and *in re*, the affectation of ANENT, the faddish bureaucratic jargon of *vis-à-vis*, the windiness of *appertaining to, relative to, relevant to, in regard to, in respect of, with reference to* and other such circumlocutions.

ABOVE-MENTIONED
Words such as *above-mentioned, above-named, above-cited, aforesaid, aforementioned* are often examples of signpost writing. The more cluttered a territory, the more it needs signposts. The more cluttered your writing, the more it needs signposts. Unclutter. Don't force your reader to backtrack to find out what *above-mentioned* refers to. If, for the sake of clarity, you want to repeat a word or a name, repeat it. The same goes for signposts such as *former* and *latter*.

ABOVE THE SALT
Mencken loved this phrase to the point of boredom. In medieval England, the position of the *saler*, or salt cellar, on the table separated the more honored guests from the less honored. The host sat above the salt. Those who sat close to the host's end of the table were above the salt and were the more honored.

ABRIDGMENT
The American tendency is to drop the *e* after *dg* before *m*, as in *acknowledgment* and *judgment*.

ABROGATE / ARROGATE
From Latin *ab + rogare*, to seek to get away from something, *abrogate* means to annul or repeal. From *ad + rogare*, to seek to get to something, *arrogate* means to assume title or authority, usually presumptuously, hence *arrogantly*.

ABSOLUTE CONSTRUCTION, *see* ABLATIVE ABSOLUTE

ABSTEMIOUS / FACETIOUS
The meanings of *abstemious* and *facetious* have nothing in common. From Latin *temetum*, liquor, *abstemious* means eating and drinking in moderation; from Latin *facetus*, elegant, fine, *facetious* means slyly witty, flippant.

But an old intelligence test had this question: "Do you notice anything in common to *abstemious* and *facetious* and to no other word in the English language?" The answer sought was that these were the only English words that had all the vowels in alphabetical order. One student, perhaps because he flunked the question, couldn't believe the answer.

After valiant research he unearthed another such word, *arsenious*, containing arsenic.

ABSTRACT / CONCRETE

Words convey ideas. Foggy words convey foggy ideas. Foggy ideas come from a foggy mind. Even the loftiest abstractions can be explained by concrete examples of persons, places and things. The point is concretely illustrated by George Orwell's famous version (in *Politics and the English Language*) of this passage from Ecclesiastes:

"I returned, and saw under the sun, that the race is not to the swift, nor the battle to the strong, neither yet bread to the wise, nor yet riches to men of understanding, nor yet favor to men of skill; but time and chance happeneth to them all."

Orwell wrote: "Objective consideration of contemporary phenomena compels the conclusion that success or failure in competitive activities exhibits no tendency to be commensurate with innate capacity, but that a considerable element of the unpredictable must inevitably be taken into account."

A Chrysler spokesman announced recently: "The corporation is endeavoring to optimize the structural integrity of the vehicle." He meant: "We are trying to make the car as safe as possible."

ACADEMY

Datelined Athens, a brief Associated Press story in the fall of 1976 reported that Plato's tree had been destroyed by a bus. There wasn't much more to the story. The species of tree wasn't identified. Nor was the bus. It may have been a school bus seeking revenge for what had happened to education since Plato sat under his tree in the grove of Akademeia, named after Akademos, a farmer who directed Castor and Pollux to a grove where they found their abducted sister, Helen.

Whatever about the myth, the fact is that *academy* comes from Akademeia by way of Akademos and has become a generic term for a society of scholars. The word will forever be associated with Plato, to whom apology is due for what passes for scholarship in some modern academies.

To be deplored is the use of *academic* in the sense of impractical or fruitlessly argumentative, as in "The question is academic."

Sic transit gloria Platonis.

P.S. Exactly a year after the reported destruction of Plato's tree, the Associated Press identified it as an olive and quoted a Greek archeologist as saying, "Plato's tree has taken root again." May it be universally transplanted.

A CAPPELLA
Note the spelling: double *p* and double *l*. From the Italian word for chapel. Singing without instrumental accompaniment.

ACCEDE
Note the similar spelling of *accede, antecede, cede, concede, precede, recede, secede,* but the different spelling of *exceed, proceed, succeed.* Though the spellings differ, all derive from Latin *cedere,* to go.

Comes then the tricky *supersede,* from *sedere,* to sit, hence to sit above.

The informal *emceed* is a BACK FORMATION from the abbreviation of master of ceremonies.

• ACCESSIONED
Librarians used to say they acquired or added a book. Then Melvil Dewey, inventor of the Dewey decimal system for classification of publications, verbed a noun and said that a book was *accessioned* to a library. The use caught on and books are now *accessioned,* in the sense of "recorded as acquired."

ACCIDENTALLY
Commonly misspelled *accidently.*

ACCOMMODATION
Vacationing copy editors squirm when they see billboards advertising motel "accomodation." The pikers won't stay there. If there's no room for an em, they figure, it's no place for a pica. So they see whether there's room for 'em in an inn, which has two ens, which all crossword buffs know add up to an em, which *accommodation* should have two of.

ACCORDING TO
A legitimate form of attribution. "The city is going broke, according to the mayor" has the same meaning as "The city is going broke, the mayor said."

In reporting, *according to* carries no connotation of doubt or suspicion. But don't overdo it.

There's one difference, however, between *according to* and an attribution in the past tense like *he said*. When *according to* comes at the beginning of a sentence, the tenses are the same as those used by the speaker: "According to the mayor, the city is going broke and will soon be bankrupt." But when *he said* comes at the beginning, the tenses follow the principles of the sequence of tenses: "The mayor said the city was going broke and would soon be bankrupt." See SEQUENCE OF TENSES.

ACCORDION
Like UKULELE, the name of this musical instrument is frequently misspelled. The ending is *ion*, as in *clarion*, not *ian*. The word comes from Latin *ad* + *cor* (genitive *cordis*), to the heart, hence accord, harmony.

ACCOST
From Latin *costa*, a rib or side, *accost* means to come near the ribs, to sidle up to, hence its appropriateness in the sense of sexual solicitation.

ACCURACY
The word comes from Latin *curare*, to take care. For reporters and editors, accuracy is more than a virtue. Like fairness and honesty, it's a duty. Get your information right and write it right. Be accurate. Take care.

ACCUSED
An *accused* man is a man. So an *accused* murderer is a murderer. Yet he isn't legally a murderer if he has been merely accused, not convicted. Reporters should watch their terminology. Say "the suspect" or "the accused" or "the defendant." See also ALLEGED.

ACE
It's a good word for a hole-in-one, an untouched serve that wins a point, a pilot who has downed more than five enemy planes. But as a word for a great reporter, *ace* smacks of a comic strip.

ACHILLES' HEEL
Achilles' heel is not to be confused with *Achilles' tendon*, though the phrases derive from the same myth, namely, that Achilles' mother tipped him upside down and dipped him in the River Styx to make him invulnerable, but the heel she held him by stayed dry and was his downfall when it was pierced by Paris' arrow. Your *Achilles' heel* is your weak

spot, figuratively. Your *Achilles' tendon* is the strong tendon that runs from the calf muscle to the heel bone, which for Achilles was one of them dry bones.

ACID TEST
A cliché for a moment of crisis. It comes from the test administered to metal thought to be gold, which resists corrosion from acids that corrode other metals.

ACKNOWLEDGMENT, *see* ABRIDGMENT

ACOUSTICS
Are nouns ending in *-ics* singular or plural? The question is discussed under -ICS. Though the answer isn't always simple, the American Heritage makes a clear distinction for *acoustics:* singular for "the scientific study of sound"; plural for "the total effect of sound." Thus: "Acoustics involves experimentation with sound"; "The acoustics in many old newsrooms are abominable."

ACRO–
Many English words derive from Greek *akros*, highest, extreme. Among them:
   —*acrobat*, high goer, one who walks on tiptoe.
   —*acronym*, high name, for words formed from the first letters of a name, such as *CREEP* (Committee for the Re-Election of the President); or from the first letters of several words, such as *Wasp* (white Anglo-Saxon Protestant); or from parts of a series of words, such as *sonar* (sound navigation ranging).
   —*acrophobia*, fear of heights.
   —*acropolis*, high city, the fortified height of a city, especially Athens.
   —*acrostic*, high line or row, referring to a series of lines whose first letters form a name or a sentence.

ACROST
A barbaric pronunciation of *across*.

ACTIVE VOICE / PASSIVE VOICE
Voice, in Opdycke's definition, is "that inflection of a verb that shows whether its subject is the doer of the action indicated or is acted upon."

If the subject performs the action, the verb is in the active voice. If the subject is acted upon, the verb is in the passive voice.

Active voice is dynamic. Passive voice is static. Active voice is vigorous voice, unashamed to say whodunit. Passive voice is preferred by the weak, the cowardly, ashamed to name the fink who told them what they are evasively telling you. Active voice is the voice of a Zola, a John the Baptist. Passive voice is the voice of diplomacy, of international chanceries, both civil and ecclesiastic.

When you have a choice, choose active. This is particularly important in headlines. Because good heads vigorously try to tell the "who" of a story and tell it quickly, good heads try to use active voice. "Ford Is Beaten by Carter" has neither the speed nor the action of "Carter Beats Ford."

Sometimes, however, action has to give way to speed when the "whom" of a story is more important than the "who," when the "whom" is really the "who." For example, this head is in the active voice but it is slow in telling the most important part of the story: "Plane Crash Kills / 4 Cabinet Members." Switch the head to passive voice to get to the most important part of the story fast: "4 Cabinet Members / Killed in Plane Crash."

Decide which is more important: who did it or whom it was done to.

ACTIVITY

An overworked word, usually redundant. Newman gives some sad examples of this kind of verbosity. He describes the newscaster who asked the weathercaster whether there would be "more major thunderstorm activity." Thunderstorms have become thunderstorm activity, and showers have become shower activity. The reason, Newman says, is "the national affection for unnecessary word activity."

In athletic crises, benches and bullpens are hives of activity. Ogden Nash created a relief pitcher named MacTivity to enliven the breathtaking announcement: "There is MacTivity in the bullpen."

ACTUALLY

The word has its legitimate uses in emphasizing wonderment ("Did he actually drink a dozen double martinis?") but it has become almost meaningless through mindless overuse ("Actually, I enjoy Christmas") or mindful affectation ("Actually, I went to Harvard"). It is beloved of phony Anglophiles, who use it at the drop of a commonplace and pronounce it *eckshully*.

Still, *actually* is easier on the nerves than YUNNO.

AD

Though some dictionaries still consider *ad* colloquial and informal as an abbreviation for advertisement or advertising, the word has passed into standard usage and is here to stay.

'Twas not ever thus. Mencken, never a lover of admen, traced the history of *ad* and said: "The American advertising man, in the glorious days when the more forward-looking of them hoped to lift their art and mystery to the level of dogmatic theology, astronomy, ophthalmology and military science, carried on a crusade against the clipped form *ad*, but it came, alas, to nothing."

That was in 1945. Today, *ad* is solidly entrenched as acceptable usage, especially in *want ad*. American admen should have no qualms about *ad*. They are not squeamish in coining words, some of which survive and some of which don't.

A.D.

In informal usage, the American Heritage allows *A.D.* after a year number, as in "Augustus died 14 A.D." Strictly, this doesn't read right because *A.D.* is the abbreviation for *anno Domini*, in the year of the Lord. So *14 A.D.* would mean "14 in the year of the Lord." Better: *A.D. 14*.

But don't say, "Augustus died *in* A.D. 14," which would be the same as saying, "Augustus died in in the year of the Lord 14." And don't use *A.D.* with century, as in "the 2d century A.D.," which would mean "the 2d century in the century in the year of the Lord."

14 B.C. makes sense: the fourteenth year before Christ.

You can easily avoid the issue if you never use *A.D.* Assume that a year is after Christ unless it is followed by *B.C.*

ADAGE

An *adage* isn't an *adage* unless it's old. So "an old adage" is redundant. Worse is the phrase "as the old adage says" (even worse is "as the old adage hath it"). If you want to use an *adage*, don't say that what you're about to say is an *adage*. Just go ahead and use it. Don't apologize for using it by prefacing it with an announcement to your reader or listener that he shouldn't think you don't know an *adage* when you see one. See also CLICHÉ.

ADDED

As a verb of attribution, *added* is not a synonym for *said*. Try to restrict the use of *added* to something mentioned incidentally, an afterthought, not part of the running theme of a story or discourse. *Added* is an "Oh, by the way" verb, as in: "The patrolman thanked the driver for his aid in identifying the getaway car. 'Oh, by the way,' he added, 'I'm booking you for defective headlights.'"

Above all, abandon the tiresome sequence of *said, continued, added.* Some beginning writers, and some hacks, think attribution calls for *said* first, *continued* second, *added* third, to be repeated in that order throughout a story, with an occasional *explained*, down to a triumphant *concluded*. See SYNONYMOMANIA.

ADDER

The root is Anglo-Saxon *naedre*, snake. From *naedre* came *nadder*. A *nadder* became *an adder*.

Such erroneous division is responsible for other words in our language: *a napron* became *an apron; a nauger* became *an auger; a numpire* (from *non-per*, not one of a pair, hence, supposedly, an impartial judge) became *an umpire.*

In reverse, *an ewt* became *a newt;* and *an ekename*, an extra (eke) name, became *a nickname.*

ADEQUATE ENOUGH

Adequate is enough. Enough is adequate. Enough is enough.

AD HOC

A Latin tag, literally "toward this," *ad hoc* means "arranged for a special purpose," as in: an ad hoc committee, a temporary committee formed to report on something specific; ad hoc membership in the graduate faculty, a temporary appointment for the sake of a particular graduate course or thesis.

The phrase is not a verb, despite a cabinet officer's statement to Congress: "One cannot ad hoc tax reform." Good grief! Newman's comment on this bureaucratese was: "He might have added that there are no bargains at ad hoc shops." And don't ad hoc to red meat.

ADIT

Just as *exit* comes from Latin *exire*, to go out, *adit* comes from Latin *adire*, to go in. Except as a mining term for a nearly horizontal entrance, *adit* is now rarely used for entrance. It should be. It balances *exit*, it is shorter for signs and it appears in many crossword puzzles.

ADJECTIVE / ADVERB

To learn the difference between an adjective and an adverb is perhaps too much to expect of those whose gods are jocks and whose oracles sports announcers. If "he throws the ball real good" is really good enough for coaches and sportscasters, the message comes through really well enough for the fans, but surely not for reporters and copy editors. *Real* is an adjective; *really* is an adverb.

Adjectives qualify nouns ("an old tree") and pronouns ("He is old"). Adverbs modify verbs ("She drives skillfully"), adjectives ("Her driving is really skillful") and other adverbs ("She drives extremely well").

Note, however, a different usage with copulative (linking) verbs. Copulative verbs, as their name implies, merely join. They join subject and predicate. They are static, not dynamic. The most common copulative verb is "to be." Other verbs frequently used copulatively are: *appear, become, feel, look, seem, smell, taste.* (For a complete list of copulative verbs, see Opdycke.)

Copulative verbs take adjectives, not adverbs: "I am bad," not "I am badly." But note the difference between the copulative and dynamic uses of verbs of sense like *feel* and *smell.* "I smell bad" means I need a bath. "I smell badly" means that something is wrong with my nose. The most common misuse is with *feel.* When you're unhappy, you're feeling bad, not badly. You feel badly when something is wrong with your sense of touch.

Do you drive slow or slowly? Preferably slowly, but *slow* can be used as an adverb. Barzun gives a rather complicated principle: "In general, if the mode or manner signified by the adverb can be attributed to the result of the action as well as to the process, the shorter form is the more idiomatic." His examples are clearer: "Thus one *stands high* on the list, *drinks deep* from the stream, *flies low* over the trees, and so on." When in doubt, let your attuned idiomatic ear be your guide.

ADJURE, *see* ABJURE / ADJURE

ADMIT

In the sense of *confess* or *acknowledge*, don't *admit to* something. You admit your ignorance of idiom when you say, "I admit to my ignorance." Similarly, you admit having seen someone, not *to* having seen someone. You, because you are a person and not an abstraction, never admit *of.* A question, which is an abstraction, "admits of (leaves room for) several answers."

AD NAUSEAM
Meaning "to the point of nausea," *ad nauseam* is commonly misspelled *ad nauseum* to the point of nausea. See also NAUSEATED / NAUSEOUS.

ADULT / ADULTERY
The words have different derivations. *Adult* comes from Latin *ad* + *alescere*, to grow up. *Adultery* comes from Latin *ad* + *alter*, towards another, towards a different thing or person.

ADUMBRATE
You may prefer the Anglo-Saxon *foreshadow*. But recognize the root of *adumbrate* as Latin *umbra*, shade, shadow, and see the same root in other shady, shadowy words, such as *somber*, *sombrero*, *umbrage*, *umbrella*.

ADVANCE PLANNING
Have you planned backward lately?

ADVERB, *see* ADJECTIVE / ADVERB

ADVERSE / AVERSE
Both words connote opposition. Use *averse* when the subject is reluctant, disinclined ("Some instructors are averse to giving high grades"), and *adverse* when the opposition is hostile, contrary to the desires of the subject ("Most students have an adverse opinion of instructors who grade low").

ADVISER / ADVISOR
Each spelling is acceptable, but dictionaries and stylebooks tend to prefer *adviser*, which is also the more common form in political and educational reference. At any rate, be consistent.

AFFABLE *see* INEFFABLE

AFFECT / EFFECT
The distinction between these words is a stumbling block for many writers. It shouldn't be. To *affect* is to influence, to bring about a change in ("Too much liquor affects your health"). To *effect* is to produce, to make happen ("Too much liquor effected his downfall").

Effect is also a noun ("Too much liquor has a bad effect on you").

Affect is a noun only in psychological terminology, meaning a feeling or emotion.

A metropolitan newspaper recently had this sentence in a story about interstate highways: "The commissioners noted how an I-70 exit to Hays effected that city." This is an apt example of the wrong use of *effected*. The exit didn't produce the city, didn't bring it into being. The exit influenced the city's trade, brought about a change in the number of visitors. The exit *affected* the city.

He affected you. He influenced you. He effected a masterpiece. He produced a masterpiece. The masterpiece had a big effect on his career.

On the back of the driver's license in a Midwestern state appears this statement: "I hereby make anatomical gift to take affect upon my death." Such bureaucratic illiteracy is enough to make anyone give up all his intellectual and anatomical gifts and the ghost.

AFFINITY
The original meaning of *affinity* was relationship by marriage, as distinct from *consanguinity*, relationship by blood. The root is Latin *ad + finis*, near the border, neighboring.

AFGHANISTANISM
A newspaper term that describes the sad propensity of some editorial writers and columnists to pontificate about topics far removed from the interests of their readers. The editorialists thus run little chance of controversy or contradiction. Meanwhile, local problems scream for attention.

Afghanistanism also describes the attitude of news editors who prefer frothy features to investigatory stories of community involvement. Some news editors send reporter-photographer teams to cover juicy crimes across country but refuse to look out their own windows to see what's going on in their own ghettos and find out why.

P.S. In the winter of 1980, Afghanistan became a topic very close to the interests of readers. Perhaps *Afghanistanism*, as a term for esoteric pontification, will have to be changed to something less exoteric, such as Chadism or Liechtensteinism.

AFORESAID, *see* ABOVE-MENTIONED

AFRAID
Try to avoid *afraid* unless the context calls for fear, fright, terror, alarm. Don't use it casually, as in "I'm afraid not" or "I'm afraid I disagree with you" or "I'm afraid we have a previous engagement." Why not "I'm sorry

I have bad news for you," rather than "I'm afraid I have bad news for you"?

Afraid is one of Bernstein's "atomic flyswatters," powerful words that convey quite moderate meanings, like sending men on boys' errands or, in one of today's vogue words, overkill.

Here are other such adjectives (add their adverbs): *amazing, awful, divine, dreadful, earthshaking, enormous, fabulous, fantastic, frightful, gorgeous, horrible, mad, petrified, sensational, stupendous, super, terrible, terrific, tremendous, unbelievable, wonderful.*

AFTER

The comparative form of Anglo-Saxon *af*, meaning "off, away," was *after*, "more off, more away." *After* is a good word, better than *following* or *subsequent to*.

Its opposite, *before*, is another good word, much better than *prior to*. If you don't use *posterior to*, why use *prior to*? Would you say, "Posterior to the game, we had a few drinks"? So why say, "Prior to the game, we had a few drinks"? Make it: "Before and after (and even during) the game, we had a few drinks."

● AFTERMATH

The word comes from Anglo-Saxon *math*, which means "mowing." (This has nothing to do with the root of *mathematics*, which is Greek *manthanein*, to learn.) An *aftermath* was a second mowing, a gathering of hay for the second time. It has lost this literal agricultural meaning but it still means a figurative second harvest, a consequence or result, especially a disastrous result of a disastrous event. Fire may be an aftermath of an airplane crash. Disease may be an aftermath of debauchery.

But don't use *aftermath* to describe something that merely follows something else, as in "A reception for the musicians will be an aftermath of the concert."

AGAPE

Some modern versions of the ancient Christian love feast would leave ancient Christians agape at the agape. Today's orgies are what sociologists call "sexual educational group dynamics."

AGENDA

Originally, the word was a Latin plural (things to be done). Today, the usage is singular: "The agenda for the meeting is already overloaded." Originally, the singular was *agendum*, a word now rarely used. Today, *agendum* has become "an item on the agenda" or "an agenda item." *Agendas* is gaining ground as the plural of *agenda*.

✦ AGGRAVATE

The word is not a synonym for *annoy*. To *aggravate*, from Latin *ad* + *gravare*, to make more grave or more heavy, means to make something bad worse. Its use for *annoy* is rated informal by the American Heritage. You aggravate something. You annoy someone. ("He aggravated his cold by getting his feet wet. This annoyed him.")

AGGRESSIVE

Note the spelling: double *g*.

AGLEY

A fine Scottish word from *gley*, to squint, hence askew or awry, as in Burns' "To a Mouse": "The best laid schemes o' mice an' men / Gang aft a-gley."

AGNOSTIC

Although some young people profess to be atheists, they are neither intelligent enough nor experienced enough to have reached so final a conclusion of dogmatic arrogance. If they don't believe in God but don't know enough to deny the possibility of His existence, they could call themselves agnostics.

Paul saw an altar in Athens inscribed *Agnosto Theo*, "To the Unknown God." The English word *agnostic* was coined in 1869 by Thomas Huxley, English biologist and grandfather of Julian and Aldous. A strong evolutionist at the height of the Darwinian controversy, Huxley vigorously objected to his opponents' calling him an atheist, which he wasn't. So he invented *agnostic*, which, says Moore, "offers a refuge for the humble honest doubter, halfway between the dogmatism of the churches and the arrogance of the materialists."

AGOG

The word is appropriate to describe the prose of reporters who write falsely ecstatic leads such as "All Rome was agog tonight as Jackie O and Prince Charles reunited" or "All Tampa Bay was agog today as the moment of truth arrived for Super Bowl CXVI" (and note the *as* clause, illegitimate offspring of the old "as thousands cheered" school of gee-whizbang reporters).

Agog is from Old French *en gogues*, "in merriments." Save it for occasions less mundane than spectacles of brute prowess, whether sexual or sportive.

AGONY COLUMN

The phrase, originally British, refers to the classified advertising section, usually labeled "Personal," in which messages appear for missing relatives or friends. In college publications, these are often gags and should be screened by the advertising acceptability department lest there be vindictive hurt or defamation. Indeed, in these early days of typesetting by impersonal computer, experience has already taught some publishers legal lessons in guarding against unauthorized insertion of scurrilous ads.

AGORAPHOBIA *see* –PHOBIA

AGREEMENT OF SUBJECT AND PREDICATE

Singular-plural inconsistency is probably the most common error in print and broadcasting. The problem usually arises with collective nouns, which may be treated either as singular or as plural, but not as both singular and plural in the same sentence. For example, in "Montgomery Ward is opening their new store today," the writer has decided that his subject is singular and so he uses a singular verb but then he forgets (or is ignorant) and uses a plural pronoun to refer to a singular subject.

Listen to enough broadcasting, especially commercials, and you'll begin muttering, and end screaming, "Oh, does they?" and "Oh, do he?"

British usage tends to treat collectives as plural: "The government are expected to raise taxes"; "Arsenal have been losing lately." American tendency is singular: "The state legislature is cutting down on appropriations for higher education"; "Missouri has lost three games in a row."

American tendency, however, is to be inconsistent within the same sentence: "The government is expected to lower taxes because they think this will encourage spending"; "Missouri has lost their quarterback."

The solution is to make up your mind whether the collective is singular or plural and then be consistent.

See also ANTECEDENT.

AHOLD

Except as an illiterate provincialism, there's no such word. In the sense of "grasp," you get hold of something, or "a hold," but not "ahold." Idiomatically, in the sense of "get in touch with," you get hold of someone, not "ahold."

AILUROPHOBIA, *see* -PHOBIA

AIN'T
Originally a contraction of "am not," *ain't* has extended in illiterate speech to mean "is not," "are not," "has not," "have not." The American Heritage calls the usage nonstandard, Evans calls it unacceptable, and Fowler calls it an uneducated blunder. All these authorities, however, have reservations about universal condemnation of the first person singular interrogative form *ain't I* as a contraction for *am I not*. Nevertheless, one should hesitate to use it. *Ain't I* once may have been grammatical, but time has driven it from educated speech and writing, except as a deliberate colloquialism. For further discussion, see AREN'T I.

À LA
The author of *HTK* berated a newspaper for having used *à la* with a noun of masculine gender, *à la bourgeois*. He should have known that though French *à la* is feminine, it is used as an abbreviation of *à la mode de* (in the manner of) and agrees with *mode*, which is feminine. *Mode de* is omitted in phrases such as *à la Bella Abzug* or *à la Barbra Streisand* and *à la* (not *au*) *Nixon* and *à la* (not *au*) *Carter* (not to be confused with *à la carte*—see TABLE D'HÔTE). Chicken à la King is not necessarily a regal dish; it is named for the chef who first concocted it.

ALABAMIAN
Inhabitants of Alabama prefer *Alabamian*, with an *i*. Similarly, *Indianian*, for an inhabitant of Indiana (or duck the issue and use *Hoosier*).

⬧ ALAS
When someone says "Alas," you can bet evens he's going to add "poor Yorick." And you can bet odds on his adding "I knew him well." As he took the skull of Yorick, the king's jester, from the clown in the churchyard, Hamlet said: "Alas, poor Yorick! I knew him, Horatio."

Alas is from Latin *lassus*, weary, hence regretful, pitying. Wearying, indeed, is this threadbare quotation.

ALCOHOL
Not all *alcohol* is eyewash, but it used to be. *Al-kohl* is Arabic for the powder with which Arab girls paint their eyes. Antimony is heated and vaporized to produce a black powder that acts as a stain. Wine, when heated, produces a vapor that cools into an essence, a spirit. Because the processes are similar, the word for eye powder, *al-kohl*, became the word

for spirit of wine, *alcohol*. In its adjectival form, it is frequently misspelled *alcholic*.

ALEXANDER

One of the more potent alcoholic mixtures is an Alexander, made from brandy (or gin), crème de cacao and sweet cream. From Greek *alexein*, to defend, and *andros*, of man, came *Alexandros*, defender of men. Perhaps the potion was so named because only somebody with the guts of Alexander the Great could defend his stomach against so lethal a weapon. See also ROB ROY.

✦ ALGER, HORATIO

Horatio Alger was the name of the author (1834–99), not the name of one of his characters, none of whom, incidentally, became a millionaire. They usually rose from rags to respectability, not riches, by pursuing the path of righteousness.

ALGONQUIN ROUND TABLE

The name of the informal luncheon club at the Algonquin Hotel in New York during the Jazz Age. Among its members, mostly literary or theatrical figures, were Franklin P. Adams, Alexander Woollcott. Heywood Broun, Harold Ross, Marc Connelly, George S. Kaufman, Dorothy Parker, Robert Benchley, Edna Ferber, Tallulah Bankhead, Harpo Marx (but not his brothers). This mutual admiration society is amusingly analyzed in the chapter "We Charming Few" in Richard O'Connor's *Heywood Broun*, biography of the founder of the American Newspaper Guild, now the Newspaper Guild.

ALIAS

From the Latin adverb *alias*, otherwise, its adverbial form is short for *alias dictus*, otherwise called. As an English noun, an *alias* is another name, an assumed name.

ALIBI

From the Latin adverb *alibi*, elsewhere, it is an English noun and in law means an attempt to prove that one was elsewhere than the place of crime at the time it was committed. Extension of this meaning to any excuse is called colloquial by Webster and informal by the American Heritage, but this use in writing is acceptable to 41 percent of the American Heritage panel of experts. As a verb, *to alibi* is approved by only 21 percent of the panel as acceptable writing. In common usage, however, *alibi* denotes any excuse and connotes a contrived excuse at least tinged with dishonesty. *Alibi* will grow in acceptability, both as noun and as verb.

ALL
When *all* goes before a pronoun in the objective case, it takes *of*: "All of us will be there." When *all of* goes before a noun, the *of* may be dropped: "All (of) the students will be there." The *of* doesn't have to be dropped. You may want to keep it for rhythm or you may want to drop it for tightness. Let your ear be your guide.

As a pronoun, *all* may be either singular or plural. If *all* signifies everything or the whole or the only thing, it is singular: "All I want is a room somewhere"; "All I ask is a tall ship and a star to steer her by" (even though the predicate is plural). If *all* signifies each person or thing in a group, considered individually, it is plural: "All were charged with petty larceny"; "All were considered literary works."

ALL-AMERICA
The adjective is *All-America*, the noun *All-American*: "He is a member of the All-America football team"; "He is an All-American."

ALL-AROUND / ALL-ROUND
As a hyphenated adjective before a noun, *all-round* is preferable, meaning versatile, skilled in various aspects, as in "an all-round athlete." In cricket, *all-rounder*, a noun, is a term applied to a player who both bats and bowls well.

ALL BUT ONE
Although *all but one* seems to convey a plural idea, a noun following the phrase is singular, as in "He lost all but one tooth." Similarly, *all but one* takes a singular verb when the phrase is followed by a noun, as in "All but one ship was sunk."

Bernstein says this "looks like poor grammar." He prefers to call it "good idiom." It may look like poor grammar but it really isn't. *All but*, in this construction, is an adverbial phrase (or a compound adverb) modifying the adjective *one*, which is singular and therefore qualifies a singular noun, which takes a singular verb. (The same principle applies to *more than one*.)

When, however, *all but one* is not immediately followed by a noun, the verb is plural, as in "All but one of the ships were sunk" or "Of the twenty ships, all but one were sunk" (but why not say nineteen?). The use of *of the* changes the grammatical construction. *One* becomes a noun, not an adjective, and it is the object of the preposition *but*, meaning except; and the subject is *all*, which is plural because it signifies each ship in the fleet, considered individually, wherefore the verb is plural.

If all this seems complicated, you can duck the problem if you use an *of* phrase or if you can count.

● ALLEGED

Don't *allege* a person. *Allege* a thing. Don't say "the alleged murderer." Say "the suspect" or "the accused" or "the defendant." Say "the alleged crime" or "the alleged murder." See also ACCUSED.

ALLEGORY

Allegory is sustained metaphor, veiled representation of implied meaning. Classic examples are Christ's parables, Spenser's *The Faerie Queene*, Bunyan's *Pilgrim's Progress* and Orwell's *Animal Farm*. In newspaper features, the weakness of allegory is that it quickly leads to boredom when attempted by clumsy writers who have little wit for humor. This is especially true of prolonged sports metaphor. Not everyone is a Russell Baker or an Art Buchwald.

ALLITERATION

From the ear of a discerning craftsman, alliteration, the repetition of the same sounds or syllables, is effective. Often it's sophomoric, as in this headline: "Student Spirit Sparkles / As Spring Semester Starts." Worse was this head from the Buchanan High School paper in the TV show "Welcome Back, Kotter": "Boom Boom Blows Big Battle / As Buchanan Basketballers Bow." High-school papers teem with alliteration for the sake of alliteration. When alliteration is the best rhetorical way to convey a message, as in some advertising, use it. Otherwise, avoid.

ALLOTTED

Note the double *t*. The word is commonly misspelled with one *t*.

To form the regular past tense or past participle or present participle from an infinitive of more than one syllable, double the final consonant after a single vowel when the final syllable is stressed. Thus: *allot, allotted, allotting*; *occur, occurred, occurring*; *rebel, rebelled, rebelling*. But: *benefit, benefited, benefiting*; *cancel, canceled, canceling*; *kidnap, kidnaped, kidnaping* (AP to the contrary). And (after double vowel): *prevail, prevailed, prevailing*; *repeat, repeated, repeating*; *succeed, succeeded, succeeding*. See also BUS.

ALL RIGHT
Two words, not *alright*, which is not all right, not at all right.

ALL-ROUND, *see* ALL-AROUND / ALL-ROUND

ALL THE FARTHER
A provincialism, as in "Is this all the farther we're going?" instead of "Is this as far as we're going?"

ALL TOGETHER / ALTOGETHER
When the meaning is "everybody at one time or in one place," the term is *all together*, as in "Now, all together, on the downbeat" or "We were all together for Christmas." When the meaning is "completely or all told," the term is *altogether*, as in "It is altogether fitting that we should dedicate this field" or "The Bobcats made only three first downs altogether" (they made three, all told, not at the same time).

ALLUDE / REFER
From Latin *ludere*, to play, *allude* means to mention indirectly; from *referre*, to carry back or to direct to, *refer* means to mention directly ("When he alluded to his first love, he was referring to his mother"). Allusion is only implicit reference.

ALMOST / NEARLY
We tend to use *almost* rather than *nearly* in contexts such as a description of feeling ("He felt almost scared to ask her") and a negative construction ("The tires had almost no mileage on them"). But these are matters of common usage rather than distinction of meaning. Though some authorities say *almost* is closer to *totally* than *nearly* is, the distinction is so subtle that, according to Bernstein, one "would have to retreat to the next room to cogitate before deciding which to use." So forget it. But see MOST.

A LOT
Two words, dammit. Pardon the anger, but years of seeing *alot* in the copy of both students and professionals would unbalance the equanimity of much milder men.

ALPHABET
From *alpha*, *beta*, the first letters of the Greek alphabet. There are many alphabets. Here is the U.S. Navy Phonetic Alphabet: Alpha, Bravo,

Charlie, Delta, Echo, Foxtrot, Golf, Hotel, India, Juliet, Kilo, Lima, Mike, November, Oscar, Papa, Quebec, Romeo, Sierra, Tango, Uniform, Victor, Whiskey, Xray, Yankee, Zulu.

Here is another: A for 'orses; B for pork; C for fishes; D for ential; E for Peron; F for vescent; G for police; H for respect; I for lootin'; J for oranges; K for ancis; L for leather; M for sis; N for dig; O for the garden wall; P for a dime; Q for billiards; R for mo; S for you; T for two; U for me; V for la France; W for a buck; X for breakfast; Y for God's sake; Z for breezes.

ALPHONSE-GASTON
The *Alphonse-Gaston* routine ("After you"—"No, after you") originated in a Hearst comic strip. Its British equivalent, Claude–Cecil, originated in a BBC radio series of World War II.

ALTAR / ALTER
Note the spellings ("If you take a matrimonial trip to the altar, your life will be altered").

ALTERNATELY / ALTERNATIVELY
When the meaning is "one after the other," the term is *alternately*. When the meaning is "one or the other," the term is *alternatively*.

ALTERNATIVE
The derivation is Latin *alter*, one of two, or other of two, not *alius*, other. Some authorities therefore restrict *alternative* to a choice between two. Fowler calls this a fetish, a literary rule unduly revered. The American Heritage panel is rather closely split, 58 percent to 42 percent, against the restriction. Because we have words such as *choice* and *option* for selection among many, why not use *alternative* for selection between two? In this sense, then, *two alternatives* is redundant, as is *the other alternative*.

ALTOGETHER, *see* ALL TOGETHER / ALTOGETHER

ALTRUISM
French *altruisme* was coined by Auguste Comte, founder of positivism, to mean other-ism, as opposed to I-ism or egoism.

ALUMINUM
The British call it *aluminium*. When Humphry Davy discovered the metal in 1808, he called it *alumium* (from Latin *alumen*, alum), which in

1812 he changed to *aluminum*, which later became *aluminium* to harmonize with the -*ium* of other elements, such as calcium and potassium (but what about aurum and platinum and other pre-1812 discoveries?). Webster chose *aluminum* for his 1828 dictionary and this remains the American spelling.

ALUMNI
Latin for foster sons, from *alere*, to nourish. *Alumnus* is masculine singular, *alumna* feminine singular, *alumni* masculine plural, *alumnae* feminine plural. The generic word for all former students, whether graduates or not, is *alumni*, embracing both men and women.

AM / FM
Short for amplitude modulation and frequency modulation. The American Heritage defines amplitude modulation as "the encoding of a carrier wave by variation of its amplitude in accordance with an input signal" and frequency modulation as "the encoding of a carrier wave by variation of its frequency in accordance with an input signal." All clear?

A.M. / P.M.
Abbreviation for Latin *ante meridiem*, before noon, and *post meridiem*, after noon. Lowercase in AP style. Note that "10 a.m. in the morning" and "3 p.m. in the afternoon" are redundant. See TODAY / TOMORROW / YESTERDAY for newspaper style for time elements and the order of time, day, place.

AMATEUR / NOVICE
Distinguish between these words. An *amateur*, from Latin *amare*, to love, is one who engages in something, with or without skill, as a pastime rather than as a profession. A *novice*, from *novus*, new, is a beginner or one who is preparing for a profession.

AMBIGUITY
You could lead a happy life thinking it's better to be fooled occasionally than to be suspicious constantly. But not on a copy desk. With accuracy, consistency, fairness and imagination, suspicion is a cardinal virtue for a copy editor. Not only must a copy editor know something about everything and where to find out everything about anything, but also he must distrust his own mother. If his mother tells him she loves him, he should check it out.

Suspicion is especially important when a copy editor writes headlines, which are set larger than body type and attract more attention than copy. (For ambiguity in copy, see JUXTAPOSITION.) A headline writer must check and recheck a head for clarity and single meaning or he may find himself with another embarrassing headline story to add to his reminiscences.

A headline doesn't tell an accurate story if its language is ambiguous, open to more than one interpretation. For example, in some contexts an innocent noun is found guilty of having more than one meaning: "Beauty Unveils Bust at Ceremony." (This and some of the other examples are taken from a collection of American newspaper headlines compiled by Earle Tempel, *Humor in the Headlines*; others are taken from *HTK*.) Or: "Mr. McClusky Will Give / Free Goose to 4-H Girls."

Sometimes the culprit is a verb: "Missouri Pacific to Drop / Passengers from 3 Trains." Or: "Avoid Having Baby / At the Dinner Table." Worse: "President Eats Turkey, / Lays a Cornerstone."

Words that are both verbs and adjectives can lead to ambiguity: "Police Stoned in Hartford" or "Escaped Leopard / Believed Spotted."

Bernstein, in *Headlines and Deadlines*, gives an example of ambiguity that arises from words that are both verbs and nouns: "U.S. Rules on Tax / Adopted by State." Did the United States give a ruling on tax measures adopted by some state or has some state adopted U.S. tax measures as its own? Is *rules* a verb or a noun?

Then there are words that are both nouns and adjectives. An Associated Press story reported that Vern Miller, then Kansas attorney general, expected police to enforce anti-gambling laws at county and state fairs. A paper ran this head: "Miller Expects / Fair Gambling / Enforcement." (The head is also split. See SPLIT HEADS.)

When you aggravate the misuse of a noun for an adjective by using as an adjective a noun that is also a verb and using it in front of a word that can be either noun or verb and putting these two words in front of yet another noun-verb, the result, like this sentence, is chaotic. Bernstein gives this example: "Jones Will Fight / Hinges on Baby."

Look at the mess you can get from adjectival clutter: "Catholic Women Hear / Seeing Eye Dog Talk."

The ordinal adjective *first*, coupled with a news mania for uniqueness, can lead to ambiguity: "Fatal Attack / Wasn't First / For Nasser."

Ambiguity sometimes arises from a person's name: "Broad to Be Honored / As Man of the Year." Oldtime tennis buffs will get two messages from: "Helen Wills Moody / On 3-Week Honeymoon."

Often the problem is one of pronunciation: "Actor Accidentally Shot in Debut." In this context, the classic printable favorite is this head over a story about an explosion in a Kentucky outhouse: "Farmer Interred Is Not Dead."

Sometimes ambiguity of time makes a head ludicrous: "Cemetery Gets Praise / From Former Resident." Or: "Girl Becomes Methodist / After Delicate Operation."

Very often the ambiguous interpretation comes from unfortunate JUXTAPOSITION, as in the prepositional phrase in: "Auto Hits Pedestrian / Without a Tail Light." Or a SQUINTING MODIFIER: "Man Shot in Head / Accidentally Dies." Or a misplaced antecedent: "Man Pulls Needle from Foot / He Swallowed 66 Years Ago."

Be suspicious.

AMBULANCE
The pace of an ambulance is much faster than a walk, but the word comes from Latin *ambulare*, to walk (as in such words as *amble*, *ambulatory*, *perambulate*, *somnambulist*), by way of French *hôpital ambulant*, the itinerant hospital following an army.

AMERICA'S CUP
Note the official title of this yacht race. It's *America's*, not *America* or *American*. The name came from the schooner *America*, winner of the first race for which the cup was presented, in 1851, by the Royal Yacht Squadron of England. Though it is indeed true that the race has never been won by other than an American vessel, this isn't the reason for the title.

AMICUS CURIAE
A legal term that refers to a person who suggests or states a matter of law in a case to which he is not a party. The literal translation from Latin is "friend of the court."

AMICUS USQUE AD ARAS
A Latin phrase now rarely used, *amicus usque ad aras* deserves perpetuation as a description of one who will stick by another except for religious differences. Its literal translation is "a friend as far as to the altars."

AMOK, *see* AMUCK

AMONG / BETWEEN
Anglo-Saxon *be-twa*, by two, suggests that *between* should be used to express the relation of two things. True, but it should be used also to ex-

press the relation of a thing to several other things individually. Thus we speak of relations between the Big Ten universities when we relate each to each of the nine others; and we choose between several applicants for a job, relating the qualifications of each to the qualifications of each of the others.

When the relation is collective and vague, the word is *among*, from Anglo-Saxon *on-gemang*, in a crowd ("He looms high among his contemporaries"). *Among* should not be used for only two.

AMORAL / IMMORAL / UNMORAL

You are *amoral* or *unmoral* if you have no moral code. You are *immoral* if you act against your moral code.

AMPERSAND

Once upon a time, children were taught two symbols after *z* in the alphabet, with their meanings: &c., *et cetera;* & *(per se) and* (meaning that &, by itself, means *and*). The children were taught to say "et-per-se-and," which became "and-per-se-and," which became "ampersand."

The symbol & is said to have come from a shorthand for *et* (and), used in some old Latin manuscripts. Then some early impressionist teacher saw a sitting cat in & and called the symbol "and-pussy-and," which led to other equally strange corruptions.

Don't use & in the name of a business firm or other group unless the firm or group itself uses it: *Quill and Scroll,* but *Editor & Publisher, U.S. News & World Report.*

AMUCK

Though the root is Malay *amoq*, furious, the word has been spelled *amuck*, rather than *amok*, for the last three hundred years, especially in *to run amuck*, which has nothing to do with *muck* but means to run around furiously in all directions at the same time. There's no law against *amok*, but, as Evans says, "it's pretentious and invites an embarrassing probe of the user's knowledge of Malayan." Fowler calls *amok* a didacticism.

AMULET

Usually worn around the neck, an amulet has nothing to do with arms, any more than a fetish has anything to do with feet. From Latin *amoliri letum*, to ward off death, an amulet was a charm strung around the neck of a baby in the days of high infant mortality. The superstition survives among older infants, religious and irreligious.

ANACHRONISM
From Greek *ana* + *chronos*, beyond time. By extension, an *anachronism* is a statement involving incongruity of time, as in "Napoleon zipped up his greatcoat and started his march to the Communist capital," which is doubly anachronistic, or "The unearthed horseshoe, stamped 150 B.C., possibly came from one of Julius Caesar's horses," which is also fraudulent.

ANACOLUTHON
From Greek *an* + *akolouthos*, not following, inconsistent, *anacoluthon* is a technical term for the grammatical error of switching from one construction to a grammatically different construction within the same sentence: "He testified he saw a man driving along the highway and who seemed to be drunk." The construction has been switched from a participial phrase to an adjectival clause; put *who was* before *driving*. See PARALLELISM.

Sleepy reporters commit anacoluthon in this kind of sentence: "The patrolman said he had never seen 'an accident so tragic in all his career.'" The patrolman surely said "*my* career."

ANAGRAM
From Greek *ana* + *grammatizein*, to transpose letters, an *anagram* is a word or phrase formed from a reordering of the letters of another word or phrase. "Court of general session" becomes "scenes of rogues on trial." But Espy's attempt to turn "Queen Victoria's jubilee" into "I require love in a subject" has an *r* too many. Likewise, "the death of Robert G. Ingersoll, the famous agnostic" has an *a* too many for "Goes, gathering the belief that no Lord comforts us." Make it *a'gathering* and you have a perfect 43-letter anagram. Play with words.

ANALOGOUS
Note the spelling: not *lag*, but *log*. From Greek *analogos*, proportionate, resembling.

ANALYSIS / SYNTHESIS
The meanings of the words become clear from their roots: *analysis* comes from Greek *ana* + *lyein*, to loosen up; *synthesis* comes from Greek *syn* + *tithenai*, to put together.

ANAPHORA
A rhetorical device in which a word or phrase is repeated (from Greek *ana* + *pherein*, to carry again, to repeat) at the beginning of successive

clauses or sentences. *Anaphora* is common in the Bible (see, for example, the Beatitudes). With light touch, it rings rhetorically rhythmical, but in heavy hands, rhetoric can become bombast, and rhythm doggerel, as in the pompous puffery of politicians who string one "a man who" after another "a man who" after another "a man who" till anaphora sinks into dysphoria.

ANATOMY, *see* -TOMY

AND
And now we come to the nonsense that one shouldn't begin a sentence with *and*. And why shouldn't one? But don't overdo it.

AND/OR
This unsightly gimmick is a legalism unnecessary in prose, probably unnecessary in law. It rears its ugly head in contexts such as "The offense is punishable by a $100 fine and/or 30 days in jail." Translate into English: "The offense is punishable by a $100 fine or 30 days in jail or both."

ANDROGYNOUS
The derivations by which we distinguish between *polyandry* and *polygyny* come together in *androgynous*, from Greek *aner* (genitive *andros*), man, and Greek *gyne*, woman, hence possessed of both male and female characteristics, hermaphroditic (from the son of Hermes and Aphrodite, Hermaphroditus, who while bathing became joined in one body with a nymph).

AND THAT
Fowler contemns those who "put their trust in a rule of thumb" that says an *and that* clause must be preceded by a *that* clause. (The same principle applies to *and which, and who, but that, but which, but who* and objective and possessive forms thereof, including *whom* and *whose*.) He takes more than 3,000 words in one entry to vent his contempt.

In milder fashion, Barzun disagrees with the rule and takes refuge in the principle that *and that* is allowable if a preceding *that* can be understood in "hidden form" (a refuge of grammatical sinners), as in "This is the girl I love and who loves me."

No matter. Despite these truly august authorities, use the rule of thumb. Bernstein says the rule is "applicable in nine sentences out of ten—which should be good enough for any rule" (his tenth sentence omits a preceding *that* for the sake of euphony).

That, *which* and *who* in this discussion are relative pronouns. The same principle applies to *that* as a nounal conjunction, as in "He said that he was getting tired of reading so much discussion about the problems of grammar and that he was going to watch TV."

See THAT for a discussion of the omission of *that* before nounal clauses. See THAT / WHICH for the distinction between *that* and *which*.

ANECDOTE
From Greek *an* + *ekdotos*, not given out, not published, hence kept secret, *anecdote* came to mean something published that was previously secret. An anecdote is now a short story involving humor or what used to be called "human interest."

ANEMONE
From Greek *anemos*, wind. *Anemone* won't blossom in many news stories, but it is mentioned here to illustrate the verbal delights of those who know some Greek and Latin. When they see or hear *anemone*, as Moore says, they are "reminded of the wind that tosses the frail white blossoms in March, or when they come across such a phrase as 'the circumambient dark' can imagine the darkness walking round, like a wolf about a camp-fire, as the dangerous dark deepens." Words like these have lives of their own.

ANENT
As common usage, *anent* went out with penny postage. It is a mark of those who feel that writing has to be stilted to be impressive. Use *about*, *concerning*, *on*, *regarding*.

ANESTHETIC / ESTHETIC
From Greek *an* + *aisthesis*, without feeling, *anesthetic* is the opposite of *esthetic*, apprehended through the senses, hence appreciative of the arts or, informally, good taste. Under anesthesia, one has no feeling. *Esthetic* is sometimes spelled with a diphthong, *aesthetic*, but *anaesthetic* is rare. Morris quotes critic John Chapman's definition of gout as "aesthete's foot."

ANFRACTUOUS
A BUCKLEYISM. The word is straight Latin and means winding, twisting and turning, sinuous, tortuous, roundabout. If in some context none of these conveys the nuance of *anfractuous*, go ahead and use it. Such a con-

text, however, is hardly imaginable. The word reeks of Samuel Johnson at his most pompous.

ANGLICE
This adverb, from Latin, means "in the English form" and refers to English names for foreign places, such as Dunkirk for Dunkerque, Florence for Firenze, Leghorn for Livorno, Naples for Napoli. The use of the foreign form invites a charge of affectation. Though you've spent three weeks in Europe, talk English—and don't put a stroke across 7.

ANGLOPHILE, *see* PHIL-

ANGLOPHOBIA, *see* -PHOBIA

ANGOSTURA
A brand name, hence uppercase, for Angostura bitters. As the label on the bottle vigorously points out, *Angostura* has nothing to do with angostura bark except that they both originated in Angostura (now Ciudad Bolivar), a city in Venezuela. The label also proclaims the merits of the bitter aromatic tonic as "a pleasant and dependable stomachic" and a weapon in man's never-ending war against the social disgrace of flatulence.

ANNIVERSARY
From Latin *annus versus*, a year turned. Some newspapers insist that *anniversary* be inserted after *birthday* in all copy. Admittedly, one has only one birthday and one celebrates the anniversaries of that day as the years turn. But one should also use a·little common sense and the common form of "twenty-first birthday" or "birthday party."

ANNUIT COEPTIS
Wanna make a buck? Show one to someone and ask what is on the back of it and what the words mean. The reverse side of the dollar bill includes the reverse side of the Great Seal of the United States, which says "Annuit Coeptis" (adapted from the Aeneid, "He [God] has been favorable to the things begun" or "God has smiled on our undertakings") and "Novus Ordo Seclorum" (also from Virgil, "a new order of the ages"). Nobody is asking everybody to be a Latin scholar, but if our national symbols (and academic seals) have Latin mottoes, we ought to know the translations.

ANOINT
Commonly misspelled *annoint*. See also UNCTUOUS.

ANOMIE, *see* –NOMY

ANONYMOUS
From Greek *an* + *onoma*, no name. English abounds with words from the same root. Among them: *antonym, homonym, metonymy, onomastic, onomatopoeia, pseudonym, synonym.*

ANOTHER
"About 60,000 people attended the game; another million saw it on TV." You can't have another million unless you've had a previous million. Say "a million others." See also EACH OTHER / ONE ANOTHER and OTHER THREE / THREE OTHERS.

ANSWERED
In a news story, *answered* is a LOADED VERB of attribution if it is used to mean "refuted" or "silenced," as in "He answered his critics by pointing out (another loaded verb) his accomplishments as a legislator." Make it "He replied to his critics by describing what he had done as a legislator."

ANTAPHRODISIAC
Preventive of sexual desire, from Greek *anti* + *aphrodisiakos*, from Aphrodite, the Greek goddess of love, identified by the Romans with Venus, whence *venereal*. The World War II veteran who today says, "That saltpeter is finally catching up with me," is confusing *antaphrodisia*, the prevention of sexual desire, with *anaphrodisia*, the decline thereof.

ANTARCTIC / ARCTIC
Pronounce that *c* in the middle of each of these words and spell them right.

ANTE
The Latin word for *before*, hence in poker the word for the stake you put up before you receive cards. It's also a verb, as in "Someone didn't ante (up)," which crime will prompt some card accountant (there's one in every poker school) to mutter, "Pot's right?" or "Someone anted (or anteed) twice." The word has extended to other business enterprises. As

an adjective, *penny ante* has come to mean cheap or stingy; as a noun, it means chicken feed or other chicken combinations.

ANTECEDENT

Tell a class, "A pronoun agrees with its antecedent in person, number and gender but it takes its case from the clause in which it stands," and you'll see glassy eyes and realize that most of today's students learned their language at their mothers' knees and at other joints, such as schools of creative relevance, impressionistic expressionism and ungrammatical permissiveness. You realize you have to define eight grammatical terms in what seemed a simple statement: *pronoun, agreement, antecedent, person, number, gender, case, clause.*

Under discussion here is *antecedent*, from Latin *ante + cedere*, to go before. In grammar, an antecedent is the word or group of words that a pronoun stands for or refers to (sometimes called *referent*).

In "The men who are going are blind," the antecedent of the pronoun *who* is *men*, which is third person, plural number, masculine gender, wherefore the verb is plural ("*are* going"). The case of the pronoun is nominative, therefore, *who*, not *whom* or *whose*, because it is the subject of the verb in the clause "who are going." (In "The men whom you are taking are blind," *men*, the antecedent of the pronoun *whom*, is nominative case, but *whom* is objective case because it is the object of the verb in the clause "whom you are taking.")

Contrast this sentence: "One of the men who are going is blind." Here, the antecedent of the pronoun *who* is still *men*, not *one*, wherefore *who* is still plural and takes a plural verb. *One*, however, is a singular subject and takes the singular verb *is*. The principle may be better understood if the sentence is transposed to read: "Of the men who are going, one is blind." You wouldn't dream of saying, "Of the men who is going, one is blind" or "Of the men who are going, one are blind."

Etymologically, *antecedent*, in its grammatical usage, is often a misnomer because an antecedent doesn't have to go before the pronoun it stands for or refers to. For example, in "In all her life, Alice had never seen anything so curious," *Alice* is the antecedent of *her* but comes after *her*.

See also WHO / WHOM.

ANTEDILUVIAN

From Latin *ante + diluvium*, before the deluge, before the Great Flood described in Genesis, hence antiquated.

ANTENNA
In zoology, the plural of *antenna* is *antennae*. In radio-TV, the plural is *antennas*. The word is Latin for sail yard.

ANTEPENULT
The third last syllable of a word. Thus *lu* is the antepenult of *antediluvian*. From Latin *ante* + *paene* + *ultimus*, literally the one before almost the last. So *ultimate* (*ult*) is the last, *penultimate* (*penult*) the second last (next to last), *antepenultimate* (*antepenult*) the third last.

ANTERIOR
The comparative degree of Latin *ante*, before, literally more before, *anterior* is the opposite of *posterior*, the comparative degree of *post*, after, literally more after. See also AFTER.

ANTHOLOGY
From Greek *anthos* + *legein*, flower gathering, hence a collection of beautiful literary pieces. By extension, *anthology* has come to be used for a book of readings, not necessarily literary, on some educational theme. Some anthologies bear little resemblance to the etymological concept.

ANTHROPO-
The Greek combining form for *man*, in the generic sense of human being, not in the specific sense of masculine gender. Hence: *anthropoid*, resembling man, apelike; *anthropology*, study of the origin and development of man; *anthropomorphism*, attribution of human qualities to things or beings not human (see also TAPINOSIS); *anthropophagy*, eating of human flesh.

ANTICLIMAX
The rhetorical figures of *climax* and *anticlimax* come from Greek *klimax*, ladder. Rhetorically, climax involves a succession of steps or statements ascending in importance; popularly, the climax is the highest point. Rhetorically, anticlimax, the opposite of climax, involves a succession of steps or statements descending in importance to the ludicrous; popularly, an anticlimax comes after a climax. (The American Heritage gives this example of a sudden descent from the impressive or significant to the ludicrous or inconsequential: "For God, for country, and for Yale.") Note the spelling of the adjective *anticlimactic* (not *anticlimatic*) and be sure to pronounce the second *c*.

ANTIMACASSAR
Makassar (or Macassar) is a city on the island of Sulawesi, formerly Celebes, in Indonesia. Unguents from there were the ingredients of a once popular hair-oil, Macassar. To guard against stains from this grease, lacy covers were put over the backs of chairs and sofas. The cover was called an *antimacassar*.

ANTIPASTO
Though a good antipasto is a meal in itself, the word means "before the food" in Italian. See HORS D'OEUVRE.

ANTONOMASIA
When you call Babe Ruth the Sultan of Swat, or when you call a strong man a Tarzan, you are practicing *antonomasia*, from Greek *anti* + *ono-mazein*, to name instead. *Antonomasia* is the substitution of an epithet or other phrase for a proper name, or the substitution of a proper name for a common noun to identify someone as a member of a group or class.

Modern examples are The Bird, for pitcher Mark Fidrych, and a Cosell, for a motor mouth. Old examples are: The Voice, for Frank Sinatra; The Man, for Stan Musial; the Oomph Girl, for Ann Sheridan; a Babbitt, for a man of parochial outlook; a Scrooge, for a skinflint; a Hitler, for an unscrupulous megalomaniac.

The Irish still call the father of a family Himself, and the father calls the real head of the house Herself.

ANTONYM
From Greek *anti* + *onoma*, opposite name, hence a word whose meaning is the opposite of that of another word, as *true* is the antonym of *false*, and vice versa.

A NUMBER
Takes a plural verb, as in "A number of people are now sorry they didn't vote," whereas *the number* takes a singular verb, as in "The number of people who didn't vote is large." The same principle applies to *total* and *variety*.

ANXIOUS / EAGER
Though these words sometimes overlap (you can be anxious about going somewhere, yet eager to go), use *anxious* to connote worry or apprehension, *eager* to connote desire or enthusiasm. The roots indicate the dis-

tinction: *anxious* is from Latin *angere*, to cause pain, to choke; *eager* is from *acer*, sharp, keen.

ANY
From the Anglo-Saxon word for *one*. But *any* may be either singular or plural, depending on the context. When *any* means *any one*, it is singular, as in "Any of these brands is expensive." When *any* means *some*, it is plural, as in "Are any of these brands expensive?"

ANY AND ALL
The phrase is redundant. "Any visitor is welcome" is the same as "All visitors are welcome." So why say, "Any and all visitors are welcome"?

ANYBODY / ANYONE
Each is singular: "Anybody (anyone) is allowed to express his (not *their*) opinion." *Anyone*, as one word, refers to persons in general; *any one*, as two words, refers to one person or thing in a specific group. For example, "Anyone can choose any one of the applicants (options)." *Anybody*, as one word, refers only to persons; *any body*, as two words, refers to a corporate or corporeal body. For example, "Anybody can join any body of volunteers to search the river for any body." The same principles apply to *somebody* and *someone*.

ANY MORE
Two words. Note that *any more* can't literally be used in a positive statement, such as the provincialism "Annie lives here any more." Use *any more* in a negative statement ("Annie doesn't live here any more") or in a statement with a negative implication ("Annie rarely lives here any more") or in a question ("Does Annie live here any more?").

ANYONE ELSE
If you say, "Alice writes better headlines than anyone in the class," Alice is not a member of the class. If she is a member of the class, say, "Alice writes better headlines than anyone else in the class."

ANY OTHER
The *anyone else* principle applies also to *any other*. If you say, "Florida has more beaches than any state in the country," you are saying Florida has more beaches than Florida, because Florida is a state. Make it "any other state."

A-1
The tops, from A-1 at Lloyd's, which used to grade hulls by alphabet and rigging by numbers.

AORTA
If you visit Australia, you'll want to know something about the language. *Aorta* in Strine, the Australian language, is not the anatomical term for the arterial trunk, but the vessel through which courses the lifeblood of Strine public opinion, as in: "Aorta mica laura genst all these cars cummer ninner Sinny. Aorta have more buses. An aorta put more seats innem so you doan tefter stan aller toym—you carn tardly move innem air so crairded. Aorta do something about it." It sounds like the great American "they oughta."

For a hilarious course in Strine, see Afferbeck Lauder's *Let Stalk Strine*, and read all about egg nishners, baked necks, sag rapes, sly drools, terror souses, dismal guernsey, Orpheus Rocker, War Sigma Tilda and Australia's glory girls, Gloria Soames and Gloria Sarah Titch. You don't have to read the entries in afferbeck lauder. For the price of the book, ask Emma Chisit.

AP / UPI
Abbreviations for the Associated Press and United Press International. Note that a newspaper is a *member* of the Associated Press, a cooperative nonprofit agency that levies assessments on its members to meet its costs, whereas a newspaper is a *client* of (or subscriber to) United Press International (UPI), the other large American wire service, which sells its service on a contract basis. See the fourth edition of Hohenberg for an up-to-date treatment of the wire services.

APERITIF
This French word comes from Latin *aperire*, to open, as in *aperient*, opening the bowels, but *aperitif*, a drink before a meal, has lost its original meaning, and the drink has other purposes.

APHESIS
From Greek *apo* + *hienai*, to send off, to let go. *Aphesis* (shortened from *aphaeresis*) is the loss of the first letter or syllable of a word, as in *cute* from *acute*, *squire* from *esquire*, *special* from *especial*, *drawing room* from *withdrawing room*. The new word is called aphetic. See also ADDER.

APHRODISIAC, *see* ANTAPHRODISIAC

APOCOPE
When you drop a final *g*, as in *comin'* and *goin'*, you are apocopating (see SYN-), from Greek *apo + koptein*, to cut off. *Apocope* is the loss of the final sound(s) or syllable(s) of a word (see also APHESIS). Examples are *curio* from *curiosity*, *auto* from *automobile*, *hypo* from *hypodermic*, *cinema* from *cinematograph*, *stereo* from *stereophonic*, *piano* from *pianoforte*.

APOCRYPHAL
An *apocryphal* story or work is one whose stated source cannot be proved and is probably spurious, from Greek *apo + kryptein*, to hide away, hence hidden, spurious.

APOGEE
The astronauts brought this word into more popular use. The *apogee*, from Greek *apo + ge*, away from the earth, is the point farthest from the earth in the orbit of the moon or of an artificial satellite. Its opposite is *perigee*, from *peri + ge*, near the earth.

APOLOGY
John Henry Newman's *Apologia Pro Vita Sua* was not a statement of regret for his life, but a justification of it, from Greek *apo + logos*, speech in defense, by way of Latin *apologia*. The old meaning of *apology*, defense, lingers in the rarely used *apologia*, but *apology* has softened to the modern meaning of expression of regret.

APOPEMPTIC
A BUCKLEYISM. The word comes from Greek *apo + pempein*, to send off or away, and means something sung or addressed to someone departing. Despite Buckley's occasional forays to preserve the word, commencement orators probably won't be called apopempticians. *Ave*, valedictory. *Vale*, apopemptic.

APOSIOPESIS
When editors use dashes (or other typographical gimmicks) to avoid using words they think may offend, they are engaged in *aposiopesis* (accent on the penult). They are also engaged in foolishness, because the

dashes offend. And sometimes the dashes invite justifiable curiosity, as happened when almost all American newspapers in the fall of 1976 aposiopesized the famous infamous words of Earl Butz, secretary of agriculture, in a racist story he told to—of all people—John Dean of Watergate and Pat Boone of Cleansville.

If the story has to be used and if the words are essential to the story, use the words.

In rhetoric, *aposiopesis*, from Greek *apo + siopan*, to be quite silent, is a device whereby a speaker gains attention by suddenly breaking off in the middle of a sentence as if unwilling or unable to finish the thought, as in "I'll say this about Butz——no, I can't."

A POSTERIORI / A PRIORI

Reasoning *a posteriori* is induction, going from the particular to the general. Scientists work from observation of a multiplicity of phenomena and induce conclusions therefrom. They go from effect to cause.

Reasoning *a priori* is deduction, going from the general to the particular. Philosophers work from known or assumed princples and deduce conclusions therefrom. They go from cause to effect.

The words are Latin: *a posteriori*, from the latter; *a priori*, from the former.

Sometimes *a priori* is confused with *prima facie*, which means on first appearance, before closer inspection, as in *prima-facie evidence*, the raising of a presumption of fact. The terms should not be confused.

APOSTROPHE

As a punctuation mark, the apostrophe (') is used for, among other things, contractions, such as *isn't, wasn't, won't, wouldn't*, from Greek *apostrophos*, the accent of elision or omission. Some newspapers use this kind of contraction in news stories because the *not* in negative verb forms can be carelessly dropped in typesetting, thus producing the opposite meaning.

The apostrophe is also used to indicate omission of part of a number, as in *the '20s*. Most American newspapers, following AP style, don't use the apostrophe in the plural of numbers (two *7s*, not two *7's*). It is commonly used in the plural of single letters (two *d's*), especially when there is danger of ambiguity, as in two *as* (*a's*) or two *is* (*i's*).

For examples of the ignorant use of the apostrophe in plurals, see PLURALS. Also see POSSESSIVES.

In rhetoric, apostrophe, from Greek *apo + strephein*, to turn away, is a feigned turning away from an audience to address an absent or imaginary person or object.

APOTHEOSIS, *see* THEO–

APPARENT
It is apparent (obvious) that the apparent (seeming) contradiction in the meaning of *apparent* is troublesome. The trouble with *apparent* can be seen in the contrary meanings given it by Webster (visible, evident, seeming) and the American Heritage (readily seen, plain, obvious).

In speech, inflection can convey the intended meaning. But in many written contexts, because *apparent* means both obvious and seeming, the word is ambiguous. So why not say *obvious* when you mean obvious, and *seeming* when you mean seeming?

Apparently (obviously), the same principle applies to the apparently (seemingly) contradictory use of the adverb *apparently*. See also EVIDENTLY.

APPENDECTOMY, *see* –TOMY

APPLE OF MY EYE
The pupil of the eye was once thought to be solid and spherical, shaped like an apple. David prayed, "Guard me as the apple of thy eye." Moses said of Jacob that the Lord "kept him as the apple of his eye." Solomon advised, "Keep my law as the apple of thy eye." Jeremiah lamented, "Let not the apple of thy eye cease." Zachariah said the Lord told Zion, "He that toucheth you, toucheth the apple of my eye." Like so many beautiful quotations from the Bible, the phrase has been ground into a cliché.

APPLE PIE
When used in editorials and speeches that see the United States as the land of "baseball, motherhood and apple pie" and praise someone as being "as American as apple pie," the term is a cliché. New clichés are needed. Why not the land of "pro football, divorce and pizza pie"? Or "as American as French fries"?

The apple-pie bed, Shipley suggests, gets its name either from the way the sheets are folded, like the crust on an apple turnover, or from French *nappe pliée*, folded sheet.

APPOSITION

Reporters and sleepy copy editors often forget the appositive comma in a sentence in which the phrase in apposition (from Latin *ad + ponere*, to put near) is long. For example: "Ford, the congressman from Michigan who was catapulted into the White House as a result of vice-presidential and presidential malfeasance is regarded by his former colleagues on Capitol Hill as honest and industrious." There has to be a comma after *malfeasance*.

The comma is often forgotten even in shorter appositive phrases, such as: "John Jones, a retired plumber died today." Put a comma after *plumber*.

Commas are not used when a phrase is so welded to a name as to be part of it, as in "Frederick the Great" or "Attila the Hun" or "Wilt the Stilt." And note the difference between "Winston Churchill, the venerable British statesman, died today" and "The venerable British statesman Winston Churchill died today." In the second sentence, the words before *Winston Churchill* are almost a title.

But appositive commas are needed when the indefinite article is used, as in "A venerable British statesman, Winston Churchill, died today."

Also note that you have more than one brother when you write, "My brother Charles is a physician," but you have only one brother when you write, "My brother, Charles, is a physician."

APPROXIMATELY, *see* ABOUT

APRICOT

The more common pronunciation has a long *a*, as in *day*. Through Greek, Arabic, Portuguese and French, *apricot* is from Latin *prae + coquere*, to cook beforehand, hence to ripen early, as in *precocious*.

A PRIORI, *see* A POSTERIORI / A PRIORI

APRON, *see* ADDER

APT / LIABLE / LIKELY

The three words have nuances of meaning. *Apt* involves probability based on known tendency. *Liable* involves probability of unpleasant consequence. *Likely* involves simple probability. Bernstein gives this clear example: "Teen-agers are apt to speed on an open road. If they do they are liable to be arrested. Then they are likely to be sorry."

The most common misuse is of *liable* for *likely* when nothing disadvantageous is involved, as in "You are liable to see him jogging any evening." Make it *likely*. A clue to the meaning of *liable* is its derivation from Latin *ligare*, to bind, hence to be legally obliged, as in *lien*.

AQUA PURA
A term beloved of writers who fear to repeat a word or who stretch for elegant variation. Water is water.

ARC
We put a *k* in the past tense and the participles of such verbs as *frolic*, *mimic*, *panic*, *picnic*. If you use *arc* as a verb, put a *k* in its parts, *arcked*, *arcking*. *Arced* and *arcing* look and sound almost obscene. Anyway, except in electrical usage, why not *arch*?

ARCH- / ARCHI- / -ARCHY
These two prefixes and one suffix all come from Greek *archein*, to be first, to rule. Dozens of English words come from this root. Here are a dozen: *anarchy*, *archaic*, *archangel*, *archbishop*, *archeologist*, *archetype*, *archipelago*, *architect*, *archive*, *autarchy*, *monarchy*, *oligarchy*.

ARCHY AND MEHITABEL
If they refer to a cockroach and a cat, these two names should be lowercase because archy, the cockroach, wasn't strong enough to hold down the shift key on the typewriter of Don Marquis, American newspaperman (1878–1937) and author of *archy and mehitabel* (1927), a book of blank verse with no capital letters. It was composed by archy on Marquis' typewriter at night while Marquis was absent from the newsroom. It describes the amorous adventures of mehitabel, a cat whose motto was "wotthehell, archy, toujours gai."

ARCTIC, *see* ANTARCTIC / ARCTIC

AREA
This is one of Nickles' "territorial words," words "that set illusory boundaries around the occupations and preoccupations of mankind." Hack writers take "in government spending" and make it "in the area of government spending." Another territorial word is *field*. Hacks take "an expert in education" and make it "an expert in the field of education." Other such words are *circle*, *domain*, *province*, *realm*, *sphere*. Most of the time they are unnecessary abstractions. Be simple. Unclutter.

ARENA

In the days before supermarkets, you tagged along with your mother from store to store, from grocer to baker to butcher. The butcher store had sawdust on the floor to soak up the blood. Before sawdust, sand was used, as it was used in a Roman amphitheater, a place of bloodshed, the center of which was called the arena. *Arena* is the latin word for *sand*. By METONYMY, the word for *sand* became the word for *sandy place*. The bloody notion of *arena* is preserved today in the language of pugilism and politics, which are not dissimilar.

AREN'T I

The strictly grammatical form of the first person singular present negative interrogative is *am I not*, contracted to *amn't I*. Speakers shrink from *am I not* as stuffy, and from *amn't I* as prissy. So *aren't I* has crept into the language. Though it is grammatically contradictory because of the singular subject and plural verb, *aren't I* is "colloquially respectable," as Fowler says, and now almost universal. The American Heritage usage panel voted 27 percent in favor of *aren't I* in writing and 60 percent in speech. The vote here is in favor in both, on the side of colloquial respectability and universal usage. See also AIN'T.

ARISTOCRACY, *see* –CRACY

ARITHMETIC

From Greek *arithmos*, number. One of the seven classical liberal arts, arithmetic is being hastened to extinction by pocket calculators and digital computers. Some children are now growing up unable to tell time except by a digital watch or clock. Look, ma, no hands. See also LIBERAL ARTS.

ARMISTICE

From Latin *arma*, arms, and *sistere*, to stand still, to stop, hence a suspension of hostilities, a truce. (Compare *solstice*, one of the two times a year when the sun seemingly stands still.) The armistice of World War I, the war to end wars, occurred November 11, 1918, the anniversary of which was celebrated as Armistice Day until 1954, when in the United States the name was changed to Veterans Day (no apostrophe in AP) because the war to end wars didn't.

AROMA
Don't use *aroma* for every kind of smell. The Greek word for spice, it means a pleasant smell. Use *stench* and *stink* for unpleasant smells. *Scent*, *fragrance*, *perfume* and *bouquet* connote delicacy. *Odor*, like *smell*, is generic.

ARROGATE, *see* ABROGATE / ARROGATE

ARSE
Webster calls it vulgar. The American Heritage says it's chiefly British. Partridge has 67 entries for it. Though its origin from Greek *orros*, rump, is polite enough, *arse* is hardly a word for polite society. Americans prefer *ass*.

ARSON
From Latin *ardere*, to burn, as in *ardent*, *ardor*. Some Britons say it comes from arsin' around with matches.

ARTERIOSCLEROSIS / ATHEROSCLEROSIS
The first word comes from Greek *arteria*, artery, and *skleros*, hard, hence hardening of the arteries. Atherosclerosis is a form of arteriosclerosis, and the word comes from Greek *athera*, gruel. The pus formed on the arterial walls by atherosclerosis is like gruel.

ARTICLE: A; AN; THE
Some grammarians classify the indefinite articles *a* and *an* and the definite article *the* as adjectives. Others classify them as a separate part of speech. The preference here is to classify them as demonstrative adjectives.

A is used before consonant sounds, *an* before vowel sounds: a book, a one-night stand, a university; an egg, an olive, an umbrella. The *o* of *one* has the consonant sound of *w*, as in *won;* the *u* of *university* has the long consonant sound of *y*, as in *yew;* the *u* of *umbrella* is a short vowel sound, as in *ugh*.

When a beginning *h* is sounded, it's a consonant sound, hence *a history*. When a beginning *h* is not sounded, the word begins with a vowel sound, hence *an honor*.

Some grammarians hold that when a beginning *h* is not stressed, the correct form is *an*, as in *an historic* occasion. So would you say *an hotel*, *an harpoon?* This form is a dying relic of British usage. It's as archaic as Beadle Bumble's "The law is a ass, a idiot."

The American Heritage is misleading when it says *an* is used "before words beginning with a vowel or with an unpronounced *h*." So *an eulogy, an union?* The key is the sound, not the letter.

The same principle applies before abbreviations that begin with a vowel sound: an FCC ruling, an LL.D., an M.D., an NAACP policy, an R.N., an SEC regulation. Sometimes, however, a reader will almost automatically translate an abbreviation into what it abbreviates. He will tend to translate *L.A. Times* into Los Angeles Times, hence *a L.A. Times* editorial. It's a question of judgment. What is the reader saying to himself?

The is pronounced with a short *e* before consonant sounds and with a long *e* before vowel sounds.

Luce writing spread the practice of dropping *the* from the beginning of a sentence, as in "Most important problem of the tourist trade is the decline of the value of the dollar." The folly of this practice is obvious if the sentence is transposed: "The decline of the value of the dollar is most important problem of the tourist trade." Worse, write the sentence without any *the*: "Most important problem of tourist trade is decline of value of dollar." As a reminder of the need for the definite article, Bernstein amends the psalmist's line to "If I forget *the*, O Jerusalem, let my right hand be forgotten" (Douay).

An exception to the need for *the* is its omission before *police* in newspaper copy, as in "Police today continued their investigation" or "A suspect has been arrested, police said."

The in the name of a newspaper or magazine is usually lowercase when the publication is mentioned in other publications ("He gets most of his opinions from the *New York Times* and the *New Yorker*"), but uppercase when a publication with *The* in its name is referring to itself.

AS

This handy word is adverb, conjunction, preposition, pronoun. Here they all are in one sentence: "As (preposition) a rookie, he was as (adverb) calm as (conjunction) a veteran such as (pronoun) Blanda."

As a conjunction, *as* is overworked by breathless writers who string *as* clause after *as* clause, joining unjoinables, oblivious of the need for the refreshing pause of a period. Sportswriters are especially guilty of overworking *as*. For example:

"The Kansas Jayhawks edged the Oklahoma State Cowboys last night as streak-shooting Herb Nobles swished a 31-foot desperation heave as the gun went off and time ran out on the luckless 'Pokes as they lost their 12th straight in Allen Field House to even their season record at 7–7 and their conference mark at 1–1 as the 'Hawks continued their winning skein as they registered their second consecutive victory in conference play with no defeats as they boosted their season figures to 11–3 as thousands cheered."

And as tonstant weader fwowed up. Only a meaningless ass loves the meaningless *as*.

AS / LIKE

In standard usage, *like* is not a conjunction. As a preposition, *like* means "similar to" or "similarly to." If you can substitute either "similar to" or "similarly to," the word you're looking for is *like*. You would say, "She should be similar to (like) me" or "She should act similarly to (like) me." You would not say, "She won similar to I predicted" or "She won similarly to I predicted." So the right word in the last two examples is *as*.

"Tell it like it is" is a COSELLISM and a BARBARISM, as is "Gasper tastes good like a cigarette should."

The failure to distinguish between *as* and *like* is one of the most common blunders in written and spoken English. "Like I said"? No, "As I said." Some of us don't talk good like we used to could.

AS FOLLOWS

Though *follows* is singular, *as follows*, rather than *as follow*, is correct before a list of items, as in "The students on the honor roll are as follows:"; though *students* and *are* are plural, the idiomatic *as follows* is correct, perhaps because it is a shortened form of a phrase such as "*as* they are named in the list that *follows*."

AS IF / AS THOUGH

If is an adverbial conjunction of condition: "If he stays, she will leave." A condition of her leaving is his staying.

Though is an adverbial conjunction of concession: "Though he is fat, he is beautiful." You concede that he is fat, but you think he is beautiful.

In "He looks as if he is disgusted," *as if* is a conjunction compounded from *as* and *if* in the old construction "He looks as he would look if he were disgusted." Substitute *as though* for *as if* and you get "He looks as he would look though he were disgusted," which isn't what you mean and doesn't make sense. See also THOUGH.

AS IF / LIKE

As is said in AS / LIKE, if you can substitute either *similar to* or *similarly to*, the word you're looking for is *like*. Would you say, "He looks similar to he is disgusted" or "He looks similarly to he is disgusted"? So make it: "He looks as if he is disgusted."

The misuse of *like* for *as if* is widespread, especially in speech. Even in the learned corridors, nay, classrooms, of schools of journalism one hears repeatedly "It looks like it's gonna rain," "He looks like he had a bad night." It looks as if teachers should correct themselves and their students.

Use the subjunctive mood with *as if* when the sentence is in past or conditional tense and the *as if* clause expresses a condition contrary to fact. These are correct: "He played as if he were the only one on the team" (he wasn't the only one on the team); "He would drive as if he were trying to qualify at Indy" (he wasn't trying to qualify at Indy).

AS MANY

"She sang in four operas in as many nights." Why *as many*? Why not *four*? Don't be afraid to repeat a word.

ASPIRATE / ASPIRE, *see* –SPIRE

ASSASSIN

Note the spelling: double *s* twice. *Assassin* comes from Arabic *hashshashin*, eaters of hashish, a secret society of Moslem fanatics founded in Persia in the eleventh century and dedicated to the principle that the only good Christian was a dead one. Before they set out on murder missions, their sheikh, The Old Man of the Mountains, made sure they were highly fortified with hashish, a crutch of false courage that has extended beyond Persia.

ASSERT

From Latin *ad* + *serere*, to join to oneself, to claim, to maintain, to state positively. Don't use *asserted* as a simple synonym for *said*. Save it for strong statements. See SYNONYMOMANIA.

ASSUAGE

From Latin *suavis*, sweet, hence to make less severe, to pacify, to smooth. *Suave*, smoothly polite, blandly pleasing, has the same origin.

ASSUME / PRESUME

In the sense of "take for granted," the words are almost interchangeable. Shaw gives this fine distinction: to *assume* is "to infer without proof"; to *presume* is "to infer as true without actual proof to the contrary." One assumes something for the sake of argument. One presumes that night will fall.

In other senses, the words are not interchangeable, as can be seen from their etymology. *Assume* comes from Latin *ad + sumere*, to take to oneself, to adopt ("He assumed the role of devil's advocate"). *Presume* comes from *prae + sumere*, to take before, to take in advance ("He presumed to take the first place at table").

Some authorities use the get-together between Sir Henry Morton Stanley and Dr. David Livingstone in Tanganyika to illustrate the distinction between *assume* and *presume* in the sense of "take for granted." They say that Stanley, explorer and correspondent for the New York *Herald*, wasn't trying to start an argument with Livingstone, explorer and medical missionary, when he said, "Dr. Livingstone, I presume."

One undistinguished nonauthority insists that Livingstone's real name was Presume and that what Stanley said to him was "Sir, please state your full name," to which Livingstone replied, "Dr. Livingstone I. Presume." Incidentally, Stanley's real name was John Rowlands.

ASSURANCE / INSURANCE

In the United States, the financial term is *insurance*. In Britain, *insurance* is in general use, but some companies use *assurance* for life insurance, and *insurance* for marine, fire and accident. One explanation of the distinction is that the holder of a life or annuity policy is *assured* of benefits sooner or later, whereas the holder of a fire or accident policy is *insured* but has no assurance of ever having a fire or an accident. One is assured *of* something and insured *against* something. See also ENSURE / INSURE.

ASTERISK

So often heard and misspelled as *asterick*. An *asterisk* (*) is a little star, so called from its shape. From the diminutive of Greek *aster*, star.

AS THOUGH, *see* AS IF / AS THOUGH

AS THOUSANDS CHEERED, *see* AGOG and AS

ASTRAPHOBIA, *see* –PHOBIA

ASTROLOGY

One of the problems of news judgment is how much you should give readers what you think they want and how much you should give them what you think they need. It helps to know that what you think they want is what they want and that what you think they need is what they need.

Sometimes you should play God and give readers what you think they need but don't want. And sometimes you shouldn't give them what you think they want but don't need.

Astrologers (from Greek *astron*, star, and *legein*, to speak) pretend they can predict the course of human events from the course of celestial bodies. Despite the popularity of astrology as indicated by readership studies, why run a column on a pseudoscience? Why perpetuate the racket?

ASTRONAUT

A sailor among the stars, from Greek *astron*, star, and *nautes*, sailor.

ASTRONOMY

From Greek *astron*, star, and *nemein*, to arrange, hence the scientific study of the celestial bodies and phenomena beyond the earth. Astronomy is one of the classical liberal arts. Astrology is one of the classical con arts.

AS WELL AS

If you seek total confusion, read the reams the grammarians have written about *as well as*. Some call it strictly a conjunction, others both conjunction and preposition, others both phrasal conjunction and phrasal preposition.

Perhaps *as well as* is best treated as a conjunction meaning "and not only," not meaning "besides." So:

"They will have to give, as well as take (not *taking*), a little."

"We, as well as they (not *them*), are going."

"He, as well as she, is (not *are*) going." (The *as well as* phrase is set off by commas and is only a secondary subject.)

"He, as well as they, is (not *are*) going." (Same principle as in the previous example.)

Must the *as well as* phrase be set off by commas? Well, not necessarily in your copy, but preferably in your mind.

And what do you do if *I* is involved? According to the principle, you would have to say, "I, as well as she, am going," which is awkward. So politely reconstruct to "She, as well as I, is going." Or avoid the entire issue and say, "We're both going." See also PLUS.

ASYNDETON
A rhetorical figure in which conjunctions are omitted, as in "Ready, set, go" and "I came, I saw, I conquered." From Greek *a* + *syndetos*, without conjunctions. See also POLY-.

AT / IN
Vague is the old dictum that *in* is to be used for large places and *at* for small. What about all the places in between? And who is to define "large" and "small"? The only guide is idiom. But don't use the provincialism "I met him down to the store."

ATAXIA, *see* TAXIDERMY

ATHEISM, *see* THEO-

ATHLETE
Only two syllables. It's not *ath-a-lete*, though many athletes, and former athletes who are now sportscasters, throw in the extra syllable. Youngsters hear this and, as they imitate their heroes' sports style, they imitate their heroes' speech style, and so we have a generation running around and saying *ath-a-lete* and *ath-a-letic* and *ath-a-letics*.

Athlete comes from Greek *athlein*, to contend for a prize. *Ath-a-lete's foot* comes from athletes' foot-in-mouth disease.

ATLANTIC / ATLAS
The Greeks and Romans called the sea beyond the Atlas Mountains, in northwestern Africa, *pelagos Atlantikos* and *mare Atlanticum*, whence English *Atlantic*. The Atlas Mountains were so rugged that they were thought to support the heavens, which is how they got their name, from Atlas, the Titan in Greek mythology who was condemned to support the heavens on his shoulders. A volume of maps is called an *atlas* because the frontispiece of the early books of maps usually had a picture of Atlas holding the world.

ATOM, *see* -TOMY

AT RANDOM
A *random* sample is not designed *at random*, which means without definite purpose, unsystematically, from Old French *randon*, haphazard. A random sample is purposely designed to give every member of a population an equal chance of being represented.

ATROCIOUS
Commonly misspelled with a double *t* and commonly misused. Note the derivation, Latin *atrox*, cruel, fierce, and don't use *atrocious* as a synonym for *bad*. Save *atrocious* for the exceptionally violent, brutal, savage, much more wicked than simply bad.

ATROPHY
In both noun and verb, the stress is on the first syllable, and the last syllable is pronounced as in *fee*. From Greek *a* + *trephein*, to nourish not. *Trophy* comes from a different Greek root, *trepein*, to turn; a trophy was originally a monument erected where an enemy was turned back.

AT THE PRESENT TIME
Now.

AT THIS POINT IN TIME
Now.

ATTIC
A feature of the Attic (from *Athens*) style of architecture was a small top story with square columns, hence the English *attic* for a small room at the top of a house.

ATTORNEY
An *attorney* is not necessarily a lawyer. An *attorney* is anyone legally appointed to do business for someone else. From Old French *atorner*, to appoint.

ATTORNEY GENERAL
The plural is *attorneys general*. The AP abbreviation is Atty. Gen.

ATTRITION
From Latin *ad* + *terere*, to rub again, *attrition* means a wearing down, a gradual diminution in number or strength. Here are other words from the same root:

—*contrition*, a state of being "rubbed with," bruised, broken down with sorrow, humbly penitent.

—*detriment*, a rubbing away, causing damage, harm, loss.

—*detritus*, something rubbed away, disintegrated, left over.

—*termite*, a worm that wears away at wood at will.

—*tribulation*, a state of being worn down or something causing being worn down, ground under, pressed down (the *tribulum* was an instrument for grinding corn).

—*trite*, worn out by use, hackneyed.

AUDITION

Though the verbing of nouns is usually ugly, and unnecessary when suitable verbs already exist to convey intended meaning, sometimes the use of a noun as a verb meets a need. *To audition* is a good example. It avoids the awkwardness of "to grant a hearing to" or "to give a trial performance." And though *to audition* comes from Latin *audire*, to hear, it usually involves not only hearing, but also seeing. See VERBING NOUNS.

AUGEAN

When editorial writers call on government to clean house, they may call for "the cleansing of the Augean stable." The reference is to Augeas, king of Elis, who left his large stable of oxen uncleaned for thirty years. Hercules cleaned it in one day by diverting through it the rivers Alpheus and Peneus. *Augean* thus came to mean exceedingly filthy or corrupt.

AUGER, *see* ADDER

AU JUS

When one's French is confined mostly to menus, one may show one's ignorance of French. When a diner orders roast beef from a menu that has "roast beef au jus," he may add, "But easy on the au jus," which is like saying, "But easy on the in juice." *Au jus* is straight French for "in juice," served with the natural juices of the meat. See also CHAISE LONGUE.

AULD LANG SYNE

When you're celebrating New Year's Eve, you'll inexorably arrive at the embarrassing moment when you'll all join hands and sing a song nobody ever quite seems to know all the words to. "Auld Lang Syne," a Scottish song of uncertain origin, was partly rewritten by Robert Burns. Its name is Scottish for "old long since," hence the good old days long past, the days we didn't know were good till they were long past.

AUSPICIOUS

The word has been cheapened by public speakers who seem unable to omit "on this auspicious occasion" from their Babbittry. From Latin *avis* + *specere*, to look at birds, to observe omens in the flight of birds, *auspicious* has come to mean attended by favorable omens, indicative of success, prosperous. See also GUEST SPEAKER.

AUTARCHY / AUTARKY

The words have different roots and different meanings. *Autarchy* is from Greek *auto* + *archein*, to rule by oneself, to rule with absolute power. *Autarky* is from Greek *auto* + *arkeein*, to suffice by oneself, to be independent. Autarky is the policy of national economic self-sufficiency, independent of imports.

AUTHENTIC / GENUINE

The similar roots of these words from different languages indicate their similar meanings. *Authentic* is from Greek *authentes*, one who does anything with his own hand. *Genuine* is from Latin *gignere*, to beget. Both words mean reliable, trustworthy. But *authentic* has the added meaning of "not fictitious," and *genuine* has the added meaning of "not spurious." An authentic account of something is one that corresponds to facts; truth is involved in authenticity. A genuine Lincoln manuscript is one that can be proved to have been written by Lincoln himself. A work of art can be both authentic and genuine. Sargent's portrait of Theodore Roosevelt depicts Roosevelt as he was and it was painted by Sargent. One could prove that Michelangelo's *Moses* is genuine, but it would be hard to prove authentic.

AUTHOR

As a verb, *author* is rejected by 81 percent of the American Heritage usage panel. Hooray for 81 percent of the American Heritage usage panel! An author writes a book. He doesn't author it. See VERBING NOUNS.

AUTOCRACY, *see* –CRACY

AUTONOMY, *see* –NOMY

AUTOPSY

From Greek *autos* + *optos*, seen for oneself. An *autopsy* is an examination of a body to learn the cause of death. It is also called a *post-mortem*, Latin for "after death."

AUXILIARY VERB

An auxiliary verb is one that helps (Latin *auxilium*, help) to form the tenses, voices and moods of other verbs. For example: "I *have* seen him," "I *have been* seen," "I *must* go." English has eight auxiliary verbs: *be, can, do, have, may, must, shall, will*. These have fifteen other forms: *am, are, is, was, being, been, were* from *be; could* from *can; did, does* from *do; had, has* from *have; might* from *may; should* from *shall; would* from *will*.

Sometimes an auxiliary verb may be used as a principal or notional verb (one that of itself expresses the notion of action or state), as in "I have a book," "He is a student," "We do good work." In "Let me out so that I may run," *may* is an auxiliary, indicating the potential (or subjunctive mood) of running. But in "He may run if he wishes," *may* is a notional verb, indicating permission to run.

AVANT-GARDE

French for vanguard, *avant-garde* is applied to anyone in the forefront of his art as an experimenter and innovator. *Avant-garde* has deteriorated to mean anything from daring to downright disgusting.

AVENGE / REVENGE

Avenge is a verb; its noun is *vengeance*. *Revenge* is both verb and noun. Their meanings depend on the point of view of the person avenging or revenging.

Avenge connotes the achieving of justice ("I'll avenge the slaying of my daughter by tracking down her killer and bringing him to the bar of justice"). *Revenge* connotes the achieving of personal satisfaction ("I'll revenge that parking ticket by putting sand in that cop's gas tank").

Someone seeking vengeance is trying to vindicate. Someone seeking revenge is being vindictive.

AVER

When was the last time you heard someone quote someone else by saying, "'I'll have a beer,' he averred"?

In its legal sense, to *aver*, from Latin *verus*, true, is to verify, to prove or justify a plea. Don't use *averred* as a simple synonym for *said*. Save it for its legal sense or for dogmatic declaration. See SYNONYMOMANIA.

AVERAGE

An *average* is a measure of central tendency. Three averages are in common use: mean, median, mode. In a set of numerical grades, for example, the *mean* is the total of the grades divided by the number of students; the *median* is the middle grade; the *mode* is the grade most frequently occurring. In the set 40, 45, 50, 56, 60, 65, 65, 65, 76, the mean is 58, the median 60, the mode 65.

AVERSE, *see* ADVERSE / AVERSE

AVID
From Latin *avere*, to long for, *avid* should be restricted to the notion of craving eagerly, excessively desirous, greedy. It has become a cliché, as in "an avid sports fan."

AVOCADO
Note the spelling. And the plural is *avocados:* no *e*. The derivation is as tasteless as the fruit is tasty: from Spanish *aguacate* (perhaps corrupted by Spanish *bocado*, tidbit), from Nahuatl (Uto-Aztec) *ahuacatl*, testicle (from the shape of the fruit). See also ORCHID.

AVOCATION / VOCATION
The prefix in the derivation of *avocation*, Latin *a* + *vocare*, to call away from, shows the distinction between the words. One's calling is one's vocation. For respite from one's calling, one is called away from it to a hobby.

AVUNCULAR
A diminutive of Latin *avus*, grandfather, *avuncular* is the adjective for *uncle*. It originally referred to a maternal uncle but it is now applied to all kinds of uncle, including Sam and pawnbrokers.

   Aunt, from Latin *amita*, father's sister, is now applied to all kinds of aunt. It has no adjectival form except perhaps the contrived *auntlike*. For the feminine form of the masculine adverb *avuncularly*, foolish *-wise* addicts will contrive *auntwise*. See –WISE.

AWARD
Awards are prizes that surely every red-blooded American has won at least one of. The bestowal of awards is a national pastime promoted by the press to provide copy, especially on sports and other business pages. If by malevolent chance you have never won an award, you should win one for never having won one. Then the papers will say, "John Smith was awarded the prize for . . ." But, unless Smith was the award, Smith wasn't awarded. The prize was. See also FALSE PASSIVE.

AWFULLY

Overused and often misused. Strictly, *awfully* means appallingly, dreadfully, horribly. Hence phrases such as "an awfully decent person" or "an awfully good time" are strictly contradictory. See also AFRAID.

AWHILE

An adverb. One word ("He stayed awhile"). Because *awhile* means "for a time," *for awhile* would mean "for for a time." Because the noun *while* means "period of time," *for a while* is correct. Either *awhile* or *for a while*.

BABBITT
George F. Babbitt, the lead character in Sinclair Lewis' novel *Babbitt* (1922), epitomized the smugness of smalltown businessmen, schooled but uneducated, banded in clubs for self-protection and the perpetuation of parochial outlook. *Babbitt* became a word for such a person. See ANTONOMASIA.

BABY SITTER
AP spells *baby sitter* as two words but hyphenates *baby-sit* and *baby-sitting.*

BACCALAUREATE
The word comes from Latin *bacca lauri*, laurel berry, and implies the laurel conferred on one who receives a bachelor's degree. (To the celebrations come the Laurels and the Plaudits, professional partygoers.)

BACK FORMATION
The French gave us the noun *liaison* and we got along fine till somebody decided to coin the verb *liase* from it. The process is called back formation.

The Greeks gave us the noun *enthusiasm*, from which somebody coined the ugly verb *enthuse*, branded colloquial by Webster and disapproved by 76 percent of the American Heritage usage panel, but growing in use.

Back formation is not necessarily evil. Time and need are the criteria. *Liase* hasn't lasted and isn't needed. Many back-formed words, however, have become accepted, such as *diagnose, donate, drowse, laze, orate, resurrect, sidle.*

Sculpt isn't needed but seems to be gaining ground on *sculpture* as a verb. The unneeded and graceless *commentate* is still regarded by wordsmiths as barbaric, taste be praised. *Buttle* is disappearing as fast as butlers.

Burgle a century ago may have been facetious, but it has grown in acceptability, and almost anything is better than the hideous *burglarize.*

BACTERIA
The word is plural. Hence bacteria *are*. The singular is *bacterium*, from Greek *bakterion*, a little staff, a reference to the shape of the microorganism. *Bacillus*, a species of bacterium, is from Latin *bacillum*, a little rod, again a reference to shape. From the same root comes *imbecile*, a person without a staff, without something to lean on, without support, hence feeble-minded.

BAD / BADLY, *see* ADJECTIVE / ADVERB

BAD BLOOD
To say of people who hate each other that there is "bad blood between them" is to use what Evans calls "an anemic cliché."

BADE
Pronounced *bad*. *Bade* and *bid* are forms of the past tense of *bid*. Use the past tense *bade* in the sense of "ordered, invited, greeted, said farewell." Use the past tense *bid* in the sense of "offered to buy" and in bridge.

BAGDAD-ON-THE-SUBWAY
The inhabitants of Gotham, a village in Nottinghamshire, dissuaded King John from living there by behaving like imbeciles. Six hundred years later, the legend persuaded Washington Irving to give the name Gotham to New York. Then O. Henry called it Bagdad-on-the-Subway, a much more authentic and picturesque term than Mayor John Lindsay's Fun City. The Big Apple has had some rotten problems.

BAILIWICK
Wick (from Latin *vicus* to Middle English *wik*) means village, and a bailiwick is a bailiff's territory, hence the modern meaning of one's private domain or area of authority.

BALANCE
A balance scale has two plates, from Latin *bi* + *lanx*, double plate. Don't use *balance* when you mean *remainder*. A *balance* is the difference between two things, such as credit and debit, as in "bank balance." The remainder is what is left over from the whole, as in "the remainder (better *rest*) of the week." The American Heritage usage panelists are almost evenly split on this distinction: 47 percent for, the remainder against.

BALDING

Time magazine likes the adjective *balding*, meaning "becoming bald." Bernstein objects to it. He prefers *baldish*. The American Heritage, which calls *balding* "informal" and doesn't mention *baldish*, says *balding* is accepted by 55 percent of its usage panelists. Representative responses from them are those of Isaac Asimov, "distasteful but necessary," and Katherine Anne Porter, "entirely vulgar."

BALLISTICS

The word comes from Greek *ballein*, to throw, hence the study of projectiles. Many English words derive from the same root. Among them:
  —*diabolic*, thrown across, hence traducing, calumniating, slanderous; slander long having been considered a great evil, *diabolic* was applied to the vice, hence *devil*, *devilish*.
  —*emblem*, something thrown in, inserted, hence inlaid work.
  —*embolism*, the lodging of something inserted in a tube or canal too small for its passage, something "thrown into" the blood, such as a clot or an air bubble.
  —*hyperbole*, something thrown beyond, hence exaggeration; the geometric *hyperbola* comes from the same roots.
  —*metabolism*, something thrown elsewhere, changed, hence the chemical changes in living cells.
  —*parable*, something thrown beside, compared, set beside, juxtaposed; from the same roots come *palaver*, *parabola*, *parlance*, *parley*, *parliament*, *parlor*, *parole*.
  —*problem*, something thrown forward, put forward, proposed.
  —*symbol*, something thrown with, put together; originally a token of identification, something broken in two so that the bearers could match the parts for identification, hence a sign.

BALLOT

From Italian *ballota*, a bullet, diminutive of *balla*, a ball. White and black balls were once used in secret balloting, as they are today, at least metaphorically, in some clubs and societies; hence to blackball somebody, to reject from membership.

BALLPARK FIGURE

Bureaucratic jargon for *an estimate*, made popular by the Nixon gang's penchant for sports metaphors.

BALLYHOO
Shipley and Webster say the word comes from Ballyhooly, a village in County Cork, Ireland, seemingly noted for the uproarious bluster of its inhabitants, as the inhabitants of the Cork village of Blarney were noted for their wheedling flattery. The American Heritage says the origin of *ballyhoo* is unknown. Certainly, however, *bally* is a British euphemism for *bloody*. Partridge says *ballyhoo* is perhaps from *ballyhooly truth*, a music-hall corruption of "the whole bloody truth."

BANSHEE
From Gaelic *bean sidhe*, woman of the fairy folk, a *banshee* is a female spirit who wails outside a house to warn the family that one of its members is about to die. Many Irishmen say they have heard a banshee. All Irishmen know someone who has.

BANZAI
The word is Japanese for "(may you live) 10,000 years" and has become part of the language in the United States since World War II as a result of the suicidal bayonet charges by Japanese troops yelling "banzai."

BAPTIZE
From Greek *baptein*, to dip in water. Mencken, quoting Grose's *Classical Dictionary of the Vulgar Tongue*, uses *baptized* to refer to "spirits that have been lowered with water."

BARBARISM
The ancient Greeks said the language of foreigners sounded like "bar-bar-bar." They nicknamed foreigners "the bar-bar people," hence *barbarians*. People who speak or write ungrammatically commit barbarisms. See also RHUBARB.

BARBECUE
Note the spelling. It isn't *barbeque*, despite the signs on Jiffyburger Alley, Anytown, U.S.A. The word comes from Taino through Haitian Creole and Spanish *barbacoa*, a framework of sticks on posts.

BARD
The word is Gaelic. A *bard* was a professional poet who composed and sang songs about his tribe's heroes. Thomas Moore's minstrel boy was

indeed a warrior bard. But to use *bard* to refer indiscriminately to any poet is, as Evans points out, "to indulge in a low grade of frigid jocularity," and to call Shakespeare "the Bard of Avon" is "to come feebly into the rear of an outworn fashion with a lamentable piece of stilted nonsense."

BARMECIDE FEAST
A gift that looks like something valuable but is really nothing. From the *Arabian Nights* story of a wealthy Persian family, the Barmecides, one of whom served a hungry beggar an imaginary feast.

BARNBURNER
One who comes on strong, like the man who burned his barn to rid it of rats.

BARRATRY
From French *barater*, to cheat, *barratry* is the crime of buying or selling of positions in church or state and, in maritime law, the fraudulent breach of duty by a ship's master resulting in loss to a ship's owner.

The word has a third meaning: the practice of stirring up groundless lawsuits, prevalent today in many cases of insurance, professional liability, exaggerated rights and selective indignation.

BASED ON
A common dangling participial phrase, as in "Based on his record, I would promote him." This means that you are based on his record, because the participle belongs to "I," the subject of the clause. Make it: "Based on his record, my opinion is that he should be promoted" or, better, "I would promote him because of (on the basis of) his record." See DANGLING PARTICIPLE.

BASICALLY
Have you noticed that you've been hearing *basically* a lot more than you used to? It's catching up with other knee-jerk words like *yunno* and *hopefully*:

"How did you like the movie?" "Basically, I liked it."
"What do you think of Carter?" "Basically, he's an honest guy."
"Can Watson putt?" "Basically, he's a good putter."
Whatever happened to *on the whole, in general, mostly*?

BASIC ENGLISH
A form of English invented in the 1920s by C. K. Ogden, an English psychologist, in the hope of establishing a simple international language. Hence he called it "basic," which is also an acronym for British American Scientific International Commercial. It consists of 850 English words: 600 nouns, 150 adjectives, 100 "structural" words, of which only 16 are verbs. There are also 100 non-English scientific terms and 250 "word groups."

Basic English wasn't intended to supplant English or to stifle style, but to promote international understanding and to simplify the teaching of English as a foreign language. Despite its simplicity, Basic English hasn't caught on. See also ESPERANTO.

BATED BREATH
If you use the cliché, spell it right. You'll see *baited breath* as often as the correct spelling, as if one's mouth were a mousetrap. The adjective comes from *abate*, hence to moderate, to hold one's breath in anticipation of something. See SONIC WRITING.

BATHOS
Don't confuse *bathos* with *pathos*. *Bathos*, the Greek word for depth, is a descent from the sublime to the ridiculous. You commit *bathos* if, for example, you ruin a stately speech by ending it with some tasteless anecdote. The adjective is *bathetic*, like *pathetic*, the adjective for *pathos*, the Greek word for suffering. *Bathos* is commonly misused as the equivalent of "sloppy sentimentality."

BATTLE ROYAL
If you want to sound like a fan of cockfighting, use *battle royal*, a cliché from the jargon of the cockpit. Originally, the term referred to medieval jousting between teams commanded by kings.

B.C., *see* A.D.

BEAT A HASTY RETREAT
A cliché. He got out fast.

BECAUSE OF / DUE TO
Verbs, other than copulatives (see ADJECTIVE / ADVERB), take adverbs. Nouns and pronouns take adjectives. *Due to* is an adjectival preposi-

tional phrase, as in "His defeat was due to carelessness." Here the adjective *due* belongs to the noun *defeat*. If you say, "He was defeated due to carelessness," *due* has nothing to belong to; *he* wasn't due, nor was *carelessness* due. *Because of* is an adverbial prepositional phrase, as in "He was defeated because of carelessness." Here *because of* belongs to the verb *defeated*.

BEDLAM
The word is a corruption of *Bethlehem*, which was pronounced *bedlam* in reference to the hospital of St. Mary of Bethlehem, in London. The hospital was what used to be called a lunatic asylum, a madhouse. Hence *bedlam* today refers to any scene of uproarious confusion, such as the newsroom of a university paper, sometimes called a night care center.

BEFORE, *see* AFTER

BEGIN / COMMENCE / START
The distinctions among these words are of context, not of meaning. Custom prescribes the proper use in a particular context, such as "begin the meal," "commence the ceremony," "start the race." *Begin* is the most common, and one wouldn't commence or start the beguine. Note that the past tense is *began* and the past participle *begun*: "He began to cry. He has begun to cry." *Commence* is the most formal. One *starts* one's engine, as in the Indianapolis 500 ritual, "Drivers, start your engines," which is also how Jimmy Hoffa used to announce the end of a Teamsters strike.

BEG THE QUESTION
Begging the question is not the same as avoiding the issue. To *beg the question* is to assume, without proof, the truth of something whose truth is being questioned. If you are trying to prove the existence of a deity, you beg the question if you state that a belief in God's existence is essential to man's sanity.

BEHALF
The terms *in behalf of* and *on behalf of* are not interchangeable. *In behalf of* means "for the benefit of, for the sake of, in the interest of," as in "Trevino played the exhibition in behalf of the Mexican earthquake relief fund." *On behalf of* means "as the agent of, on the part of, in the place of," as in "The dean thanked the school's benefactors on behalf of the faculty."

BEHEMOTH

The more common pronunciation has the stress on the second syllable, not the first. Authorities differ on whether the behemoth (from the Hebrew word for "great beasts") described in the Book of Job was a hippopotamus or an elephant. You be the judge: "He eateth grass like an ox. His strength is in his loins, and his force in the navel of his belly. He setteth up his tail like a cedar; the sinews of his testicles are wrapped together. His bones are like pipes of brass, his gristle like plates of iron." Despite the cedarlike tail, the vote here is for hippopotamus, mostly because Job's chronicler says later, "He will drink up a river and not wonder." *Behemoth* today has the meaning of something enormous in size, such as Alex Karras or Hagar the Horrible.

BEING AS

"Being as I missed the bus, I was late for class," the student said. The student is a barbarian. Like "being as how," "seeing as how," "allowing as how," *being as* is a barbarism. Make it *because*.

BELABOR

To *belabor* is to beat with a stick, to assail verbally. Barzun insists that it does not mean to "make a to-do about," which is to *labor* a point, to deal with in exhaustive detail.

BELIEVE / FEEL / THINK

The thinking wordsmith will not use these words interchangeably. One *believes* with the heart, the soul, faith. One *feels* with the senses, the emotions. One *thinks* with the mind, intellect, reason.

You believe in God, you believe in a hereafter, you believe in her, you believe that she won't let you down. Not: I don't believe we've met before (I don't think we have).

You feel hungry, you feel nauseated, you feel a song coming on, you feel sorry for him, you feel he can't be trusted. Not: He feels that the speed limit should be enforced (He thinks it should be).

BELLY

It's a good word, whether anatomical or metaphorical, as in *bellyache*, *bellyband*, *bellybutton*, *belly dancer*, *belly flop*, *bellyful*, *belly landing*, *belly laugh*, *belly up to the bar*, *yellow-bellied* and Churchill's reference to the Balkans as the Nazis' *soft underbelly*. See Evans, under *belly*, for a delightful discussion of *abdomen*, *belly*, *guts*, *stomach*, *tummy* and "the futility of attempting through euphemisms to avoid the facts of life."

BENEDICT
A newly married man, especially one who has long been a bachelor, possibly trapped into committing matrimony. From Benedick, the confirmed bachelor in Shakespeare's *Much Ado About Nothing*, sparring partner of Beatrice, whom he married after stormy courtship. *Benedick* and *Beatrice* come from Latin *benedictus* and *beatus*, both meaning blessed.

BENEFITED
The past tense and the participles of *benefit* have only one *t*. See also ALLOTTED.

BESIEGE
Note the spelling.

BEST / MOST, *see* **BETTER / MORE**

BE SURE AND SEE
This is an example of hendiadys, from Greek *hen dia dyoin*, one by two, the linking of two words with a conjunction to express one idea. "Be sure and see me" would mean two actions, being sure and seeing, whereas one action is intended, being sure to see. Make it "Be sure to see me." A more common example is "Try and do better." You're not being asked to try and to do, but to try to do. Make it "Try to do better."

BETTER / MORE
When you say "like" or "dislike," "love" or "hate," you're expressing quality. When you want to say how much you like or dislike, how much you love or hate, you need a quantitative adverb because you have already expressed quality. Thus you like this house *more* than you like that house, not *better*. You like coffee *more* than you like tea, not *better*. You love her *more and more* each day, not *better and better*, unless you're equating love with physical technique. And you wouldn't say, "I hate (or dislike) it worse." So why "I love (or like) it better"? The same principles apply to the superlatives *best* and *most*.

BETTER PART OF
"She stayed for the better part of an hour" means that she stayed for more than a half-hour. Why *better*? Are the last thirty minutes better than the first thirty? Make it "most of the hour" or "the greater part."

BETWEEN, *see* **AMONG / BETWEEN**

BETWEEN EACH (EVERY)
"He smoked furiously between each (every) act" doesn't make sense.
A plural, or two singulars, should come after *between*. Make it "between
acts" or "between one act and the next."

BETWEEN YOU AND I
A barbarism. Prepositions take the objective case: between you and me,
between her and him, between them and us.

BETWIXT AND BETWEEN
Unless the alliteration is needed for rhythm, avoid this cliché. The two
words mean the same.

BIANNUAL / BIENNIAL
Twice a year is *biannual*. Once every two years is *biennial*.

BIBLE
Uppercase when referring to the sacred book of Christianity, compris-
ing the Old and New Testaments: "The Bible has long been a best seller."
Lowercase when referring to a work considered authoritative in a discipline or occupation: Fowler's *A Dictionary of Modern English Usage*,
the bible of the English language; the *Sporting News*, the bible of baseball; the *Daily Racing Form*, the bible of horse racing.

BIBLE BELT
Mencken's term for the Southern and border states in which religious
fundamentalism rules.

BIBLIOPHILE, *see* **PHIL–**

BICAMERAL
From Latin *camera*, room, chamber. A *bicameral* legislature has two
chambers, branches, houses. A *unicameral* legislature has only one.

BID, *see* **BADE**

BIENNIAL, *see* **BIANNUAL / BIENNIAL**

BIGAMY, *see* **–GAMY**

BIKINI

Bikini has nothing to do with two kinis. Bikini, an atoll in the Marshall Islands, was the site of the first atomic bomb tests after World War II. The impact was similar to that produced by the first tiny two-piece swimsuits, hence the name *bikini*. The later *monokini* is thus falsely derived, as is the *nokini* of nude swimmers.

BIKINI HEAD

Sometimes a news story has so many angles that a copy editor has to decide whether to write a headline that tries to cover everything or a headline that covers only one of the angles. He must make a decision between a *crinoline head*, which covers everything but touches nothing, and a *bikini head*, which covers very little but touches the main points.

For example, if a story concerns a city commission meeting that covered five agenda items, all more or less equally newsworthy, a copy editor might go for a crinoline head, sometimes called a deadhead or flathead, such as "City Commission Meets." Or he might choose one of the items and write a bikini head, such as "City Raises Bus Fares." The choice depends on the size of the head and the nature of the story.

BILLABONG

From Australian aboriginal *billa*, water, and *bong*, dead, *billabong* has a sound lovelier than its derivation. A billabong is a blind river channel or a stagnant backwater. The word has become known beyond Australia because of the international popularity of the song "Waltzing Matilda," whose first line tells of the jolly swagman who camped by a billabong. Like many Americans who have never seen a home where the buffalo roam, many Australians have never seen a billabong.

BILLINGSGATE

The word means abusive language, from the notoriously foul language of the fish market at Billings Gate, one of the old city gates of London, just below the old London Bridge. The language near the new London Bridge is the plastic patois of a supermarket in Lake Havasu City, Arizona, U.S.A.

BILLION

In American usage, a *billion* is a thousand millions: 1,000,000,000.
In British usage, a *billion* is a million millions: 1,000,000,000,000.

The British word for our billion is *milliard*. *Billion* comes from

French *bi + million*, a million to the second power, but the French follow the American numeration. The Germans follow the British. Editors dealing with foreign copy should beware.

BIMONTHLY / SEMIMONTHLY
Once every two months is *bimonthly*. Twice a month is *semimonthly*. The distinction should be preserved, especially in journalism.

BIRTHDAY, *see* ANNIVERSARY

BISCUIT
From Latin *bis + coctus*, twice cooked. An American biscuit is a British scone. A British biscuit is an American cracker or cookie.

BITE OFF / CHEW
"To bite off more than you can chew," a relic of spittoon culture, was revived by Sinatra in "My Way." If you bite chaws from plugs of tobacco, use this cliché. Otherwise, forget it.

BITESIZE SNACKS
This adman's phrase is etymologically redundant. *Snack* comes from Middle Dutch *snakken*, to bite.

BITTER END
In this cliché, *bitter* doesn't refer to sour taste. A *bitter* is the end of a ship's cable or rope wound around a bitt (a post). If you're at the *bitter end*, you're at the end of your rope. The sour taste in your mouth is etymologically incidental.

BITTERSWEET
This beautiful word is an OXYMORON.

BIWEEKLY / SEMIWEEKLY
Once every two weeks is *biweekly*. Twice a week is *semiweekly*. It's too bad the British *fortnightly*, every two weeks, sounds affected over here.

BLACKGUARD
Originally, blackguards were kitchen workers in an army or a noble household, so called because the color of their pots and pans became theirs.

BLACKMAIL
From Old English *mael*, agreement, the Scottish *mail* meant rent. "White mail" was paid in silver. "Black mail" was paid in grain or cattle to plunderers along the Scottish border in exchange for protection. Hence the modern meaning of *blackmail* as extortion by intimidation.

BLAME
Only beings with a conscience—thus human beings and their institutions—can be guilty, blameworthy. So don't blame inanimates or irrational beings. And don't blame something on somebody (or some body). Blame somebody (or some body) for something.

BLINDMAN'S BUFF
The game is blindman's buff, not blindman's bluff. *Buff* is short for *buffet*, a slap.

BLITZ
Short for German *blitzkrieg*, literally "lightning war." Both *blitz* and *blitzkrieg* are now standard English. War impoverishes man but enriches his language.

BLOND / BLONDE
As an adjective, *blond* may be used of both sexes. As an adjective, *blonde* is feminine. As nouns, *blond* is masculine and *blonde* feminine.

BLOVIATE
You won't find *bloviate* in the American Heritage or in Webster's Second. Like Espy, who delights in the word, one has to "resort to the Third to find it, and resorting to the Third is a personal humiliation for me." To *bloviate* (possibly from blow) is to orate verbosely and windily. It deserves circulation.

BLOW YOUR MIND
This phrase is a child of the drug culture of the 1960s. Like its parent, it's abhorrent.

BLURB
This term for book-jacket puffery was coined by Gelett Burgess, humorist and illustrator, and defined by him as "a sound like a publisher." Burgess, famous for his "Purple Cow" quatrain, also coined **BROMIDE**. A

special edition of his *Are You a Bromide?* has on its jacket a picture of a sickly sweet young woman whom he called "Miss Blinda Blurb."

BOBOLINK
A sonic delight, both in call and in name. Originally *boblincoln*.

BODACIOUS
A slang combination of *bold* and *audacious*.

BOGEY
In golf, bogey, from *bogy*, an imaginary person, used to be what we now call par, the number of strokes an imaginary first-rate golfer, such as the imaginary Colonel Bogey, would take on a hole or for a round. In modern golf, *bogey* has lost this meaning and now means one over par. A birdie is one under par; an eagle, two under; an albatross (or double eagle), three under.

BOGGLES THE MIND
Intransitively, to *boggle* is to shy suddenly in alarm. The mind boggles at something. "It boggles the mind" is an example of the error of making an intransitive verb transitive. Transitively, to *boggle* is to make a botch of, to bungle, but this is not the sense in which it is used in "boggles the mind." The phrase is now a cliché.

BONA FIDE, *see* SONIC WRITING

BONFIRE
The word is not from French *bon*, good. *Bonfire* is from Middle English *banefyre*, a fire of bones, such as occurred in the burning of victims of plague and religious persecution.

BONHOMIE, *see* SONIC WRITING

BOOBOISIE
To remedy what they considered the paucity of words to describe victims of the Depression, Mencken and a couple of his friends put together a list of about fifty new words, which Mencken published in the Baltimore *Evening Sun*. Among them were *boobariat*, *booberati*, *boobarian*, *boobomaniac*, *boobuli* and *booboisie*. Only *booboisie* has lasted. A combination of *boob* and *bourgeoisie*, it refers to people who are stupid and gullible.

BOONDOCKS
From Tagalog *bundok*, a mountain. The boondocks are the scrub country, the backwoods, the sticks, the bush.

BOONDOGGLE
A scoutmaster in Rochester, N.Y., coined *boondoggle* in 1925 to describe the braided leather lanyard made and worn by Boy Scouts, which is what these youths were called before society got ridiculously touchy. During the New Deal, *boondoggle* came to mean any unnecessary and wasteful project.

BOOST
A blend of *boom* and *hoist*.

BOOTLEG
Long before the sad days of Prohibition, smugglers and other illegal purveyors of liquor would carry their contraband in the legs of their knee-high boots to avoid detection by government agents.

BOOTLESS
Bootless doesn't mean unshod. From Anglo-Saxon *bot*, profit, *bootless* means without profit, unavailing, fruitless. In Shakespeare's *Julius Caesar*, Caesar, constant as the northern star that Cimber should remain banished, said: "Doth not Brutus bootless kneel?" Even Brutus couldn't change Caesar's mind. And Brutus didn't change his own mind, either, as Caesar found out a second later, gasping, "Et tu, Brute? Then fall, Caesar."

BOOZE
From Middle Dutch *busen*, to carouse, to see the world with some color in it.

BORN IN WAUKEGAN
To telescope facts, reporters sometimes join unjoinables (see NON SEQUITUR). A common device is the *born in* formula, as in "Born in Southern California, he played football for the Chicago Bears" or "Born in Chicago, she studied piano at the Curtis Institute in Philadelphia." In *Watch Your Language*, Bernstein gives this comment from Marc Rose, a *Reader's Digest* editor: "Born in Waukegan, Ill., I get damn sick of the non sequiturs."

BOSTON ACCENT

The Boston accent is the subject of much research and the butt of many stories. It has been described as "one-third Harvard, one-third hick and one-third mick." A fish-starved Nebraskan arrived in Boston and asked a cab driver: "Where can I get scrod around here?" Replied the cabby: "How delightful to hear the pluperfect subjunctive!"

BOTTLENECK

A student said he was late for class because of heavy traffic at the intersection of 23d and Iowa streets, which he called "the biggest bottleneck in town." So traffic there should really flow copiously. Cut your metaphors down to size.

BOTTOM LINE

Bureaucratic jargon for net profit or loss, the final score, what's left at the end.

BOUND AND DETERMINED

A cliché.

BOURBON

The whiskey gets its name from Bourbon County, Kentucky. Unlike the name of the French royal family, bourbon whiskey is pronounced *burbun*, not *boorbun*.

BOURGEOISIE

Note the spelling. See also **BOOBOISIE**.

BOWDLERIZE

To expurgate, to censor prudishly. The Rev. Thomas Bowdler, a Scottish physician, edited *The Family Shakespeare* in 1818, expunging "whatever is unfit to be read by a gentleman in a company of ladies." But modern scholarship, according to Morris, has discovered that the original bowdlerizer was not Thomas but his sister Henrietta Maria, known as Harriet, who edited the first edition of *The Family Shakespeare* in 1807.

The edition had no editor's name on the title page but, according to Susan Shatto, a Shakespearean scholar, writing in the London *Times* of March 30, 1976, "Harriet's family and friends knew the work to be hers." Harriet didn't take the credit, because, says Shatto, "as a spinster past middle age, she might not want the public to know that her understanding of Shakespeare was sufficient to expurgate it."

Morris adds: "That puts us in mind of the remark that Samuel Johnson made to a pair of ladies who congratulated him for omitting the four-letter words from his dictionary: 'I find it interesting to note that you have been looking for them.'"

BOYCOTT

Capt. Charles Boycott was agent for the estates of the Earl of Erne, County Mayo, Ireland. In 1880, the tenants, plagued by crop failures and absentee landlords and English domination and spurred by the land reform program of Charles Parnell, Irish nationalist statesman, set up their own scale of rents and refused to pay what Boycott demanded. Encouraged by Parnell to "isolate him from his kind as if he were a leper of old," the tenants submitted Boycott to a series of criminal harassments, refusing to gather crops, forcing his servants to leave him, destroying his property, intercepting his mail and food supplies, jeering at him in the streets, hanging him in effigy, threatening his life. In short, they *boycotted* him. The word quickly became part of the English language and has spread to French, German, Dutch and Russian.

BRACHY–

The combining Greek form for *short*, as in: *brachycephalic*, having a short, almost round head; *brachydactylic*, having abnormally short fingers or toes; *brachylogy*, a short, concise speech or shortened expression; *brachypterous*, short-winged; *brachyuran*, short-tailed.

BRACKETS

From Latin *bracae*, breeches, through the French diminutive *braguette*, a codpiece (from Middle English *cod*, a bag, the scrotum), a pouch covering the crotch of the tightfitting breeches worn by men in the fifteenth and sixteenth centuries. Brackets in punctuation are of two kinds: ( ), for parentheses; and [ ], brackets, for insertion of words not in the original copy and for a parenthesis within parentheses. Thus: (See the illustration of *codpiece*, *Il Finimondo* [*The End of the World*], by [Luca] Signorelli in the American Heritage.)

BRAGGADOCIO

Note the spelling: double *g*, single *c*. *Braggadocio* is from Old French *bragard* and the Italian augmentative *-occio*. Braggadocchio, a character in Spenser's *The Faerie Queene*, was a personification of vain boasting.

BRAILLE
Named for its inventor, Louis Braille (1809–52), French musician and educator, blind from childhood. The system is spelled either uppercase or lowercase.

BRASSIERE
This French word is now English, usually shortened to *bra*. From Latin *brachium*, arm, come *brace*, support, and *brassiere* (from French *bras*, arm), garment of support, like an arm around the body. Other common words from *brachium* are *bracelet*, *bracer*, *embrace*. From the same root, the Spanish *bracero*, one who works with his arms, is now the American word for a Mexican laborer allowed to migrate to the United States to work for a specified period.

BRAVERY / COURAGE
Bravery is an innate quality. *Courage* is the quality you hope to have when put to the test. For courage, you need fear. And, negatively, you hope to have the courage not to do something. Veteran soldiers show their bravery in battle. Little children show their courage in the dentist's chair.

BREAKAGE
Ponder this as you read the racing results. Suppose that the win pool in a horse race is $500,000 and that the club's share and taxes amount to 16 percent. This leaves a pool of $420,000. Suppose that $42,060 has been invested on the winner. This should mean a dividend of $19.97 for a $2 ticket. But no. The club breaks down dividends into multiples of 20 cents. Thus your $2 ticket brings you $19.80. And the club collects $3,606 in what is called *breakage*. Incidentally, without club's share and taxes, your dividend would have been $21.39. This is what is known as never giving a sucker an even break. There's one born every minute. Good old reliable Nathan.

BREAKDOWN
The word is an example, from statistics, of what Fowler calls "popularized technicalities." *Breakdown* is an acceptable word for classification, division into categories, as in "A breakdown of the semester grades

showed that the average woman ranked higher than the average man."
But Fowler warns of "the danger that its liberal meaning may intrude
with ludicrous effect," as in "The breakdown of students by grades shows
a healthy advance by women." Fowler gives the example of "statistics
of the population of the United States of America, broken down by age
and sex."

BREAKTHROUGH
An overworked word. *Breakthrough* is properly used for a scientific or
technological advance, but don't use it indiscriminately to describe every novelty, such as: "The invention of the martini was a major breakthrough for olives."

BRIBE
Old French for a lump of bread, from *brimber*, to beg. In the Sermon on
the Mount, Christ spoke of asking for bread and not expecting to get
a stone. Now when a briber asks for bread, he expects to get paper that
will buy precious stones.

BRIDLE PATH
Note the spelling. It's not the road to an altar.

BRIEF
As Nickles remarks, "Only lawyers can compose a 50-page document
and call it a *brief*."

BRITAIN
Note the spelling: one *t*. Great Britain comprises England, Scotland and
Wales. The United Kingdom comprises Great Britain and Northern
Ireland.

BROADCAST
The past tense and the past participle of the verb are *broadcast*, as in
forecast, not *broadcasted*. *Broadcast* is both noun and verb and has
bred such offspring as *telecast* (noun and verb), *newscast* (noun), *sports-
cast* (noun), *simulcast* (noun and verb) and the various *-er* and *-ing* forms.

BROBDINGNAG
Watch that first *n*. The word is often incorrectly spelled and pronounced
Brobdignag. In Swift's *Gulliver's Travels*, Brobdingnag is an imaginary
country where everything is on an enormous scale and the inhabitants

are "as tall as an ordinary spire steeple." The adjective is *Brobdingnagian* and is now used to mean gigantic, colossal.

BROCCOLI
The root is Italian *broccolo*, cabbage sprout, and the vegetable is a species of cauliflower. E. B. White wrote the famous caption for a 1928 *New Yorker* cartoon:
"It's broccoli, dear."
"I say it's spinach, and I say the hell with it."

BROGUE
From Irish *barrog*, a grip, a hold, a bond (on the tongue), hence a strongly accented dialect, especially a certain Irish pronunciation of English. Another kind of brogue, the shoe, comes from *brog*, Irish for *shoe*, whence also *brogan*.

BROKEN LINK
Barzun's term for the construction in which two adjectives are linked to different prepositions. For example: "I am fond of, and devoted to, my mother-in-law." Don't overdo it. Try "I am fond of my mother-in-law and devoted to her." Says Barzun: "Writers who make a habit of the broken link may fairly be suspected of showing off their misplaced accuracy at the expense of style." And they make a habit of forgetting the comma after the second preposition.

BROKER
From Latin *broccare*, to pierce, to tap a cask. A wine merchant was called a broker because he was a broacher of casks, one who pierced them to sell wine at retail. *Broker* has extended to many other forms of business. *Brooch* comes from the same root.

BROMIDE
In *South Pacific*, Ensign Nellie Forbush sang of being as corny as Kansas in August, as trite and as gay as a daisy in May, bromidic and bright as a moon-happy night. From the sedative qualities of the chemical compound, *bromide* was coined by Gelett Burgess (see also **BLURB**) to describe people or expressions that tend to put one to sleep.

Burgess defined a bromide as one who "does his thinking by syndicate, follows the main-traveled roads, goes with the crowd." A bromide's conversation was marked by such bromides as "I don't know much about art, but I know what I like" and "It's bad enough to see a man drunk—but, oh! a woman!"

BROWN AS A BERRY
A bromide. Some think the reference is to the coffee berry. But, as Evans points out, Chaucer used the phrase ("His palfrey was as broun as is a berye") more than two hundred years before coffee had been heard of in England. This cliché, six hundred years old, should be stamped out.

BUBBLE AND SQUEAK
The British name for fried leftovers of meat and vegetables, said to derive from the sounds of cooking it.

BUCK
President Carter borrowed President Truman's desk sign, "The buck stops here," and said he would follow Truman's policy of accountability. *Buck* is a reference to an old form of poker in which a chip or marker, called a buck, was placed in front of the dealer to be passed by him to the next dealer to answer the old question, "Whose deal is it?" Hence "to pass the buck" is to shift responsibility to someone else, and "The buck stops here" means to accept responsibility.

BUCKLEYISM
A reviewer of a book by William F. Buckley, Jr., a collection of his newspaper columns, found himself marking many words he didn't understand or wasn't sure of. He wove some Buckleyisms into this sentence and led his review with it:

"For anfractuous tuquoqueism and immanentization of the eschaton without the chiliastic afflatus of solipsistic brachycephalics, one must etiologically etiolate the fustian rodomontade of phlogistonic energumens and their psychotropic epigoni whose sylleptic ignoratio elenchi and apodictic sciolism transmogrify the apopemptic meiosis and anaphoric interstices of the sibylline incunabula of autarkic ultramontanism, lest by jacobinical malversation the incondite tatterdemalions detumesce the osmotically jejune hagiolaters of soritically otiose taxonomists despite the inchoate enthymeme of paradigmatic animadversion and the meritocratic dirigisme of some anapaestic eponym."

Are you still there? Well, the point is that if words are to convey intended ideas, a reader has to understand the words.

There are three kinds of reader: one who understands; one who doesn't understand but will find out; and one who neither understands nor gives a damn, and he's not worth worrying about.

To find out how many of the 89 words in the lead paragraph could be understood by educated readers without being driven to a dictionary,

the reviewer called on DUPE (D̲ecidedly U̲nscientific P̲olling E̲nter-
prises), a nonprophet organization, which polled twenty journalism professors. The highest score was 60, recorded by an antediluvian lexicog-
rapher. The lowest was 35, recorded by an ovicephalic taxonomist who
smartly identified 13 prepositions, 10 articles, 7 conjunctions, 4 pronouns
and 1 auxiliary verb. The mean was a miserable 44. DUPE concluded
that because some journalism professors drive ordinary mortals to dictionaries to understand COMMUNICOLOGESE, the professors themselves
ought to be driven to dictionaries to understand English.

Buckley says he consciously strives to seek the company of his intellectual superiors. Unless he is communing with Burke and Belloc and
Chesterton and Eliot, he must be lonely.

BUCKSHEE
From Persian *bakhshish*, a tip, a gratuity, *buckshee* means free of charge,
gratis.

BUCOLIC
From Greek *bous* + *kolos*, cowherd, hence rustic. *Bucolic* is often used
pejoratively.

BUDGET
From Old Irish *bolg*, a leather bag, through Latin *bulga* and French
bougette, the English *budget* was the annual estimate of revenues and
expenditures delivered to the House of Commons by the Chancellor of
the Exchequer in a leather purse or bag. Hence the modern word for a
statement of expected income and expenses.

BUFF
In the sense of a fan or enthusiast, *buff* originated in *fire buff*, a term given
to early American volunteer firemen, either because the wealthy ones
wore buffalo-skin coats in winter or because the firemen's uniforms were
buff-colored. In either case, *buff* is from Old French *buffle*, buffalo.

Buff has extended to many other forms of enthusiasm and interest,
as in *sports buff*, *history buff*. An authority on the buffalo is a buffalo
buff, which is turning the etymological wheel in redounding, redundant
circle.

BULL
Rummaging through an 1893 dictionary of Worcestershire words, Moore
found *bull-squitter*, defined as "much talk or fuss about a little matter."

It rhymes with today's more common word, shortened to *bull*, which Partridge says originated in Australia early in this century and spread rapidly in the armed services of all English-speaking nations.

Bull, the animal, is from Anglo-Saxon *bula*, the diminutive of which is *bulluc*, bullock.

Bull, as in papal bull, is from Latin *bulla*, a seal, and gets its name from the round leaden seal attached to some papal letters. On the pope's farm in Castel Gandolfo, there used to be a sad bull irreverently called "Casti Connubii" ("Chaste Wedlock"), from Pius XI's papal bull of the same name.

BULLETIN
A brief dispatch containing late important news, usually no more than 40 to 50 words.

BULLSHOT
A cocktail made of beef bouillon and gin or vodka, a *bullshot* is a pleasant bracer on a football Saturday. If chicken broth is substituted for beef bouillon, the result is called chickenshot.

BUNKUM
When members started to leave the House during a boring speech by Felix Walker, a congressman from Buncombe County, North Carolina, in the Sixteenth Congress (1819–21), Walker suggested that those who remained should also leave because "I'm talking only for Buncombe." *Buncombe*, meaning nonsense, foolish talk, political claptrap, is now more commonly spelled *bunkum*, shortened to *bunk*. To *debunk* has the same origin. *Bunco*, or *bunko*, a swindle, a confidence trick, comes from Spanish *banca*, a card game.

BUREAUCRATESE
Bureaucratese is the language of bureaucrats (see -CRACY). Examples of the jargon abound in statements issued by governmental bodies. Here are some (and their translations):

"Innovative mechanisms of input by the technostructure can finalize solutions to societal dysfunctions." (Technology can solve society's problems.)

"The consumer affairs coordinator will review existing mechanisms of consumer input and seek ways of improving these linkages via the consumer communication channel." (Whoever gets the job will help people get some action on their complaints.)

"Given the areas of management and program emphasis both explicitly and implicitly noted in this document, current planning, development and operational proposals and programs will sort out as strongly mission-supportive, or as moderately or as dubiously mission-supportive. An identification of transferable managerial resources will thus result." (Different proposals will be handled differently.)

"The proposed project is not the type situation which is geared to impact or to postulate a conceptualization for congruency of purposes which would complement the present team assignments after several stringent political posture conditions are met to assist legislatures on an ad hoc basis as issues emerge toward a legislative agenda-of-imperatives." (What you suggest isn't going to help us run the country.)

Business, too, breeds bureaucratese. Witness this letter from the "senior programming analyst of the process computer department" of one of the country's largest corporations:

"Submitted attached is our response to your position relative to our answer concerning your question about the statement regarding our facts relating to your allegation superseding the remark on the correction to the addition of the omission in your programming specification. Should your evaluation of our review of your changes lead to revision of the amendment to your omission, our response may require discussion." (Here's what you're looking for; maybe we should talk about it.)

What further need have we of witness?

BURGEONING
From Old French, *burjon*, a bud, *burgeoning* connotes sprouting, new growth, sudden emergence. It should not be used for just any kind of growth. Quickie food franchises are growing in number, but they're not burgeoning. The population of India has been growing for a long time, but it isn't burgeoning, suddenly budding. The tulip bulbs are burgeoning in early spring.

BURGLARY / ROBBERY / THEFT
Burglary is entry, but not necessarily by breaking in, with intent to commit a felony. *Robbery* is stealing with violence or threat of violence. *Theft* is stealing without violence or threat of violence.

BURGLE, *see* BACK FORMATION

BURIDAN'S ASS

One who can't make up his mind which toll booth to enter or which parking spot to take or which stall to use is behaving like an ass, which, according to Jean Buridan, fourteenth-century philosopher, would die of starvation if placed exactly between two equal bundles of hay.

BURKE

Several of the Watergate criminals were guilty of burking. *Burke* comes from William Burke, an Irish laborer hanged in 1829 in Edinburgh for murdering at least fifteen persons by suffocation. Burke and his accomplices smothered their victims, leaving no trace of violence so that they could sell the bodies for dissection. Hence to *burke* is to dispose of quickly and quietly, shelve, suppress, cover up.

BUS

Because monosyllables that end in a single *s* regularly double the *s* before a suffix, the plural of *bus* strictly should be *busses*, but *busses* is already the plural of *buss*, a kiss, wherefore the plural of *bus* usually is *buses*.

For the same reason, the past tense and the past and present participles of *to bus* are *bused, bused, busing*, even though monosyllabic verbs ending in a consonant regularly double the consonant to form these parts (*bug, bugged, bugging*; *jut, jutted, jutting*).

So *busing* is a means of educational integration, and children are *bused* to school. When children are *bussed*, they are kissed. When George McGovern, after a presidential campaign speech in 1972 in New Jersey, thinking the microphones were closed, snapped at a reporter, "Kiss my ass," the *Jersey Journal* ran the immortal headline: "McGovern Speaks Out on Bussing."

BUT

Some authorities consider *but* a preposition when it precedes a noun or a pronoun at the end of a sentence, and a conjunction when it precedes a noun or a pronoun elsewhere in a sentence. Thus they say, "Nobody saw him but her," but "Nobody but she saw him."

When these authorities allow "Nobody but she saw him," they are saying that the sentence really extends to "Nobody saw him but she saw him." But if nobody saw him, how is it that she saw him? And then why not extend "Nobody saw him but her" to "Nobody saw him but her saw him"?

The position of *but* in a sentence is hardly a sound criterion for grammatical distinction. Instead, follow the principle that when *but* means *except*, it is a preposition and is therefore followed by the objective case ("Nobody but her saw him").

In the construction "There is no doubt but that she saw him," *but* is redundant. Drop it and say, "There is no doubt that she saw him."

And don't use *but what*. Don't say: "There is no doubt but what he will win." Make it "There is no doubt that he will win."

Similarly, *but*, as an adverb meaning *only*, is redundant in "He has but only one life to give." Omit either *but* or *only*. And watch the implied double negative in "He won't live but a month," in which *but* means *only*. Make it "He will live but a month" or "He will live only a month." See also CANNOT HELP BUT.

BUTTERFLY
Jacobs suggests that among the many criteria for naming animals was "mode of excretion." Thus the butterfly was so called because its excrement has the look and consistency of butter, just as the shitepoke heron was named because of the way it empties its bowels when frightened by a shot.

BUY
It's a good verb and not stilted like *purchase*. It has also become a noun.

BY AND LARGE
This is one of Fowler's "popularized technicalities." Strictly, *by and large* is a nautical term for sailing slightly off the wind. Hence the phrase is popularly used to express virtual generalization, but it is now often a knee-jerk term used to fill the gap between thought and speech.

BY A SCORE OF
Padding. When sportswriters say, "The Dodgers beat the Reds by a score of 4 to 3," they mean "The Dodgers beat the Reds 4–3."

BYLINE
Though the dictionaries prefer the hyphenated spelling, *byline* is the more common spelling among journalists.

BY THE SAME TOKEN
A cliché. Try *likewise* or *similarly* or *besides*.

CABAL

From Hebrew *qabbalah*, received doctrine or tradition, occult interpretation of the Old Testament, from *qabal*, to receive, hence secret scheme, conspiratorial intrigue. Coincidentally, and only coincidentally, the initials of the members of the Committee of Foreign Affairs of Charles II spelled *CABAL*: Clifford, Arlington, Buckingham, Ashley (Cooper), Lauderdale. In 1672, these men conspiratorially signed the Treaty of Alliance with France without parliamentary consent and forced England into war with Holland despite existing treaties. These advisers were known as the "cabal" and acted as a *cabal*, but they didn't originate the word.

CABLESE

When foreign correspondents file by cable, their language may be cablese, a coded jargon of copy skeletonized to save words and therefore money. Articles and some prepositions and conjunctions are omitted, and words joined. For example: *exustates*, from the United States; *unexplain*, don't explain; *scald*, so called; *ants*, and it is; *kanb*, can be; *tno*, to know. The copy editor's job is to flesh the skeleton, translate the jargon into English. Because of modern international high-speed transmission, the translation of cablese, an absorbing task for editorial cryptographers, is a dying art.

CACO–

Several English words derive from Greek *kakos*, bad, ugly, unpleasant. For example: *cacophony*, unpleasant sound; *cacography*, bad handwriting, incorrect spelling; *cacogenics*, the study or process of racial deterioration; *cacoethes*, bad habit, an itch to do something inadvisable, as in *cacoethes scribendi*, an urge to write that should be stifled. The root is almost onomatopoeic, as in the slang *cacky*, distasteful, which is an echoic form, as is the word to *defecate* in Latin (*caccare*) and other languages.

CADDIE
In a French family, the younger son was destined to be a military cadet, treated by his elders as a *cad*. In Scotland, the home of golf, a *caddie* was a boy who did odd jobs, carried packages, such as a golf bag. A golfer who underpays his caddie is a cad.

CADUCEUS
The herald's wand (Greek *karukeion*, whence Latin *caduceus*) carried by Hermes, messenger of the gods, was a winged staff with two snakes coiled around it. The *caduceus* is the symbol of the medical profession. The snake was a symbol of healing, shedding its skin to renew itself.

CAGER
Sports jargon for a basketball player. Though there's little excuse for it in copy, it's a handy short word for a tight headline.

CAIN
If you refer to "the mark of Cain," remember that it wasn't a brand of infamy, but a symbol of protection. After he killed Abel, Cain was scared of being killed, but the Lord said to him, "No, it shall not be so; but whosoever shall kill Cain shall be punished sevenfold." And the Lord "set a mark upon Cain that whosoever found him should not kill him."

CAJUN
A corruption of *Acadian*, the name given to inhabitants of Louisiana reputed to be of Acadian descent. Acadia was a French colony in eastern Canada. Southern Louisiana has a parish (county) named Acadia.

CALCULATE
The ancients calculated by counting with stones, from Latin *calculus*, a small stone, a pebble, whence also the name of the branch of mathematics.

CALENDAR
Note the spelling: *ar*, not *er*. There is a word *calender*, a machine for pressing cloth or paper between rollers to make it smooth and glossy, from Greek *kylindein*, to roll, whence also *cylinder*. But *calendar*, a list of dates, is from Latin *kalendae*, the calends, the first day of the month in the Roman calendar.

CALISTHENICS

Exercises to help you become strong and perhaps beautiful, from Greek *kallos*, beauty (adjective *kalos*, beautiful), and *sthenos*, strength. Several other English words derive from *kallos*. For example: *calligraphy*, beautiful handwriting; *calliope*, a musical instrument, literally "beautiful voice," from *Calliope*, the Muse who presides over eloquence and heroic poetry; *calomel*, mercurous chloride, literally "black beauty" (the purgative, though white, was developed from a black powder); *kaleidoscope*, view of beautiful form; *calla lily*.

CALLIPYGIAN / STEATOPYGIAN

If your behind is shapely, you are *callipygian*, from Greek *kallos*, beauty, and *pyge*, rump. If your behind is fat, you are *steatopygian*, from Greek *steatos*, fat, and *pyge*, rump. *Ars est celare arsem*.

CALLOUS / CALLUS

Both words come from Latin *callus*, hard skin. *Callus*, noun and intransitive verb, has the physical sense of "hard skin," "to form hard skin." *Callous*, adjective and verb (transitive and intransitive), has the additional figurative sense of "hardened in feeling, insensitive," "to make (become) hardened, insensitive." Careless about his calluses, a callous man will stay callused.

CAMELLIA

Note the spelling: double *l*. The name of the flower comes from George Joseph Kamel (1661–1706), a Moravian Jesuit missionary in the Philippines, who first reported it.

CAN / MAY

The words are not interchangeable in the context of possibility. "He can go" means it's physically possible for him to go. "He may go" means there's a chance he will go.

In other contexts, the distinction between *can* and *may* is gradually disappearing. Note, however, that *can't* is becoming more common than the clumsy *mayn't* in negative requests ("Can't I go?") and in negative responses to requests ("No, you can't go").

In *Winners & Sinners*, Bernstein reports this conversation:
Little Boy: "Mommy, can I go to the men's room?"
Mother: "Tommy, did you say *can*?"
Little Boy: "No, Mommy, I said men's room."

CANADA GOOSE
Canada, not *Canadian*.

CANAPE
Three syllables, the first stressed. French for *sofa*, from Greek *konopeion*, a bed covered with a canopy of mosquito curtains, from Greek *konops*, a mosquito. The modern use of *canape* for an appetizer comes either from the sense of "covering" (the delicacy that covers the bread or cracker) or from the sense of "bed" (the thin slice of bread or cracker on which the delicacy reposes).

CANARD
French for *duck*. The meaning of *canard* as a false report, a story floated to deceive the public, comes from the French expression *vendre un canard à moitié*, to half-sell a duck, to make one believe something impossible or false, to deceive (one cannot half-sell anything).

CANARY
The color comes from the bird, and the bird comes from the islands. The Canary Islands were so called because of the large dogs (Latin *canis*) that roamed on one of them.

CANCEL
There's only one *l* in *canceled*, *canceling*. See also ALLOTTED.

CANDIDATE
In ancient Rome, people seeking election wore glistening white togas to signify their purity of character, whence our word *candidate* (from Latin *candidus*, white, from *candere*, to shine) for one seeking election or selection. Other common words from the same root are *candid*, *candor*, *candle*, *incandescent*.

CANINE
The word comes from Latin *canis*, a dog, but should be used only adjectivally of dogs. If it is used seriously as a noun for *dog*, says Evans, *canine* "is pompous, and if used humorously (in mockery of the pompous use) it is threadbare." As a noun, a *canine* is a tooth, an eyetooth, shaped like a dog's.

CANNOT HELP BUT
In the construction "I cannot help but be angry," Bernstein, in *Miss Thistlebottom's Hobgoblins*, calls *cannot help but* "almost standard." Fowler calls it "indefensible" and a "curious confusion" between *cannot help being* and *cannot but be*. Strunk calls it "unnecessary." Make it "I cannot help being angry." See also BUT.

CANOSSA
"To go to Canossa" is to do penance, be humbled, climb down. The reference is to Canossa, the castle in Northern Italy where in 1077 Henry IV of Germany, the Holy Roman Emperor, submitted to the authority of Pope Gregory VII, after having been kept waiting for three days in the snow in a penitent's shirt.

CANTALOUPE
The spelling of this melon is carved in several weird ways in supermarkets. The correct spelling is either *cantaloupe* or *cantaloup*, both pronounced as in *lope*. The word comes from Cantalupo, a papal villa near Rome, where it was first grown in Europe, from seed said to have come from Armenia.

CANTER
A pace between a trot and a gallop, shortened from *Canterbury gallop*, the leisurely pace of the pilgrims as they rode to Canterbury.

CAN'T SEEM TO
In the construction "He can't seem to get to class on time," Shaw calls *seem to* unnecessary. Bernstein calls it "obviously illogical" but "clearly idiomatic and in reputable use." Of the American Heritage usage experts, 49 percent vote against it, but 51 percent can't seem to find any sound reason for objecting to it. The kid can get to class if he wants to, but he doesn't seem to want to.

CANUTE
The myth is that the old king tried to roll back the ocean. He didn't try to. He told his subjects he had as much chance of doing what they wanted him to do as he had of rolling back the ocean. Anyhow, the reference is rather stale. And it was Charlton Heston who parted the sea.

CANVAS / CANVASS
Both words come from Latin *cannabis*, hemp. *Canvas*, the cloth, was sometimes used for sifting flour, whence possibly the word came to be used as a verb to mean sifting public opinion, spelled *canvass*.

CAPITAL / CAPITOL
In the *capital* city, the building where the legislature meets is the *capitol*, sometimes capitalized as in the Capitol in Washington, D.C., where the Congress meets.

CAPRI / CAPRIS
For the island, the stress is on the front syllable. For the pants, the stress is on the rear.

CAPRICIOUS
From Italian *capo*, head, and *riccio*, hedgehog, as if one's hair were standing on end like the spines of a hedgehog, which impulsively, capriciously, rolls itself into a ball for protection.

CARAMEL
The word has three syllables.

CARAT / CARET / CARROT
The three words have the same pronunciation, but different meanings. *Carat*, a unit of weight for precious stones, comes from Greek *keration*, a little horn, through Arabic *qirat*, a bean. Beans, because of their sameness, were once used as a measure of weight. *Carrot*, the vegetable, comes from a similar Greek root, *karoton*, so named because it is shaped like a horn. *Caret*, the editing symbol for insertion of a missing letter or word or group of words, is straight Latin for "it is missing."

CARBURETOR
Note the American spelling.

CARE
The care package that a student receives from home has its origin in CARE, acronym for Cooperative for American Remittances to Europe, a charitable organization formed after World War II to send packages of food and clothing and other necessities of life to Europe. The name was later changed to Cooperative for American Relief Everywhere.

CAREEN / CAREER / CAROM

The differences in meaning can be seen from the differences in derivation. *Careen* comes from Latin *carina*, a ship's keel, and means to sway from side to side. *Career* comes from French *carrière*, a racecourse, and means to move forward at high speed. *Carom* comes from French *carambole*, the red ball in billiards, and means to strike and rebound. So: "The car careered down the turnpike, careened across the median and caromed off the retaining fence."

CARET, *see* CARAT / CARET / CARROT

CARICATURE

The sense of distorted exaggeration comes from the derivation, Italian *caricare*, to overload, from Latin *carrus*, a vehicle.

CARNIVAL

Originally, the festival before the rigors of Lent was called a *carnival*, from Latin *carne vale*, literally, "Flesh, goodbye."

CAROUSAL / CAROUSEL

The words shouldn't be confused. A *carousal* is a wild party, a drinking bout, from German *garaus*, all out, as in *garaus trinken*, to drink all out, to empty the cup. A *carousel* is a merry-go-round, from Italian *carosello*, a tournament of cavalry.

CASE

Teachers of English, at least those who care about case, thank God that English has only three cases: nominative, objective, possessive. Case is the relationship of nouns or pronouns to other words in a sentence.

Example: in "Jack has two children and he loves them but he prefers his daughter to his son," *Jack* is nominative (subject of the verb *has*), *he* is nominative (subject of the verbs *loves* and *prefers*), *children* is objective (object of the verb *has*), *them* is objective (object of the verb *loves*), *daughter* is objective (object of the verb *prefers*), *son* is objective (object of the preposition *to*) and *his* is possessive (possessing *daughter* and *son*).

For a thorough treatment of case, see Opdycke. And note that a copulative verb (see **ADJECTIVE / ADVERB**) takes the same case after it as before it. Thus "This is he." See also **THAN**.

CASKET
Those who used to call themselves undertakers used to call the burial box a coffin. Those who now call themselves morticians or grief therapists call the burial box a casket. Mencken quotes Nathaniel Hawthorne in denunciation of *casket* in 1863 as "a vile modern phrase, which compels a person . . . to shrink . . . from the idea of being buried at all." *Casket* is a euphemism.

CASSANDRA
The word has been used as a pseudonym by various columnists, notably Sir William Connor of the London *Daily Mirror*. Cassandra, daughter of Priam, King of Troy, received the gift of prophecy from Apollo. When she spurned him later, he decreed that she should never be believed. She correctly prophesied the fate of Troy and the death of Priam and Agamemnon. Hence a Cassandra is a person who foretells the truth but is not believed.

CASUAL
Watch it. It often comes out *causal*, and the two are contraries. Similarly, watch *marital* and *martial*, though these two are not necessarily contraries.

CATACHRESIS
When you *affect* instead of *effect*, or *imply* instead of *infer*, or *lay* instead of *lie*, you are guilty of catachresis, the use of words in senses that do not belong to them, from Greek *kata* + *chresthai*, to use against, to misuse.

CATACLYSM
Its derivation is mild: Greek *kata* + *klyzein*, to wash down. But it's a powerful word that should be reserved for powerful events, physical or political, such as an earthquake or a violent revolution. An inch of rain or a 10–0 baseball score is not cataclysmic. See also AFRAID.

CATALOGUE
In library usage, the trend is to drop the last two letters, as in *card catalog*. The omission somehow doesn't look right in some parts of the verb, however, as in *cataloging* and *cataloged*.

CATALYST
In chemistry, a *catalyst*, from Greek *kata* + *lyein*, to loosen down, to release, is a substance that accelerates a reaction of other substances but is virtually unchanged by the reaction. By extension, a *catalyst* is a person who resolves a problem between others by his mere presence and is unchanged by the result. Such a person is rare. Rare, too, should be the use of *catalyst*. Don't use it as a synonym for *mediator* or *conciliator* or *diplomat* or *ombudsman*.

CATARACT
From Greek *kata* + *rassein*, to dash down or strike down, *cataract* means both a downpour and a floodgate. In this sense of obstruction, *cataract* is used for an opacity or obscurity of the eye.

CATCHWORD
If you play the game of Catchword, you will meet such delightful words as *wallydrag* and *wicopy and gallimaufry* and *galligaskin* and many others.

Originally, a *catchword* was a word printed under the bottom line of a page, the word being the first word of the next page. The design was to catch the reader's attention. *Catchword* was then used for the last word of an actor's lines, the cue word for the next speaker. *Catchword* also came to mean *slogan* or SHIBBOLETH.

The game of Catchword comes from the practice of printers to head each page of a dictionary, or the facing pages of an encyclopedia, with the first and last words defined on the page. The game is a sort of literary solitaire. Strange, solitary words in bold display type catch the eye and the mind, tempt one to find their origin and meaning, expand vocabulary and heighten one's love affair with words. Try it.

And read about widgeons and wicopies and wickiups in John Ciardi's "Widgeonry," in *Someone Could Win a Polar Bear*. Ciardi got the inspiration for his poem from his habit of browsing through catchwords.

CATEGORY
Note the spelling. It's not *catagory*.

CATER-CORNERED
The word derives from French *quatre*, four, hence four-cornered, diagonally opposite. It has nothing to do with cats or kittens, but sonic evolution has spawned *catty-cornered* and *kitty-cornered*, both acceptable.

CATERPILLAR
Caterpillar does derive from *cat*. It comes from Latin *catta pilosa*, hairy cat. Note some of the other words from Latin *pilus*, hair: *pile* (as in a carpet), *pluck*, *plush*, *depilatory*.

CATHERINE WHEEL
St. Catherine of Alexandria was tortured on a spiked wheel in 307. This grisly event is perpetuated in *catherine wheel*, a spinning firework and a somersault (cart wheel), and in *catherine-wheel window*, a circular spoked window (rose window).

CATHOLIC
From Greek *katholikos*, universal, the word is lowercase when it means universal, comprehensive in taste, sympathy, understanding. It is uppercase when it refers to a member of a Catholic church. A *catholicon* is a remedy for all diseases, a panacea.

CAUCASIAN
Isn't it time we dropped *Caucasian*? Today the word is meaningless as a substitute for *white*.

One thinks of an old friend, a minister's son, reared in a rigorous home, schooled in rigorous institutions in a small community for sixteen years. Accepted for graduate study at a metropolitan university, he arrived in the big city and found freedom and fleshpots. As he filled out his registration forms, he ran into the question: "Church preference?" He replied: "Gothic."

Perhaps when we run into the race question on our bureaucratic forms, we should reply: "Human."

CAUSAL, *see* CASUAL

CELEBRITY
An overworked word. It used to have the sense of famous, renowned, but today it is used to refer to anyone from a wailing vocalist in a rock band to a 36-handicap hacker in a pro-am golf tournament.

CELSIUS
The metric system upon us, Americans had better get used to Celsius, a temperature scale named after its inventor, Anders Celsius, an eighteenth-century astronomer. The scale is also called *centigrade*, from its range of 0 to 100 degrees from freezing to boiling. The Fahrenheit scale,

named after Gabriel Fahrenheit (1686–1736), ranges from 32° freezing to 212° boiling.

To convert from Fahrenheit to Celsius, multiply the Fahrenheit reading by 5, subtract 160 and divide by 9 to get the Celsius reading, as in the formula 9C = 5F − 160.

This seems simple enough, but pity the poor student who can't figure a percentage or convert from inches to picas unless he twiddles his pocket calculator. Options are to poke your head outdoors or phone the time-and-temperature number.

CEMENT / CONCRETE
The words should not be interchangeable, except colloquially. Cement, mixed with water, is the adhesive ingredient in concrete.

CEMETERY
Note the spelling. It's not *cemetary*.

CENOTAPH
From Greek *kenos + taphos*, empty tomb, a *cenotaph* is a monument that honors a dead person whose remains lie elsewhere, or is symbolic of a group of dead people, such as victims of war or persecution. Other *taph* words are: *epitaph*, literally "on the tomb," an inscription on a tombstone or monument or a brief statement about a dead person; and *taphephobia*, fear of being buried alive.

CENSOR / CENSURE
Though the words come from the same root, Latin *censere*, to assess, judge, value, one should distinguish between them. To *censor* is to examine, expurgate, prevent publication. To *censure* is to find fault with, severely disapprove, blame.

CENTAUR WORDS
Bernstein coined *centaur words* to describe words coined by a combination of two words (for example, *smog* for smoke and fog), just as a centaur is a combination of man and horse. Bernstein's coinage is yet another in a series of several dozen to describe this kind of combination, among them being amalgams, blend words, telescope words, portmanteau words. Etymologically, *portmanteau* itself is a centaur word, a combination of French *porter*, to carry, and *manteau*, coat, literally a coat-carrier. In *Through the Looking-Glass*, Humpty Dumpty thus explained

to Alice his use of *slithy* (lithe and slimy): "You see, it's like a portmanteau . . . there are two meanings packed up into one word." Lewis Carroll coined many centaur words, but only *chortle* (chuckle and snort) and *squawk* (squall and squeak) seem to have survived in common usage.

Some centaur words start out as cute coinage, such as those concocted by Walter Winchell (*infanticipating* for pregnant, *Reno-vated* for divorced) and by *Time* magazine in its earlier days (*cinemorsel* for a beauteous movie actress, *newshen* for a woman reporter), but they fail the test of time. Others serve a purpose and linger, such as *brunch* (breakfast and lunch), *motel* (motor and hotel), *splutter* (splash and sputter), *transistor* (transfer and resistor). *Stagflation* (stagnancy and inflation) may not last. *Guesstimate* (guess and estimate) should not. But Bernstein's own *mixaphor* (mixed and metaphor) should.

CENTER AROUND
It is physically impossible to *center around*. Make it *center on*. If you want to use *around*, use it with *cluster, hover, resolve, rotate*. Use *around* with *circle* when the context is dynamic ("The protesters continuously circled around the stadium"), but not when the context is static ("Police circled the hijacked plane").

CEPHALALGIA
From Greek *kephale*, head, and *algos*, pain, a term beloved of Mencken to describe a hangover.

CESSPOOL, *see* –SPIRE

CHAIR
Until time rules otherwise, *chair* should be kept as a noun. What's wrong with "Smith presided at the meeting" or "Smith was the chairman" or "Smith was in the chair"? As Bernstein remarks, pretty soon we'll be saying that Smith "podiumed the orchestra" or "pulpited the church" or "floored the Senate." And then it'll be "Smith lecterned the lecture" and "Smith rostrumed the convention" and "Smith speakerstabled the banquet." Some fingers should be kept in the verbal dikes. See VERBING NOUNS.

CHAIRPERSON
Like *parent* and *child* and *teacher* and *student* and dozens of other words, *chairman* is common gender. Despite the *-man*, it isn't masculine. *Man* is from Anglo-Saxon *mann*, human being.

The abomination of *chairperson* weaseled into the language when misguided people confused freedom of choice and equality of opportunity with license to butcher the language. There are indeed sexist terms in the language, but a campaign to change *-man* words to *-person* words is lexicographically and sexually ridiculous.

Hupersons should person the sheepparts to epersoncipate us from all personner of personipulation of our parent tongue, the language of our foreparents. See also FEMINISM.

CHAISE LONGUE
Good grief, the phrase is *chaise longue*, straight French for *long chair*. Despite the ads, the second word is not *lounge*. Nor is the phrase *chase lounge*, which, as Evans reminds us, is an idea "fostered by boudoir comedies that this is a lounge on which the eternal chase begins or ends." And, despite common mispronunciation and widespread misconception, it certainly isn't *chaste lounge*.

CHAMOIS / CHAMMY / SHAMMY
The word for this soft leather is the word for the animal whose hide it used to be made from (it now is often made from the hide of deer, sheep and goats). More common spellings are *chammy* and *shammy*, whose plurals are *chammies* and *shammies*. The plural of *chamois* is the same as the singular, but the *s* is pronounced in the plural and not in the singular. Among Newman's miserable puns is "I wish I could chamois like my sister Kate."

CHANCELLOR
The word comes from Latin *cancelli*, lattices or gratings, which surrounded the seat of judgment in the Roman Empire and at which the *cancellarius*, the *chancellor*, stood to protect the court from the ordinary people. He was really an usher. Later, the word was used for an important secretary or a minister of state or a chief judicial or administrative officer. A chancel, the part of a church reserved for the clergy, is often enclosed by lattice or railing, and the word comes from the same source.

CHARISMA
John Kennedy made *charisma* popular. He used it and he had it. The word is Greek for *gift*, the gift of extraordinary power of leadership and ability to win the devotion of the led.

Theologically, *charisma* means a divine gift, such as the gift of miracles. Since Kennedy, the word has become overworked and is now often applied prosaically to anyone running for office who is at least capable of running a pay toilet.

CHARIVARI, *see* SHIVAREE

CHARWOMAN, *see* CHORE

CHAUFFEUR
The early steam-powered automobile was tended by a stoker, the French for which was *chauffeur*, from *chauffer*, to heat. Note the spelling.

CHAUVINIST
Before the women's rights movement, a *chauvinist* was a super-patriot, an extreme hero worshiper, from Nicolas Chauvin, a French soldier who adored Napoleon. Women who contend that men regard them as mere sex objects call men male chauvinist pigs, seemingly because such men adore themselves.

For his exaltation of Napoleon, Chauvin has become an object of ridicule, as should anyone, man or woman, who exalts one sex over the other. One should compliment the complements. Vive la différence!

CHECKMATE
When a chess player maneuvers his opponent's king into an inescapable position and cries "Checkmate," he is echoing the Arabic *shah mat*, meaning "The king is dead."

CHEESE
Milk curds did not prepare the whey for the slang phrases *big cheese* and *head cheese*, which come from Hindustani *chiz*, thing, the real thing.

CHERCHEZ LA FEMME
French for "look for the woman." The French, it seems, think that a woman is at the heart of most problems. In the United States, the slogan should perhaps be *cherchez la buck*.

CHESTERBELLOC
A combination of G. K. Chesterton and Hilaire Belloc, two of the great names of early twentieth-century English literature, all but neglected in American education. A *Chesterbelloc* is one who combines, or at least appreciates, the attributes of Chesterton and Belloc in their roles of humanist, humorist, critic, poet, novelist, journalist, cartoonist, polemicist,

essayist, historian, philosopher, theologian, to which add oenologist, zymologist and all-round bon vivant. In short, a *Chesterbelloc* is a man for all seasons.

CHIAROSCURO
A delightful OXYMORON, from Italian *chiaro + oscuro,* light and dark, hence the use of light and shade in art.

CHIASMUS
The Greek letter *chi*, X, forms an intersection. A *chiasmus* is a rhetorical intersection, an inversion of words. The Bible is replete with this figure of speech. Witness: "And God created man to his own image; to the image of God he created him" (Genesis); "All things were made through him, and without him was made nothing that has been made" (John).

CHICANE
In bridge a hand without trumps is called a *chicane*, from French *chicaner*, to quibble, to prolong a contest with trickery. As in *chicanery*, the first syllable has an *sh* sound.

A bridge hand that has no card higher than a 9 is called a *Yarborough*, after Lord Yarborough, a nineteenth-century bridge player who used to bet 1,000 to 1 against getting such a hand. (This is a sucker bet; the true odds are 1,827 to 1.)

CHICANO
Don't equate *Chicano* with *Mexican-American*. Some Mexican-Americans describe themselves as Chicanos. Some don't.

CHIEF JUSTICE, *see* JUDGE / JURIST / JUSTICE

CHILDISH / CHILDLIKE
When used of adults, *childish* is pejorative. *Childlike* connotes the admirable qualities of childhood, such as innocence and simplicity. *Childish* connotes the less admirable qualities, such as irrationality and facile enthusiasm.

CHILIASM
From Greek *chilias*, a thousand, the word refers to the belief that Christ will return to the earth to reign for 1,000 years, the millennium (Latin *mille + anni*, 1,000 years). Its adjective, *chiliastic*, is a BUCKLEYISM.

CHIONOPHOBIA, *see* –PHOBIA

CHIRO–
The Greek word for hand, *cheir*, gives us several English words. For example: *chirography*, handwriting; *chiromancy*, fortunetelling by examination of the hand, palmistry; *chiropody*, treatment of ailments of hand and foot, now usually restricted to the foot; *chiropractic*, adjustment of the joints, especially of the spine, by hand; *enchiridion*, a handbook or manual; *surgeon*, shortened form of the older *chirurgeon*, one who worked (*ergon*, work) by hand.

CHI-SQUARE
This is the name given, usually derogatorily, to the school of journalism educators who emphasize the quantitative, statistical, inductive, theoretical approach to communications research, as opposed to the Green Eyeshade school, whose members emphasize the qualitative, literary, deductive, practical approach to journalism education. The twain should meet.

   Green Eyeshade refers to the headgear that used to be worn by some copy editors.

   Chi-Square refers to a statistical test to evaluate the probability of obtaining a set of observed frequencies from a population having certain assumed or theoretical frequencies. Webster defines *chi-square* as "the sum of the quotients obtained by dividing the square of the difference between the observed and theoretical values of a quantity by the theoretical value." Yes, well.

CHOLESTEROL, *see* STEREO–

CHOOSE
The past tense of *choose* is *chose*. The past participle is *chosen*.

CHORD / CORD
The musical term is *chord*. Those folds in the larnyx that vibrate with breath to produce sound are *vocal cords*. An emotional response strikes a *chord*. A part of the central nervous system is the *spinal cord*. See SONIC WRITING.

CHORE
From Anglo-Saxon *cyrr*, a turn, business, piece of work. *Charwoman* has the same root. Ladies used to hire charwomen. Some women now advertise for charladies.

CHORTLE, *see* **CENTAUR WORDS**

CHRISTIAN
The word once signified a professed follower of Christ, a member of some Christian religion. It is now informally applied to a decent, civilized person. This was perhaps the sense in which it was used by a former U.S. ambassador to the United Nations when he said the Arabs and Israelis should "sit down and settle their differences like good Christians." See also CRETIN.

CHRONIC
Don't use *chronic* as a synonym for *severe*. From Greek *chronos*, time, *chronic* should convey some sense of long duration, lingering, as in "a chronic drinker," "a chronic invalid," "chronic rheumatism." The opposite of *chronic* is *acute*.

CINCINNATI
Note the spelling.

CIRCUMLOCUTION OFFICE
Dickens' delightful name for a government department in *Little Dorrit*.

CIRRHOSIS
From Greek *kirrhos*, orange-colored, the color of the liver of one who has the disease of cirrhosis of the liver. Note the spelling: double *r*.

CITE
The word is ambiguous. It may mean: to summon to appear; to quote as proof or authority; to mention honorably; to mention dishonorably. Because of its shortness, *cite* is a favorite word of headline writers. It should be used only when its meaning is clear from the context. See also HEADLINESE.

CLAIM
Unless there is assertion of a right or title, *claim* should not be used as a synonym for *allege, assert, charge, declare, maintain, profess, protest, propound*. See SYNONYMOMANIA.

CLAM CHOWDER, *see* **PUMPERNICKEL**

CLASSIC / CLASSICAL

The adjectives are interchangeable except in certain senses, to wit: *classic* should be used to connote "of the highest class" ("Richard Burton's classic portrayal of Hamlet") or "conforming to a standard or pattern" ("a classic case of parental neglect"); *classical* should be used to refer to ancient cultures, especially Greek and Latin ("modern neglect of classical education").

Sportswriters should be restrained from applying *classic* to every event from demolition derbies to celebrity seed spitting. And must they always refer to the World Series as "the annual fall classic"?

CLAUSE

Grammatically, a clause is a group of words that contains a subject and a verb and is not a sentence. There are four kinds of clause: *principal* (also called independent clause), *nounal, adjectival* and *adverbial* (the three last are also called dependent clauses). This sentence has all four:

"Her father warned her that she should never accept a ride from any person who offered her one when she was walking home from school."

PRINCIPAL CLAUSE: "her father warned her"; it governs the rest of the sentence and it can stand independently.

NOUNAL CLAUSE: "that she should never accept a ride from any person"; it is the object of the verb *warned* and it is the equivalent of a noun (this was his "warning").

ADJECTIVAL CLAUSE: "who offered her one"; it qualifies *person*, which is the antecedent of *who*, and it is the equivalent of an adjective (the "ride-offering" person).

ADVERBIAL CLAUSE: "when she was walking home from school"; it modifies the verb *offered* and it is the equivalent of an adverb, being introduced by an adverbial conjunction of time (*when*).

CLAUSTROPHOBIA, *see* –PHOBIA

CLEAN / CLEANSE

As verbs, *clean* was once used for all material substances and *cleanse* for spiritual or ceremonial purification. *Cleanse*, however, has now been extended to connote purgation of any kind. Whatever about the truth of the maxim "Cleanliness is next to godliness," one must admire the wit of the university administrator who arranges that the departments of hygiene and religion be juxtaposed at registration.

CLERIHEW

Edmund C. Bentley, 1875–1956, an English journalist and novelist (*Trent's Last Case*), invented a form of nonsense verse that came to be named after his middle name, Clerihew, a family name of Scottish origin.

A *clerihew* has four lines, usually of unequal length and different meter, the first two and the last two rhyming. The subject must be a real person, usually named in the first line.

Espy describes the clerihew as "the ideal put-down—gentle, compassionate, unanswerable." For examples, see Bentley's *Biography for Beginners* and *Clerihews Complete* and W. H. Auden's *Academic Graffiti*.

CLICHÉ

Busy as a beaver all day, he was as tired as a dog when he hit the hay last night. He thought he would fall into the arms of Morpheus and sleep like a log, but his pad was cold as ice and he tossed and turned and didn't sleep a wink. Well, to cut a long story short, in the wee small hours he hit the deck like a bolt from the blue to get himself a hair of the dog to warm the cockles of his heart, but, as luck would have it, this was more easily said than done because he was fresh out of what the doctor ordered. Make no bones about it, he was really over a barrel. Little did he think he would be without the necessary. He was in a pretty kettle of fish, it goes without saying. Rather than open a new can of worms, he threw in the sponge without further ado and hit the sack to await Old Sol and another day, another dollar. It was too funny for words, needless to say.

You get sick of reading and hearing clichés. Sick and tired.

A cliché, from French *clicher*, to stereotype, to cast from a mold, is an expression that is trite (from Latin *terere*, to rub, hence worn-out by use), hackneyed (from *hackney*, a horse for hire, worn-out by service).

Speech is often riddled with clichés because people speak faster than they think and because they speak in phrases rather than in words. They have picked up the phrases over the years and don't stop to think what the words mean. At their creation, the phrases were original and bright. Down the years, they have become worn-out by use. What we need are new clichés.

There is less excuse for clichés in writing than in speech. A writer has more time to seek the right word, to avoid triteness. If, however, he decides that a cliché is the best way to convey his meaning he should go ahead and use it. He should not apologize for using it by adding a patronizing phrase such as "if you'll pardon the expression," "to coin a phrase," "as the old saying goes." Such apologies are manifestations of intellectual pride, the equivalent of saying, "Look, I'm using a cliché but I want you to know I know it's a cliché."

The first paragraph of this entry contains more than thirty clichés. If you want more, see Shaw's list of more than three hundred, but don't try to read them all at one fell swoop, to coin a phrase.

CLIMACTERIC / CLIMACTIC / CLIMATIC
The adjective of *climax* is *climactic*; the adjective of *climate* is *climatic*. A *climacteric* is a critical stage of life involving change, such as menopause. Climacterics supposedly occur in odd multiples of seven years. The grand climacteric is supposedly at age 63. See also ANTICLIMAX.

CLINIC
From Greek *kline*, a bed, a *clinic* was originally a bedridden person. Clinical teaching was medical instruction in the bedside manner. Clinical baptism was deathbed conversion. *Clinic* properly pertains to medicine but has been extended to other vocations and to sports.

CLOSE PROXIMITY
The best kind.

CLOTURE
The word is not a fancy word for *closure*. *Cloture* is a parliamentary term for ending debate and voting on a measure.

COED
Formerly an acceptable word for a female student at a coeducational institution, *coed* is now in disfavor.

COERCE, *see* EXERCISE

COHORT
A *cohort* is not an individual companion or associate, as in "Haldeman and Mitchell, two of Nixon's cohorts (make it *accomplices*)" or "Calder Pickett, a journalism cohort (make it *colleague*) of mine." A *cohort* is a group of people united in some way, especially military, from Latin *cohors*, an enclosure, a company of soldiers. As Bernstein points out, the *co* in *cohort* is not a prefix meaning together. If it is, he asks, "what is a *hort?*" Other common words from the same root are *cortege, court, courtesy, curtain, curtsy.*

COKE

A diminutive of Coca-Cola, *Coke* is also a trademark and should be uppercase.

COLESLAW

There is no idea of cool or cold in *coleslaw*, from Dutch *kool sla*, cabbage salad. Some like it hot.

COLISEUM

Those colossal structures for entertainment, whether artistic or brute, derive from the Roman Colosseum, but the word is spelled *coliseum*, plural *coliseums*.

COLLABORATE TOGETHER

There's no other way.

COLLECTIVE NOUN

See AGREEMENT OF SUBJECT AND PREDICATE. For a collection of collective nouns, see James Lipton's *An Exaltation of Larks*.

COLLIDE

For a collision, from Latin *col* + *laedere*, to strike together, at least two objects must be in motion. Thus a moving vehicle doesn't collide with a parked vehicle or some other stationary object. It crashes into, hits, strikes (but not together). In possibly unconscious preservation of a British newspaper tradition, some American editors won't allow "A truck collided with a car," lest the reader impute blame to the driver of the truck. And vice versa. Readers do tend to blame whoever collided with. The issue can be avoided by "A truck and a car collided."

COLLOQUIALISM

Some authorities have sought to pigeonhole language into four rigid compartments: literary, common, colloquial, slang. Language can't be pigeonholed. Last year's slang may be this year's colloquialism and next year's common language. The test is time. And why do these authorities equate literary with stilted? Common, unstilted language is also very commonly literary.

The problem is one of label. The word *colloquial* itself illustrates the problem. It derives from Latin *col* + *loqui*, to speak together, to converse. The idea that colloquial language is a lower form of language thus puts an etymological seal of disapproval on conversation, which is not of itself less than literate (another label).

So lean lightly on labels and let language evolve through time, taste, convenience and scholarship.

But if you do label, examine Bernstein's suggestion of *casual* as a better word than *colloquial* for relaxed, easy, familiar expression. For Bernstein, *casualism* "does not imply that the expression is necessarily unsuitable for serious [another label] writing." He calls it an "orange light," not a red one. Read his measured treatment of the topic in *The Careful Writer* under "Casualisms." His analysis is noteworthy also for his comments on Webster III.

COLON
The punctuation mark colon (:) derives from Greek *kolon*, a limb, a member, a clause of a sentence. The colon, like the semicolon, is used much less today than formerly, especially in newspapers. Apart from its mechanical uses to introduce lists, formal statements and subtitles of books (it has been said that no doctoral dissertation or master's thesis is respectable without a colon in the title) and to separate numerals in time of day and sports times, the colon has acquired, as Fowler says, "a special function: that of delivering the goods that have been invoiced in the preceding words." Gore Vidal describes the colon as "a blare of French horns introducing a significant theme." A colon, like a dash, can be effectively used for dramatic pause but, like the dash, it should not be overused.

In newspapers, which prefer short sentences to long, the use of colons and semicolons is regarded as cheating on sentence length. To most newspaper editors, a sentence is a group of words between periods. When in doubt, use a period.

For a thorough examination of the colon, see Nurnberg.

COLOSTOMY
See the last sentence of -TOMY.

COMMA
The punctuation mark comma (,) derives from Greek *koptein*, to cut off. A comma cuts off a word or a phrase or a clause from another to avoid collision, to prevent ambiguity, to set off words or phrases in apposition, to list or enumerate (as in this sentence), to introduce complete quotes, to indicate a pause or change of tone in speech and to achieve various other ends of smoothness and clarity.

Too much has been written about the use of a comma before the *and* in a series. Look at the last dozen words of the last sentence in the previous paragraph. Should there have been a comma before the *and* after *speech*? Some say yes. Some say no. The best test is ambiguity. Because there is no danger of ambiguity at the end of that sentence, don't use a comma. But use a comma after *sleeping* in this sentence, "He spent his time reading, watching television, sleeping, and strolling in the woods," unless the man was sleeping in the woods.

Newspapers and other popular publications usually don't use a comma before *and* in a series. Scholarly publications usually do. Kate L. Turabian, author of *A Manual for Writers of Term Papers, Theses, and Dissertations*, an authoritative stylebook for academic research, insists on the comma before *and* in a series and she must have been pained when the front cover of the fifteenth impression of her work dropped the comma after *Theses* in the title.

When should you use a comma to separate the clauses in a compound sentence? For *and*, the old rule was that a comma should be used when the subjects of the clauses are different. Thus: "The professor is lecturing, and the students are listening." A better principle is that a comma should be used only when both clauses are long or when there is danger of ambiguity. Without a comma after *parents*, this sentence is ambiguous at first reading: "He drove to Colorado with his parents and his wife stayed home with the children."

When the clauses of a compound sentence are connected by *but*, a comma is often used before *but* for the effect of suspended contrast, even when the clauses are short. Thus: "The professor is lecturing, but the students are sleeping."

A common error in newspaper copy is the absence of a second comma in this kind of sentence: "When he was arrested, the defendant said he was beaten up by police." He didn't say this when he was arrested. He said that when he was arrested he was beaten up. Put a comma after *said*.

For a thorough treatment of the many uses and abuses of the comma, see Nurnberg.

COMMANDO

From Afrikaans *kommando*, the term referred to a small raiding force of Boer settlers or to a raid itself. *Commando* was revived in World War II after Dunkirk, when it was used for the small groups of Allied volunteers who recrossed the English Channel in destructive sorties. *Com-*

mando is now used for a member of a raiding group, as well as for the group itself.

COMMA SPLICE
This is another term for RUN-ON-SENTENCE.

COMMENCE, *see* BEGIN / COMMENCE / START

COMMENTATE, *see* BACK FORMATION

COMMITMENT
The word is commonly misspelled. There's only one *t* in the middle, unlike *committal* and *committed* and *committee*.

COMMON GENDER
Either masculine or feminine. See also CHAIRPERSON and GENDER.

COMMON OR GARDEN
This cliché is a translation of the Latin *communis vel hortensis*, applied to varieties of plants and insects and, by extension, to almost anything else. Lately, the cliché has become "your basic (whatever)."

COMMUNICATION
Like *media*, the word is overworked when applied to journalism, especially in journalism education. What newsman or any other kind of journalist calls himself a media communicator or a member of the media of mass communication? What reader or listener or viewer calls himself a communicatee?

COMMUNICOLOGESE
Scientism is the fixation that the research methods of the natural sciences are the only valid means of acquiring knowledge in any academic discipline. Scientism is the science of making a science out of something that isn't a science, such as communicology. The language of communicology is *communicologese* and it abounds in some so-called learned journals in some of the social sciences and, God help us, journalism. Here are some examples of communicologese from one issue of an academic publication for journalists:

—The presentation of material by means of two sense modalities is more effective than either simple visual or oral presentation.

—The inter-linkages between macro-social and micro-psychological changes, though rooted in social mobilization, may not be totally determined by it.

—The essence of modernity may not lie in the transition from particularistic to universalistic outlooks, but in a people's ability to compartmentalize both kinds of value structures.

—Most discriminations taken in juxtaposition would yield a dissonance result.

—Knowledge is seen in this study as often necessary for adoption but is not sufficient because of the impact of other variables such as income and situational and infrastructural factors which interfere in the decision-making process.

—The question is this: Does reliance on the mass media for environmental information discourage the audience from developing a personal commitment that alternative information sources might foster to help alleviate environmental deterioration?

As Newman says, "Abraham Lincoln was on the side of the social scientists when he said, 'God must have loved the people of lower and middle socio-economic status, because He made such a multiplicity of them.'"

COMPANION
The derivation, Latin *cum*, together, and *panis*, bread, attests to the meaning of *companion*, one who eats bread with another.

COMPARE TO / COMPARE WITH
When you put something in the same class as something else, you *compare* that *to* this. You are suggesting a likeness. You *compare* Jim Ryun's running style *to* a gazelle's. As the American Heritage says, comparison *to* involves similarities that are "often metaphorical rather than real; a general likeness is intended rather than a detailed accounting."

When you seek both similarities and differences, you *compare* that *with* this. You are studying details for kinds and degrees of similarity and difference. You *compare* Frost's style *with* Sandburg's.

Barzun sums up the distinction well: "Any writer can *compare himself with* Shakespeare and discover how far he falls short; if he *compares himself to* Shakespeare (i.e., puts himself on the same level), then he had better think again."

COMPLEMENT / COMPLIMENT
Note the spellings. *Compliment* rarely is misspelled. *Complement* often is. To *complement* is to fill, make whole, supply a lack, bring to perfection. To *compliment* is to praise, congratulate, approve.

COMPLETELY DECAPITATED
Partial decapitation is like partial pregnancy.

COMPOUND VERB
See the last paragraph of SPLIT INFINITIVE.

COMPRISE
The whole comprises the parts. The parts compose (constitute, make up) the whole. The encyclopedia comprises twenty-six volumes. Twenty-six volumes compose the encyclopedia. The encyclopedia is composed of twenty-six volumes. Shun "is comprised of."

CONCEDE, *see* ACCEDE

CONCLUDED
In stories of interviews and speeches, try to restrict *concluded* to the sense of "drew a conclusion" rather than "ended." The last quote in a story is seldom the speaker's logical conclusion, which, in a straight news story, is usually high in the story, often in the lead.

CONCORDANCE
Apart from the meaning of agreement or harmony (from Latin *con +* *cors*, of the same heart or mind), *concordance* has the technical meaning of a book that alphabetically lists all the principal words, with their contexts, in all the works of an author, or all the principal words in a book or collection of books. A concordance to the Bible and a concordance to Shakespeare are invaluable reference books for writers and editors.

CONCRETE, *see* ABSTRACT / CONCRETE; CEMENT / CONCRETE

CONCUBINE
From Latin *con + cubare*, to lie down together. From *cubare* also come *incubate, succubus, covey, cubicle.*

CONDITIONAL / CONDITIONAL PERFECT, *see* SEQUENCE OF TENSES

CONJUNCTION

From Latin *conjungere*, to join, a conjunction is the part of speech that joins words, phrases, clauses. Conjunctions have two chief classifications: coordinating and subordinating. Coordinating conjunctions join words, or word groups, of the same rank; the most common coordinating conjunctions are *and* and *but*. Subordinating conjunctions join dependent clauses to independent clauses in a complex sentence; among the many kinds are subordinating conjunctions of comparison (*than*), concession (*although*), condition (*if*), duration (*while*), manner (*how*), place (*where*), purpose (*so that*), reason (*because*), time (*when*).

Nounal conjunctions (*that, whether*) introduce a nounal clause (see CLAUSE). Relative conjunctions (*who, that, which*), preferably called relative pronouns, introduce adjectival clauses (see CLAUSE).

To avoid common errors, note:

—*because* is an adverbial conjunction of reason, not a nounal conjunction ("The reason for his success is *that* he is shrewd," not *because*); see REASON IS BECAUSE.

—*if*, strictly, is an adverbial conjunction of condition, not a nounal conjunction ("He wants to know *whether* you need him," not *if*); see IF / WHETHER.

—*like* may be a preposition, but never a conjunction ("Do *as* I do," not *like*); see AS / LIKE.

—*than* is a conjunction, not a preposition ("He is taller than *I*," not *me*); see THAN.

—*where* is an adverbial conjunction of place, not an adjectival conjunction ("This is a movie *in which* the hero dies," not *where*); see READ WHERE.

—*while*, strictly, is a conjunction of duration, not concession ("*Although* he works hard, he makes little money," not *while*); see WHILE.

CONNIVE

The primary meaning of *connive*, Latin for "shut the eyes," is to wink at wrongdoing, to pretend it doesn't exist. Strictly, *connive* doesn't mean conspire or scheme. When a student connives at another's cheating, he doesn't necesarily conspire with the other student to cheat. To *conspire* is to breathe with, to plot (see -SPIRE).

CONNOISSEUR
Note the spelling: double *n*, double *s*.

CONNOTE / DENOTE
To *connote* is to suggest a meaning beyond the exact meaning. To *denote* is to give an explicit sign or an exact definition. Remember that *connote* is broader than *denote*.

CONSANGUINITY, *see* AFFINITY

CONSECUTIVE / SUCCESSIVE
Things that happen consecutively happen one after another without interruption, without a break. Things that happen successively happen one after another regardless of the intervals between them. Webster gives the example of four *consecutive* days (four days in a row) and three *successive* leap years (not three leap years in a row). The athlete must have been really exhausted after he ran what the Associated Press called his "fourth consecutive sub-four-minute mile."

CONSENSUS
The word is often misspelled *concensus*, probably because of confusion with *census*. *Consensus* comes from Latin *consentire*, to feel together, to agree. *Census* comes from Latin *censere*, to value, to assess. *Consensus of opinion* is redundant. *Consensus* is agreement of opinion. *Consensus of opinion* would be agreement of opinion of opinion.

CONSIDER
When the Roman augurs carefully observed the stars, they considered (from Latin *sideris*—genitive of *sidus*, group of stars, constellation). Some authorities would restrict *consider* to mean "judge after careful deliberation," but the word seems entrenched in its looser meanings of *think*, *reckon*, *regard*. Thus "I consider him a coward" doesn't necessarily mean that a judgment has been made after careful deliberation.

CONSISTENCY
Rare is the person whose life is one thrilling novelty after another. Though we are encouraged to advance the frontiers of knowledge, to explore the unexplored, to develop new ideas ("new concepts in living—new life-styles," as the admen say), almost all of us spend much of our lives doing

the same things over and over again. To enjoy this, we need to discover the thrill of monotony.

We need to learn from children, who cry out in their simplicity, "Do it again," when you play the same old game with them or tell them the same old story. We need to learn from another simple being, the Supreme Being, who by definition must be simple, else He would be complicated, wherefore imperfect, wherefore not the Supreme Being. His days and nights, His sun and stars, His calendar of nature are testimony to the simple thrill of "Do it again," the thrill of monotony.

The thrill of monotony, *consistency*, is a virtue for writers and editors. Inspiration is fruitless without perspiration. Imagination must be tempered with consistency. Editors strive to bring order to words. Theirs is not a democratic society in which people can exercise their freedom by using whatever capricious, inconsistent style they choose in matters of spelling, capitalization, hyphenation, abbreviation, identification, punctuation, numeration, tabulation, symbolization. That's why we have stylebooks.

To cultivate *consistency* and to lighten their editors' load, writers should be steeped in the stylebook of the publication for which they are working. It won't cramp their literary style. Creation demands order. Writers must learn the thrill of monotony. Day after day, they must do it again.

CONSPICUOUS BY HIS ABSENCE
A cliché. Forget it. It sticks out like a sore thumb.

CONSPIRE, *see* CONNIVE; –SPIRE

CONSTRUCTIVE CRITICISM
What a writer petulantly calls for when a critic says anything uncomplimentary about his work.

CONSUMMATE
As a verb, *consummate* is stressed on the first syllable. As an adjective, it is stressed on the second syllable.

CONTACT
Authorities disagree on the acceptability of *contact* as a verb in the sense of "get in touch with." Strunk calls it "vague and self-important." Webster brands it "Colloq. U.S." Two-thirds of the American Heritage panel-

ists say it is "not appropriate to formal contexts." Fowler, however, says, "Convenience has prevailed over prejudice," and accepts it. More than twenty years ago, Evans said, "It is certainly accepted in spoken English today and will probably become the usual term in written English as well." More than a dozen years ago, Bernstein said, "The verb will undoubtedly push its way into standard usage sometime. Do you think you can wait?"

If you think the waiting time is over or if you can't wait any longer, go ahead and write, "I'll contact him." But why not choose a more specific verb to fit a specific context, such as *write, phone, see, find, meet, approach, look up, call on, talk to, interview?*

In *On Writing, Editing, and Publishing,* Barzun reminds us of the proper use of *contact* to mean "touch," as in this sentence on a very hot day: "On a day like this, I wouldn't contact anybody for the world."

CONTAGIOUS / INFECTIOUS

From Latin *tangere,* to touch, a *contagious* disease is transmitted by physical contact. From Latin *inficere,* to work in, to taint, an *infectious* disease is transmitted by such agencies as water and air. An *infectious* disease is not necessarily *contagious.*

Shaw makes a good distinction between the figurative uses of the words. *Contagious,* he says, emphasizes speed, as in "Contagious fear ran through the audience," whereas *infectious* suggests something irresistible, as in "Mark Twain's infectious humor stimulated prolonged laughter and applause."

CONTINUALLY / CONTINUOUSLY

Something happens *continually* when it lasts for a long time but with occasional interruption. "It rained continually for a week" means that it rained off and on for a week. Something happens *continuously* when it lasts without interruption. "It rained continuously for three hours" means that it rained without a break for three hours.

CONTRAIL

A contraction of "condensation trail."

CONTRITION, *see* ATTRITION

CONTROVERSIAL ISSUE

Redundant.

CONVINCE

For 362 bleeding words, Newman inveighs against the construction *convince . . . to*, instead of *persuade*, as in "I convinced him to buy a new car." He gives no reason for his anger. You may convince somebody that he should do something; or you may convince him of his folly. But why not convince him to do something? Bernstein argues that *convince* means "to satisfy beyond doubt" and therefore connotes "a static situation, which does not in itself suggest a consequent action," as would be implied by the addition of a verb form, such as the infinitive "to do something." But "convince him that he should do something" suggests consequent action and adds a verb form. Newman laments that *convince . . . to* is "now virtually accepted." Though you may not be able to convince Newman to do it, you may strike *virtually*.

COOL

The word, like *gay*, is becoming perverted in meaning. *Cool* now connotes goodness or beauty or pleasure and is applied to all the necessities of life from franchise food to electronic cacophony. In the sense of temperature, a cucumber is indeed cool, but those who use the cliché aren't thinking of temperature. They just aren't thinking.

COOPERATE TOGETHER

The best way.

COP

As a noun, *cop* is gaining respectability as a synonym for *policeman* and does not seem to be resented by policemen. It is certainly more respectable than the barnyard word the crazies scream. *Cops* is a handy word for tight headlines. The origin of *cop* is disputed. It probably came from Latin *capere*, to seize, whence also *cop a plea*, which led to *cop out*.

COPE

Don't use *cope* without *with*.

COPULATIVE VERB, *see* ADJECTIVE / ADVERB

COPYRIGHT / COPYRIGHTED

AP prefers *copyright* for the adjective ("a copyright story") and *copyrighted* for the past tense of the verb ("He copyrighted the story").

CORD, *see* CHORD / CORD

CORPUS DELICTI

Literally, Latin for "the body of a crime." Legally, the material evidence that a crime has been committed. *Corpus delicti* does not mean the body of a victim, nor is it spelled *corpus dilecti*, which would mean the body of a loved one.

COSELLISM

Howard Cosell of ABC has made popular the practice of turning off the sound on a television set during sports events. Cosell is a master of the art of making simple things complicated. His language is *Cosellism*. The baseball season becomes "the still current baseball season." A smoke bomb is "an instrumentality of destruction." A low score is attributed to "the relative paucity of scoring." Many field goals are "a veritable plethora of field goals." A manager "must husband his pitching resources."

As Newman says, "Only Cosell would speak of a football team 'procuring a first down,' or say that a fighter was 'plagued by minutiae,'" and "nobody else would say, 'The Redskins have had two scoring opportunities and failed to avail themselves both times,' or 'The mist is drifting over the stadium like a description in a Thomas Hardy novel.'"

Cosell fancies himself not only as a litterateur but also as a grammarian extraordinaire. Frank Gifford, an ABC colleague, asked him one night, "Who do you think will win?" Replied Cosell, "No, Giff, *whom*, not *who*." Gifford meekly accepted the fallacious correction instead of responding, "Sorry, Howard. Do you think them will win?"

Never before in the history of American air waves has one man's arrogance done so much to annoy so many.

COSMO-

Among the many words that derive from Greek *kosmos*, order, universe, world, are these:

—*cosmetic*, well ordered, arranged, hence beautifying.

—*cosmogony*, a theory of the origin of the universe (*gony* from *gignesthai*, to be born).

—*cosmology*, metaphysical study of order in the universe.

—*cosmonaut*, a Russian astronaut (*nautes*, sailor).

—*cosmopolitan*, a citizen of the world, a much traveled person, at home in any country, gathered from many parts of the world.

—*macrocosm*, the great world, the universe, a large system (*makros*, large).

—*microcosm*, a small world, a representative community or institution, man as an epitome of the universe (*mikros*, small).

COUÉISM

A system of psychotherapy propagated by Emile Coué (1857–1926). Based on autosuggestion, the cult is most remembered for its slogan: "Every day and in every way I'm getting better and better." The movement was impeded by the report of a bowlegged man who uttered the slogan too often and became knock-kneed.

COULD OF

A barbarism for *could have*.

COUNCIL / COUNSEL

A *council* is a governing body or assembly. *Counsel* is advice. Don't confuse the spellings. A member of a council is a councilor, one *l*. One who gives advice is a counselor, also one *l*.

COUNTERPART

A *counterpart* is something or someone similar or complementary, not an opposite or an opponent.

COUNTRY / NATION

The *country* is the territory of the *nation*. *Country* refers to geographical territory, homeland. *Nation* refers to political entity, a community of people.

COUPE

For an enclosed car with two doors, American English has dropped the French acute accent and changed the pronunciation to *coop*. The word is from French *couper*, to cut off, as is *coupon*.

COUPLE

As a collective noun, *couple* may be either singular or plural. But you will have less trouble with agreement of subject and predicate if you treat *couple* as plural. Try this for singular awkwardness: "The couple was married two years ago and it spent its honeymoon in Florida. But it was divorced last year and then went its separate ways." Change to *were, they, their*.

    Couple needs *of* after it in sentences such as "He scored a couple touchdowns in the first half" or "She had only a couple dollars in her purse." And "couple, three dollars" or "couple or three dollars" involves a switch from a collective to a cardinal number. Make it "two or three."

COURAGE, *see* **BRAVERY / COURAGE**

COURTEOUS / POLITE
Courteous people are more than *polite*; they go beyond the common good manners of politeness and help others by their kindness. Politeness may be superficial. Courtesy is ingrained.

COURT-MARTIAL
The word is hyphenated. Its plural is *courts-martial*.

COURT OF ST. JAMES'S, *see* **ST. JAMES('S)**

COVENTRY
To send to *Coventry* is to refuse to associate with, to ostracize. Coventry, an industrial city near Birmingham, England, is most famous in recent history for its indiscriminate bombing by the Luftwaffe in November 1940. During the English Civil War (1642–52), the Parliamentarians occupied Coventry and sent Royalist prisoners there, whence the phrase "sent to Coventry." Morris adds that the natives of Coventry disliked the presence of soldiers and ostracized any girl caught talking to a soldier, which practice caused soldiers sent to Coventry to regard the assignment as bad duty. See also **BOYCOTT.**

COVET
In newspaper jargon, especially sports, all trophies, prizes, awards and championships of any kind are coveted. *Covet* does come from Latin *cupere,* to desire, but it connotes unlawful or excessive desire. Possibly from its use in the English translation of the Ten Commandments, *covet* usually implies desire for someone or something that belongs to someone else.

COWARD
A person who has his tail between his legs is a coward, from Latin *cauda,* tail.

CQ
In radio, the letters CQ are used as code for "Call to Quarters" at the beginning of messages intended for all receivers.
      In newspaper editing, the letters are sometimes used in parentheses after a strange spelling to alert the typesetter that the word must be spelled exactly as it is in the copy. Thus: "John Smth (cq) died today." The sym-

bol (its origin is disputed) is being replaced by a marginal note such as "as is" or "OK" or by the use of a rectangle around the word. See also STET, which has a different meaning.

–CRACY
Greek *kratein*, to be strong, to have power, to rule, is the root of many English words, such as:

—*aristocracy*, government by the best citizens (*aristos*, best).

—*autocracy*, government by self (*autos*), by absolute sovereign.

—*bureaucracy*, government by administrative officials (French *bureau*, office or desk, from *bure*, cloth covering for desk or table), usually used derogatorily.

—*democracy*, government by the people (*demos*).

—*gerontocracy*, government by the elders (*geron*, old man).

—*plutocracy*, government by the wealthy (*ploutos*).

—*technocracy*, government by scientific technicians (*techne*, skill, craft).

Through the years, other words have been coined from -*cracy* to denote power, such as *cottonocracy*, for King Cotton, but they have died. (Will we see *oleocracy*, *petrocracy*?) A newer coinage is *mediacracy*, invented in the mid-'70s to denote the power of the media, itself an ugly word, almost as ugly as *mediacracy*, which should die—the word, not the power of the press, essential to democracy, especially in the struggle against bureaucracy.

CREDENCE
Except in the sense of diplomatic or commercial letters of credence, the word, from Latin *credere*, to believe, trust, is being replaced by *credibility*, usually followed by *gap*.

Its ecclesiastical use in *credence table*, a small table that stands next to the altar and holds the materials of the Eucharist, comes from the ancient practice of setting food and drink on a side table for foretasting by a servant as a precaution against poisoning. If the varlet survived, the victuals could be trusted. From the same practice comes *salver*, a tray or serving platter, from Latin *salvare*, to save, through Spanish *salvar*, to foretaste. From *credence* comes *credenza*, a buffet or sideboard, usually without legs.

CREEPING SOCIALISM
This was a warning cry forty or fifty years ago against governmental intervention in the lives of the governed. The cry has largely gone unheeded. Socialism no longer creeps. It gallops.

CRÈME DE MENTHE
Straight French for cream of mint, the name of the liqueur retains its French pronunciation in English. Order a *crame de monnt,* not a *cream de menthe.*

CREPUSCULAR
What a beautiful word! It comes from Latin *crepusculum,* twilight, from *creper,* dusky, and refers to birds and insects (and, by extension, humans) that become active at twilight. Itself a beautiful word, *twilight* comes from Anglo-Saxon *twi + leoht,* two lights. An annual event in bygone summers in the hamlet of Hills, Iowa, was the Hills Crepuscular, a corroboree whose high point was the ceremonial burning of an outhouse.

CRESCENDO
From Latin *crescere,* to grow, *crescendo* means a gradual increase in volume, not the loudest point. Other words from the same root are *accrue, adolescent, concrete, crescent, crew, decrease, excrescence, increase, recruit.*

CRETIN
In the patois of the Alpine valleys of Valois and Savoy, the French word for a Christian, *chrétien,* became *crétin* and was applied to the many unfortunate Alpine children who suffered from a congenital mental condition caused by thyroid deficiency. Their horrific appearance made them physically repulsive, but the peasants reasoned that the children were spiritually apart from brute animals, so they baptized them and called them *crétins.* Thus *cretin,* without the accent, is an English word for an idiot, one who has extremely deficient mentality, but nonetheless a human soul.

CRINOLINE
The fabric of a crinoline, a petticoat (also a hoop skirt), was originally horsehair and linen thread, from Latin *crinis,* hair, and *linum,* linen. A *crinoline* headline is one that covers everything but touches nothing (see BIKINI HEAD).

CRISIS
The plural is *crises.* See also CRITICISM.

CRITERIA
The word is plural. Its singular is *criterion.* Common errors are "the criteria is," "one criterium is" and "two criterions." The word comes from

Greek *krinein*, to separate, choose, judge, whence also *crisis, critic, endocrine, exocrine, hypocrite.*

CRITICISM
From Greek *krinein*, to judge, *criticism* strictly means judgment, but it has come to mean blame, condemnation, denunciation, faultfinding. True *criticism* embraces both the good and the bad.

In another sense, but from the same root, a *critical* decision is one made in a moment of crisis, the moment of judgment. In a hospital, a person may be put on the critical list, signifying that his condition has reached a crisis, that he is dangerously ill, but *critical* is not a synonym for *dangerous* unless crisis is involved. Excessive drinking is dangerous to one's health and may lead to a critical decision to save one's health and quit drinking.

CRITIQUE
A tolerable noun (better *criticism, commentary*). A lousy verb (use *criticize, comment on*). See VERBING NOUNS.

CROUPIER
From Old French *croupe*, rump, the posterior part of a horse, the crupper. A croupier is one who sits on the rump, in a secondary position, hence a person who sits at the lower end of the table, facing the host at the upper end and, at a public dinner party, acting as assistant chairman. The more common use of *croupier* is for the attendant at the fat part of a gambling table who pays the winners and collects from the losers.

CROWDED TO CAPACITY
A reporter leaves an unanswered question when he writes that a hall or a stadium was "crowded to capacity." What's capacity? The reader can't be assumed to know. Hence he won't know the size of the crowd.

CRUSADE
From Latin *cruciare*, to mark with the cross, by way of Spanish *cruzar*, to bear the cross. The original crusades were the European Christian military expeditions in the eleventh, twelfth and thirteenth centuries to recover the Holy Land from the Moslems. A newspaper *crusade* is a campaign of public service to promote a cause or to remedy an abuse.

CRYPTIC
From Greek *kryptein*, to hide, hence of hidden meaning, secret, enigmatic, mystifying. Other words from the same root are *apocryphal*, *crypt*, *cryptogram*, *cryptography*.

CUI BONO
Latin, literally "to whom (is it) for a benefit?" The phrase has become English to mean "for whose good?" or "of what use is it?" It may often be applied to published research in some disciplines, as in Webster's example: "painstaking research, to be sure, but in such a subject, cui bono?"

CUL-DE-SAC
French, literally "the bottom of a bag," hence a dead-end street, blind alley. The preferred English pronunciation is *cull*, not the French *cool*.

–CULE
A Latin diminutive, as in: *animalcule; funicular*, as in funicular railway or cable car, from Latin *funiculus*, a small rope, the umbilical cord; *minuscule*—note the spelling—*minus*, not *minis; molecule*, a little mass; *opuscule*, a small, minor work; *tubercular*, pertaining to a small knob or growth.

CULOTTES
From Latin *culus*, rump, backside, whence also *recoil*, to fall back, shrink back, spring back.

CULPRIT
In medieval English courts, when a person pleaded not guilty, the prosecutor would respond, "Culpable, prest," meaning "He is guilty and I am ready to prove it" (from Latin *culpa*, fault, blame, guilt, and *praestus*, ready). In court records, this was abbreviated to *cul. pret.*, whence *culprit*.

CURB
British spelling distinguishes between *curb*, check or restrain, and *kerb*, gutter edge. American spelling is *curb* for both meanings. Mencken pitied the English visitor to New York who wondered whether the sign "Curb your dog" meant restrain his natural impulses or take him to the gutter to yield to them.

CURFEW
From French *couvrir* + *feu*, to cover the fire, a curfew was originally an order to put out all fires at a certain time in the evening. The signal was the ringing of a bell. Thomas Gray's curfew tolled the knell of parting day.

CURIO, *see* APOCOPE

CURIOSITY
Note the spelling. Though it is the noun for *curious*, it has no second *u*.

CURMUDGEON
The origin of this delightful word for a cantankerous person is obscure. Some say it may have come from French *coeur*, heart, and *méchant*, wicked. Samuel Johnson listed *curmudgeon* as from "*coeur méchant*, Fr. an unknown correspondent." Twenty years later, a dictionary listed it as from "French *coeur*, unknown, and *méchant*, correspondent." So there is nothing new in the failure of some modern students to distinguish between modern dictionary abbreviations for *from* and *French*.

CURRENTLY
The word often is redundant, as in "He is currently living in Chicago." If you need contrast between past and present, use the Anglo-Saxon *then* and *now*, rather than the Latin *previously* and *currently*.

CURRICULUM
From Latin *currere*, to run, hence a course, a course of study, a collection of courses. The plural is either *curricula* or *curriculums*, preferably *curriculums*. See PLURALS.

CURRICULUM VITAE
Latin, literally "the course of life," hence a summary of one's career. An applicant for a position prepares a *curriculum vitae*, commonly shortened to *Vita* (not the genitive *Vitae*, as is embarrassingly seen as the heading of some applications for academic appointment or promotion).

CUSTODIAL ENGINEER
A euphemism for caretaker, janitor.

CUTTY SARK
Scottish for short shirt or skirt. The name of the brand of Scotch whisky comes from a lightly clad figurehead on the bow of a ship.

CYBERNETICS
Coined by Norbert Wiener, American mathematician, from Greek *kybernetes*, helmsman, governor, *cybernetics* refers to the control processes of various systems, such as computers. It is singular.

CYNIC
The followers of Antisthenes thought that happiness was attainable only by the satisfaction of one's natural needs in the cheapest and easiest way and that nothing natural could be improper or indecent. So they performed all their bodily functions in public, which did not endear them to their neighbors, who called them *kynikos*, doglike. Hence the English word *cynic* for a currish, selfish, faultfinding, contemptuous person. Oscar Wilde defined a *cynic* as "a man who knows the price of everything and the value of nothing." Perhaps the word also came from the Cynosarges, the gymnasium outside Athens in which Antisthenes was forced to teach because his mother was not Athenian by birth. Another English word from the Greek word for *dog* is *quinsy*, inflammation of the throat, from *kynanche*, dog's collar, from *kyon*, dog, and *anchein*, to choke. See Moore for an instructive exchange between his schoolmates and schoolmaster on the derivation of *cynic*.

CYNOSURE
From Greek *kynosoura*, dog's tail, from *kyon*, dog, and *oura*, tail, the *cynosure* is the northern constellation, three of whose stars seemed to the Greeks to be shaped like a dog's tail sticking upwards. The Greeks also called the brightest star of the constellation the *kynosoura*, whence the English word for the center of attraction. The more common pronunciation is *sign-a-sure*, as in *Dinah Shore*.

DACHSHUND
That dog with the low-slung undercarriage was used in Germany for tracking badgers, whence its name: German *dachs*, badger, and *hund*, dog. Note the spelling.

DACTYLOLOGY
Sign language, from Greek *daktylos*, finger, toe, digit. Other words from the same root are: *dactyl*, a poetical foot of three syllables, long-short-short, from the three joints of a finger; *dactylogram*, fingerprint; *dactylography*, identification of fingerprints; *date*, from the shape of the fruit; *pterodactyl* (*pteron*, feather, wing), a flying reptile with an enormously developed fourth digit, extinct except in some sculptures of the JAYHAWK.

DAISY
From Anglo-Saxon *daeges-eage*, day's eye, because some species show their yellow center in the morning and close in the evening.

DAN / BEERSHEBA
"From Dan to Beersheba" means "from limit to limit." Dan and Beersheba were the northern and southern limits of Palestine. Boundaries in that troubled part of the world have changed. The cliché hasn't.

DANDELION
From French *dent de lion*, lion's tooth, from Latin *dens leonis*, because the leaves of the weed are sharply indented.

DANGLING PARTICIPLE
In ABLATIVE ABSOLUTE, this example of the dangling participle construction is given: "Swimming in strong surf, her bikini fell off." The participle *swimming* is dangling because it doesn't belong to the subject of the main clause, *bikini*. Her bikini wasn't swimming. She was. This undangles the construction: "Swimming in strong surf, she lost her bikini." Better: "While she was swimming in strong surf, her bikini fell off." Here the wishy-washy participle has been replaced by a finite verb.

The principle is that every participle, particularly at the beginning of a sentence, must have a noun or pronoun it can belong to, modify. (Another term for dangling participle is unattached modifier.) Opdycke gives this principle of word order: "When a sentence begins with a participle, the first substantive (noun or pronoun) not in the possessive case in the main clause is modified by that participle." Thus in "Strolling through the park, Jack's hat blew off," *strolling* grammatically belongs to *hat*, which is ridiculous; the hat wasn't strolling. Make it "While Jack was strolling through the park, his hat blew off."

Another ludicrous type of dangler stems from imperatives, as in this road sign: "If wet, drive slowly." So don't speed unless you are dry. And this admonition comes on a can of bug killer: "If swallowed, seek medical advice." If you have been swallowed, you may find it hard to seek medical advice, which probably would be too late, anyway.

DARK AGES
On the day Romulus Augustulus, the last Western Roman emperor, died in 476, nobody announced to the world: "World, put out the lights. Today we start the Dark Ages."

Historical periods are named by historians in retrospect. Because historians saw little intellectual light in the period from the fall of Rome to the Renaissance of the fourteenth century, they named the period the *Dark Ages*. In later retrospect, they saw more intellectual light in the period from Charlemagne, crowned Holy Roman Emperor in 800, to the Renaissance, so they shortened the Dark Ages to the period from the fall of Rome to Charlemagne. The term "Middle Ages" is now applied to the period from the fifth century to the fourteenth century and includes the Dark Ages.

DASH
The dash (—) is a handy punctuation mark to signify interruption of thought, a sharp break in a sentence or delayed effect. But don't overdo it, especially to patch up long, wordy sentences. Dashy writing can become jerky writing. For the use of dashes to replace offensive words or letters, see APOSIOPESIS.

DATA
The word is plural. Its singular, which is rarely encountered, is *datum*. "These data don't support the hypothesis," not "This data doesn't support the hypothesis."

DATELINE
In American newspapers, almost all nonlocal stories begin with their place of origin. Originally, the date was added to the place, whence *date-line*. Few American papers now use the date in a dateline, but *dateline* is still the term for the place of origin. See also INTERNATIONAL DATE LINE.

DAUGHTER-IN-LAW
Your sons' wives are your daughters-in-law, not daughter-in-laws. If your son is living with a woman without benefit of matrimony, you may call her your daughter-outlaw. You are her father-outlaw or mother-outlaw. Similarly, the man who lives with your unmarried daughter is your son-outlaw.

DAYLIGHT-SAVING TIME
American newspaper style abbreviates *daylight-saving time* by the eight American time zones, of which the most frequently used are EDT (Eastern Daylight Time), CDT (Central), MDT (Mountain), PDT (Pacific). Note that *daylight-saving* is hyphenated and that the second part is *saving*, not *savings*.

DEBONAIR
From Old French *de bon aire*, of good air, good breeding, good disposition. Shipley traces the term to falconry: a hawk *de bon aire* flies high from its aerie, its nest on a high place. The term now means graceful, affable, carefree. It used to mean *gay*, but this word has taken on another meaning, unfortunately for the language. See GAY.

DEBRIEF
Nickles calls *debrief* "an outrageous verb, among the worst modern coinages of the unliterary mind, yet accepted without protest in recent dictionaries and sanctioned by general use."

The prefix *de-* sometimes has the sense of reversal, the taking away of something, as in *debunk, decompose, devaluate*. Hence *debrief* was coined by some bureaucratic half-wit to mean the taking of information or intelligence from someone after a mission for which he had been briefed. But the man still has the information. In this sense, as Nickles says, *debrief* makes as much sense as *decircumcise*. If you want to find out what someone has found out, why not question, interrogate?

DEBRIS
The *b* comes before the *r*, despite the frenzied plea of the public address announcer at a basketball game: "The team will be penalized if you don't quit throwing derbis."

DEBUT
A good noun, a lousy verb, whether intransitive ("Tracy Austin debuts as a professional") or transitive ("Cardin will debut his fall fashions"). The American Heritage usage experts vote 93 percent against the intransitive, 97 percent against the transitive. See VERBING NOUNS.

DECANTER
From Latin *canthus*, rim of a wheel, lip of a vessel, to *decant* is to pour from one container into another, preferably gently. A decanter is a bottle, often of cut glass, from which liquor is served. Other words from the same root are *cant* (in the sense of *slant* or *slope*), *canteen*, *canton*.

DECATHLON
The word has no *a* between the *h* and the *l*. It isn't *decath-a-lon*, which one often hears, even in TV commercials featuring an Olympic decathlon champion (see ATHLETE). The word is from Greek *deca*, ten, and *athlon*, a contest.

DECIMATE
For mutiny or cowardice, Roman leaders would choose one of every ten soldiers by lot for execution. Thus a legion was decimated, from Latin *decem*, ten. *Decimate* has extended to mean to kill a large part of a group or destroy a large part of an area. But don't use it with such adverbs as *totally* or *completely* or with a fraction other than one-tenth.

DECLARATION OF INDEPENDENCE
"Write as you talk" is sound advice if you talk well, but the advice and the writing degenerate if you "write like the people talk." Mencken discovered this when some scholars took seriously his burlesque translation of the Declaration of Independence into the American vulgate.

Wrote Mencken, in part: "When things get so balled up that the people of a country have to cut loose from some other country and go it on their own hook, without asking no permission from nobody, excepting maybe God Almighty, then they ought to let everybody know why they done it, so that everybody can see that they are on the level, and not trying to put nothing over on nobody."

Scholars, who are supposed to have the ability to help others see through things, ought themselves to have a sense of humor, the ability to see through things.

DEDUCTION, *see* A POSTERIORI / A PRIORI

DE-ESCALATE
One doesn't ride up an escalator and down a de-escalator. An escalator, originally a trademark from Latin *scala*, ladder, moves both up and down. Only recently, by BACK FORMATION from *escalator*, came *escalate*, to increase or enlarge in intensity. More recently, by redundantly reverse back formation from *escalate* and by courtesy of some euphemist in the Pentagon, came *de-escalate*, to decrease or lessen in intensity. Forget it.

DEFENSE
When the fanatics scream, "*dee*-fense, *dee*-fense," they offend against aural propriety and the proper pronunciation of *defense*, which stresses the last syllable, not the first. And when the coaches and scribes speak of "defensing a play," they offend by verbing a noun. Defend territory and defend against a play. Defend against the offense (which, in this sense, stresses the first syllable, but the last syllable in the sense of resentment or transgression).

DEISM
See *theism* in THEO-.

DEITY
The *e* is pronounced as in *see*, not as in *day*.

DÉJÀ VU
A French phrase that has become English, literally "already seen," *déjà vu* describes the sensation of having already experienced something that one is really experiencing for the first time, akin to *paramnesia*, literally "resembling loss of memory."

DELIRIOUS
The word is a dead metaphor, having lost its ancient metaphorical meaning of "getting out of a rut," from Latin *de + lira*, literally "away from

the furrow" in plowing. Anyone who did something unusual was said to be delirious. Today, *delirious* describes a temporary state of mental disturbance, and one who does something unusual is said to be doing his own thing, a cliché best forgotten.

DELUSION / ILLUSION
Bernstein gives a good example of the distinction between these words. "If you watch the magician 'saw a woman in half,' you are observing an *illusion*," he says, and "if you think he really did it, you are suffering from a *delusion*." An *illusion* is a false perception. A *delusion* is a false belief. Both words come from Latin *ludere*, to play. Other words from the same root are *allusion, collusion, elusion, interlude, ludicrous, prelude*.

DEMOCRACY, *see* –CRACY

DENIZEN
The word has nothing to do with *den*. A *denizen* is an inhabitant, a resident, from Latin *deintus*, from within, as opposed to a foreigner, from Latin *foras*, from without, out of doors, abroad, whence also *forest*.

DENOTE, *see* CONNOTE / DENOTE

DENOUEMENT
A French word that has become English, meaning the solution or unraveling of a plot or a problem, originally from Latin *nodus*, knot, hence an untying. The French acute accent on the first *e* is usually dropped in English.

DEPRECATE / DEPRECIATE
The distinction has become tricky because *deprecate* is now sometimes used to mean *depreciate* in the sense of self-belittlement, as in *self-deprecating, self-deprecatory*. The American Heritage experts are almost evenly split on the acceptability of *deprecate* in this sense. But the distinction should be preserved.

Etymologically, the distinction is clear. *Deprecate* comes from Latin *deprecari*, to pray away from, to seek to avert, hence to disapprove. *Depreciate* comes from *depretiare*, to take the price away from, to decrease in value, hence to belittle, disparage. An economist deprecates the state of the dollar, which has depreciated over the years.

DE RIGUEUR
If you use this French phrase, meaning "required by strict etiquette, socially obligatory," spell it right. Put a *u* both before and after the *e*.

DERRIÈRE
An English euphemism for the rump, the rear end, the behind, *derrière* is French for *behind*. See also PREMIÈRE.

DESERET
The *Deseret News* of Salt Lake City is not the *Desert News*. *Deseret* is a word for *honeybee* in the Book of Mormon. It signifies industry, which is the motto of Utah, also known as the Beehive State.

DESSERT
From French *desservir*, to stop serving, to clear the table, hence the last course.

DETENTE
The word derives from Latin *detendere*, to unstretch. An old French word, *detente* became internationally fashionable in the '70s to connote a relaxing of strained relations between the United States and the Soviet Union. Conversely, some thought the policy stretched things too far on one side. The French acute accent on the first *e* has been dropped by American newspapers.

DEUCE
A card with two spots, or the two pips on a side of a dice cube, or a dice throw of two ones. *Deuce* comes from Latin *duos*, the masculine accusative of *duo*, two. In tennis, the score of deuce is so called because two successive winning points are needed for game (from French *à deux le jeu*, two to play). *Deuce*, as an expletive, probably comes from the crusty comment of a crapshooter who throws a deuce.

DEUS EX MACHINA
Latin, literally "God from a machine." A *deus ex machina* is any improbable character or device, such as a miracle ending, artificially introduced into a situation or story to resolve a problem.

DEUTERO-
A combining form meaning second or secondary, from Greek *deuteros*, second. Several English words have this form. Among them: *deuteragon-*

ist, an actor who plays a secondary role (see also PROTAGONIST); *deuterium*, the hydrogen isotope of mass number 2, also called heavy hydrogen, discovered by Harold Urey, chemist, cosmogonist and Nobel laureate; *deuterocanonical*, belonging to a second, or later, canon (list) of genuine biblical works; *deuterogamy*, second marriage (see –GAMY); *deuteron*, the nucleus of the deuterium atom, consisting of one proton and one neutron; *Deuteronomy*, the fifth book of the Bible, which repeats the Ten Commandments and other laws (*nomos*, law), first stated in Exodus.

DEVELOP
Note the spelling. The old alternative, *develope*, is now a misspelling.

DEVELOPING COUNTRIES
Bureaucratese for newly independent nations, previously developed as colonies. Similar bureaucratese is *development area* for a part of a city being rebuilt. Some latter-day Dickens will write an urban masterpiece titled *An In-Depth Survey of Two Development Areas*.

DIAGNOSE
A condition is diagnosed, not a person.

DIALECT
Don't try to write in regional or foreign dialect unless you are completely conversant with it in ordinary conversation. A phony accent is easy to spot, whether in speech or in writing. Don't be a carpetbagger. Don't be stage Irish.

DIALOGUE
Formerly more or less restricted to the lines of a play or an exchange of words in a novel, *dialogue* now seems to be replacing good words like *talk* and *chat* and *conversation*. In its new use, it is frequently preceded by *meaningful*, which is getting to be one of the most meaningless words in the language. "We had a meaningful dialogue" may mean anything from a semantic discussion to a casual exchange of pleasantries at a cocktail party.

DIAPHRAGM
Note the spelling. *Diaphragm* comes from Greek *diaphragnyai*, to fence off by a partition wall.

DIARRHEA
Note the spelling: double *r*. The diphthong has been dropped from the older spelling, *diarrhoea*. The word comes from Greek *dia + rhein*, to flow through. Other words from the same root are *catarrh* (*kata + rhein*, to flow down) and *hemorrhoid* (*haima + rhein*, to discharge blood).

DIATRIBE
A *diatribe* will wear you out, as its etymology indicates: Greek *dia + tribein*, to rub out completely, to wear away.

DICHOTOMY, *see* –TOMY

DICKENS
What the dickens did you do that for? Who the dickens do you think you are? Why the dickens didn't you tell me? The euphemistic *dickens* has nothing to do with Charles. The word was used by Shakespeare in *The Merry Wives of Windsor*, when Mrs. Page says, "I cannot tell what the dickens his name is . . ." O'London said *dickens* was probably a contraction of *devilkins*. The American Heritage says it is possibly a euphemistic alteration of (*Old*) *Nick*.

DICKER
The word may sound like slang, but it is ancient and respectable. *Dicker* comes from Latin *decuria*, a set of ten, which was a unit of commerce. A decuria of hides became *decher* in German, which passed into English and became *dicker*, the word used by the early American colonists in their bargaining with the Indians for skins and furs. *Dicker* has lost its connotation of number and of hides and has come to mean to bargain, to argue, to haggle.

DIDDLE
In the senses of swindle and dawdle, *diddle* comes from Jeremy Diddler, an imaginative petty swindler in James Kenney's farce *Raising the Wind*. Poe wrote an essay on "Diddling considered as one of the exact sciences." Then there was the man who asked for a pound of kiddleys and was told that the correct pronunciation was *kidneys*. He replied: "I said 'kiddleys,' diddle I?"

DIDN'T USED TO
"He used to read a lot" signifies something habitually done in the past. In this usage, *used to* is an auxiliary verb, as is *did* in "He did read a lot."

Because *did used to* is a double redundant auxiliary, we don't say, "He did used to read a lot." How then can we, grammatically and sensibly, say, "He didn't used to read a lot"? If the two auxiliaries can't be used properly in a positive statement, how can they be used properly in a negative statement?

Just as the negative of *did* is *did not*, contracted to *didn't*, so the negative of *used to* is *used not to*, contracted to *usedn't to*, as in "He used not to read a lot" or "He usedn't to read a lot." It may sound strange to some American ears, but the British have gotten along fine with *usedn't* for many years (but not with GOTTEN). *Usedn't* is grammatically correct. It also makes sense.

The same principle applies to questions, both positive and negative, *to* being dropped, as in "Used he read a lot?" or "Usedn't he read a lot?" Not: "Did he used to read a lot?" nor "Didn't he used to read a lot?"

Some otherwise respectable authorities notwithstanding, the use of *use to*, instead of *used to*, is barbaric.

DIE

As Nickles says, "For simple, stark nobility, no verb can replace *to die*." Yet the English language abounds in euphemisms, both flowery and facetious, for *died*. Though nothing can change the inevitability of death, and few things can soften its blow, preachers and morticians resort to verbs such as *passed away, passed on, expired, succumbed, breathed his last, gathered to his fathers, gone to rest, gone to his reward, called home*. The late Bill Vaughan's favorite was *gone where the woodbine twineth*. Death may be unpleasant, but it is a fact. *Died* tells the fact simply, starkly, nobly.

DIFFERENT

Different is an adjective in the positive degree, not the comparative degree. Comparative adjectives take *than* (stronger than, more beautiful than). *Different* takes *from*. Peter is different from Paul. Alice is more beautiful than Francine Sue (is beautiful). But not: Alice is different than Francine Sue (is different?).

Come then those who would allow *different than* before what Evans calls a "condensed clause." Bernstein, in *Miss Thistlebottom's Hobgoblins*, gives this example: "The feeling of weightlessness affected him this time in a different way than ever before." *From*, he says, "would produce some such clumsy locution as 'The feeling of weightlessness affected him this time in a different way from the way it ever before had.'" (How about

"The feeling of weightlessness affected him this time differently from previous times"?) Nickles gives this example: "Morality today is different than in older times." He says *than* avoids the verbosity of "Morality today is different from that which prevailed in older times." (How about "Today's morality is different from yesterday's"?) Because of "concise-ness," 44 percent of the American Heritage experts allow *than* in "How different things seem now than yesterday." (How about "How things seem to have changed since yesterday"?)

As Bernstein said earlier, in *The Careful Writer*, the "almost mysti-cal argument" that *different* is "felt" to be a comparative leads to the kind of language used as a slogan by an interstate trucking company: "Faster than rail, regular than mail."

DINGBAT
Archie Bunker's endearing term for his wife is also a printing term for any typographical decoration that has no specific name.

DINOSAUR
From Greek *deinos*, fearful, terrible, and *sauros*, lizard. Though of Greek derivation, *dinosaur* was coined by Sir Richard Owen, British zoologist, in 1841.

DIOCESE
The word for this ecclesiastical district comes from the Greek word for housekeeping or administration, *dioikesis*, from *oikos*, house. The more common pronunciation of *diocese* has the stress on the first syllable, and the last syllable is pronounced *sis*. The plural, *dioceses*, has the stress on the first syllable, and the last two syllables have a sound like *sisses*. These are other words from the same root:
—*ecology*, study of the household, the biological science of the rela-tionships of organisms to their environments (falsely used by ama-teur environmentalists for the wilderness itself).
—*economy*, management of the household (*nemein*, to manage); *home economics* is etymologically redundant.
—*ecumenical*, belonging to the whole world as a household, belong-ing to the inhabited world, hence universal, especially in the sense of ecclesiastical unity.
—*parish*, a group of neighbors (*para* + *oikos*, near the house), hence a subdivision of a diocese, or a civil district, a county (as in Louisiana).

DIPHTHONG
Note the spelling: an *h* follows both *p* and *t*. *Diphthong* comes from Greek *di + phthongos*, two voices, two sounds, the joining of two vowels. *Diphtheria* has a similar spelling but comes from *diphthera*, leather, a reference to the rough membranes that coat the air passages in this disease.

DIPLOMA / DIPLOMAT
The Greek word *diploma* meant something doubled, a piece of folded paper, from *diploos*, twofold. Ancient credentials came in the form of a document of two wax tablets or a folded sheet of writing material. This diploma was borne by public officials, including traveling diplomats. Today's educational diploma is intended to certify a graduation from a certain stage of learning, but it is sometimes merely a certification of registered attendance.

DIPSOMANIAC
One who has an uncontrollable craving for alcoholic liquor, from Greek *dipsa*, thirst, and *mania*.

DIRECT OBJECT
In "I gave him a book," *book* is the direct object of the verb *gave*, and *him* is the indirect object, governed by the understood preposition *to*. The indirect object precedes the direct object when a preposition is understood. The direct object precedes the indirect object when a preposition is stated, as in "I gave a book to the library." "Throw Mama from the train a kiss" is attempted murder of Mama and real murder of the language. See also CASE.

DIRGE
A contraction of Latin *dirige*, the imperative singular of *dirigere*, to direct. A *dirge* is a funereal lament and gets its name from the first word of "Dirige, Domine, Deus meus, in conspectu tuo viam meam" ("Direct my way in Thy sight, O Lord, my God"), the antiphon of the first psalm of the first nocturn in the old Latin Office for the Dead.

DISADVANTAGED
The word is properly applied to someone who for physical, psychiatric, social, economic or educational reasons has not had ample opportunity

for intellectual or cultural advancement. *Disadvantaged* is improperly applied as a euphemism for someone who is intellectually or culturally cloddish for other reasons, another popular educational euphemism for whom is *underachiever*.

DISASSOCIATE / DISSOCIATE
AP prefers *dissociate*.

DISASTER
Disasters were said to occur because of the evil influence of some star, from Greek *dis* + *astron*, something ill-starred.

DISCLOSE / REVEAL
Don't use *disclosed* or *revealed* as a synonym for *said* unless what is being reported is a genuine disclosure, a revelation, an exposure, something of importance previously unknown or secret. Don't use *disclosed* or *revealed* for the mundane, as in "'My car gets 25 miles to the gallon,' he disclosed" or "'My feet are killing me,' he revealed."

DISCOMFITURE / DISCOMFORT
The words have different meanings. *Discomfiture* is the experience of being thwarted, frustrated, put to rout ("His blind luck with his putter caused me great discomfiture and I lost by seven strokes"). *Discomfort* is lack of comfort, mild distress ("The temperamental air conditioner caused me some discomfort in bed last night"). *Discomfort* is both noun and verb. The verb for *discomfiture* is *discomfit*. *Discomfiture* always involves *discomfort*, but not vice versa.

DISCOVER / INVENT
Something *discovered* is something that already existed but hadn't been found or known. Harold Urey *discovered* heavy hydrogen. Something *invented* is something that hadn't already existed. Eli Whitney *invented* the cotton gin.

DISCREET / DISCRETE
Both words have the same derivation, Latin *discretum*, past participle of *discernere*, to distinguish, to separate. *Discreet* means prudent, exercising good judgment. *Discrete* means separate, individually distinct.

DISGRUNTLED
An old English word for a pig's snout was *gruntle*, also the word for a pig's snort, whence the human *grunt*. When pigs are in good humor, they gruntle. When humans are in bad humor, they are *disgruntled*.

DISINTERESTED / UNINTERESTED
If you are *uninterested*, you have no interest; you are indifferent. If you are *disinterested*, you may be interested, but you have no self-interest; you are impartial, unbiased.

DISMAL
In each month of the medieval calendar, there were two unlucky days, called *dismal*, from Latin *dies mali*, days of evil. They were also known as "Egyptian days," from their reputed discovery by Egyptian astrologers. These were the days: Jan. 1, 25; Feb. 4, 26; March 1, 28; April 10, 20; May 3, 25; June 10, 16; July 13, 22; Aug. 1, 30; Sept. 3, 21; Oct. 3, 22; Nov. 5, 28; Dec. 7, 22. Those Egyptians were right about Dec. 7.

DISMAL SCIENCE
Carlyle's name for political economics.

DISPARAGE
The word originally meant "to marry unequally," from Old French *desparagier*, to deprive one of one's lineage, extraction (*parage*), hence to lower in rank or estimation, to belittle.

DISPOSALL
A trademark. Uppercase.

DISTAFF
The distaff side has become a cliché for a description of work by women, the maternal branch of a family or women in general. *Distaff* comes from Anglo-Saxon *distaef*, the staff for holding flax or wool for spinning. The male equivalent of the distaff side was the spear side.

DITTO
From Latin *dictum*, past participle of *dicere*, to say, hence a reference to something already said. Ditto marks (") are placed under a word or words, usually in tabulated copy, to avoid repetition.

DIVED / DOVE
AP prefers *dived*.

DIVINE, *see* AFRAID

DIXIE
The name for the Southern states was originally a nickname for New Orleans, from a $10 bill issued by a bank there and marked *Dix* (French *ten*) for the benefit of French Creoles.

DOA
Police and hospital lingo for "dead on arrival." Note that the arrival is the arrival of the body at a hospital. It is not the arrival of the police at a scene of death, which usage Nickles calls a "genteel misuse by police officials when they refer, for example, to 'a female found DOA in her home.'"

DOESN'T TELL STORY
If you have to reduce all the rules and recommendations of news headline writing to two, they would be: the head must fit and it must tell the story. A head that doesn't fit won't appear in print. A head that doesn't tell the story shouldn't appear in print.

If the main job of a news head is to summarize the story accurately and completely so that a reader can look at the head and decide whether he wants to read the story, a news head that doesn't tell the story doesn't do its main job. A good copy editor must have sound news judgment. While he is editing a story before writing its head, he must keep asking himself what the real news is, what's new about the story. He should be framing what Bernstein, in *Headlines and Deadlines*, calls a "news point sentence," a sentence that summarizes the whole story. From this sentence he can write a head that will tell the story.

Many heads don't go far enough in telling a story. For example, over a story about Jimmy Carter's reaction to Andrew Young's description of certain prominent figures as racists, one newspaper wrote this head: "Carter Reacts to Criticism." Of whom? The copy editor could have told the story more specifically with something like "Carter Supports Young."

The most common kind of head that doesn't tell the story is the deadhead or flathead, the kind of head that says: "Group Meets" or "Mayor Speaks" or "Bias Discussed." What happened at the meeting?

What did the mayor say? What was the outcome of the discussion? Insist on reasonable head space to tell a story. See also BIKINI HEAD.

DOLLAR
The first dollars were *thalers*, from *Joachimsthalers*, silver coins made in the valley (*thal*) of St. Joachim, near Prague, in the early sixteenth century.

DOROTHY
What some non-Kansans think every Kansas girl is named. And all Kansas dogs are named Toto.

DOUBLE POSSESSIVE
"A story of Ernie Pyle" is a story about Ernie Pyle. "A story of Ernie Pyle's" is a story by Ernie Pyle. The *of* and the apostrophe make for a double possessive, which is idiomatically proper. The same is true for pronouns: "a story of his."

DOUBTLESSLY / UNDOUBTEDLY
The words *doubtlessly* and *no doubt* are often thrown in by a writer or speaker who really isn't sure or merely hopes he is right or just won't bother to give a reason for his opinion. *Doubtlessly* and *no doubt* are weaker than *undoubtedly* and *without doubt*, which connote certainty. *Doubtless* is both adjective and adverb. *Indubitably* is stuffy.

DOUBT THAT / DOUBT WHETHER
The use of *that* or *whether* after *doubt* depends on the kind of sentence and the kind of doubt. *That* should be used in a negative statement or in a question: "I don't doubt that Evert will win"; "Do you doubt that Evert will win?" *That* should also be used in a positive statement in which doubt is really unbelief, lack of confidence: "I doubt that Evert will win," meaning you won't be much surprised if she loses. But *whether* should be used in a positive statement in which doubt is real doubt, uncertainty: "I doubt whether Evert will win," meaning you just don't know which way the match will go. And see BUT; CANNOT HELP BUT; IF / WHETHER.

DOWN UNDER
Australians and New Zealanders don't refer to themselves as coming from Down Under, any more than they refer to Americans and Canadians as coming from Up Over.

DRACONIAN
A law or punishment barbarously harsh, after Draco, a magistrate of Athens, whose code of laws in 621 B.C. was said to be extremely severe.

DRAWING ROOM, *see* APHESIS

DREADFUL, *see* AFRAID

DROMEDARY
A one-humped camel, originally a camel trained for riding, from Greek *dramein*, to run. Some other words from the same root:
—*aerodrome*, or *airdrome*, older words for *airport*.
—*Dramamine*, a trademark for a drug used to treat motion sickness, whether by air, sea, car or camel.
—*dromomania*, obsession with roaming.
—*hippodrome*, originally an oval track around which horses (*hippos*, horse) used to run; now an arena for horse shows or a circus.
—*palindrome* (which see for examples), a running again (*palin*, again), a word, phrase, verse, sentence or paragraph that is the same when read forward or backward.
—*prodrome*, a running before, a warning symptom.
—*syndrome*, a running together (*syn-*, together), a group of symptoms that occur together and characterize a disease or other condition.

DROWNED
One *drowns* accidentally ("He drowned in raging surf"). One is *drowned* feloniously ("He was drowned by an envious rival").

DRUNK / DRUNKEN
Benjamin Franklin learned a lot between the ages of 16 and 31. At 16, in the *New England Courant*, he listed 19 synonyms for *drunk*. At 31, in the *Pennsylvania Gazette*, he listed 228. Drunkenness, he said, is so vile that it is "reduced to the wretched necessity of being expressed by distant roundabout phrases and of perpetually varying those phrases as often as they come to be well understood to signify plainly that a man is drunk." Today's distant roundabout phrases for *drunk* are uncounted.

As an adjective, *drunk* is the usual form for a predicate ("The man was drunk"), but *drunken* is the preferred form before a noun ("The man was charged with drunken driving"). As a noun, *drunk* was once slang for *drunkard*, but it seems to have become standard. *Drunk* is certainly accepted in the sense of a binge ("He is recovering from a six-day drunk").

DRY
The plural is *drys* when the word is used for an anti-liquor lobby.

DRY AS DUST
The cliché comes from Dr. Jonas Dryasdust, a ponderous antiquarian who was created by Walter Scott and to whom Scott addressed the prefaces of several of his books.

DUE TO, *see* BECAUSE OF / DUE TO

DUMBBELL
Lifters of dumbbells develop the same muscles as bell ringers, but without the bells, whence the term.

DUMFOUND
Though *dumfound* is a blend word from *dumb* and *confound*, the more common spelling has no *b*.

DUNCE
The opponents of the teachings of John Duns Scotus contemptuously referred to his followers as "Duns men," whence *dunce*.

DUPE, *see* BUCKLEYISM

DYED-IN-THE-WOOL
The cliché for "long unchangeable" comes from the process of dyeing wool before it is spun. A young reporter, probably a Democrat, recently referred to a distinguished professor as a "died-in-the-wall Republican." See SONIC WRITING.

DYSPEPSIA
If you suffer from *dyspepsia*, the cause may be bad cooking, from Greek *dys*, bad, and *pessein*, to cook.

DYSPHEMISM
From Greek *dys*, bad, and *pheme*, speech, *dysphemism* is the antonym of *euphemism* (see EU-). A dysphemism is the substitution of a belittling or offensive term for an inoffensive one, such as *pill-pusher* for a doctor, or *shrink* for a psychiatrist.

EACH

When *each* is the subject of a clause, it takes a singular verb and singular referents, as in "Each is doing his best to succeed." When *each* comes after a plural subject, it doesn't govern the verb, which is therefore plural, as in "They each are doing their best to succeed" or "Jack and Jill each are doing their best to succceed." When *each* comes after a copulative verb or an auxiliary verb, to emphasize individuality, the number of a subsequent noun is singular, as in "They are each a candidate for an Academy Award" or "They each have won an Academy Award." See also EITHER.

EACH AND EVERY

Redundant.

EACH OTHER / ONE ANOTHER

If two persons are having a conversation, each is talking to the other; they are talking to *each other*. If three persons are having a conversation, each is talking to one and to another one; they are talking to *one another*.

The principle seems simple and sensible, but authorities are split on it. For example, 55 percent of the American Heritage experts accept *each other* for more than two, and 54 percent accept *one another* for only two. A stronger case can be made for the acceptance of *one another* for only two than for the acceptance of *each other* for more than two. But why not accept the principle?

EAGER, *see* ANXIOUS / EAGER

EAR

In newspaper jargon, an *ear* is the space on each side of the flag, which is the nameplate of the newspaper on the front page. Ears are often boxed and may contain weather information, the name of the edition, references to stories inside the paper, or even ads. Such important space shouldn't be wasted.

EARTH
Uppercase in specific reference to the planet.

EASEL
From Latin *asellus*, a little ass, through Dutch *ezel*, ass, from the similarity of the shape of an easel to that of a carpenter's horse.

ECDYSIAST
Mencken received a letter in 1940 from "a practitioner of the fine art of stripteasing" who wanted him to "help the verbally underprivileged members" of her profession by coining a word to replace *stripteasing*, "which creates the wrong connotations in the mind of the public." Though Mencken suspected the sly hand of a press agent, he responded because "I always answer letters of working-girls politely." He thought it might be a good idea to relate stripteasing to "the associated zoological phenomenon of molting" and he flirted with *moltician* before rejecting it because of its likeness to *mortician*. He then came up with *ecdysiast*, from Greek *ekdysis*, the stripping of an outer layer of skin.

S. I. Hayakawa and Stuart Chase had also been consulted, but Hayakawa said he had nothing to suggest because he had never seen a stripteaser in action, and Chase, "busy with the salvation of humanity on a dozen fronts," according to Mencken, did not reply.

Though *ecdysiast* came to be recognized by the dictionaries, Gypsy Rose Lee, queen of all ecdysiasts, scornfully rejected the word in an interview with H. Allen Smith, hollering: "Ecdysiast, he calls me! Why, the man is an intellectual snob. He has been reading books. Dictionaries. We don't wear feathers and molt them off. . . . What does he know about stripping?"

ECLECTIC
An eclectic is a person whose opinions are chosen from various sources, from Greek *eklegein*, to single out, pick out, choose.

ECOLOGY / ECONOMY / ECUMENICAL, *see* DIOCESE

ECSTASY
Note the spelling: the word ends in *asy*, not *acy*.

EDUCANTO / EDUCATIONIST
An *educationist* is a former teacher who sacrifices content for method and who cloaks scientistic mindlessness with a jargon called *Educanto*,

coined by James D. Koerner in *The Miseducation of American Teachers*. *Educanto*, says Koerner, "can reduce any mildly sensitive layman to a state of helpless fury in a matter of minutes" and "can also induce severe nausea"; Educanto "masks a lack of thought, and in fact makes thought of any important kind extraordinarily difficult."

To an educationist, teachers are "resource personnel," "directors of experiences," "adult models," "communicators," "learning-aids officers," "structurers of frameworks," "catalytic agents," "creators of learnings environments," "school situations analyzers." Educationists talk about "the progressive familial subcultural mental retardation," "the cathartic construction projective dimension," "the normative generalization reference cue," "the situation response relationship reinforcement," "the extrinsic dualistic organization of coordinate administration."

Koerner thus sums up the knowledge gained by a graduate in Educanto: "You will know that dynamically reinforced growth of your ideational and cross-fertilized learnings has occurred, hopefully through intravariable autorivalry, enriched need arousal, purposeful goal-oriented behavior, and persistent achievement motivations. Your self-actualization, together with your real-life readiness for situational and refractive testing against Yoakam's Readability Formula, will be concretioned. You will be ready to socialize to your peer group, whose modal behaviors as practitioners of Educanto have been randomized within the framework of reference of the contextual analogies of Flannery's Critical Incident Index so that all isolates have been integrated into the appropriate activity constructs—and both over-achievers and fortunate deviates whose role-playing compulsions have excititioned peer wrath and even Glanser's Syndrome are assigned intervisitational field laboratory experiences for greater concomitant learning experiences."

The graduate is then turned loose on the nation's children "to undermine by imperceptible degrees, and finally to suppress entirely, the English tongue."

EDUCATED GUESS
The phrase is a cliché, despite its being dignified by the American Heritage as an estimation "based primarily on experience and some factual knowledge." As Nickles says, "The viability of this phrase, to hazard a conservative estimate, is still anybody's guess." *Guesstimate* is BUREAUCRATESE.

EFFECT, *see* AFFECT / EFFECT

EFFETE

The word was made popular by Spiro Agnew's crack at the "effete corps of impudent snobs who characterize themselves as intellectuals," but popular currency gave *effete* the meaning of sophisticated or snobbish, or even effeminate, instead of sterile, worn-out, exhausted, barren, from Latin *effeta* (*ex + fetus*), worn out by childbearing.

E.G., *see* I.E.

EGALITARIANISM

From French *égalité*, equality. As a doctrine of equality, *egalitarianism* is tarnished by those who interpret equality to mean the inalienable right to be equal to one's superiors and superior to one's equals. As an educational doctrine, *egalitarianism* is similarly tarnished by those who would lower standards, especially standards of language, in the name of populism.

EGOISTIC / EGOTISTIC

To be *egoistic* is to have a narrow view of the world as if it revolved around oneself only. To be *egotistic* is to refer to oneself continually and boastfully. Both words come from Latin *ego*, the personal pronoun *I*.

EGREGIOUS

Standing out from the flock, from Latin *e grege*, from the flock, hence outstanding, conspicuous, exceptional, almost always in the bad sense of "blatant" or "outrageous," as in "Schenkel committed several booboos in his commentary on the golf tournament, the most egregious of which was his line: 'If Joyce Kilmer could be here, she would really love the trees.'"

EITHER

When *either* is the subject of a clause, it takes a singular verb and singular referents, as in "Either of the paintings is worth its price."

When *either* and *or* join singular subjects, the verb is singular, as in "Either Jack or Jill is going downhill." When *either* and *or* join a singular subject and a plural subject, put the plural subject second and make the verb plural, as in "Either the president or his representatives are expected to attend" or "Either he or they are expected to attend."

When *either* and *or* join subjects of different person, make the verb agree with the nearer subject, as in "Either he or you are responsible for this mess" or "Either she or I am responsible for this mess." If this sounds awkward, change the construction to "Either he (she) is responsible for this mess or you are (I am)" or duck the issue with a verb that doesn't change in person, as in "Either he (she) or you (I) must bear the responsibility for this mess." The same principles apply to *neither . . . nor*.

Don't use *either* as a substitute for *each* or *both*. Not: "There are billboards on either side of the highway." Make it "billboards on each side" or "billboards on both sides."

As for pronunciation, are *either* and *neither* "eether" and "neether" or are they "eyether" and "neyether"? As the Irishman replied, "ather," as in *bather*.

EKE
The word is from Anglo-Saxon *ecan*, to increase, and is usually accompanied by *out*. To *eke out* is to add something with great difficulty to something that is insufficient, as in "She eked out her low income as a writer by working as a waitress for long hours." Don't use *eke out* in the sense of "prolong," as in "He tried to eke out his life by scavenging from garbage cans." See also ADDER.

ELDER / OLDER
Use *elder* and *eldest* only with persons and *older* and *oldest* with either persons or things. Restrict *elder* and *eldest* to describe the relative age of members of a family, as in "his elder brother" or "their eldest child," or the seniority of rank of members of a business, as in "the eldest partner," who may not be the oldest. Don't use *elder* with *than*.

ELECTORAL
The stress is on the second syllable, not the third, as is commonly heard every four years in reference to the Electoral College or the electoral vote.

ELECTRICITY / ELECTROCUTION
When rubbed, amber produces sparks and causes attraction and repulsion. The Greek word for amber is *elektron*, whence *electricity* and *electronics* and all other *electro-* words. *Electrocute* is a blend word from *electricity* and *execute*, coined in 1889 when New York became the first state to establish electrocution as the death penalty. Some Latin purist who helped compile the stylebook of one prominent Midwestern newspaper protested this coinage, as did Fowler, and insisted on *electrocise*, from Latin *caedere*, to kill. But the protest, as Fowler conceded, is idle.

ELEVEN
When shepherds of old ran out of fingers for counting, the next sheep was *endleofan*, Anglo-Saxon for "one left over," eleven. Similarly, *twelf* was "two left," twelve.

ELLIPSIS
An *ellipsis* is an omission of one or more words, and a printing mark (. . .) for omission, from Greek *elleipein*, to leave out.

Ellipsis may be true or false. If what is omitted does not affect grammatical construction, the ellipsis is true, as in "He is happy, she sad," wherein *is is* also the verb understood after *she*. If what is omitted does affect grammatical construction, the ellipsis is false, as in "They either have or will learn a foreign language," wherein *learned* is needed after *have*. A common form of false ellipsis occurs in the construction "Jim is as tall or taller than Joe," wherein *as* is needed after *tall*.

False ellipsis is permissible in a construction in which what is missing isn't really missed, such as *am* after *I* in "She is happy, I sad," or *wear a tie* after *I* in "He wore a tie, as did I."

As a printing mark, the *ellipsis* (or *ellipses points*) is used to signify the omission of words irrelevant to the context.

EM
A printing term for the square of any size of type, originally from the space occupied by the letter *M*. An *em* pica, almost exactly one-sixth of an inch, is a measure of width. See also ACCOMMODATION.

EMBARRASS
The word is commonly misspelled. Note the double *r* and double *s*. See also HARASS.

EMBLEM / EMBOLISM, *see* BALLISTICS

EMCEED, *see* ACCEDE

EMERITUS
From Latin *emereri*, to obtain or merit by service, the title *emeritus* is given to a retired person, along with the rank held before retirement, as in *professor emeritus*. As a noun, *emeritus* has the plural *emeriti*.

EMINENT / IMMINENT

"A tornado is eminent," the TV announcer intoned. A tornado does indeed come from on high, but it threatens when it comes low. *Eminent* and *imminent* have the same Latin root but different prefixes and different meanings: *eminent* from *eminere*, to project out, be prominent; *imminent* from *imminere*, to project toward, threaten.

EMOTE

Theatrical slang. BACK FORMATION from *emotion*.

EMPATHY / SYMPATHY

The words have the same Greek root but different prefixes and different meanings: *empathy* from *empatheia*, suffering in; *sympathy* from *sympatheia*, suffering with. *Empathy* is stronger and more personal than *sympathy*. *Empathy* involves vicarious identification and extends beyond feelings of pity or commiseration to an understanding of the very soul of another.

EMPHASIZE, *see* LOADED VERB

ENCLOSED

In business letters, or anywhere else, *enclosed herewith* is a redundancy. And *enclosed please find* is an archaic absurdity.

ENCYCLOPAEDIA / ENCYCLOPEDIA

The diphthong is retained in *The Encyclopaedia Britannica*, but not in *The Encyclopedia Americana*.

ENDEMIC / EPIDEMIC

The words have the same Greek root but different prefixes and slightly different meanings: *endemic* from *endemos*, in the people; *epidemic* from *epidemos*, among the people. *Endemic* refers to something that is peculiar or native to a people or locality, such as a habitually prevalent disease or some permanent aspect of the human condition. *Epidemic* refers to something that spreads rapidly among people, such as a disease that strikes a region or some fad. Webster gives this example: "Fear, which is an endemic latent in every human heart, sometimes rises into an epidemic."

ENDORSE
Because *endorse* comes from Latin *dorsum*, the back, through French *en dos*, put on the back, "endorse on the back" is etymologically redundant, but universally accepted. And one may endorse without signing on the back.

END RESULT
Unless the context involves a series of results, *end result* is redundant JARGON.

ENERVATING
The word is often wrongly used to mean stimulating, exciting. The opposite meaning is correct: sapped, drained, weakened, from Latin *enervare*, to take the nerves or sinews from.

ENOCH ARDEN
An *Enoch Arden* marriage is one involving a woman whose husband is presumed dead but isn't. In Tennyson's poem "Enoch Arden," the shipwrecked Enoch returns after more than ten years and finds that his wife is remarried and happy and he decides to let things be.

ENORMITY / ENORMOUSNESS
Both words are from Latin *e + norma*, out of the rule, but *enormity* refers to an act out of the moral rule and connotes heinousness, outrageousness, whereas *enormousness* refers to a condition out of the physical rule and connotes immense physical size.

ENQUIRE / INQUIRE
In American usage, *enquire* and *enquiry* are rarely seen. The British tend to use *enquiry* as a formal word for a question and *inquiry* for an investigation. *Inquire* has the stress on the last syllable. The more common pronunciation of *inquiry* has the stress on the second syllable, not the first.

EN ROUTE
Two words. But why not use the English "along the way" or "on the way to"?

ENSURE / INSURE
Though *insure* is a later form of *ensure*, *insure* seems to be in almost general use, not only for "making secure financially," but also for "making

sure" and "making safe," as in "The adviser insured that the student would be busy" and "The padding insured the athlete against injury."

ENTHUSE, *see* BACK FORMATION

ENTHUSIASM, *see* THEO–

ENTITLED / TITLED
Distinguish between these words. *Entitled* involves a right ("You are entitled to equal opportunity"). *Titled* involves a name ("The book is titled *The Professional Journalist"*).

ENTOMOLOGY, *see* –TOMY

ENTREE
In British dining, the entree is a preliminary course, which makes more etymological sense than in American dining, in which the entree is the main course. The French acute accent on the penultimate *e* has largely been dropped.

ENVY / JEALOUSY
Envy is stronger than *jealousy* and embraces coveting, as can be glimpsed from the derivations of the words: *envy* from Latin *invidere*, to look at with malice; *jealousy* from Latin *zelus*, zeal, emulation.

EPHEMERAL
Quickly passing, beginning and ending in a day, from Greek *epi* + *hemera*, on a day. Some ancient journals were called *ephemerides*.

EPICENE
English lacks *epicene* pronouns for *he/she*, *him/her*, *his/her*(*s*). From Greek *epikoinos*, common to many, promiscuous, *epicene* has the primary meaning of "common to both sexes," but it also has come to mean effeminate or even sexless.

EPICURE
Epicurus (c.340–270 B.C.), Greek philosopher, neither taught nor practiced the doctrine of sensual gratification as the greatest good, but *epicure* came to signify a debauched person. Epicurus taught and practiced the doctrine of happiness and serenity by means of a virtuous life.

Epicure now describes a person of refined or fastidious taste, especially in food and drink.

EPIDEMIC, *see* ENDEMIC / EPIDEMIC

EPIGRAM

From Greek *epi* + *graphein*, to write upon, an *epigram* was originally an inscription, then a short, concise poem with what Fowler calls "a sting in the tail." It now is a sharply phrased, witty expression, often satirical.

EPILOGUE / PROLOGUE

From Greek *epi* + *legein*, to say something besides (what has been said), an *epilogue* is a short poem or speech addressed to an audience at the end of a play, or a postscript to a literary work. From Greek *pro* + *legein*, to say something before, a *prologue* is an introduction to a play, or a preface to a literary work.

EPIPHANY

The Twelfth Day of Christmas, the day the lords are leaping, is January 6, the feast of the Epiphany, from Greek *epiphainein*, to manifest, hence the word for the manifestation of Christ to the Gentiles as represented by the Magi (three lords a' leaping). Incidentally, the gift on the fourth day of Christmas was four colly birds, not "calling birds," four blackbirds (from Anglo-Saxon *col*, coal).

EPISCOPAL / EPISCOPALIAN

A member of the *Episcopal* (adjective) Church is an *Episcopalian* (noun).

EPITAPH, *see* CENOTAPH

EPITHALAMIUM, *see* SHIVAREE

EPITHET

The word is now used more for a derogatory term ("prime bastard, punk kid") than for a mere appellation ("Gene the Machine, Jimmy the Greek"). The derivation is Greek *epi* + *tithenai*, to put on, add to, hence an added name.

EPITOME, *see* –TOMY

EPOCH

An *epoch* is the start of a period of change, as can be seen from its derivation, Greek *epoche*, a pause, a position in time, from *epechein*, to hold on, to stop. *Epoch* should not be used synonymously with *era*. An *epoch* starts an *era*. The invention of interchangeable parts was an epoch in the history of manufacturing and began the era of mass production by assembly line.

EPONYM

Mae West is the *eponym* of the inflatable life preserver. Quisling, puppet head of Norway during the German occupation of World War II, is the *eponym* of a traitor. From Greek *epi* + *onoma*, upon a name, an *eponym* is a person from whom a people, place, era, practice or object gets its name. Fowler has an informative list of eponymous words in common use.

EQUALLY AS

The phrase is redundant. In "Mary is equally as smart as Joan," drop *equally*. In "Joan has a good vocabulary, but there are other attributes that are equally as desirable in a writer," drop either *equally* or *as*, preferably *as* because of emphasis.

EQUINOX

The two times when day and night are about equal are the vernal equinox (about March 21), the start of spring (Latin *ver*), and the autumnal equinox (about September 23), the start of autumn. From Latin *aequa* + *nox*, equal night.

EREWHON, *see* UTOPIA

ERITAS

Nancy Maloley's burping cow, Norman Cousins' golf-hating congressman, Franklin's Polly Baker, Mencken's bathtub and a jug of Admiral W. J. Marshall's no-cal bourbon, among other great hoaxes of American journalism, are enshrined in the Eritas Memorial Library in Colorado Springs, invented by columnist James Kilpatrick in 1973. The Eritas collection is a must for all journalists and other students of satire.

ESCALATE, *see* DE-ESCALATE

ESCAPER

One who employs is an employer. One who is employed is an employee. One who escapes is an escaper. What's an escapee? Though Bernstein says *escaper* "doesn't strike the modern ear as right," *escaper* has long been in the dictionaries and is gaining ground on the absurd *escapee*. Maybe some modern ears are surd.

ESCHATOLOGY

From Greek *eschatos*, last, extreme, furthest, *eschatology* is the theological study of the last or final things, such as death, judgment, heaven, hell, which are sometimes called "The Four Last Things." Do not confuse with SCATOLOGY.

ESPERANTO

Lazarus Ludovici Zamenhof, a Russian philologist and oculist, devised the artificial language of Esperanto in 1887. The name came from Zamenhof's pseudonym, "Dr. Esperanto" (one who hopes). Zamenhof hoped Esperanto would become the world's official international language. It hasn't.

As Moore says, "It must surely be a great bore, and a most unrewarding labour, to learn a language that possesses neither a literature nor any historical associations." If an international language were really needed, Moore would plump for Latin, rather than "its bastard descendant, this bloodless, backboneless, witless deformity called Esperanto."

ESPRIT DE CORPS, *see* SONIC WRITING

ESSENTIAL / NECESSARY

The old distinction between these words was that *essential* applied to the conceptual and *necessary* to the physical, a distinction akin to the Thomistic distinction between *essence* and *existence*. The distinction seems to have died and *essential* and *necessary* have become almost interchangeable. *Essential*, however, still seems stronger than *necessary*. Somehow, if you are told that something is essential for you, you feel more obliged to get it or do it than if you are told it is necessary.

What is *essential* is part of what makes something what it is, part of its essence. What is *necessary* is part of a cause-effect relationship, whereby something won't exist without something else needed for its existence.

Fowler gives the example of his own dictionary, whose alphabetical arrangement is "unessential, but not unnecessary." A dictionary without alphabetical arrangement would still be a dictionary, he says, "but the laws of causality make the publishers demand and the writer supply alphabetical order, and without it the purpose would be very badly served."

ESTHETIC, *see* ANESTHETIC / ESTHETIC

ET AL.
Short for Latin *et alii*, and other persons. So why not talk English and say "and others"? But if you use *et al.*, note that *et* has no period, whereas *al.* does.

ETC.
Short for Latin *et cetera*, and other things. Use it informally, if you really must, to indicate that a list is only partial. But don't use it at the end of a list that began with a phrase like *such as* or *for example*. And don't end a letter with *Yours etc.* (or &c.) unless you want to leave your correspondent in doubt about how you regard him. Above all, don't use *etc.* as a cover for ignorance when you have run out of ideas.

ETERNAL TRIANGLE
The cliché is becoming less apt in these days of husband-and-wife swapping. We need a new cliché. Perhaps "ephemeral quadrangle."

ETHICS, *see* –ICS

ETIQUETTE
The French word originally meant a ticket or label, from Old French *estiquer*, to stick, from the practice of sticking the military procedures for the day, the *etiquette*, on a post for the watch to see.

ETYMOLOGY
The study of the derivation of words, from Greek *etymon*, the true sense of a word, from *etymos*, true, real. Short *e*, as in *get*.

EU–
The Greek word *eu*, good, well, pleasant, is an English prefix of the same meaning. Many English words derive from *eu*. Among them:

—*Eucharist*, a showing of good favor, thanksgiving (*charis*, favor, thanks, grace).

—*eugenics*, study of hereditary improvement, good breeding (*eugenes*, well-born).

—*eulogy*, commendatory oration, high praise (*legein*, to speak).

—*eupepsia*, good digestion (*pessein*, to cook); see also DYSPEPSIA.

—*euphemism*, use of pleasant words, substitution of a seemingly inoffensive term for a seemingly offensive one (*pheme*, speech); see also DIE and DYSPHEMISM.

—*euphony*, pleasant sound, sweet voice (*phone*, sound, voice); see CACO-.

—*euphoria*, well-being, great happiness, a feeling easy to bear (*pherein*, to bear).

—*euphuism*, affectation of elegance in style, from the flowery style of *Euphues: Or the Anatomy of Wit*, by John Lyly, sixteenth-century English novelist and playwright (*phuein*, to cultivate). Don't confuse with EUPHEMISM.

—*eurhythmics*, harmonious bodily movement (*rhythmos*, measured motion, symmetry).

—*euthanasia*, easy or painless death, a euphemism for "'mercy' killing" (*thanatos*, death); see SONIC WRITING.

EUNUCH
The word for a man whose testicles have not developed has nothing to do with "*eu*, good, well, pleasant," but derives from Greek *eune*, bed, and *echein*, to keep, hence a guardian of the bed, a castrated functionary put safely in charge of a harem.

EUREKA
As an exclamation of delight over discovery, *eureka* comes from the triumphant cry of Archimedes (*heureka*, "I have found [it]!") when, while bathing, he discovered the principle of measuring the volume of an irregular solid by the displacement of water. He thus successfully performed his assignment to test the purity of the gold crown of Hiero, the tyrant of Syracuse, presumably after drying himself. Another word from *heuriskein*, to find, discover, is *heuristic*, serving to stimulate investigation.

EVENTEMPERED
Not necessarily a compliment. An *eventempered* person may be habitually lethargic or always surly.

EVERYBODY / EVERYONE

The words take a singular verb and singular referents: "Everybody (everyone) is expected to do his best." When singular agreement leads to awkwardness or absurdity, as in "Everybody was standing, but he is now sitting," change the construction: "They were all standing, but they are now sitting."

Everyone should be written *every one* (two words) when *everybody* cannot be substituted for *everyone*, as in "Every one of them is doing his best" or "Every one of the dogs has attacked him." See ANYBODY / ANYONE.

EVERY EFFORT

When some bureaucrat tells you, "Every effort is being made to look into the matter," be assured that (1) nothing has yet been done, or (2) nothing will ever be done, or (3) nothing can possibly be done. You may as well forget the whole matter. Certainly, forget the cliché.

EVERY OTHER

"He will have a full schedule this week and every other week for the rest of the year." Does this mean "every week" or "every second week"? Because of the ambiguity of *every other*, say *every* when you mean "every," and *every second* when you mean "every second."

EVERY PLACE

Two words.

EVIDENTLY

Unlike the ambiguous meaning of APPARENT, the meaning of *evident* presents no problem: clear, obvious. Like *apparently*, however, the adverb *evidently* has the contrary meanings of *obviously* and *seemingly*. In speech, inflection can convey the intended meaning. But in writing, *evidently* may be ambiguous, as in "He was evidently drunk." Was he obviously, unquestionably drunk? Or was he seemingly, probably drunk? So why not say *obviously* and *unquestionably* when you are sure, and *seemingly* or *probably* when you are not sure?

EX–

In copy, make it "the former president." In headlines, "ex-president" is OK. *Ex-* with a compound title, however, creates a problem. Does "ex-French general" mean that the man is no longer French? Does "ex-Miss America" mean that your ideal has committed matrimony? More than a dozen years ago, Bernstein recommended *ex* without a hyphen for use in headlines. The idea didn't catch on. It should.

EXCEPT, *see* BUT

EXCEPTION PROVES RULE
When someone whines, "The exception proves the rule," he is usually trying to exculpate himself. An exception doesn't prove a rule if *prove* means *demonstrate*. An exception doesn't demonstrate the truth of a rule; it tries to demonstrate the opposite. Nor does an exception demonstrate the existence of a rule, for how could the rule not be known to exist if an exception to it is known?

An exception proves a rule if *prove* means *test*. *Prove* comes from Latin *probare*, to try, examine, test. An *exception* puts a rule to the *test*. A printer's proof sheet puts typesetting to the test of being checked against the original copy. Moses told the Israelites that the Lord had brought them through the desert for forty years "to afflict thee and to prove thee," to test whether they would keep the commandments.

Use a seeming exception to test the soundness of a rule, not to justify a deviation by resorting to a cliché.

EXCLAMATION POINT
Don't overdo the exclamation point (!), also called *exclamation mark*. Don't use exclamation points as if your every mundane statement were a breathtaking shriek of sheer ecstasy. You have outgrown the sophomoric entries in your diary and your pubescent protestations of undying love. And don't use exclamation points to point up your wittiness. Save exclamation points for genuine exclamations ("What a beauty!"), interjections ("Good grief!"), certain kinds of wish ("May we meet again!") and those precious moments of life that call for unrestrained emotion, such as the arrival of the millennium or the repeal of the personal income tax, whichever comes first. See INTERROBANG.

EXCORIATE
To *excoriate* somebody is to remove a piece of his flesh literally, or to tear his hide off figuratively, from Latin *corium*, skin, hide, leather (originally "piece of flesh").

EXCUSE / PARDON
A *pardon* implies guilt. An *excuse* denies guilt. A plea for pardon is a request for forgiveness, release from guilt. A plea of excuse is a statement

of innocence, release from blame. "Excuse me" is weaker than "Pardon me" and is the more common term of courtesy in social intercourse.

EXECUTIVE
In business, *executive* used to be a term restricted to the highest officers. Today it is often applied to anyone who is above at least one person in the pecking order. *Executive* has also become a term of snobbery, as in such phony phrases as "executive credit plan," "executive luncheon special."

A deliberative body goes into executive session when it wants to exclude the public, including the press, the public's representative, either to preserve legitimate secrecy or to cloak questionable conduct.

EXERCISE
One gets physical exercise when he has a workout. One gets emotionally exercised when he gets worked up. *Exercise* comes from Latin *ex* + *arcere*, to take out of confinement, to ease restraint, to put to work. From the same root is *coerce*, to force to work, to dominate.

EXHILARATING
You wouldn't spell hilarious "hilirious." So don't spell *exhilarating* "exhilirating." Both words come from Latin *hilaris*, merry.

EXODUS, *see* ODOMETER

EXORCISE
To chase out devils by use of a holy name or adjuration, from Greek *horkos*, oath.

EXOTIC
The original meaning of *exotic* is "foreign," from Greek *exo*, outside. Because of the glamour that some automatically associate with foreign products, *exotic* has come to be applied to anything unusually charming or strangely beautiful or rare and expensive.

EXPERTISE
Strictly, *expertise* is the sum of knowledge in any discipline, not an individual's knowledge or expertness.

EXPIRE, *see* DIE; -SPIRE

EXPLAINED

In *The Young Immigrunts*, Ring Lardner has this dialogue: "Are you lost daddy I arsked tenderly. Shut up he explained." Many reporters use *explained* with as much sense. Don't use *explained* as a verb of attribution unless what the speaker said was indeed an elucidation of complicated facts.

EXPLOSION

In the sense of "violent outburst," *explosion* went along calmly for centuries until *The Population Explosion* was published and suddenly the word exploded to mean all kinds of swift increase, more mild than menacing, from the cultural explosion to the crabgrass explosion to the computer explosion to the fast food franchise explosion. After such faddish misuse of the word, Nickles says, "the inevitable *sexual explosion* must be adjudged an anticlimax."

EX POST FACTO

Latin, literally "from what is done afterwards." An *ex post facto* construction is one in which something is impossibly attributed to somebody or something after the event, as in "The dead man phoned his wife shortly before he collapsed in the phone booth" or "The witness said he called the fire department when he saw flames beginning to emerge from the burned-out store."

FABIAN

By ANTONOMASIA, Quintus Fabius Maximus was called Cunctator (The Delayer) because he preferred wary skirmishes to direct assaults in the defense of Rome and thus baffled Hannibal. Hence a *Fabian* policy is one that employs cautious strategy or delaying tactics in the promotion of a cause and seeks gradual progress. The Fabian Society, among whose early members was George Bernard Shaw, was formed in 1884 in London to promote the gradual spread of socialism. 1984 may be an apt year for its centennial.

FABULOUS

Though *fabulous* was originally the adjective of *fable*, it has come to be the adjective of just about anything, from hotels to haircuts to hamburgers. In a letter to the London *Times*, a literate gentleman once rightly complained about an advertisement for a book described by its publishers as "fabulously true." See also AFRAID.

FACILITATE

A windy word for "make easier, aid, assist, help."

FACILITY

As a building, informally, a *facility* is an outhouse. As a building, formally, a *facility* is a flatulent word tacked onto anything from a concert hall to a prison. *Facilities* is a handy generic word for a collection of buildings and assembly rooms with different purposes, as in "The university will open all its facilities during homecoming." But call a gymnasium a gymnasium, not a recreational facility, and a school a school, not an educational facility.

FACT

A *fact* is a *fact*. In "The governor stressed the fact that his administration had done an excellent job," what is stressed is not necessarily a fact. And when a fact is a fact, *the fact* is often unnecessary, as in "He mentioned the fact that President Buchanan was a bachelor"; drop *the fact*.

But when a preposition or a verb cannot introduce a nounal clause, *the fact* is necessary, as in "He was referring to the fact that Palmer had never won the PGA" or "He didn't like the fact that smoking was prohibited at the meeting."

FACTITIOUS / FICTITIOUS
These similar words have different meanings: *factitious*, artificial, sham, contrived, from Latin *facere*, to make, do; *fictitious*, imaginary, feigned, nonexistent, from Latin *fingere*, to form, invent, feign. Phony publicity is *factitious*. A phony name is *fictitious*.

FACTOR
Fowler calls *factor* "one of those words which are so popular as thought-saving reach-me-downs that all meaning is being rubbed off them by constant use." *Factor* is indeed overworked and worn-out. A factor is something that contributes to an effect, but it has become a factotum for such words as *component, consideration, constituent, element, event, fact, ingredient, occurrence, part*. Think a little and choose a more appropriate word for the context. And don't use the redundant *contributing factor*.

FACTOTUM
A person or thing that is used to do all kinds of work is a *factotum*, from Latin *fac*, imperative of *facere*, do, and *totum*, all, everything. An administrative assistant is a *factotum*. So is *factor*.

FAERIE / FAIRY
If you refer to Spenser's *The Faerie Queene*, spell it right. Spenser's *faerie*, Old French for enchantment, was a land of enchantment. As an alternative spelling, perhaps *faerie* or *faery* should be reintroduced into the written language to avoid the homosexual connotation now entrenched in *fairy*.

FAHRENHEIT, *see* CELSIUS

FAIL
Failure implies lack of attainment of an objective ("He failed to make the Olympic team") or lack of execution of an obligation ("She failed to file her tax statement") or expectation ("He failed to acknowledge our invitation"). Don't use *fail* in a purely negative sense ("He failed to sleep well last night"; make it "didn't sleep well").

FAIRNESS

In reporting and editing, accuracy alone is not enough. *Fairness* is essential to the responsibility of informing society. Unfortunately, some recent highly publicized investigatory stories have been misunderstood by some people and have led to the idea that a reporter's responsibility is to "get somebody." The press does have the responsibility to investigate public affairs. It also has the responsibility to report them fairly.

Every controversy has at least two sides. Every story of controversy should report both or all sides. Anyone mentioned in an unfavorable light in a controversial story should have a chance to respond in the same story. If the person cannot be reached, editors should decide whether the story is so urgent that it has to be run immediately. If it is run, the story should say that the person could not be reached. And a follow-up story should report the response when the person is reached.

Fairness is the responsibility of everyone in the press, and its lessons should be thoroughly learned and faithfully practiced by young men and women who aspire to become professional journalists.

FALSE PASSIVE

Though some grammarians disagree, when you transpose a sentence from active voice to passive voice, the DIRECT OBJECT becomes the subject. "Peter won a prize" becomes "A prize was won by Peter." And "Peter gave Paul a prize" should become "A prize was given (to) Paul by Peter," because *prize* is the direct object. *Paul* is the indirect object. So "Paul was given a prize by Peter" is false passive. Always ask yourself what was given. Paul wasn't given. The prize was.

Worse is the use of *presented with*, as in "Morgan was presented with the MVP award." First, Morgan wasn't presented; the award was. Second, *with* is meaningless, unless both Morgan and the award were presented to somebody else.

FAME, *see* INEFFABLE

FAMILIARITY

Doesn't always breed contempt. And, as Churchill observed, "Without a certain amount of familiarity, you will never breed anything."

FANATIC

Religion is at the root of *fanaticism*, from Latin *fanum*, temple, whence also *profanity*, irreverence (outside the temple). As an abbreviation of *fanatic*, *fan* (as in "football fan") is disputed, but both the abbreviation and the dispute make sense.

FANNIE MAE / FANNY MAY
The nickname for the Federal National Mortgage Association is *Fannie Mae*, and its bonds are *Fannie Maes*. The candy is *Fanny May*.

FANTASTIC, *see* AFRAID

FARCE
A performance stuffed with jokes is a *farce*, from Latin *farcire*, to stuff, whence also *infarct*, something stuffed in, a result of obstruction of circulation in an organ, as in myocardial infarction, disease of the muscle tissue of the heart.

FARTHER / FURTHER
For physical distance, *farther* and *farthest* are preferred; otherwise, *further* and *furthest*.

FASCIST
The graffiti of some modern vandals are as illiterate as they are insulting. Well, half as illiterate. *Pig* is usually spelled correctly, but *Fascist* is invariably *Facist*. *Fascist* comes from Latin *fascis*, bundle, through Italian *fascio*, bundle, group, union. Fasces, bundles of sticks through which an ax blade projected, were the symbol of authority of Roman magistrates and became the symbol of union under the absolute authority of Mussolini.

FATE, *see* INEFFABLE

FATHER-IN-LAW
Plural *fathers-in-law*. For *father-outlaw*, see DAUGHTER-IN-LAW.

FATHER'S DAY
Note the apostrophe and its position.

FEASIBLE / POSSIBLE
What is *feasible* is *possible*: what can be done can happen. But what is *possible* is not necessarily *feasible*: some things that can happen can't be done. A plan to ban automobiles downtown is *feasible* (or *possible*).

A drought next summer is *possible;* but a drought can't be *feasible.* See also PRACTICABLE / PRACTICAL.

FEEDBACK
Computer jargon for "Tell us what you've found out," as in "Extrapolate the interrelationship of the input and the feedback." See also EDUCANTO / EDUCATIONIST.

FEEL, *see* BELIEVE / FEEL / THINK

FEISTY
Some writers, mature in years but not in spirit, says Nickles, "care only for novelty, not for etymology." As example he cites *feisty* in its prevailing sense of "belligerent" or "spirited," a meaning borrowed from "the hoary Appalachian dialect" by adolescent minds ignorant of its derivation from *fisting dog,* "a scrappy little mongrel that broke wind," from Anglo-Saxon *fistan,* to break wind. *Fizzle* comes from the same root.

FELL SWOOP
When Macduff learns that his wife and children have been "savagely slaughter'd" by Macbeth, he cries, "All my pretty ones? / Did you say all? O hell-kite! All? / What, all my pretty chickens and their dam / At one fell swoop?" The hell-kite is Macbeth, who had swooped on his victims, Macduff's little chickens, like a hawk. *At one fell swoop* has since become a cliché. If you use it, know that *fell* has nothing to do here with *fall,* but means inhumanly cruel, savage, from Latin *fello,* a wicked person, whence *felon,* perhaps through *fel,* gall. Anyone who uses the cliché, says Evans, "deserves to be required to explain publicly just what he thinks it means."

FEMINISM
In *Winners & Sinners,* "a bulletin of second-guessing" originated by Bernstein for the staff of the *New York Times,* Bernstein gives three examples of trivial feminism in the *Times:*

"He is the first Irish person to be canonized since Laurence O'Toole . . ."; the copy originally read *Irishman.*

"Americans are to staff three early-warning stations . . ."; the first edition said they were to *man* the stations.

". . . Luitsen Kuiper, the head of the seven-person team"; the writer himself changed *seven-man team* to the unidiomatic *seven-person team.*

Says Bernstein: "We all should realize that 'man' in one meaning always has been and still is a generic term for human being and when used as such carries no sense of masculinity. Women have enough real issues of equality that they are justified in fighting for without devoting energy to such trivia as appear in those cited instances. Above all, let's not make The Times look silly." See also CHAIRPERSON.

FERMENT / FOMENT
In their literal senses, *ferment* and *foment* are distinct. To *ferment* is to undergo chemical conversion by the addition of some substance such as yeast, from Latin *fermentum*, leaven, yeast. To *foment* is to bathe with warm water or lotion, as in a compress or poultice, from Latin *fovere*, to warm.

In their figurative senses, however, *ferment* and *foment* are almost interchangeable. Both mean "to cause trouble, to agitate," as in "Outsiders fomented (or fermented) campus unrest." But *foment* is used more than *ferment* in a bad sense ("His crafty behavior fomented student revolt"; "Her fertile brain was fermenting with ideas") and in the sense of bringing about trouble rather than adding to it.

FEUD
Note the spelling. Often it comes out *fued*.

FEWER / LESS
"She now eats fewer meals and less candy." Use *fewer* for countables and *less* for collective quantity. The sense of collective quantity prevails in sums of money, periods of time, measures of distance and weight: less than $200 a week, less than six months, less than three miles, less than 200 pounds. See also UNDER.

FEZ
The felt headgear is named for Fez, a city in Morocco. If you can't think of a Moroccan's name, perhaps his fez will be familiar.

FIAT
The command or decree is Latin, "Let it be done," the third person singular present subjunctive of *fieri*, to become.

The car is Italian, an acronym for Fabbrica Italiana Automobile (di) Torino, the Italian Automobile Factory of Turin.

FIBBER'S CLOSET

In the old radio show "Fibber McGee and Molly," starring Jim and Marian Jordan, Fibber's closet was always loaded with most of his possessions, which would cascade when the closet was opened. *Fibber's closet* became synonymous with any overloaded mess. Another relic of the show is Molly's rejoinder: "'Tain't funny, McGee."

FICTITIOUS, *see* FACTITIOUS / FICTITIOUS

FIDDLE WHILE ROME BURNS

A cliché and, if the subject is Nero, a historical falsehood.

FIELD, *see* AREA

FIFTH COLUMN

In the Spanish Civil War, a rebel general, leading four columns of troops against Madrid, broadcast that there was a fifth column within the city, a force of Franco supporters. Hence a *fifth column* is any subversive group within defense lines. *Fifth columnist* was a popular term in the 1950s for a Communist sympathizer in the United States.

FILIBUSTER

A *filibuster* was originally a buccaneer, a freebooter, from Dutch *vrij* + *buit*, free booty or plunder. Though *filibuster* is still used for an adventurer engaged in private military action, its common use today is for the practice of legislative obstructionist tactics or for the person who practices such tactics. Shipley says the meaning has shifted "from piracy to congressional privateering." And note the spelling: only one *l*.

FILIPINO / PHILIPPINE

The Philippine Islands used to be Las Islas Filipinas, from Spanish *Felipe*, King Philip II of Spain. The spellings are tricky. The inhabitant retains the Spanish *F* and one *p*. The country begins with *P* and has double *p* in the middle. One way to remember the correct spelling is to think of a man's name, Philip Pine, but then you have to remember that there is only one *l* in this form of *Philip*. You might as well just photograph *Philippine*.

FINALIZE, *see* –IZE

FINITE VERB

A finite verb is limited (wherefore *finite*) by person, number, tense and mood. In "He ran," *ran* is a finite verb, limited by third person, singular number, past tense and indicative mood. *To run* is an infinitive (unlimited) and *running* is a participle (part verb), neither of which is limited by person or number and neither of which can be a predicate ("He to run" and "He running" are not sentences). One of the marks of crisp, clear writing is the use of the finite verb.

FIRST OF ALL

Drop *of all*.

FIX

Henry James, Anglophile, is said to have replied to a niece who offered to "fix" his tea: "Pray, my dear young lady, what will you fix it with and what will you fix it to?" James had a fixation about *fix* and was stuck on its etymological sense, from Latin *figere*, to fasten.

But *fix* in American usage has come to be used for almost anything you want to use it for. Mencken records that as long ago as the early nineteenth century, British visitors to the United States were astounded at the versatility of *fix*. One said it meant "to do anything." Another said it had "perhaps as many significations as any word in the Chinese language" and he listed some of them: "to be done, made, mixed, mended, bespoken, hired, ordered, arranged, procured, finished, lent or given." Dickens, in 1842, wrote home that he had heard *fix* used for laying a tablecloth, dressing oneself, being treated by a doctor and mulling claret, among other tasks.

Today, one hears and reads about fixing food, drinks, faces, hair, teeth, nails, clothes, houses, furniture, negatives, gadgets, machinery, wagons, cats, dogs, dope addicts, dates, traffic tickets, sporting events and on and on and on. *Fix* is indeed a sloppy word, automatically and carelessly used without thought for the most suitable word for the context. Fix your thinking.

Other common words from the same root are *affix, fixation, fixture, microfiche, prefix, suffix, transfix*.

FIZZLE, *see* FEISTY

FLACK / FLAK

Coined by *Variety* but borrowed from German *flak* (antiaircraft artillery or the bursting shells therefrom), *flack* is a mildly derisive term for a press agent, a member of an occasionally derisible profession. *Flak* is an abbreviation of German F̲liegera̲bwehrk̲anone, aircraft defense gun.

FLAG, *see* EAR

FLAMMABLE / INFLAMMABLE
The prefix *in-* has meanings other than *not*, the most common of which is simply *in*, which is its meaning in *inflammable*, which is the same as *flammable*, which is spreading because some people think *inflammable* means "not flammable," which it doesn't. The words are interchangeable, both meaning "capable of being easily ignited."

FLAUNT / FLOUT
The words are often misused, *flaunt* more often being misused for *flout*. To *flaunt* is to wave proudly, to show off, to display ostentatiously, boastfully ("The new graduate flaunted his diploma as he marched through the faculty after commencement"). To *flout* is to defy, to mock, to treat with contempt, to scoff at ("The new graduate flouted tradition by wearing only shorts at commencement").

FLAUTIST / FLUTIST
Either. *Flutist* is older. *Flautist* blew into English through the influence of Italian *flautista*, flutist.

FLEET STREET
British journalism, by METONYMY. Fleet Street is the center of the London newspaper district. The street was named for "the Fleet" (Anglo-Saxon *fleot*, inlet), a nearby creek, now a sewer, as is much of London journalism.

FLOTSAM AND JETSAM
A cliché for things discarded, odds and ends, junk. The distinction between *flotsam* and *jetsam*, and between the other components of a wreck, *lagan* and *derelict*, is now only of legal interest. Flotsam, Jetsam, Lagan & Derelict sounds like an apt name for a firm of maritime lawyers.

FLOUNDER / FOUNDER
A blend word from *founder* and *blunder*, to *flounder* is to move clumsily, struggle, often with *around*. To *founder* is to become disabled, collapse, cave in, sink, from Latin *fundus*, bottom. Thus: "The business

floundered around for years from one crisis to the next till it finally foundered in bankruptcy."

FLOUT, *see* FLAUNT / FLOUT

FLUORESCENT
Note the spelling: the *o* comes after the *u*, not before. Think of *fluoride*, not *flour*.

FLUTIST, *see* FLAUTIST / FLUTIST

FM, *see* AM / FM

FOLIO
In printing, a *folio* is a page number. At the top of a newspaper page, other than page one, the line that contains the name of the paper, the date and the page number is called the folio *line*.

FOLKS
As a deliberately folksy substitute for *people*, *folks* is corny in formal speech and writing.

FOMENT, *see* FERMENT / FOMENT

FOREGO / FORGO
To *forego* is to go before, to precede (rarely seen except in the participles *foregoing* and *foregone* and in the name of a great racehorse). To *forgo* is to abstain from, to renounce, to give up. Thus: "After the Vatican Council, the bishop decided to forgo some of the privileges of office he had cherished in foregoing years." *Forgo* may also be spelled *forego*, but not vice versa.

FOREIGN CURRENCY
Editors should indeed translate foreign currency into American, but they should also mention the foreign amount. It is disconcerting to read that someone in England was fined $203 for some offense. Why the odd figure? Make it "$203 (100 pounds)" or whatever the current equivalent is. The same principle applies to foreign measures till the metric system is widespread and understood in the United States.

FOREIGNER / FOREST, *see* **DENIZEN**

FOREIGN PLURALS, *see* **PLURALS**

FOREWORD
In the sense of preface or introduction, note the spelling. It often comes out *foreward* or *forward*.

FORGO, *see* FOREGO / FORGO

FORLORN
Keats, in "Ode to a Nightingale," sighed: "Forlorn! The very word is like a bell! / To toll me back from thee to my sole self!" *Forlorn* has been described as the loneliest word in the language and, because of its sound, one of the saddest.

FORLORN HOPE
The phrase is an English spelling of Dutch *verloren hoop*, lost troop, hence an undertaking that has only thin hope of success.

FORMER
Samuel Johnson abhorred the signpost writing of *the former* and *the latter*. "As long as you have the use of your pen," he said, "never be reduced to that shift." See also ABOVE-MENTIONED.

FORMULATE
Except in the devising of scientific or mathematical formulas or in a highly complicated technical problem, *formulate* is a grandiose word for *form*.

FORNICATION
From Latin *fornix*, arch, vault, *fornication* has deteriorated, says Jacobs, "from the fornical architecture of the low-vaulted Roman brothels to the pudendous activity within."

FOR THE PURPOSE OF
To.

FORTUITOUS / FORTUNATE
What happens by chance or accident is *fortuitous*. What is *fortuitous* may also be *fortunate*. But what is *fortunate* is not necessarily *fortuitous;*

it may have happened not by chance or accident. Thus: "My bumping into Harry the Horse at the track was both fortuitous (I ran into him accidentally) and fortunate (he touted me onto a winner)."

FOR YOU TO
Don't use *for you to*, or a similar phrase, when it immediately follows a verb, as in "I would like for you to meet him"; drop *for*. But *for* is used when the phrase follows a noun ("I would like an appointment for you to meet her") or an adjective ("I would be pleased for you to meet her").

FOUNDER, *see* FLOUNDER / FOUNDER

FRACTION
Because a *fraction* may be a small or a large part of a whole, some authorities object to the use of *a fraction* in the sense of a small part, as in "Downtown business is a fraction of what it used to be." Fowler calls the usage a "sturdy indefensible," illogical but common. But when *a fraction* is preceded by *only*, which is usually the case, the sense of smallness is suggested. *Only a fraction* is sturdily defensible.

FRAMEWORK
In its nonphysical sense, *framework* is overworked. *Within the framework of* is a thoughtless circumlocution for one of these words or phrases: *as part of, by, in conformity with, in the light of, through, under.* And except as a set of physico-mathematical coordinate axes, the creaky *frame of reference*, as Nickles says, is "ready to collapse from overwork."

FRANKENSTEIN
One wet Swiss summer, Mary Wollstonecraft Shelley, Percy's second wife, swapped ghost stories with her husband and Byron. Mary told the story of Frankenstein, a physiology student who creates a monster, which persecutes and ultimately ruins him. She later published the story as *Frankenstein; or, The Modern Prometheus.* Though she gave the monster no name, generations have mistakenly given it the name of its creator, Frankenstein. Figuratively, a Frankenstein monster, or Frankenstein's monster, is any work that destroys, or threatens to destroy, its originator.

FREAK
Not an adjective. The adjective of the noun *freak* is *freakish* or *freaky*. *Freak* is also a poetic verb, to speckle or streak with color. With *out*, it

is also a verb in the drug culture, suggested by Partridge as deriving from the weird visions of color experienced by LSD addicts.

FREE LANCE
Two words for the noun. Hyphenate the adjective and the verb. And hyphenate *free-lancer*.

FRIENDS
When capitalized, *Friends* refers to Quakers, members of the Society of Friends. See SOME OF MY BEST FRIENDS.

FRIGHTFUL, *see* AFRAID

FRISBEE
Uppercase. It's a trademark.

FRISCO
San Franciscans prefer *San Fran* as an abbreviation.

FRIVOLOUS
Note the spelling. Not *frivilous*. You wouldn't say *frivility*.

FROM
1969–74 is a period. Richard Nixon was president *in 1969–74*, or *from 1969 to 1974*, but not *from 1969–74*. *In* a period, or *from* a year to another year, but not *from* a period. The same principle applies to other periods of time. See HENCE, THENCE, WHENCE.

FULFILL
Either *fulfill* or *fulfil*, but not *fullfill* or *fullfil*. Never "full" at the beginning.

FULL STOP
What the British call the American period (.).

FULSOME
The word doesn't mean full or abundant. It means over-full, offensively excessive because insincere. *Fulsome* praise is empty, not full.

FUN
A respectable noun, a slovenly adjective. For the thoughtless, *fun* has become an all-purpose adjective to describe any experience from the mildly amusing to the wildly uproarious.

FUNICULAR, *see* **–CULE**

FURLONG
From Anglo-Saxon *furh* + *lang*, a *furlong* is as long as a furrow, which is 40 poles (a pole, 5½ yards, is the width between furrows) or 220 yards, one-eighth of a mile, the length of a furrow on a square field of 10 acres (48,400 square yards).

FURTHER, *see* **FARTHER / FURTHER**

FUSED PARTICIPLE
The term is Fowler's. He has almost 2,000 words on the subject in one entry. Briefly, a participle is fused when it is joined to a noun or pronoun not in the possessive case when the possessive case is needed grammatically and semantically, as in "He doesn't like Alice staying out late at night"; make it *Alice's*. What isn't liked is not *Alice*, but *Alice's staying out late*. Indeed, he likes Alice and that's why he doesn't like Alice's staying out late. Similarly: "He doesn't like you staying out late at night"; make it *your*.

Insistence on the possessive case in this construction, however, can lead to absurdity, as in "He didn't want to run the risk of something bad's happening to Alice" or "Rape had recently been reported in the neighborhood, and he didn't want to take a chance on that's happening to Alice."

A sound principle is to use the possessive case with a proper name or a personal pronoun to avoid the fused participle. And use finite verbs to avoid awkward participial constructions: "He didn't want to run the risk that something bad would happen to Alice" or "He didn't want to take a chance that Alice would be raped."

Above all, remember this about participles: If you don't use 'em, you won't fuse 'em.

FUTURE / FUTURE PERFECT, *see* **SEQUENCE OF TENSES**

FUTURE PLANS
They usually are.

G

GAFFER
This word for an old man is a contraction of *godfather*. Almost never heard these days is its feminine counterpart, *gammer*, a contraction of *godmother*.

GALORE
Irish *go leor*, enough, hence abundant, plentiful. Macdonald calls *galore* a "women's-magazine locution." Fowler says it is "chiefly resorted to by those who are reduced to relieving dullness of matter by oddity of expression" and it is "no part of the Englishman's natural vocabulary, except as a jocular colloquialism (*Whisky galore!*)." But *galore* is certainly a part of an Irishman's natural vocabulary and the word is commonly heard outside Ireland, which has fewer Irish than the rest of the English-speaking world.

GAMBIT
Strictly, a gambit is an opening move or remark or ploy in which something is sacrificed in the hope of later gain, from Italian *gambetto*, "a tripping up," from *gamba*, leg. This is its use in chess.

Loosely, *gambit* is used for any opening move in a discussion or negotiation. As such, it is acceptable to 63 percent of the American Heritage usage panel. See also STALEMATE.

GAMUT
The lowest note in the medieval musical scale was called "gamma ut," from *gamma*, the Greek letter for *G*, the note for one tone below the first note of the scale, and *ut*, the name given (see below) to the first note of the scale (modern *do*). *Gamut* was later applied to the whole series of musical notes, hence an entire range of anything. (In a review of a Broadway performance by a very young Katharine Hepburn, Dorothy Parker wrote that Hepburn had run "the gamut of emotions from A to B.")

The names of the notes of the scale came from syllables in the Vespers hymn of the feast of the Birthday of St. John the Baptist, each emphasized syllable being one note higher on the scale than the previously emphasized one (as in "*Doe*, a deer, a female deer; *Ray*, a drop of golden sun . . ."; from Rodgers and Hammerstein's *The Sound of Music*): "U̱t queant laxis ṟesonare fibris / M̱ira gestorum f̱amuli tuorum, / S̱olve polluti la̱bii reatum, / S̱ancte I̱ohannes." *Ti* is now more commonly used than *si*, and *ut* has been supplanted by the more sonorous *do*.

–GAMY

Among the many English words from Greek *gamos*, marriage, are these:
- —*allogamy*, cross-fertilization (*allos*, other).
- —*bigamy*, marriage to two persons at a time.
- —*deuterogamy*, marriage after the death or divorce of one's spouse (*deuteros*, second).
- —*digamy*, same as *deuterogamy*.
- —*endogamy*, marriage within one's tribe, caste, social group (*endon*, within).
- —*exogamy*, opposite of *endogamy* (*exo*, outside).
- —*monogamy*, marriage to only one person at a time (*monos*, one, single, alone).
- —*polygamy*, marriage to more than one person at a time (*polys*, much, many).

GANDHI

For both the Mahatma and Indira, the spelling is *Gandhi*, not *Ghandi*. As in the alphabet, *h* comes immediately before *i*.

GANTLET / GAUNTLET

One of the problems with these words of different spelling and different meaning is that the more common pronunciation of each is the same, the first syllable being pronounced "gaw," as in *paw*. Their derivations clarify their distinction:

Gantlet comes from Swedish *gatlopp*, a running down a lane, from *gata*, street, lane, and *lopp*, course, running, wherefore a *gantlet* is (1) a lane between two lines of men who beat some unfortunate as he tries to run through it, as in "run the gantlet," and (2) a stretch of railroad track on which two sets of track overlap to avoid switching in a narrow place.

Gauntlet comes from French *gantelet*, diminutive of *gant*, glove, wherefore a *gauntlet* is (1) a protective glove and (2) a challenge, as in "fling down the gauntlet," from the former use of a glove as a symbol of defiance.

GAP
An overworked faddish word to describe any kind of opening from a little crack to a grand canyon, qualified by a noun to produce unmeasured figures such as *credibility gap*, *generation gap*, *information gap*. The fad needs a stopgap.

GATEKEEPER
COMMUNICOLOGESE for *editor*, a *gatekeeper* is one who mans a gate to control what copy will get through him and how it will be played. Rarely in the history of the press has an editor ever identified himself as a gatekeeper.

GAUGE
Note the spelling: *a* before *u*.

GAUNTLET, *see* GANTLET / GAUNTLET

GAY
Because of its arrogation by homosexuals to describe themselves, we are losing *gay* in its happy sense of bright, lively, carefree, exuberant. As historian Arthur M. Schlesinger Jr. says, "*Gay* used to be one of the most agreeable words in the language. Its appropriation by a notably morose group is an act of piracy." Alas, mehitabel!

GAZEBO
The first person singular future tense of second conjugation Latin verbs ends in *-ebo*, as in PLACEBO. *Gazebo* is dog Latin for "I shall gaze," whence a *gazebo* is a structure that commands a pleasant view, such as a balcony or belvedere (beautiful viewing) or summerhouse. The stress is on the second syllable, and the more common pronunciation has a long *e*, as in *bee*, not *bay*.

GAZETTE
Many early newspapers had *Gazette* as part of their name, from Italian *gazzetta*, diminutive of *gazza*, magpie, the name for a small tin coin which was the price of an official Venetian newspaper in the sixteenth century.

GENDER
Unlike the grammar of many other languages, the grammar of modern English, thank heaven, ascribes gender in terms of sex: masculine (male sex), feminine (female sex), neuter (neither sex), common (either sex).

MASCULINE: *father, Charles, colt, he.*
FEMININE: *mother, Caroline, filly, she.*
NEUTER: *book, lamp, it.*
COMMON: *author, citizen, doctor, friend, journalist, teacher.*

Much of the misguided, though well-intentioned, convolution of language to cleanse it of any taint of sexism would be dispelled if people would realize that English has a fourth gender, common to both sexes. See also CHAIRPERSON and FEMINISM.

GENEALOGY
Note the *a* in the middle of the word. It's *genealogy*, not *geneology*.

GENUINE, *see* AUTHENTIC / GENUINE

GERRYMANDER
While Elbridge Gerry was running for a third term as governor of Massachusetts in 1812, he permitted the Democratic legislature to redistrict the state so as to concentrate the strength of the Federal party in a few districts. Gilbert Stuart, painter, saw a map of the new districts on the wall of a newspaper office, thought its irregular outline resembled the body of an elongated animal, added head, claws and wings to it and said, "That will do for a salamander." The newspaper editor, probably Benjamin Russell of the *Columbian Centinel*, remarked, "Better say a gerrymander."

Gerrymander has survived to mean any electoral division that gives an unfair advantage to a party, or any similar altering of a situation to one's advantage.

Gerry lost the gubernatorial election, but was elected vice president of the United States in the same year. He pronounced his name with a hard *g*, but *gerrymander* has a soft *g*, as in *Jerry*.

GESTAPO
The Nazi secret police, an abbreviation of Geheime Staatspolizei, secret state police.

GIBBERISH
The more common pronunciation has a soft *g*, as in *jib*. *Gibberish* is imitative, like *jabber, gabble, giggle.*

GIBE / JIBE / JIVE
To mock or heckle is to *gibe*, also spelled *jibe*. Both spellings are also used for the noun, meaning a derisive remark, a taunt. But to be in agreement

with, to fit in, is to *jibe*. In this sense, to *jive* is often and mistakenly used. To *jive* is to talk the jargon of jazz or some other lingo, often unintelligible, or to jitterbug. As a noun, *jive* means the music itself or its jargon or some nonsensical chatter.

GILD THE LILY
A cliché and a false quotation from Shakespeare's *King John*, in which Salisbury complains about the "wasteful and ridiculous excess" of John's second coronation. To crown him a second time, says Salisbury, is "To gild refined gold, to paint the lily, / To throw a perfume on the violet, / To smooth the ice, or add another hue / Unto the rainbow." Go paint the lily, or gild the clouds with sunshine, but don't gild the lily.

GLAMOUR
A Scottish variant of *grammar*, from English *gramarye*, magic, because grammar was synonymous with learning, and learning was considered magic by the unlearned. Cheapened from its original meaning of magical enchantment, *glamour* has come to be associated with the phony charm of those whom press agents call celebrities. Unlike most English -*our* words, *glamour* has retained the *u* in American spelling, but *glamorous* is more common than *glamourous*.

GLOAMING
A beautiful word, from Anglo-Saxon *glom*, twilight. See also CREPUSCULAR.

GLOVE
Foreigners who learn the rudiments of English from Hollywood and Tin Pan Alley must wonder at the seeming obsession Americans have with gloves. The rainbow around our shoulder fits us like a glove and we're so misty we can't tell our hat from our glove and we want back our rose and our glove. The song merchants don't really care about *glove*, but they've already used *dove* and *above* and *shove* and they're forcing a meaningless rhyme for *love*.

Those who get their language from Nashville don't have this problem: *lurv* can be rhymed with more than a dozen words, among them such appropriate choices as *curve, nerve, perv* and *hors d'oeuvre*.

GLUTTON / GOURMAND / GOURMET
The *gourmand* and the *gourmet* have good taste in food, but the *gourmet* eats more fastidiously and the *gourmand* eats more. The *glutton* eats anything and too much of everything.

GOBBLEDYGOOK

In 1944, Maury Maverick, Texas congressman, coined *gobbledygook* to describe bureaucratic jargon. He said that he wasn't sure why he chose the word and that it must have come to him in a vision: "Perhaps I was thinking of the old bearded turkey gobbler back in Texas who was always gobbledy-gobbling and strutting with ludicrous pomposity. At the end of this gobble there was a sort of gook."

As chairman of a federal agency, Maverick issued this order to his subordinates: "Be short and say what you're talking about. Let's stop *pointing up* programs, *finalizing* contracts that *stem from* district, regional or Washington *levels*. No more *patterns*, *effectuating*, *dynamics*. Anyone using the words *activation* or *implementation* will be shot."

He said he was fed up with gobbledygook such as "maladjustments coextensive with problem areas . . . alternative but nevertheless meaningful minimae . . . utilization of factors which in a dynamic democracy can be channelized into both quantitative and qualitative phases."

Witness the gobbledygook in this directive to internal revenue agents: "The effect of the amendment, as explained on the floor of the Senate, if finally enacted into law, would be to permit, after having made an adjustment in an item affecting the excess profits tax, in a year to which the amendment is made applicable, which has an effect on the normal or surtax for the year, any resulting adjustment necessary in the normal or surtaxes may be accomplished although the statute of limitations for assessment of any deficiency or making any refund of such taxes, has expired."

Evans hails *gobbledygook* as "a happy coinage, combining the self-important, indignant, incomprehensible gobbling of a turkey cock with the idea of a sticky and loathsome muck into which the unhappy listener or reader sinks with a bubbling cry."

Pity the listener and the reader. Talk and write in clear English. See also BUREAUCRATESE.

GOES WITHOUT SAYING
So why say it?

GOLF LINKS
Along with their other great gifts to harried humanity, the Scots have given us golf, both a game and a religion. *Golf* is Scottish dialect from Middle English, possibly from Middle Dutch *colven*, to play a game with sticks or clubs (Dutch *kolf*, club). The ancient Scots played and worshiped golf on links, "common land which is found by the seashore,

where the short, close turf, the sandy subsoil, and the many natural obstacles in the shape of bents, whins, sand holes, and banks, supply the conditions which are essential to the proper pursuit of the game," according to *The Encyclopaedia of Sport*.

Properly, then, a *golf course* is not a *golf links* unless it is by the sea and on land covered with coarse grass and sand and the other horrors necessary to the proper pursuit of this purgatory. Loosely, however, *golf course* and *golf links* are interchangeable in the United States. Whatever the name of the field of blood, golf, like life, isn't meant to be fair.

GOOGOL

Coined by Edward Kasner, American mathematician, a *googol* is the number 10 raised to the power 100, or the number 1 followed by 100 zeros. A *googolplex* is the number 100 raised to the power googol, or the number 1 followed by a googol of zeros. The terms may soon be helpful in simplified reporting of the federal budget.

GORDIAN KNOT

King Gordius of Phrygia tied the knot of the yoke of a wagon so cunningly that an oracle declared that whoever could untie it would rule Asia. Alexander the Great promptly slashed through it with his sword. Hence "to cut the Gordian knot" is to solve an intricate problem by swift, drastic measure. If you use the cliché, don't confuse its meaning by applying the phrase to anyone who acts recklessly in trying to solve a problem and thus causes worse problems.

GORGEOUS, *see* AFRAID

GOSSIP

From Anglo-Saxon *godsibb*, godparent, godchild, close friend, crony, a *gossip* was one who talked incessantly about his own or other people's relatives. The word now embraces both the talker and the talk, the tattler and the tattle, the newsmonger and the newsmongering.

GOT / GOTTEN

As a past participle of *get*, *got* denotes acquisition or completed action, as in "I have got better gas mileage from this car than from any other" or "I have just got the money from the bank." In this sense, *gotten*, another past participle of *get*, may be substituted for *got* in American usage, but not in British.

In the sense of simple possession, however, *have got* is redundant, as in "I have got only a few dollars to my name" (drop *got*) or "I haven't got the time" (*don't have*) or "Have you got a moment?" (*do you have*).

GOTHAM, *see* BAGDAD-ON-THE-SUBWAY

GOURMAND / GOURMET, *see* GLUTTON / GOURMAND / GOURMET

GOVERNMENT
There's an *n* in the middle of *government*, omitted by the many who misspell it *goverment*, possibly because they so pronounce it.

GRADUATED
Strictly, a college graduates a student, moves him up a step (Latin *gradus*, step, degree, grade), but "He graduated from college" is older and more common than "He was graduated from college." Both forms are acceptable. Similarly, "He graduated in 1979" and "He was graduated in 1979." But *from* is needed if *college* or its equivalent is used: not "He graduated college."

GRAFFITI
Note the spelling: double *f*, single *t*. And note that *graffiti* is a plural word; its singular is *graffito*. The word is a diminutive of Italian *graffio*, a scratching, a crude inscription on a wall or door, especially of a public convenience. When a society turns to toilets for its humor, the writing is on the wall.

GRAMMAR
From Greek *graphein*, to write. *Grammar*, the first of the seven classical liberal arts, is the art that systematically describes how words are used in a language and how they are related. Grammar classifies words into what are traditionally called the parts of speech and their sub-classes.

Mainly because of its neglect in primary education, whether through permissiveness or through ignorance, grammar is a dying art in the United States. Some thoughtful teachers and writers, however, are attempting to revive the art and they are meeting with some success in various parts of the country, despite the opposition of the "anything goes" school of sloppy thinkers. Surely the dark night of barbarism has not so enveloped the country that one cannot correctly identify and use the parts of speech without being dubbed a pedant. For ungrammatical writers and speakers, there ought to be a sin tax. See also **PARTS OF SPEECH**.

GRAY / GREY
Americans tend to prefer *gray*, Britons *grey*. And there are those who think *gray* has a darker shade than *grey* because to them *a* seems darker than *e*. Perhaps a better case could be made for choice by appearance in context, as in *gray day*, *grey eyes*. As for the dog, the spelling is *greyhound*, the origin of the first syllable of which is uncertain, but is certainly not connected with color.

GREAT BRITAIN, *see* BRITAIN

GREEN EYESHADE, *see* CHI-SQUARE

GRIEVOUS
The *i* comes before the *e*, not after the *v*: *grievous*, not *grevious*. The misspelling may cause the often heard mispronunciation, but probably the mispronunciation causes the misspelling.

GRISLY / GRIZZLY
A gruesome sight is *grisly*. Hair flecked with gray is *grizzly*. Some bears are grizzly. Being attacked by a grizzly is grisly and may turn your hair grizzly.

GROG
One of the many synonyms for liquor, *grog* comes from "Old Grog," the nickname of English Admiral Edward Vernon, from the grogram (coarse fabric) cloak he habitually wore. In 1740, Vernon ordered that his sailors' daily ration of rum be cut to half rum and half water, which feeble bracer the sailors called *grog*. Incidentally, Lawrence Washington, George's half brother, served under Vernon and named Mount Vernon after him.

GROUND SWELL
Barzun points out that a *ground swell* (one word in AP), "far from being the magnificent uplifting that successful politicians want for victory, is a motion of the sea that stirs up the bottom, muddies the water and throws up debris in all directions."

GRUNT, *see* DISGRUNTLED

GUERRILLA
A diminutive of Spanish *guerra*, war, *guerrilla* is more commonly spelled with double *r*.

GUEST SPEAKER

Christ said, "Where two or three are gathered together for my sake, there am I in the midst of them." In the United States, however, where two or three are gathered together, for chrissake, there is a guest speaker.

This tribal ritual starts with a speaker who introduces a speaker who introduces the guest speaker, who introduces his speech with some weighty words like "It is indeed a pleasure and a privilege for me to be with you here today and I certainly want to thank Mr. Babbitt for inviting me, and Mr. Arbuthnot for introducing me."

The few who are still listening are then invited to "share a funny story I was reminded of as I was coming here today," a story he has carefully rehearsed and has told a hundred times. The story, which invariably involves three persons, has already lost whatever punch it might have had, because the guest speaker has announced that what he is about to say is a story, and funny at that, thereby disillusioning and patronizing his audience. When the story ends, the guest speaker condescendingly signals a change of tone with the somber line "Seriously, however . . ." He has lost his audience, or deserves to have.

The points of this rambling entry are several:

1. A speaker or writer should not waste the precious moments of an opening by uttering banalities; go straight into your act.

2. A speaker or writer should not tell his listeners or readers that he is going to tell them something; just tell them.

3. A speaker or writer should not telegraph his moods; let the listener or reader decide whether what you say is funny or interesting or serious or ironic or whatever you happen to think it is.

GYMNASIUM

The Greeks exercised in the nude, whence *gymnasium* and *gymnastics*, from *gymnos*, naked. The gymnosophists, Hindu ascetic philosophers found by Alexander the Great, thought in the nude.

GYN-

Many English words derive from the Greek word for woman, *gyne*. Among them: *gynandry*, the state of a female whose external genital organs resemble those of the male (*aner*, *andros*, man); *gynarchy*, government by women (*archein*, to rule); *gynecocracy*, also government by women (*kratein*, to have power), "petticoat rule" in a depreciative sense; *gynecology*, study of the diseases of women and their reproductive physiology; *polygyny*, the practice of having more than one female mate at a time (*polys*, much, many).

HACK
A *hack* writer is one whose style is stale and trite or one who hires himself out to write pulp, from *hackney*, a horse for hire, worn-out by service, from Hackney, in Middlesex, England, where these horses used to be raised. See CLICHÉ.

HADN'T OUGHT
A barbarism for *ought not* or *should not*. See OUGHT / SHOULD.

HAIL / HALE
One *hails* a friend in greeting or hails a cab by shouting "Taxi!" One *hales* (hauls) someone into court.

HALCYON
One's *halcyon* years are those good old days of peace, tranquillity, happiness, prosperity, from Greek *alkyon*, kingfisher, which was said to nest at sea and calm the winds and waters while the eggs were hatching. The hatching period was the seven days before and after the winter solstice, about December 22 in northern latitudes. These were the "halcyon days," an expression now used for any period of golden serenity.

HALF-MAST / HALF-STAFF
To signify mourning or to signal distress, naval flags fly at *half-mast*, others at *half-staff*.

HALF THE BATTLE
After his first two anthologies had been published, *Bird Thou Never Wert* and *Sorry I Stirred It*, Bill Vaughan, brilliant columnist of the *Kansas City Star*, invented a "Constructive Critic" who asked him, "How come you are able to think up such punk titles for your books?" Vaughan replied, "Just a knack, I guess. Some people have it; some don't. Shakespeare was terrible on titles, although very good in other ways. Can you imagine calling a play 'Hamlet' instead of 'How to Avoid Probate in Denmark'?" Said the Constructive Critic, "Shakespeare aside, the big

thing to remember is that for your kind of book a good title is half the battle." So Vaughan titled his third book *Half the Battle* and made no apology for the cliché. "It comes when I am halfway through the battle of life," he said. "Exactly halfway if I live to be 104."

HAND DOWN
Juries, whether grand or petit, don't hand down indictments or verdicts. They hand them up or return them. In law, only judges hand something down. See also WIN HANDS DOWN.

HANGED / HUNG
The past tense and past participle *hanged* is preferred to *hung* in the sense of "killed by hanging." In other senses, *hung*.

HANG-UP
A barnyard word for fixation, inhibition, irritation, vexation.

HARA-KIRI
Note the spelling, from Japanese *hara*, belly, and *kiri*, cutting.

HARASS
From Old French *harer*, to set a dog on. Other carnivorous words with a similar meaning are *hound* and *badger*. The more common pronunciation of *harass* has the stress on the first syllable, not the second. Note the spelling: single *r*, double *s*. See also EMBARRASS.

HARDLY
Because *hardly*, like *barely* and *scarcely*, has the force of a negative, it forms an improper double negative when used with a negative, as in "I couldn't hardly stand the pain." Also, though "hardly . . . when" is the equivalent of "no sooner . . . than," *hardly* is not a comparative and thus should not be used with *than*. "We had hardly arrived than the curtain went up" should be "We had hardly arrived when the curtain went up" or "We had no sooner arrived than the curtain went up."

HARE'S BREATH, *see* SONIC WRITING

HARVEY
Elwood P. Dowd's pooka. Everybody has one.

HASSLE
Perhaps a blend word from *haggle* and *tussle*.

HAVE GOT TO
In usage such as "We have got to start saving," *got* is redundant, even for emphasis. To express necessity or obligation, make it "We have to start saving," or "We must start saving." For *have got* in the senses of acquisition and possession, see GOT / GOTTEN.

HEADLINE HUMOR
If a joke told in private lays an egg, in display type it will drop a litter of lead balloons. Yet beginners in headline writing suffer from a maddening alliterative itch to be the Jack Benny or the Ogden Nash or the Frank Sullivan of the 72-point set. Only patient teaching and bitter experience will convince them that their sad humor and saccharine rhymes and sorry bromides put them in the class of George Jessel and Edgar Guest and Mr. Arbuthnot. 'Tain't funny, McGee.

Rarely does a story call for a rhymed head, and then a rhymed head calls for a skilled craftsman. Squeezing rhyme into the narrow confines of a headline is as demanding as fitting verse into the mathematical requirements of a haiku or a sonnet. Usually, the result is jingle doggerel, as in this head over a story about a presidential prayer breakfast, "Jerry Ford / Begs Lord / For Accord," or this one over a story about O. J. Simpson, "Juice / Loose / As Goose." The sadness or joy of this rhyming head depends on the beholder: "Judge Says Nude Not Rude / When Mood Not Lewd."

Occasionally, one sees an intelligent pun in a head, such as this over a controversial story about creation and evolution, "Genesis Row Causes / Second Prof's Exodus," or this philosophical gem, "The End Justifies the Jeans / In Gina Lollobrigida's Case." This head for a hockey story steals the puck: "Canadian Club Finishes Fifth." And there is imagination in "Summer TV Cup / Re-Runneth Over."

HEADLINES
Many students find synoptic writing a hard art to master. Newspaper copy editors have to master not only the art of writing a synopsis but also the far more difficult art of writing a synopsis of a synopsis. They write news headlines.

Just as a news lead should summarize a story, a news headline should summarize the lead. A news headline is a summary of a summary.

Headline writers digest a digest. They take precise words with precise meanings and fit them into precise dimensions. Their tool is a chisel, the fine semantic chisel of exact language with exact meaning and exact dimension.

Language must haunt headline writers. Theirs is the kind of mind that delights in the gymnastics of word games, acrostics, anagrams, limericks, palindromes, literary crossword puzzles. Theirs is the kind of mind that takes the mathematical accuracy and imaginative flair of the bridge or chess master and translates them into measured words, metrical ideas.

HEADLINESE

The headline writer must master a vocabulary of short words that will fit between narrow column boundaries. Too often, however, the need for short words breeds the jargon of headlinese. What journalese is to reporters, headlinese is to copy editors. "Wife Swap Pact Rocks Prexy" seems to be trying to convey the idea that the head of some institution is more than somewhat upset because two of his male employees are trading outdated models without benefit of a used wife dealer.

The catatonic cacophony of headlinese comprises three discordants: (1) the pitch of some copy editors that a headline has to "sound like a headline," as if it were written in some language other than English; (2) the theme of the progressives who think a headline is square unless, as Bernstein says in *Headlines and Deadlines*, it is "jazzed up"; and (3) the disgruntled wail of those who would compress an eight-note scale into four-letter words for the folks out there in Birdland. The result is a babel of babble like the croaking chorus from *The Frogs* of Aristophanes and Tin Pan Alley's "Walla Walla Bing Bang."

Perhaps a copy editor's best test for headlinese is the question: "How often do I hear this word used in ordinary conversation with its headline meaning?" If hardly ever, the word is headlinese.

A complete list of pet headlinese words would be out-of-date as soon as the next editor got stuck for space, and a list as long as a southpaw rookie twirler's wing would be needed for copy editors of sports stories. Examples are given in various entries as they occur alphabetically.

Headlinese, said Chesterton almost fifty years ago, "is one of the evils produced by that passion for compression and compact information which possesses so many ingenious minds in America."

"Everybody can see how an entirely new system of grammar, syntax and even language has been invented to fit the brevity of headlines," he said. "Such brevity, so far from being the soul of wit, is even the death of meaning and certainly the death of logic."

HEADQUARTERS
Preferably plural. As a verb, *headquarter* hasn't made it yet, as can be seen in its rejection by 90 percent of the American Heritage usage panel.

HEARSAY
Note the spelling. Not *heresay*.

HEARSE, *see* REHEARSAL

HECTIC
The older meaning of *hectic* was feverish, flushed, from Greek *hektikos*, habitual, characterizing the habitually feverish condition of a consumptive. By extension, *hectic* is now applied to any condition characterized by feverish activity, great excitement, wild confusion.

HEIGHT
Often mispronounced and sometimes misspelled. *Height*, unlike *length* and *breadth* and *width* and *depth*, has no *h* at the end.

HELIO–
Many English words derive from the Greek word for sun, *helios*. Here are a dozen (all pronounced as in *heel*):
- —*aphelion*, the point of a planet's orbit farthest from the sun.
- —*apheliotropism*, turning away from the sun, as roots do (*trepein*, to turn).
- —*helianthus*, sunflower.
- —*heliocentric*, relating to the sun as a center.
- —*heliograph*, a signaling apparatus that reflects sunlight with a movable mirror.
- —*helioscope*, an instrument for viewing the sun without injury to the eyes.
- —*heliostat*, a mirror automatically moved to reflect sunlight on one spot.
- —*heliotherapy*, treatment of disease by exposure to sunlight.
- —*heliotrope*, a plant that turns toward the sun, a color reddish blue-red in hue and of medium saturation and low brilliance.

—*helium*, a gas, first observed spectroscopically in the sun's atmosphere.

—*parhelion*, a mock sun, a bright spot appearing at the side of the sun.

—*perihelion*, the point of a planet's orbit nearest to the sun.

Helicopter, however, comes from Greek *helix*, *helikos*, spiral, and *pteron*, wing.

HELL
The impoverished state of the vocabulary of many can be seen in the contradictory use of *hell* in similes: as slow as hell, as fast as hell; as easy as hell, as hard as hell; as fat as hell, as skinny as hell; as cold as hell, as hot as hell; as happy as hell, as sad as hell; and on and on and on till one becomes as tired as hell of such lazy thinking. For a helluva long discussion of *hell*, see Mencken.

HELP, *see* CANNOT HELP BUT

HELPMATE
The word comes to us from a false understanding of the verse in Genesis in which, according to the King James Version, the Lord God says, "It is not good that the man should be alone; I will make him an help meet for him." *Meet* meant suitable, but *help* and *meet* became hyphenated and then one word and eventually *helpmate*. The Douay Version translates the verse: "It is not good for man to be alone; let us make him a help like unto himself."

HEMA- / HEMO-
Many English words derive from the Greek word for blood, *haima*. Among them:

—*hematology*, scientific study of the blood.

—*hematoma*, a tumor or swelling filled with blood (*-oma*, suffix indicating tumor).

—*hematose*, bloody.

—*hemoglobin*, the respiratory substance in red blood cells.

—*hemophilia*, a tendency to profuse bleeding, even from slight wounds.

—*hemorrhage*, discharge of blood (*rhegnynai*, to break, burst forth)— note the spelling (double *r*, followed by *h*).

—*hemorrhoid*, painful mass of dilated veins in swollen anal tissue (*rhein*, to flow), usually plural and called *piles*—note the spelling.

—*hemostat*, an agent that stops bleeding, or a clamp for compressing a bleeding vessel.

HENCE / THENCE / WHENCE

All three words include the notion of *from*. *Hence:* from here, from this place, from this time, from this source. *Thence:* from there, from that place, from that time, from that source. *Whence:* from where, from which place, from which source, from which reason. So *from hence* and *from thence* and *from whence* are redundant; drop *from*.

HERB

Americans prefer to drop the *h* in the pronunciation of *herb;* the British keep it. Americans, however, pronounce the *h* in almost all words derived from *herb*, such as *herbaceous, herbal, herbicide, herbivorous;* the British are consistent.

HERESY

From Greek *hairesis*, a taking-for-oneself, a choosing, *heresy* originally meant private opinion. Moral and dogmatic theology, however, changed the meaning of *heresy* to disagreement with ecclesiastical doctrine. As Moore observes, *heresy* "still carries an echo of the screams of the racked and a stench of burnt flesh." Today, some of us tend to regard as heresy any opinion contrary to our own. In the seventeenth century, Hobbes wrote in *Leviathan:* "They that approve a private opinion, call it opinion; but they that mislike it, heresy."

HERMAPHRODITE, *see* ANDROGYNOUS

HERSELF, *see* ANTONOMASIA; PRONOUN

HETERO–

Common words that derive from Greek *heteros*, other, other than usual, different, are: *heterodox*, of opinion differing from the standard; *heterogeneous*, of different kind; *heterosexual*, attracted to the other sex.

HEURISTIC, *see* EUREKA

HIBERNATES IN WINTER

That's the best time.

HICCUP

Perfect onomatopoeia.

HICK
This word for a rube is an old familiar form of Richard, as *rube* is a nickname for Reuben.

HIERARCHY
Government by "the holy people," or "the holy people" themselves, from Greek *hieros + archos*, sacred ruler. *Hierarchy* has extended to mean any pecking order, any group of people classified by rank or authority. Note the spelling.

HIEROGLYPHIC
Both adjective and noun, from Greek *hieros + glyphein*, sacred carving, a system of writing by pictures to represent words or sounds, hence anything hard to read, obscure, indecipherable.

HIMSELF, *see* ANTONOMASIA; PRONOUN

HIPPODROME, *see* DROMEDARY

HIPPOPOTAMUS
Greek *hippos ho potamios*, horse of the river. See BEHEMOTH.

HIRCINE / HIRSUTE
The words are similar in form but different in derivation and meaning. *Hircine* comes from Latin *hircus*, the he-goat, hence goatlike, smelly, lecherous. *Hirsute* comes from Latin *hirsutus*, hairy, shaggy, bristly.

HISS
"'Drop dead,' he hissed." Try that on your sibilator.

HISTORIC / HISTORICAL
A *historical* work deals with history but it will not be *historic* unless it is memorable enough to be assured of a place in history. From Greek *histor*, a learned man. See ARTICLE: A; AN; THE.

HISTRIONIC
From Latin *histrio*, an actor, *histrionic* is usually applied to overacting, excessive emotion. Its noun, *histrionics*, is plural.

HIT

Headlinese. *Hit* is overworked in headlines. To denote opposition, there are plenty of other short-count words, such as *ban, bar, chide, clash, defy, fight, lash, split, veto, vie, void, war.*

HITCHHIKE

Double *h* in the middle of the word. The "hitchhiker syndrome" is the compulsion of a successful hitchhiker to entertain the driver.

HITHERTO

The word means *up to now* (not *then*), *up to this time* (not *that*), *until now.* Incorrect: "In 1977, Al Geiberger shot a 59, a score that had hitherto been considered impossible in a PGA tournament." Make it *previously* or *theretofore* (up to then, up to that time) or even *thitherto.*

HOBNOB

Drinkers used to toast each other with "Hob or nob," from Anglo-Saxon *haebbe + naebbe*, have and have not, hit or miss, come what may. To *hobnob* now means to associate familiarly, with or without drink.

HOBSON'S CHOICE

A choice between what is offered and nothing. Thomas Hobson, a seventeenth-century liveryman in Cambridge, England, told every customer he could have any horse he wanted, as long as it was the one nearest the door. *Hobson's choice* should not be used in the context of dilemma or mere indecision.

HOI POLLOI

As a fancy term for the masses, the rabble, *the hoi polloi* is itself barbaric. *Hoi* is a Greek plural definite article and *polloi* is Greek for *many.* So *the hoi polloi* translates as *the the many.*

HOIST, *see* PETARD

HOLOCAUST

From Greek *holos + kaustos*, wholly burnt, *holocaust* strictly refers to wholesale destruction by fire. It is not a mere synonym for *disaster, calamity, catastrophe. Holocaust*, however, has become a term for Hitler's pogrom against Jews.

HOLOGRAPH

A document, especially a will, written wholly in the handwriting of its author. From Greek *holos + graphein*, to write wholly, to write in full.

HOME ECONOMICS, *see* DIOCESE

HOMO–

Though they are often confused, Greek *homos*, same, and Latin *homo*, man, are etymologically unrelated. From the Latin word we get such words as *homicide*, *homage*, *hombre*. From the Greek word we get such words as: *anomaly*, not the same result, deviation from the normal rule; *homocentric*, having the same center; *homogeneous*, of the same kind; *homogenized*, of the same consistency; *homonyms*, words that have the same pronunciation but different meaning and origin (*beer* and *bier*) and often the same spelling (*bear*); *homosexual*, of the same sex, said of a relationship between males or between females and unrelated to *homo*, man.

HONORABLE, *see* REVEREND

HONORED IN THE BREACH, *see* MORE HONORED IN THE BREACH

HOPEFULLY

This is a knee-jerk word like YUNNO. And most of the time it doesn't make sense. It makes sense when you say, "Hopefully, he awaited the jury's verdict," because he was full of hope. It doesn't make sense when you say, "Hopefully, the plane will be on time," because the plane is not arriving full of hope. You mean "I hope the plane will be on time." As Barzun says, "The twist from the proper direction of the word takes place when the speaker attributes his hope to its object."

Strunk says the use of *hopefully* to mean "I hope" or "it is to be hoped" is "silly": "Although the word in its new, free-floating capacity may be pleasurable and even useful to many, it offends the ear of many others, who do not like to see words dulled or eroded, particularly when the erosion leads to ambiguity, softness, or nonsense."

In *The Careful Writer* (1965), Bernstein says the use of *hopefully* to mean "it is hoped that" is "solecistic." Six years later, in *Miss Thistlebottom's Hobgoblins*, he softens and says, "The word is in common use and perhaps in reputable use and one wonders whether attempts to resist it are not exercises in futility." Another six years later, quoted in the *New*

Yorker, Bernstein says, "I've never heard a cogent argument against it [hopefully]," to which William Morris, founding editor of the American Heritage, replies: "One argument is that an inanimate object can't hope. But I'm afraid that the war is being lost." The conversation was interrupted when Bernstein dropped his glass. "Hopefully, that won't happen again," he said.

The problem used to be that English had no word for "it is hoped" comparable to *regrettably* for "it is regretted." In 1965, Bernstein wrote, "What is needed is a word like *hopably*, which is not here being nominated for the job." Six years later, he wrote, "It would be comforting if there were such a word as *hopably* . . . but there isn't."

There is now. *Hopeably*, with an *e*, has begun to appear in respectable books, journals, magazines and newspapers and in conversation. As *regretfully* is to *hopefully*, so *regrettably* is to *hopeably*. So, hopeably, the silly, offensive, ambiguous, soft, nonsensical, solecistic use of *hopefully* will diminish.

HORRIBLE, *see* AFRAID

HORS D'OEUVRE
French, literally "outside of work," hence beyond the ordinary meal, a side dish. One hears the phrase butchered in pronunciation from the singular *whore's doover* to the plural *horse's doovers*. Correct: *oar derv*, *oar dervs*. Mencken said *hors d'oeuvre* always was "a stumbling block to Anglo-Saxons" and was especially mauled in Prohibition days when the name was given to "the embalmed fish and taxidermized eggs" served with cocktails. Maury Maverick, of gobbledygook fame, suggested *dingle-doo*, which, like the Italian *antipasto*, is "much less painful to the national larnyx."

HOSPITAL
Even when there is more than one hospital in town, American idiom puts the definite article before *hospital* in usage such as "He was taken to the hospital." British idiom drops the article, just as it is dropped in "He was taken to prison." The British idiom makes more sense, but idioms are idioms because they don't make sense.

HOST
As a verb, *host* is unacceptable to 82 percent of the American Heritage usage experts, and rightly so.

HOT CAKES

When something sells fast, the cliché expert says it is selling like hot cakes, which won't sell well unless sold fast. But the cliché expert isn't thinking of hot cakes. He is merely grabbing a tired old phrase and uttering it without thinking.

HOWEVER

The ban against the use of *however* as an adverb of contrast at the start of a sentence is a myth. Put *however* wherever it best conveys contrast, usually immediately after what is being contrasted. Example: "Both John and Jim are bright students. John, however, studies harder." Or: "The Cubs looked good in the exhibition season. We'll have to wait for the regular season, however, to see how good they really are." If two whole sentences are being contrasted, the second sentence may properly start with *however*. However, don't overdo it.

HUBRIS

An old word newly popular. Greek *hubris*, insolence, arrogance, contempt.

HUDDLE

An American football ritual in which the players show their rear ends to the crowd before a play. After a successful play, another ritual demands that the players pat one another on the rear end to demonstrate their boyish glee.

HUNG, *see* HANGED / HUNG

HYDROPHOBIA, *see* –PHOBIA

HYPERBOLE

Exaggeration, something thrown beyond, from Greek *hyper*, over, above, beyond, and *ballein*, to throw. (See BALLISTICS.) The Greek prefix gives more than a hundred English words the added meaning of "excessively," as in *hyperactive, hypercritical, hypersensitive, hypertensive.*

HYPHEN

The punctuation mark hyphen (-) derives from Greek *hypo + hen*, under one, into one. If there were a rule about when to join words, when to separate them and when to hyphenate, it might be: (1) join them; (2) if you can't join them, separate them; (3) if you can neither join nor separate them, hyphenate. But there is no rule. Who is to say what words "can't" be joined or separated? The secret is common sense. When in doubt, consult a respectable dictionary or stylebook. There are, however, a few standard principles, such as:

Don't hyphenate an *-ly* adverb and an adjective: "highly proficient," not "highly-proficient." This principle applies whether the words come before a noun or after a verb: "A highly proficient electrician is needed for this job" and "An electrician who is highly proficient is needed for this job."

When *well* adverbially modifies a participle before a noun, hyphenate: "a well-executed move." But separate after a verb: "The move was well executed."

Watch for ambiguity. As Nurnberg points out, there's a difference between "a man-eating shark" and "a man eating shark," and between "My company employs a hundred-odd men and women" and "My company employs a hundred odd men and women." Strunk refers to the merger of two newspapers in Chattanooga, Tenn., the *News* and the *Free Press*, which became the *Chattanooga News-Free Press*.

Rephrase hyphenation such as "the Kansas City-Denver highway." The towns are not Kansas and City-Denver. Make it "the highway between Kansas City and Denver" or "the highway from Kansas City to Denver."

Avoid hyphenitis, inflammation of the hyphen, a painful disease to which young writers and stuffy scribes are especially susceptible.

HYPHEN IN HEADLINE
Both parts of a hyphenated word should be uppercase in an upstyle headline. For example: *Baby-Sit, Ex-Wife, H-Bomb, Teen-Ager.*

HYPO–
The Greek prefix *hypo–*, below, beneath, under, is a root of more than a hundred English words. For example:

—*hypochondria*, under the cartilage (*chondros*) of the breastbone, the abdomen, formerly considered the seat of melancholy, hence morbid anxiety about health, invention of imaginary ailments.

—*hypocorism*, beneath the caress (*korizesthai*, to caress, from *koros*, child), hence a pet name, an endearing diminutive (*Jimmy, darling, sweetie*).

—*hypocrisy*, judgment (*krinein*, to separate, choose, judge) underneath, hence feigning, insincerity, acting a part.

—*hypodermic*, under the skin (*derma*), popularly abbreviated to *hypo* for hypodermic injection, needle, syringe.

—*hypotenuse*, something stretched (*teinein*) under, hence the line of a triangle "holding up," subtending, opposite the right angle.

—*hypothesis*, something put (*tithenai*) under, proposed, supposed, hence a tentative explanation, an assumption to be verified.

HYSTERECTOMY, *see* –TOMY

HYSTERIA

Because they considered women more likely to be emotionally disturbed than men, ancient medical men concluded that the source of the vapors was the malfunction of an organ unpossessed by males, the uterus (Greek *hystera*). Hence our word *hysteria* for wild emotionalism, surely an etymological misconception.

I

ICEBERG

The tip of an iceberg is the part that projects above sea level, about one-ninth of the entire mass. The phrase "just the tip of the iceberg," meaning only the visible part of a problem, was originally a brilliant metaphor but is now a dull cliché.

ICHTHY-

A combining form for *fish*, from Greek *ichthus*, fish, as in *ichthyology*, the study of fishes, and *ichthyophagous*, feeding or living on fish. *ICHTHUS* was an early Christian symbol for Jesus, formed from the first letters of "Iesous CHristos THeou Uios Soter" (Jesus Christ, Son of God, Savior). Early Christians used the symbol of the fish to recognize one another. The abbreviation *IHS* is seen in religious art.

ICONOCLAST

Originally, a destroyer of sacred images, from Greek *eikon*, image, and *klastes*, breaker. A modern *iconoclast* tries to tear down cherished or traditional beliefs or institutions.

-ICS

Are nouns ending in -*ics*, such as *ethics*, *politics*, singular or plural? Try these distinctions:

Use a singular verb with an -*ics* noun when it strictly denotes the name of an art or science, as in "Ethics deals with moral principles" or "Politics deals with government."

Use a plural verb when an -*ics* noun refers to activities or practices, as in "His ethics resemble those of a louse" or "Such politics sicken me."

Use a singular verb when an -*ics* noun is followed by a copulative verb and a singular noun, as in "Ethics has become the big story in Washington" or "Politics is his consuming passion."

IDENTIFICATION, *see* WHO HE?

IDIOM

Grammatically, an *idiom* is an expression for which there is no logical explanation, from Greek *idios*, one's own, proper to oneself, peculiar to oneself, separate. Examples: "Aren't I?"; "a book of mine"; "an estimated 100 people"; "if worst comes to worst."

Beware, however, of fleeing to idiom as a refuge of sinners when you err grammatically. The plea of idiom is a poor defense for ignorance. And remember that idioms don't just suddenly spring up in the language. They become embedded over a long period.

Other common words from *idios* are *idiosyncrasy* (note the spelling: *crasy*, not *cracy*) and *idiot*. In ancient Greece, an idiot was a private person, one who held no public office. Language indeed changes with time.

IDYLL

American long *i*, as in "idle"; British short *i*, as in "Hey diddle diddle, the cat and the fiddle."

I.E.

The abbreviation *i.e.* for Latin *id est*, that is, should not be confused with *e.g.*, the abbreviation for *exempli gratia*, for the sake of an example, for example. "He based his life on Murphy's Law, i.e., if anything can go wrong, it will." "His copy was full of grammatical errors, e.g., disagreement between subject and predicate." But avoid such Latin tags. Say "that is" and "for example."

IF / WHETHER

Strictly, *if* is an adverbial conjunction of condition. In "I'll quit smoking if you'll help me," your helping is a condition of my quitting. But in "I want to know if you'll help me," your helping is not a condition of my knowing. Strictly, *whether*, a nounal conjunction meaning "that-or-that-not," should be used in the second example, as if one were saying, "I want to know that you will help me or I want to know that you will not help me."

Loosely, however, *if* is commonly used instead of *whether*. But *whether* should be used when the nounal clause is at the beginning of the sentence, as in "Whether the candidate is honest is the problem." See also AS IF / AS THOUGH; AS IF / LIKE; MOOD.

IF AND WHEN
Either *if and* or *and when* should be dropped from this cliché. Similarly, from *unless and until*, drop either *unless and* or *and until*.

IF NOT
In writing, the phrase is ambiguous. When you write, "She was the most attentive, if not the brightest, student in the class," do you mean she was the most attentive but not the brightest, or the most attentive and perhaps the brightest? If you mean "but not," write *but not*. If you mean "perhaps," write *perhaps*. In speech, the ambiguity is avoided by tone of voice, inflection, a difficult art to master in writing.

IGNORAMUS
Latin for "we do not know," *ignoramus* was once the term used by grand juries when they returned a "no bill" for lack of evidence. The word became popular in the seventeenth century as a result of a play titled *Ignoramus*, whose chief character was a lawyer of the same name, a satirical symbol of the ignorance and arrogance of some lawyers. *Ignoramus* has extended to mean anyone who doesn't know something he ought to know.

ILLUSION, *see* DELUSION / ILLUSION

IMBECILE, *see* BACTERIA

I MEAN, *see* LIKE, I MEAN; YUNNO

IMMACULATE CONCEPTION
Used jokingly, the term is a religious slur and highly offensive to Roman Catholics. It is also used ignorantly to refer to the birth of Christ. The doctrine of the Immaculate Conception refers to the conception of Mary in the womb of her mother without stain of original sin.

IMMINENT, *see* EMINENT / IMMINENT

IMMORAL, *see* AMORAL / IMMORAL / UNMORAL

IMMORTALS
The name (uppercase) given to the forty members of the French Academy, whose chief responsibility is to preserve the purity of the French

language and to decree correct usage so that fifty million Frenchmen can't be wrong.

IMPACT

A faddish, all-purpose word that has come to mean all things to all bureaucrats and admen, *impact* strictly denotes a violent bump or crash. As Barzun says, "If you have to report the impact of a meteorite in your backyard, use the word without hesitation, but forgo it in describing the effect of a new detergent on the lives of young mothers." Such verbal abuse he calls "metaphoric pidgin."

Impact is frequently misused for *effect*, as in "His warnings had no impact on me," or for what Nickles calls "stylish but useless jabber," as in "children spoiled by (the impact of) permissiveness." (Proper and more truthful usage would be "children spoiled by the lack of occasional impact of parental hand on filial bottom.")

Instead of *have an impact*, choose a more appropriate verb such as *affect, change, decrease, increase, heighten, lessen, persuade, sway*. And instead of *impact*, try *effect, change, consequence, result, repercussion, impression, influence, significance*.

Impacted, as in "impacted wisdom tooth," means wedged together.

IMPASSABLE / IMPASSIBLE

A road that cannot be traveled is *impassable*. A person who is unfeeling or unaffected by pain is *impassible*.

IMPEACH

From Latin *impedicare*, to put in fetters (*pes*, foot), to entangle, *impeach* means to bring charges against, to call to account, to indict. *Impeach* does not mean to try, to find guilty, to convict, as it was mistakenly used by those who confused the possible impeachment of President Nixon by the House of Representatives with trial by the Senate. President Andrew Johnson was impeached by the House and tried and acquitted by the Senate.

IMPENETRABLE, *see* UNGOTHROUGHSOME

IMPLEMENT

As a verb, *implement*, in the sense of "carry out" or "fulfill," is old but, in the lingo of bureaucrats and educationists, it has all but replaced *carry out* and *fulfill* and has become a faddish word. Instead of automatically mouthing *implement*, seek a more specific word to fit a specific context, such as *accomplish, achieve, carry out, discharge, execute, fulfill, keep, make, observe, perform*.

IMPLY / INFER

To *imply* is to suggest, to hint, to state indirectly. To *infer* is to draw a conclusion, to derive by reasoning, to deduce. Example: "When I said you were hard to live with, I wasn't implying that I didn't love you, and you shouldn't have inferred that I was contemplating divorce." Bernstein aptly illustrates the distinction: "The *implier* is the pitcher; the *inferrer* is the catcher."

IMPOSTER / IMPOSTOR

The words have the same derivation, Latin *imponere*, to place on, to impose, but they have different meanings. An *imposter* is one who levies an impost, a tax, especially a customs duty. An *impostor* is one who takes on the identity of another to deceive. *Impostor* is by far the more common word. Note its spelling.

IMPRACTICABLE / IMPRACTICAL, *see* PRACTICABLE / PRACTICAL

IMPRIMATUR

A censor's stamp or a stamp of approval: Latin for "Let it be printed."

IMPUGN / IMPUNITY

The words are similar in sound but different in meaning and origin. The verb *impugn*, to assail, to oppose as false, comes from Latin *impugnare*, to fight against. The noun *impunity*, exemption or freedom from punishment or penalty, comes from Latin *impunitas*, no punishment.

IN, *see* AT / IN; WANT IN

INCARNADINE

This fiercely beautiful word comes from the Latin genitive *carnis*, of flesh, hence flesh-colored and, by extension, blood-red.

After the murder of Duncan, Macbeth cries: "Will all great Neptune's ocean wash this blood / Clean from my hand? No; this my hand will rather / The multitudinous seas incarnadine."

After a succession of mostly monosyllabic words, Moore observes, Shakespeare unexpectedly introduced tremendous new words "which like lofty Spanish galleons had sailed into the language as lately as the Armada into the English Channel." *Multitudinous* had never been used in English before and "as an epithet for the sea it was audacious and beautiful; it suggested the vastness of ocean by conjuring up a picture of innumerable ripples and waves." *Incarnadine* had been used as an adjective for a dozen years "when Shakespeare by a stroke of his quill in the mighty line turned it into a verb." Bloody beautiful.

INCIDENTALLY
Commonly misspelled *incidently*.

INCLUDE
Don't use *include* or its parts unless you are listing only some members of a group. Don't say, "The members of the four-man team include Brown, Smith, Jones and Robinson." Make it *are* or "The four-man team comprises (or consists of) . . ." Don't say, "The book was translated into five languages, including French, German, Italian, Spanish and Portuguese." Put a colon instead of the comma after *languages* and strike *including*. But these are correct: "The bullpen includes four left-handers" and "The book was translated into nine languages, including French, German, Italian, Spanish and Portuguese."

INCOMPLETE SENTENCE
When a sentence begins with a relative pronoun whose antecedent is not in the sentence, the sentence is incomplete. Example: "Carter is proving the truth of the charges against his friend by personally denying them. Which is a bad omen of a sense of desperation." The second sentence in the example is incomplete. The antecedent of *Which* is the whole statement of the first sentence. Make it *This*, which is a demonstrative pronoun, not a relative.

Some writers like to pepper their prose with incomplete sentences. Too much pepper spoils the taste. A pinch is enough. An incomplete sentence may sometimes be good for sudden effect. Which shouldn't happen often. Which shouldn't have happened here.

INCREDIBLE
The frequency with which some people describe things as *incredible* is almost unbelievable. They really don't mean they can't believe something. They mean that something is hard to believe, that something seemed impossible but actually happened. Tone down *incredible* with some such modifier as *almost*.

INDEX

In all usage other than mathematical, the plural of *index* is *indexes*. The mathematical plural is *indices*.

INDIANIAN, *see* ALABAMIAN

INDICT / INDITE

Though *indict* is pronounced *indite*, note the spelling. To *indict* is to charge with an offense. The confusion in spelling is aggravated by a similar word of different meaning: *indite*, which means to compose, to set down in writing.

INDIRECT OBJECT, *see* DIRECT OBJECT

INDIVIDUAL

As an adjective, *individual* is impeccably used to distinguish between the particular and the general, as in "The individual pieces of furniture contributed to the charm of the whole room" or "The show's success was due to cooperative effort rather than individual performance."

As a noun, *individual*, in the sense of *person*, may be used to distinguish between a single human being and a group, as in "The greater good of society supersedes the rights of an individual." *Individual*, however, should be eschewed as a mere substitute for *person*, even humorously or belittlingly. In the classic sense, a person is an individual endowed with reason. In the example "Two individuals sought to influence the witness' testimony," *individuals* is unacceptable to 62 percent of the American Heritage panel. Make it *persons*. See also PEOPLE / PERSONS.

INDUCTION, *see* A POSTERIORI / A PRIORI

INEFFABLE

What is beyond expression, what cannot be uttered, is *ineffable*, from Latin *ex + fari*, to speak out. From the same root come *affable* (easy to speak to), *fame* (a result of much speech about), *fate* (what is spoken by the gods), *infant* (one unable to speak), *preface* (what is spoken before).

INFARCT, *see* FARCE

INFECTIOUS, *see* CONTAGIOUS / INFECTIOUS

INFER, *see* **IMPLY / INFER**

INFINITIVE, *see* **FINITE VERB; SPLIT INFINITIVE**

INFLAMMABLE, *see* **FLAMMABLE / INFLAMMABLE**

INFLUENZA
The word for the disease is Italian for *influence*, because astrologers attributed the disease to the influence of heavenly bodies.

INGENIOUS / INGENUOUS
An *ingenious* person acts with inventiveness, originality, cleverness, from Latin *ingenium*, inborn talent, natural quality. An *ingenuous* person acts with undisguised openness, artless frankness, sometimes with extreme naivete, without hiding feelings or attempting deception, from Latin *ingenuus*, noble, honest, frank. If you ingeniously invent a better mousetrap, don't ingenuously neglect to patent it.

INK
Headlinese for *sign*. Holdout moundsmen ink pacts. Ordinary humans sign contracts. See VERBING NOUNS.

IN LOCO PARENTIS
Latin for "in the place of a parent," a role officially stripped from institutions of higher learning in modern times as a result of the demise of parietal regulations, but a role still played by the professoriate when problems arise as a result of the demise of parietal regulations.

INNOCENT
Some ultranervous editors, scared that the *not* in a plea of "not guilty" will be accidentally dropped from copy, insist that *not guilty* be changed to *innocent*, which, as Bernstein says, is "insufficient reason to excuse an absurdity." If a defendant pleaded innocent, he could be required to prove his innocence, whereas a plea of "not guilty" is simply a negation of a charge the prosecution is required to prove. AP, however, uses *innocent*.

INNOCUOUS
Note the spelling: double *n*. Like *innocent*, *innocuous* comes from Latin *in* + *nocere*, not to harm or hurt.

INNOVATION
Because an innovation (from Latin *novus*, new) is something new or the presentation of something new, "new innovation" is redundant.

INNOVATIVE
A distinguished professor at Indiana University, Richard M. Dorson, recently suggested to a panel reviewing grant applications that any proposal mentioning *innovative* be eliminated. Such a policy, he said, would have eliminated 95 percent of the applications. In *The Chronicle of Higher Education*, Dorson remarked: "No one took me seriously. We are all befogged by the conventions of academic discourse, and whoever flouts those conventions is—a popularizer."

INNUENDO
Note the spelling: double *n* after *i*. The plural is *innuendoes*. The word is the gerund of Latin *innuere*, to nod to, hence "by hinting."

INOCULATE
Note the spelling: single *n*. From Latin *inoculare*, to implant or engraft, from *oculus*, eye or bud, to *inoculate* is to implant a virus to effect immunity. The derivation has nothing to do with the eye of the needle with which an inoculation may be performed.

INOPERATIVE
Something *inoperative* is something that doesn't work or isn't working. The White House of the early 1970s degraded the word by using it to mean "circumstantially inconvenient," as in "What we said yesterday about the administration's unequivocal position on obstruction of justice is inoperative today."

IN ORDER TO (THAT)
The first two words are almost always unnecessary, as in "He studied hard in order to improve his grades." Make it simply *to*. Similarly, *in order that* can usually be simplified to *so that* or *that*.

INPUT
When an administrator states (an administrator rarely "says"), "We would be highly appreciative if you would provide the maximum input of your expertise in the implementation of this assignment," he is desperately trying to avoid saying in straightforward English, "Please tell me what you think about this." See BUREAUCRATESE.

INQUIRE, *see* **ENQUIRE / INQUIRE**

INSIGNIA
Strictly, *insignia* is a plural word, the singular of which is *insigne*. See
PLURALS.

INSINUATE
Literally, to wind one's way into, from Latin *sinus*, curve, bosom. Of the
same derivation are *sinuous* and *sinus*.

INSPIRE, *see* **–SPIRE**

INSULIN
The islands of Langerhans, named for their discoverer, Paul Langerhans,
nineteenth-century German physician, are the smaller glands of the pancreas. They secrete *insulin*, from Latin *insula*, an island.

INSURANCE, *see* **ASSURANCE / INSURANCE**

INSURE, *see* **ENSURE / INSURE**

INTERESTING
An overworked descriptive, especially to be avoided as a description of
what you are about to relate. Don't say, "It is interesting to note that . . ."
or "I heard an interesting story today about. . . ." Let the reader or listener decide, after the note or story, whether it interested him.

INTERFACE
Computer jargon has converted this noun, meaning a surface forming a
common boundary, into a pseudoscientific verb meaning something like
"get together" or "work harmoniously." The theme song of the interfacers
is "Look for the Silver Interfacing."

INTERJECTION
Some grammarians treat interjections (such as *O, oh, ah, alas, hah*) as
a distinct part of speech. Others prefer to classify them as introductory
or parenthetical adverbs, which is the preference here. See **PARTS OF
SPEECH.**

INTERNATIONAL DATE LINE
Usually shortened to "date line," the *international date line* is an imaginary line through the Pacific Ocean at about 180 degrees longitude, east

of which, by international agreement, the date is a day earlier than the date to the west. Thus Sunday east of the line is Monday west of it. For the inhabitants of Pearl Harbor, December 7, 1941, was a Sunday, which was Monday, December 8, in Japan. A copy editor should take care to adjust the time element in stories whose DATELINE is on the other side of the *date line*.

INTERNECINE
Though it comes from Latin *necare*, to kill, *internecine* no longer necessarily implies killing or mutual (*inter*) destruction but has shifted in meaning to describe any damaging struggle or conflict within a group.

INTERPRETATIVE / INTERPRETIVE
Either. The older form is *interpretative*. Whichever your preference, note that *fact* tells what happened, *interpretation* tells why it happened and *opinion* tells whether it should have happened.

INTERRELATIONSHIP
Because the prefix *inter-* means between or among, words such as *intercommunication*, *intercommunion*, *interreaction*, *interrelation* and *interrelationship*, which already contain the notion of "betweenness" or "amongness," are redundant, especially when followed by *between* or *among*.

INTERROBANG
"What do you know about the new energy proposals" is clearly a question and requires a question mark. But "What do you know," especially when pronounced "Waddya know," is often more exclamation or greeting than question and seems to require an exclamation point. The decision seems to depend on whether an answer is expected.

For those who can't or won't make the decision, a punctuation mark called the *interrobang* (sometimes spelled "interabang") was invented by Martin K. Speckter, a New York adman and designer, and is available in some typefaces. The *interrobang*, the word itself a combination of *interrogation* and *exclamation*, is a combination of question mark and exclamation point, over a single period, as in "How about that‽"

According to *Time* magazine (July 21, 1967), Speckter had "long brooded over the proper punctuation for such rhetorical questions of daily life as 'Who forgot to put gas in the car' or 'What the hell.'" Some typographical experts, said *Time*, salute the interrobang for "its unique ability to express the ambiguity, not to mention the schizophrenia, of modern life." *Time* quoted the *Browser*, monthly bulletin of Harvard University Press, as saying the interrobang "might with profit appear editorially at the end of all remarks from the political platform and the pulpit."

Well, waddya know? See also PRONEQUARK.

INTO
The word is a preposition but it has become a faddish adjectival phrase as a substitute for *interested in*, *busy with*, *devoted to* ("She is into computers").

INTRANSITIVE / TRANSITIVE
A *transitive* verb is one that requires a direct object to complete its meaning, one whose action crosses over (Latin *transire*) to a receiver. An *intransitive* verb is one that does not require a direct object to complete its meaning, one whose action does not cross over to a receiver. In "Fred loves Alice," *loves* is a transitive verb whose direct object is *Alice*. In "The dog barked," *barked* is intransitive.

Some verbs are both transitive and intransitive, depending on the context: in "Fred slammed the door," *slammed* is transitive; in "The door slammed," *slammed* is intransitive. Also, the same verb with different meanings may be transitive or intransitive, as in "Fred gobbled the turkey" and "The turkey gobbled."

Copulative verbs (see ADJECTIVE / ADVERB) are intransitive.

INTRIGUE
Try to restrict the verb *intrigue* (from Latin *intricare*, to entangle, to perplex) to the connotation of puzzlement caused by some form of skulduggery or covert behavior, as in "Hoffa's disappearance intrigues the police" or "The recent clandestine comings and goings of my neighbor, normally a homebody, intrigue me." Don't use *intrigue* as an all-purpose synonym for words such as *interest*, *excite*, *delight*, *fascinate*, all of which might be applied to an unconventional hair style or a new backfield formation, neither of which connotes machination.

INVALUABLE
Pity the befuddled foreigner who presumes that *in* before an adjective always negates it and that therefore *invaluable* means "not valuable."

The *in* of *invaluable* is an intensifier and gives the word the meaning of "inestimably valuable." The opposite of *valuable* is *valueless*. See also FLAMMABLE / INFLAMMABLE.

INVENT, *see* DISCOVER / INVENT

INVERTED COMMAS
British quotation marks.

IPSO FACTO
Latin for "by the fact itself, by that very fact." One who suffers an *ipso facto* excommunication is cut off from the boons of membership by virtue of the very deed committed, without recourse to juridical process.

IQ
Short for *intelligence quotient*. An IQ test measures the ability to pass an IQ test.

IRONICALLY
Let the reader or listener decide whether what you are about to say is ironic. Don't preface your statement with "Ironically" and certainly not "Ironically enough."

Irony, from Greek *eiron*, one who dissembles in speech, one who says less than he thinks, is a rhetorical figure in which the literal meaning is different from the intended, or opposite to it, as in "His background as an actor brilliantly prepared him for his role as governor."

Irony is a mild form of *sarcasm*, biting humor, from Greek *sarkazein*, to tear the flesh (*sarx*, flesh), to bite the lips in rage, to speak bitterly. For Socratic irony, see SOCRATIC METHOD.

IRREGARDLESS
Regardless of the school of a-word-is-a-word-if-the-people-utilize-it, there is no such word as *irregardless*, except when used for hyperbolic humor, and even then it isn't very funny.

IRRELEVANT
Note the spelling. The word isn't *irrevelant*. See RELEVANT.

IRRELEVANT IDENTIFICATION
If religious or racial or any other incidental identification is essential or helpful to an understanding of a story, the identification should be used.

Otherwise, such identification is *irrelevant*. So, too, in a headline. If someone mentioned in a story is a Jew or a Catholic or a Holy Roller and this fact has nothing to do with the real news of the story, it must not be mentioned. But religious identification would not be only relevant but also essential to an understanding of the news of the story under this head: "Pope Appoints Jew / Vatican City Mayor."

Many Catholic papers in the pre-Johannine era suffered from irrelevant identification. These were the days, memory sadly reminds one, when some Catholic editors were so defensively chauvinist that they blamed Masonic Linotype operators for any typographical errors. The mood is typified by this headline classic in a Catholic newspaper: "Nazis Bomb Belfast; / No Catholics Killed." And perhaps some Aryan compositor was responsible for: "Child Care / Should Be / Gentile Art." But religion had to be identified to give this head relevance: "Priest Turns Holy Roller / As His Car Turns Turtle."

This kind of racial identification is racist: "Black Physician / Booked for Rape." But this, depending on the context of the story, could be relevant: "Black Educator / Fights Integration." This certainly is relevant: "Italian Historian / Says Ericson / Found America."

And just as some reporters can't identify a woman without calling her beautiful or pretty or attractive (when was the last time you read a news story that described a woman as ugly or homely or repulsive?), so some copy editors seem obsessed with identifying by hair color, as in this head over a story about a remorseful woman who had robbed seven banks: "Holdups Rued by Blonde." Her hair color had nothing to do with the story, which, however, did describe her deceptive attire in "high heels and stockings" when she pulled her capers. The head would have been slightly less irrelevant had it identified her as "High-Heeled Heistress" or "Nylon Nellie."

ISOSCELES
An *isosceles* triangle has two equal sides, from Greek *isos*, equal, and *skelos*, leg. English has scores of words prefixed by *iso-*, equal, alike, the same, such as *isobar, isomer, isometric, isomorph, isotherm, isotope.*

ISRAEL
The name of this nation is so frequently in the news that one would think writers would know how to spell it. Yet one sees *Isreal* as often as the correct *Israel*. The other correct forms are *Israeli* for the adjective and the singular noun and *Israelis* for the plural noun, not *Israelites*, as one often sees in student copy.

IT

Despite the objections of some rigid linguisticians, the neuter pronoun *it* may often be used without an antecedent, as in "It's raining" or "Baby, it's cold outside." Another idiomatic use of *it* without antecedent is in such phrases as "beat it," "cool it," "lump it," "move it," "rough it" and certain scatological expressions.

It may sometimes help to use *it* at the beginning of a sentence that would otherwise produce an awkward construction, as in this sentence, in which the true antecedent of *it* is the sixteen-word conglomeration from *to* to *construction*.

For emphasis, *it* may also be anticipatory, as in "It is your studies you should be concentrating on, not your social life." Note that the anticipatory *it* is singular: "It is your studies," not "It are . . ." And follow the principles of pronoun agreement (see ANTECEDENT) in constructions such as "It is I who am (not *is*) to blame," in which the true antecedent is the first-person *I*, not the third-person *it*, even though *it* stands for "the one."

Often, however, *it* is merely circumlocutory, as in "It is one of his many weaknesses that he doesn't like to delegate authority" (make it "One of his many weaknesses is that . . .") or "It is an obvious fact that he doesn't like to delegate authority" (make it "Obviously, he doesn't . . .").

ITALIAN / ITALIC

The name for an inhabitant of Italy is pronounced with a short *i*, as in *it*. "Eyetalian" is barbaric. The word for the species of type, designed by an Italian printer in the late fifteenth century, is pronounced with either a short *i* or a long *i* (the short is more common).

IT ALL BEGAN

"It all began one steamy afternoon when 'Ding Dong Daddy' Dumas, so known among his fellow cowpunchers because of the way he did his stuff, rode his sweaty steed along the dusty Texas trail. Not too far down the road he sighted a crick and decided to set up camp for the night. Little did he know that many moons later his campsite would become a bustling community named Dumas."

So write so many pulp writers of the It-All-Began school. The phrase is now a cliché and is sometimes seen as the lead phrase of a complicated news story or as a recapitulatory phrase after a complicated lead. Forget it. Likewise forget the anachronistic "little did he know." And how far down the road is not too far?

ITERATE
From Latin *iterum*, again, to *iterate* is to say or do again. Hence *reiterate*, like *repeat again*, is redundant for something said or done only twice.

ITINERARY
The word has five syllables, the penultimate of which often is mistakenly dropped.

IT IS INDEED A
You signal sleepy time when you start a speech with something like "It is indeed a pleasure and a privilege for me to be . . ." (See GUEST SPEAKER.) Let the listeners decide from the content of your speech whether you have a right to be pleased. Don't tell your listeners you are happy to say what you are about to say; make them happy by what you say.

ITS / IT'S
Misuse of *its* and *it's* is possibly the most sickening example of literary ignorance. The roots of the confusion should have been extirpated shortly after kindergarten. Yet the misuse is common among college students and even college graduates. Optimistically but unrealistically, let it be said once and for all that *its*, without apostrophe, is the possessive form of *it*, as in "A college diploma is losing its original significance," whereas *it's*, with apostrophe, is a contraction of *it is*, as in "It's sad to see illiterate college graduates."

IVORY TOWER
A hide-out for intellectuals who incur elephantiasis of the brain from lofty aloofness from the world that is passing them by.

-IZE
The suffix *-ize* has helped beget many legitimate verbs, such as *bowdlerize*, *demoralize*, *immunize*, *lionize*, *memorize*, *theorize*, *vulgarize*. Unfortunately, *-ize* has also helped beget some bastards, such as *containerize*, *customize*, *featurize*, *finalize*, *personalize*, *prioritize*, *Vietnamize*, *winterize*.

Mencken listed about a hundred *-ize* monstrosities, and the list has abiogenesized over the years. Particularly abominable to Mencken was *obituarized*, culled from an article in the *Literary Supplement* of the London *Times*, which moved him to mutter, "Seeing a monster so suggestive of American barbarism in the Times affected me like seeing an archbishop wink at a loose woman."

Bernstein would apply this test for the acceptability of -*ize* coinages: "The question that must be asked is not, Does this word sound important? but rather, Is this word necessary?" When new -*ize* words appear, he says, one should skeptically view them with "a kind of damn-your-ize attitude."

J

JANIZARY
Originally the name of the old Turkish infantry, from Turkish *yenicheri*, new troops. Like *gendarmes*, *janizary* (or *janissary*) is occasionally used as a xenophilic affectation for *soldiers* or *police*. Frost used it in his delightful "Departmental" (or "The End of My Ant Jerry") as a convenient rhyme for *Jerry*, *bury* and *commissary*.

JARGON
In "The Rime of the Ancient Mariner," Coleridge spoke of birds that "seemed to fill the sea and air with their sweet jargoning." *Jargon* comes from French *jargonner*, to warble, twitter, chatter meaninglessly, whence its contemporary meaning of gibberish, hybrid language, the lingo of a trade or profession. For examples, see such entries as BUREAUCRATESE; CLICHÉ; COMMUNICOLOGESE; EDUCANTO / EDUCATIONIST; HEADLINESE; JOURNALESE; PENTAGONESE; SPORTSESE; WEASEL WORDS.

JAYHAWK
The free-soil and anti-slavery guerrillas of Kansas before and during the Civil War were called Jayhawkers, after the jayhawk, a fabulous Kansas bird that lives by plundering the nests of other birds and has eyes that stick out at the sides so that it can see in all directions at the same time, even backwards, in which direction it sometimes flies to see where it has been. The jayhawk is the emblem of the University of Kansas, whose alumni are Jayhawkers. For an authentically apocryphal tour de farce on the jayhawk, see Mencken.

JEALOUSY, *see* ENVY / JEALOUSY

JEANS
No, the sea of blue that inundates any campus at any hour was not created by Levi Strauss. Jean, a twilled cotton cloth, was first manufactured in Genoa.

JEEP

The origin of the word is disputed. The more common opinion is that *jeep* is a monosyllabic slurring of *G.P.*, abbreviation for "General Purpose." Others derive it from a character in the "Popeye" comic strip, "Eugene, the Jeep," an animal whose mobility extended to the fourth dimension. As a generic term for small military vehicles, *jeep* has passed into the public domain and is lowercase; as a trademark for some vehicles produced by American Motors Corporation, *Jeep* is uppercase.

JEOPARDY

From French *jeu*, a game, and *parti*, divided, even, hence a drawn game, an even chance, wherefore the modern meaning of risk, danger, vulnerability, exposure to injury or loss.

JEREMIAD

A prolonged prophecy of doom, lamenting the sad state of something, or even everything. The word derives from the biblical lamentations of Jeremiah.

JEROBOAM

Solomon thought Jeroboam "a valiant and mighty man" and made him king of Northern Israel, but Jeroboam abused his power, "caused Israel to sin" and was "destroyed from the face of the earth." Jeroboam lives on, however, as the name of a mighty wine bottle, to be cracked only by the valiant. A *jeroboam* (stress on the penult) holds about four-fifths of a gallon, abuse of which tempts a fate like unto Jeroboam's.

JETSAM, *see* FLOTSAM AND JETSAM

JEW

Jews have been persecuted and maligned for so many centuries that some writers and speakers balk at calling a Jew a Jew, as if there were some implication of offensiveness in the word itself. So they resort to such circumlocutions as "of the Jewish faith," "of the Jewish persuasion." A Jew is a Jew is a Jew, just as a Christian is a Christian is a Christian. For a thorough discussion of the proper and improper uses of *Jew*, see Mencken. Also see IRRELEVANT IDENTIFICATION and SOME OF MY BEST FRIENDS.

JEWISH SYNAGOGUE

There's no other kind. Similarly redundant is "Jewish rabbi."

JIBE / JIVE, *see* GIBE / JIBE / JIVE

JINGOISM
Blustering support of a bellicose policy in foreign affairs. *Jingo* became popular from its use in an English music-hall song of 1878, when Disraeli sent a fleet to Turkish waters to oppose Russia's advance: "We don't want to fight, but by Jingo if we do, / We've got the ships, we've got the men, we've got the money too." The origin of *by jingo* as a mild oath is obscure, but some derive it from *jinko*, Basque for God.

JOB'S COMFORTER
The poor old patient Job had three friends whose attempts at consolation made him feel even more miserable. Thus *a Job's comforter* is one who sympathizes in such a way that the victim becomes convinced that he has brought all his troubles upon himself.

JOHN HANCOCK
By now a cliché for a signature, after John Hancock's large and prominent signature on the Declaration of Independence. Another cliché for a signature is "John Henry," which, incidentally, has nothing to do with the railroad man.

JOHN Q. PUBLIC
An overworked personification for a member of the public, an average citizen, or the public as a whole.

JOIN TOGETHER
The combination of *join* and *together* is usually redundant, as in "Join those words together" or "Let's all join together in singing our national anthem." But there are occasions when, for emphasis or formality, *join* and *together* should be joined, as in "All races in the community joined together to combat vandalism" or "What therefore God has joined together, let no man put asunder." Ask yourself whether the combination helps the prose flow. The same principles apply to *band, consult, gather, link, meet*. Note, however, the utter redundancy of "joint collaboration."

JOURNALESE
In newspapers, as in all other publications, there is good writing and there is bad writing. Journalese, the lingo of hack newspaper writers, is bad writing, often produced under deadline pressure, but nonetheless

inexcusable. One of the tasks of editors and journalism instructors is to improve newspaper writing and eradicate journalese. See also HEADLINESE.

JUDGE / JURIST / JUSTICE
Don't equate *judge* and *jurist*. And don't equate *judge* and *justice*. A *jurist* is someone skilled in the law. All judges are, or should be, jurists. But a *jurist* is not necessarily a *judge*. And few judges are justices. A member of the U.S. Supreme Court and of certain state courts is a *justice*. The title of the head of the U.S. Supreme Court is "Chief Justice of the United States" (no *Supreme*, no *Court*). The eight other members of the U.S. Supreme Court are associate justices. For a detailed list of court titles, see AP.

JUDGMENT, *see* ABRIDGMENT

JUMP
To *jump* a newspaper story is to continue it from one page to another. A jump should rarely be shorter than a quarter of a column, and a story should never jump backwards, that is, to a page previous to the first part of the story.

The lines indicating continuation are called *jump lines*. The head-line above the continuation is called a *jump head;* it may be a complete headline or merely a label word referring to the first part of the story.

Editors disagree on the policy of jumping stories. Some papers, such as the *New York Times* and the *Los Angeles Times*, jump almost every Page One story. Others jump none, which policy is dictated by space but deprives the reader of a full account of important stories.

If possible, for reader convenience, stories on one page should not jump to different pages. A convenient page for jumps is the back page of a section, but many publishers are loath to sacrifice the higher revenue of back-page advertising.

JUNTA
If you want to sound Spanish, pronounce *junta* with an *h*. The Spanish word, from Latin *jungere*, to join, has become English and acquired the *j* sound and a short *u*, as in *junk*.

JURY-RIGGED
Nothing illegal about this adjective, a nautical term for something con-structed in an emergency for temporary use, probably from Latin *ad-jutare*, to help.

JUST DESERTS
When you get what you deserve, you get your *just deserts*. The noun is often misspelled *desserts*, as if you ate only the last course or were asserting your right to it.

JUXTAPOSITION
Things are in *juxtaposition* when placed side by side, from Latin *juxta*, near, close together. Words or phrases are in false juxtaposition when their position in a sentence causes ambiguity. Barzun gives this example: "The Congressman sat informally on the carpet and discussed food prices and the cost of living with several women."

These falsely juxtaposed sentences are only some of many found in one issue of a large metropolitan newspaper:

—"Color and texture of the meat are important because they must appeal to the consumer's eye when displayed in supermarket meat cases."

—"On March 5, 1977, at the First Presbyterian Church, the two plan to marry."

—"The council was to consider revoking Johnson's license to haul trash in the city next week."

—"After October, police have promised a crackdown."

—"When the engine quit, the pilot said he lost altitude rapidly."

—"Mao's body will be preserved in a Peking building under glass." (Peasant under glass.)

Rephrasing and attention to punctuation will eliminate false juxtaposition. Think before you write and after you have written. See also **AMBIGUITY**.

KALEIDOSCOPE
Put three Greek words together and you have a view of beautiful form: *kalos*, beautiful; *eidos*, form; *skopos*, view.

KANGAROO COURT
The origin of *kangaroo* is not aboriginal. The best guess is that when Captain Cook, exploring the east coast of Australia in 1770, asked aboriginals what they called this strange animal, they didn't understand his question and he interpreted their aboriginal "I don't understand you," which sounded like "kangaroo," as the name.

Likewise disputed is the origin of *kangaroo court*, an unauthorized tribunal, such as one conducted by prison inmates. The term probably refers to the way such courts took giant kangaroo-like leaps to unproven conclusions. Another suggestion is that the term came from the courts set up during the California gold rush to try those accused of jumping claims.

KEGLER
SPORTSESE for bowler, from German *kegeln*, to bowl.

KIDNAP
Though AP adheres to the principle discussed under ALLOTTED, it makes an exception for the participles and past tense of *kidnap*, prescribing *kidnapping* and *kidnapped*. The exception seems to be based on the flimsy grounds of avoidance of the "nape" sound. The double *p* forms, however, will probably become standard as a result of newspaper conformity.

KILT
A Scot wears a *kilt*. If he wears kilts, he is like a Malayan wearing two sarongs. *Kilt* is singular. *Kilts*, too, is singular when it refers to a woman's skirt designed like a Scottish kilt.

KIN
Plural. See KITH AND KIN.

KIND OF A
You may have an individual of a species. But you may not have a species of an individual. Furthermore, *a* means *one*. You wouldn't say, "I don't like that kind of one man." So how can you justify "I don't like that kind of a man"? The same goes for *sort* and *type* and other words denoting category.

Remember, too, that *kind* is singular. Hence "these kind" or "those kind" is a solecism, despite the spawners of spurious idioms.

KINDLY
In the sense of "Kindly take care of this matter," *kindly* is stronger and more formal than *please* and tends to connote the idea of "Do this—or else." In the sense of benevolence or graciousness, *kindly* is both adjective and adverb: "He is a kindly man" and "He kindly took care of my children."

KING CHARLES' HEAD
The phrase refers to a topic that sooner or later, mostly sooner, will irrelevantly creep into and then dominate the writing or speech of someone obsessed with the topic, regardless of the subject under discussion. The allusion is to the obsession of a lovable eccentric in Dickens' *David Copperfield*, Mr. Dick, who spent ten years trying to write a historical "Memorial," which "never made the least progress, however hard he laboured, for King Charles the First always strayed into it, sooner or later, and then it was thrown aside, and another one begun."

Westbrook Pegler's King Charles' head was Eleanor Roosevelt. A. J. Liebling's was newspaper publishers. And some modern columnists have their King Charles' heads. One widely syndicated columnist will start a piece on the U.S. Supreme Court but quickly branch off into castigation of U.S. behavior in Vietnam. Another can't write a column on any subject, from economy to energy, without usually elaborating on President Lyndon Johnson's dependence on his counsel. Yet another can't seem to concentrate on any topic without some preachment on prison reform. Worse are the sports columnists who can't resist the breathless intrusion of the information that they are sports columnists, privy to the platitudes of the nation's idols. Their fate should be that of King Charles I.

KITH AND KIN
The expression is an example of what Nickles calls "fossil phrases," elderly expressions that "cling to life in English, sustained more by their value as petrified clichés than by a clear understanding of what they meant in their youth." *Kith* used to mean acquaintances and friends, and *kin* meant relatives. Evans calls *kith and kin* a meaningless cliché that has survived because of alliteration. "A fitting punishment for anyone who uses it," says Evans, "would be to require him to use the word *kith* at once in some other context." Well, some lisping Petruchio might tame a shrew with "Kith me, Kate."

KNEE-JERK WORDS
Just as a knee jerks with an involuntary kick in reflex action, a mouth jerks with involuntary words in reflex action when thought cannot catch up with speech. Thus we have knee-jerk words and phrases such as *you know* ("'yunno"), *I mean*, *like*, *um*, *ah*, *er*, words uttered thoughtlessly to punctuate lack of thought.

KNOCK UP
Britons traveling in the United States should be quickly alerted to the American meaning of *knock up*. In Britain, *to knock up* is to awaken, as in a request to a hotel desk for an early-morning call, "Please knock me up at six." The passive *knocked up* in Britain means tired out, exhausted, which sensation is purely, or even impurely, incidental to the American connotation of the phrase. See also PECKER.

KNOT
A *knot* is a nautical measure of speed, not distance. A ship travels at 20 knots, not 20 knots per hour. One knot is one nautical mile per hour, the equivalent of 1.15 land miles per hour. Thus a ship traveling at 20 knots would be covering 23 land miles per hour. *Knot* comes from the old practice of calculating nautical speed by reeling a line with equally spaced knots over the stern and counting the number of knots reeled into the water in a minute.

KNOW FROM ADAM
As an indication of unfamiliarity, "I wouldn't know him from Adam" is a cliché. You might, however, check whether he has a navel.

KNOW-HOW
Partridge says *know-how*, as a noun, came into vogue in 1943 as military slang for skill or knack. Bernstein calls it a fad word. The American Heritage calls it informal. But it's a handy word to describe ingenuity in the solution of complicated problems.

KNOWLEDGEABLE
Ugh! The suffix *-able* suggests potential, whereas *knowledgeable* is misused to connote actual knowledge, instead of the potential or capacity for knowledge. Why not, according to context, *informed, intelligent, shrewd, enlightened, discerning, learned, erudite, wise, knowing?* If, however, you use *knowledgeable*, don't forget the *e* after the *g*, unlike *acknowledgment*.

KOWTOW
Mandarin Chinese for "knock the head," to show respect by kneeling and touching one's forehead to the ground, whence its English meaning of obsequious deference or phony fawning.

KUDOS
Despite AP, the cliché *kudos* (Greek for glory, fame, praise) is singular, not plural. Its mistaken use as a plural has led to the barbaric "kudo" as a singular.

KU KLUX KLAN
The first word in the name of this vomitory organization is *Ku*, not *Klu*.

LABOR, *see* **BELABOR**

LACKADAISICAL
Not *laxadaisical*.

LACONIC
Sparta was the capital city of Laconia, whose inhabitants, as Shipley says, were "parsimonious of patter," concise in their speech. When Philip of Macedon threatened to invade Laconia, he declared, "If we come to your city, we will raze it to the ground," to which the Laconian leader replied, "If." Hence the English word *laconic* for terse, concise, succinct, pithy.

LADY
Though *lady* has largely been replaced by *woman* in formal American usage, except in plural salutation in a lecture or as a plural genteel label for a toilet room, the word still has a connotation of gentility, as distinct from genteelness. *Lady* has come a long way from its Anglo-Saxon origin, *hlaefdige*, one who kneads a loaf, a bread baker. Most modern women see no need to loaf. Many bring home the bakin'.

LAGNIAPPE
Creole for a trifling gift from a merchant to a customer, *lagniappe* traveled from Latin America (Spanish *la napa*, the gift) to Louisiana.

LAISSEZ FAIRE
French for "Let them do," loosely "Let people do whatever they want to do." *Laissez faire* (sometimes used infinitively, *laisser faire*) is the doctrine that opposes governmental intervention in economic affairs without the consent of the governed. The adjectival form is hyphenated.

LAMPOON
French *lampons*, let's drink, was the refrain of seventeenth-century drinking songs, satirical and scatological, whence the English *lampoon* for a piece of satire, humorous or abusive or both.

LANGUAGE ARTS
Educanto for English. Bernstein calls the term a "pretentious plural" for the teaching of "reading, spelling, writing, listening, speaking into a microphone, and, if there is any time left over, grammar." Barzun, in *On Writing, Editing, and Publishing*, calls *language arts* "pseudo-scientific," springing from "Neanderthal glimmer." See EDUCANTO / EDUCATIONIST.

LASER
Acronym for Light Amplification by Stimulated Emission of Radiation. A *laser*, according to the American Heritage, is "any of several devices that convert incident electromagnetic radiation of mixed frequencies to one or more discrete frequencies of highly amplified and coherent visible radiation." Got that?

LAST / LATEST
What is *latest* is not necessarily *last*. Both are superlatives of *late*, but *latest* means "last up to now" and excludes what may happen later, as in "The body of John Smith, the latest victim of the flood, was found this morning." But "I reject your latest offer and inform you that your last chance to bid will be at Friday's auction" and "Admirers of Muggeridge hope his latest book will not be his last."

LAST BUT NOT LEAST
A cliché to which, says Evans, "we are led by alliteration's lilt and lure."

LATTER, *see* ABOVE-MENTIONED; FORMER

LATTER-DAY SAINT, *see* MORMON

LAUREL, *see* BACCALAUREATE

LAY / LIE
The verbs are commonly misused, as in: "I was told to lay down for an hour every afternoon"; "I lay down whenever I have a headache"; "I was laying down when the phone rang"; "I laid down and watched television." Some of the confusion exists because the present tense *lay* is also the past tense of *lie*. No confusion should exist if one understands the difference between a transitive verb and an intransitive verb (see INTRANSITIVE / TRANSITIVE).

Lay is transitive. Its present participle is *laying*, past tense *laid*, past participle *laid*. Thus: "I now lay bricks for a living"; "I am laying bets that the Orioles will win the World Series"; "I laid a dictionary on every student's desk yesterday"; "I have laid hands on some fine antiques over the years."

Lie is intransitive. Its present participle is *lying*, past tense *lay*, past participle *lain*. Thus: "I lie down whenever I have a headache"; "I was lying down when the phone rang"; "I lay down and watched television"; "I have lain down for a nap every afternoon since my operation."

LEAD
A journalist's term for the opening paragraph or paragraphs of a story. In a straight news story, as opposed to a feature story, the *lead* is supposed to summarize the most important facts of the story, which are then developed and substantiated in the rest of the story. In a feature story, the most important facts may be withheld from the lead for delayed effect. For a thorough treatment of leads, see Hohenberg.

LEAD BALLOON, *see* TRIAL BALLOON

LEADING ARTICLE
The British term, sometimes shortened to *leader*, for the top editorial in a newspaper.

LEAVE / LET
In the sense of "not disturb," *leave* and its other verb forms are acceptable substitutes for *let* only when followed by a noun or pronoun and *alone*, as in "Leave John (him) alone" or "Left alone, John (he) did his job well."

In the sense of "not to mention," as in "Democrats, let alone Republicans, resented the president's attempt to railroad his energy bill," *leave alone* is not an acceptable substitute for *let alone*.

Expressions such as "Leave us go" and "Leave us not" are either provincialisms or sad attempts at sophisticated jocularity.

LEAVE NO STONE UNTURNED
A cliché almost 2,500 years old. Approaching cliché status is its ornithological twist, "leave no tern unstoned."

LECTERN / PODIUM
She was a promising young reporter and she had been taught to substantiate her leads. She covered a speech by Rep. Shirley Chisholm and described it in her lead as "a passionate plea for equal rights for women."

To justify this in the body of the story, she said Chisholm "pounded the podium." This means that Chisholm stomped at least one of her feet, like a circus horse taught to count.

The reporter meant *lectern*. A podium is a raised platform, a dais, on which lecturers or conductors stand, from Greek *podion*, small foot, base. A lectern is a reading desk with a slanted top on which lecturers or preachers may place their notes or texts, from Latin *legere*, to read. Pretty soon, however, as more nouns become verbs, some reporter will write, "She podiumed the lecture." See VERBING NOUNS.

LEFT WING
The origin of *left*, Anglo-Saxon *lyft*, weak, worthless (applied to the usually weaker hand), should not dishearten the political left. *Left wing* came from the French parliamentary practice of seating the nobility on the right of the presiding official, the traditional place of honor, leaving the left to the commons. Because the nobility would tend to be conservative, and the commons radical, the conservatives were called the parties of the *right*, and the radicals the parties of the *left*. The adjectival form is hyphenated, as is the noun for a member of the left, *left-winger*.

LEND / LOAN
Though *loan* is acceptable to some authorities as a verb, especially in business usage, the more common verb is *lend*, the past tense and past participle of which are *lent*.

LENGTH / STRENGTH
Both words have a *g*, which is sounded, despite the commonly heard *lenth* and *strenth*. See also HEIGHT.

LENS
So called from the resemblance of its shape to the seed of a lentil, the Latin for which is *lens*. The plural is *lenses*.

LENT
From Anglo-Saxon *lengten*, spring, the season when the days grow longer, comes *Lent*, the penitential season of the forty weekdays from Ash Wednesday to Easter Sunday.

LEPANTO
If you want a seismic example of how to write in sonic booms, read Chesterton's "Lepanto," a poem in which, says Moore, "we really hear the drums, and the brave trumpets blowing, and the cannon in the distance."

LEPRECHAUN

This tricky little old Irish elf gets his name from Irish *luchorpan*, little body. He may be seen late at night by any Irish reveler and at all Notre Dame games.

–LEPSY

A suffix indicating taking or seizing, from Greek *lepsis*, from the future stem of *lambanein*, to take, seize. Many English words derive from this stem. Among them:

—*analeptic*, medically restorative, strengthening, picking up.

—*catalepsy*, seizure involving muscular rigidity and environmental unawareness.

—*epilepsy*, seizure involving muscular convulsion and sensory malfunction, sometimes called "falling sickness."

—*narcolepsy*, seizure by sleep, sudden and uncontrollable attacks of deep sleep (*narke*, stupor, torpor, numbness).

—*nympholepsy*, seizure by nymphs, frenzied obsession for something unattainable.

—*prolepsis*, something taken before, a rhetorical ploy in which one anticipates and answers objections to weaken their force when later presented.

—*syllable*, a taking together of letters.

—*syllepsis*, a taking together of words governed by a single word used in a different sense for each of the words governed, as in "He failed his final exams and his parents," in which *failed* is the sylleptic word; see also ZEUGMA.

LESBIAN

In one of her poems, Sappho, who lived on the island of Lesbos, invoked Aphrodite to help her gain the love of a woman, whence the assumption that Sappho was homosexual, whence the word *lesbian* for a female homosexual. But, says Moore, "nobody knows whether Sappho was 16 or 60 when she wrote those lines, nor whether it was merely the fashion for the girls of Lesbos to express themselves to each other in extravagant ways—as the Elizabethan young men did, to the confusion of some modern scholars."

LESS, *see* FEWER / LESS

LESSER

Like *less*, *lesser* is a comparative form of *little*, but it is a double comparative. *Lesser* is often used in euphonious contrast with *greater*, as in

Genesis: "And God made two great lights: a greater light to rule the day, and a lesser light to rule the night."

LET, *see* LEAVE / LET

LEVEL
No one these days, it seems, teaches in grade school, in high school or in college. One teaches at the grade-school level, at the high-school level, at the college level. Then we have the local level, the national level, the international level, the poverty level, the smog level, the noise level, the freezing level, salary levels, troop levels, casualty levels and on and on and on till one loses one's levelheadedness.

As an abstraction, *level* is almost always clutter. When tempted to use it, ask yourself whether it is necessary, whether it helps meaning, clarity, style. Rephrase: not "She reached the managerial level," but "She became a manager"; not "at the eighth-grade level," but "in the eighth grade"; not "the 5 percent unemployment level," but "5 percent unemployment." Try an adverb: not "at the local level," but "locally"; not "at the personal level," but "personally"; not "at the administrative level," but "administratively."

Do your level best to translate plane jargon into plain English.

LEVI'S
The American Heritage drops the apostrophe in this trademark. AP retains it. The more common form has the apostrophe, from the possessive of the first name of Levi Strauss, the manufacturer of this riveted garment. Note the uppercase *L*. See also JEANS.

LIABLE, *see* APT / LIABLE / LIKELY

LIAISON
Note the spelling. There's an *i* both before and after the *a*.

LIBEL
Libel is injury to reputation. A publication is answerable before law for libelous material, whether the libel appears in a story, an editorial, a headline, an advertisement, a letter to the editor, a syndicated column, a cartoon, a picture, a comic strip or any other kind of printed or pictorial matter.

The law of libel has changed dramatically in recent years and will continue to change. Writers and editors for all publications must keep up-to-date with the changes.

Editors should be wary of overplaying the amount sought in a libel suit. The amount is meaningless. A claimant may ask for any amount he wants, and sometimes the amount is ballooned for publicity. The facts of the suit, not the amount, are the real test of newsworthiness of a libel case.

Headline writers should be particularly cautious about libel. In fact, perhaps also in law, the bigger the head the bigger the libel, because the display type of headlines is bigger than the body type of stories and is therefore more prominent and read by more persons. A tight count makes "Smith Is Rapist" easier to write than "Witness Accuses Smith of Rape," but so far no court in the United States has admitted tight count as a defense against libel.

LIBERAL ARTS

College recruiters and counselors stress the importance of "a good, solid foundation in the liberal arts" as preparation for any career. Few specify the classical liberal arts: grammar, logic, rhetoric, arithmetic, geometry, music, astronomy.

The first three were called the *trivium*, the four others the *quadrivium*. These arts were called *liberal* because they distinguished the freeman from the bondman. The modern liberal arts include such disciplines as the natural sciences, history, philosophy, languages. Few writers today get "a good, solid foundation" in the trivium. All should.

LIE, *see* LAY / LIE

LIFESTYLE

A faddish word for "way of life" or "way of living." Some authorities spell it as two words; some hyphenate it; AP spells it as one word.

LIGHT-YEAR

A measure of distance, not time, a light-year is the distance that light travels in one year at "the speed of light," 186,282 miles per second. Thus, such expressions as "We are light-years away from eliminating poverty" are untimely.

LIKE, *see* AS / LIKE

LIKE BETTER, *see* BETTER / MORE

LIKE FOR YOU TO, *see* FOR YOU TO

LIKE, I MEAN

A combination of knee-jerk words, *like, I mean* is an example of what Nickles calls "null sounds." A fondness for *like* as a senseless expletive— 'On Saturday nights, we, like, go to the movies'—amounts to a neurotic verbal tic," he says, "as does the interpolation of *I mean* where the meaning is already clear."

LIKELY

As an adverb, *likely*, unlike similar adverbs such as *probably* and *possibly*, should be preceded by a qualifying adverb such as *most*, *quite*, *rather*, *very*. For *likely* as an adjective, see APT / LIABLE / LIKELY.

LIKE TO DIED

The use of *like to* or *liked to* before the past tense of a verb, as in "I like to died" or "I liked to died laughing," is at best a provincialism and at worst a barbarism. The phrases are illiterate substitutes for *almost* or *nearly*.

LIMBO

"In limbo" is Latin for "on the border." From its theological meaning of an abode between heaven and hell comes its use as a term for an intermediate state, a place of confinement, a condition of neglect or oblivion.

LIMELIGHT

Though incandescent lime has been replaced by modern methods of stage lighting, *in the limelight* remains in the language to describe someone receiving much public attention or notoriety.

LIMERICK

This nonsense verse form was invented by Edward Lear in the 1840s but was not called *limerick* till the 1890s, when the refrain "We'll all come up, come up, to Limerick" was inserted between nonsense verses, often bawdy, recited in Irish pubs. Limerick is a county, whose capital city is also Limerick, in southwest Ireland.

A limerick has five lines, of which the first, second and fifth rhyme, and the third and fourth. Strictly, the first, second and fifth lines are of three metrical feet, and the third and fourth of two feet, which restrictions bothered a certain young Irish limerick writer, as explained by the composer of this nonsense:

There was a young man named O'Brien
Whose verse was of weird design.

His friends said, "The thing
Doesn't go with a swing."
And he replied, "I guess you're right and I think I know why—I'm
trying to fit too much into the last line."

LINAGE / LINEAGE
The more common spelling of the term for print measurement is *linage*.
The term for ancestry is *lineage*.

LINEAMENT / LINIMENT
The words are sometimes confused. A *lineament*, from Latin *linea*, a
line, is a distinctive outline or feature of a body or figure, especially of
the face ("Onassis' face showed all the lineaments of the stereotyped
Levantine"). A *liniment*, from Latin *linere*, to anoint, is a rubbing oil
("His wife soothed his aching back with liniment").

LINKING VERB, *see* ADJECTIVE / ADVERB

LINKS, *see* GOLF LINKS

LINOTYPE
A trademark for a typesetting machine that is becoming a museum piece
in the United States as a result of electronic technology.

LION'S SHARE
If you use this cliché, know its proper meaning. In one version of the
fable, Aesop's lion got all the meat except for a few scraps snatched by
the fox. In the other version, the lion got all. Properly, the *lion's share*
means all or almost all of something, not merely a majority.

LIQUEFY
The more common spelling is *liquefy*, not *liquify*.

LITANY
From Greek *lite*, prayer or supplication, a *litany* is a prayer in which in-
vocations are responded to by repetitive supplications. Loosely, *litany*
has come to mean "list," but it should not be used in this sense unless the
list is long and repetitive.

LITERALLY
Don't confuse with *figuratively*. Though the angry professor was tall,
he wasn't tall enough to fit this description of his anger by a student:

"He literally hit the ceiling." Nor was this description literally correct: "The pope is literally the father of his flock." Don't use *literally* as an intensifier. Its literal meaning is "exactly, according to the strict meaning of the word." When confused with *figuratively*, the word *literally* conveys a meaning the exact opposite of that intended.

LITOTES
From Greek *litos*, plain, simple, *litotes* is a rhetorical device to express understatement by the use of a negative for an affirmative, as in "This story has not a few inaccuracies," meaning that it has many, or "Ted Williams was no slouch at the plate," meaning that he was a great hitter. The most quoted example of litotes is St Paul's description of himself as "a Jew from Tarsus in Cilicia, a citizen of no mean city," meaning illustrious. *Litotes* is stressed on the first syllable, not the second, and the *i* is generally long.

LITTERATEUR
Note the spelling. Unlike *literature*, the French *litterateur* has a double *t* after the first two letters.

LITTLE DID HE KNOW, *see* IT ALL BEGAN

LIVABLE
What is wearable can be worn. What is endurable can be endured. So, logically, what is livable can be lived. Logic calls for *in* after *livable* to provide the meaning of "what can be lived in." But logic gives way here to idiom, and *livable* has come to mean "fit to be lived in" or "fit to live in." The more common spelling has no *e* before the *a*.

LIVID
The word comes from Latin *lividus*, bluish, and has the connotation of "black and blue," like the coloration of a bruise. *Livid* has also come to mean pallid or ashen, but it does not mean reddish or red. By extension, however, *livid* is now used to describe a furious person, whatever color his face becomes. If his face becomes red, it isn't livid, but he may be.

LOADED VERB
Verbs such as *emphasize*, *note*, *point out*, *stress* are called *loaded verbs* when they editorialize rather than report. There is a big difference between "Smith said the man was a cheat," which is straight reporting, and "Smith pointed out that the man was a cheat," which is the equiva-

lent of saying that it is a fact that the man is a cheat and that Smith is emphasizing the "fact." See also REBUT / REFUTE.

Another form of editorial loading is adjectival. Observe the difference in meaning when a reporter switches a predicate adjective to an attributive (before the noun) adjective: "Smith said that the school's admissions policy was biased and that it would lead to problems with HEW," which is straight reporting, and "Smith said the school's biased admissions policy would lead to problems with HEW," which is an editorial judgment that the policy is biased.

LOAN, *see* LEND / LOAN

LOATH / LOATHE
The adjective, meaning reluctant or disinclined, is *loath* (also *loth*). The verb, meaning detest or abhor, is *loathe*.

LOBBYIST
In British usage, a *lobbyist* is not a legislative flack, but a reporter who haunts the lobby of the House of Commons seeking news.

LOBOTOMY, *see* –TOMY

LOCATE
Strictly, to *locate* is to put in place or designate a site for, as in "The university planners have decided to locate the new gymnasium behind the library" (thus changing the maxim to "Mens sana ante corpus sanum"). Loosely, *located* has become synonymous with *situated*, which strictly means "already in a certain place," as in "The new solar house is situated opposite our old home."

Both *located* in its loose sense and *situated*, however, are best dropped after forms of *to be*. Simply say, "The bank is opposite the post office," not "is situated" and certainly not "is located." And don't use *locate* as a synonym for *find*.

LOCK, STOCK AND BARREL
A cliché, originating in the total parts of a gun.

LOG
The word for the record of the performance of a ship or an aircraft, its *log*, derives from the practice of measuring a ship's rate of motion by the trailing of a piece of wood, a log chip.

LOGISTICS
Takes singular verb. See –ICS.

LONGSHOREMAN
Originally *alongshoreman*.

LOVE, *see* GLOVE

LOWERCASE
The term is spelled as one word according to AP, in keeping with the style used by printers. Some old job cases of type were arranged in pairs, the upper case containing the capital letters, the lower case the small letters.

LUCULLAN
A *Lucullan* feast is a sumptuous banquet, after Lucius Licinius Lucullus, a wealthy Roman consul of the 1st century B.C., famous as a lavish entertainer.

LUDDITE
One who violently resists technological change. The Luddites were a gang of English workers of the early nineteenth century who rioted and wrecked new textile machinery in protest against the unemployment caused by the Industrial Revolution. They took their name from Ned Lud, a half-witted Leicestershire youth of the late eighteenth century who smashed his employer's stocking frames.

LURCH
What you are left in when you have been left helpless. *Lurch* was a sixteenth-century game similar to backgammon. A player suffered a lurch when at the end of a game he had scored nothing or was badly beaten. The phrase *left in the lurch* is now a cliché, but it helps songwriters who need a dandy rhyme for *church*, as in "You left me in the lurch. / You left me waiting at the church."

LUSTRUM
A period of five years. Latin for purification. The Romans underwent a ceremony of purification, the *lustrum*, after the census every five years. Other words of this derivation are *illustrate, illustrious, luster*.

MACHREE

A beautiful Irish term of endearment, from *mo* + *chroidhe*, my heart.

MACRO-

A combining form for *large* (Greek *makros*), as in *macrocephalic*, *macrocosm*, *macroeconomics*, *macrophysics*, *macroscopic*.

MAD, *see* AFRAID

MADAM, I'M ADAM

The oldest PALINDROME, by which Adam politely introduced himself to Eve when he woke up and found her ribbing him. Nobody before Christ was better bred than Adam, and in early courtship, as Jacobs points out, good breeding does not permit "such intrusive details" or "such insolent subterfuges" as "'Haven't we met before?' 'Do you speak English?' 'Can I buy you a drink?' or 'Have you seen my etchings?'" Or even "What's a nice girl like you doing in a place like Eden?"

MADISON, DOLLEY

Note the spelling of the first name of the wife of the fourth president.

MAE WEST, *see* EPONYM

MAGDALEN(E)

If you are referring to Magdalen College, Oxford, or Magdalene College, Cambridge, pronounce the name Maudlin. Indeed, *Magdalen* is the source of *maudlin*, mawkishly emotional, effusively sentimental, traits given to Mary Magdalene by puritan painters who, as Moore says, showed her as "snivelling into a handkerchief, red-eyed, even red-nosed, and thoroughly unattractive," lest they be thought to be glorifying vice by depicting a prostitute as pretty or happy. The language, "always quick to reflect our hypocrisies, took due note of this," Moore says, and *maudlin* took on its modern meaning.

MAÎTRE D'

The too often snooty, money-grubbing character who presides over a restaurant or a night club is called a *maître d'*, short for French *maître d'hôtel*, master of the house, major-domo, chief steward, head waiter. A university football coach had trouble recruiting players from Mater Dei (Mother of God) High School in Southern California until he learned that his pronunciation of the name of the school, "Maître D'," was more than somewhat erroneous.

MAJOR

The trouble with *major*, as an adjective, is that it is strictly a comparative (*greater*) but is loosely used either as a positive (*great*) or as a superlative (*greatest*). "A major problem" has come to mean a great problem. "The major problem" has come to mean the greatest problem. *Major*, the comparative degree of Latin *magnus*, great, has no English positive; the superlative is *maximal*.

   Major has become overworked. A little thought would provide a more appropriate positive adjective, such as *big, great, important, serious, chief, main, principal*.

MAJORITY

When *majority* refers to a specific number, it takes a singular verb, as in "The Democratic majority in the Senate is 22." When *majority* refers to the larger group, it takes a singular verb if there is a notion of collective unity, as in "The Democratic majority is opposed to White House interference," but a plural verb if there is a notion of individuation or "most," as in "The majority of Democrats are opposed to the president's energy bill."

   Unless you are contrasting a majority with a minority, *most* is better than *majority* most of the time. And don't use *majority* to refer to the greater part of something that is not countable, as in "The majority of the area is zoned for commercial use"; make it "most of the area" or "the greater part of the area."

   "Great majority" means "much more than half." "Greater majority" and "greatest majority" are incorrect unless you are comparing numbers, as in "Nixon had a greater majority in 1972 than in 1968" and "Roosevelt's greatest majority was in 1936."

   Try to resist the temptation of automatically inserting *vast* before *majority*.

   And note the distinction between *majority* and *plurality*. In an election in which there are more than two candidates, a candidate who gets more votes than the other candidates combined (that is, more than half the votes) has a majority; a candidate who gets more votes than any other candidate, but not more than the other candidates combined, has a plurality.

MAKES HIS HOME
If broadcasters are to be believed, people don't "live" anywhere. They "make their home."

MALAPROPISM
Marijuana, the student wrote, is a crotch for the young. Nixon, the editorial said, will be remembered for his empirical presidency. The umpire, according to the sportswriter, needed the services of an optimologist. The student teacher said she had been assigned to Horseman School.

All these are *malapropisms*, ludicrous confusions of words of similar sound but different meaning. The term derives from Mrs. Malaprop, a character in Sheridan's *The Rivals* who loved what she thought were elegant words, but ebulliently misused them. Her most famous line is "She's as headstrong as an allegory on the banks of the Nile." Sheridan got her name from French *mal à propos*, literally "badly to the purpose," inappropriate, out of place, whence we have the English adjective *malapropos*.

So the United States has forty-eight contagious states, and Arabs wear turbines, and those dogs with the brandy casks are Sarah Bernhardts. See also SONIC WRITING.

MAN AFTER HIS OWN HEART
Samuel tells Saul in 1 Samuel that the Lord has sought "a man after his own heart" to replace Saul (He chose David). The phrase, usually with *my* instead of *his*, has long since become a cliché in many languages.

MAN IN THE STREET
An overworked term for "the ordinary citizen," "the public."

MANNA
When someone receives an unexpected gift of great value, he may say, "It was like manna from heaven." Biblically, "from heaven" is redundant. That's where the manna came from when the Lord fed the Israelites in the desert of Sin. They cried, "Man hu," Aramaic for "What is this?"

MANNER BORN

Cannons roar and trumpets bray as Claudius drains his draught of Rhenish wine. Hamlet explains to his visitor, Horatio, that the revelry is a customary Danish salute to prowess in drinking. Hamlet disapproves of the custom, "though I am a native here, and to the manner born," meaning that he has grown up with the practice. "To the manner born" is often rendered, erroneously, "to the manor born." See also MORE HONORED IN THE BREACH.

MARATHON

The race covers 26 miles, 385 yards (about 42.2 kilometers), the distance covered by the Greek messenger who ran from Marathon to Athens to bring the news of a Greek victory over the Persians at Marathon. The word is used to mean any test of endurance. But also see –THON.

MARGIN

When an announcer says the Steelers beat the Cowboys by a margin of 35 to 31, he is trying to tell you in his periphrastic way that the score was 35 to 31. The margin was 4.

MARITAL, *see* CASUAL

MARQUEE / MARQUIS / MARQUISE

Though all three words have the same derivation, French *marquis*, "count of the march (frontier)," from *marche*, frontier country, they have several different meanings. A *marquee*, pronounced "mar-key" and stressed on the second syllable, is a tent or canopy, from *marquise*, the linen draped on an officer's tent, from *marquis*. A *marquis*, pronounced in English "mar-kwis" and stressed on the first syllable, is a nobleman who ranks above an earl or count and below a duke. A *marquise*, pronounced "mar-keys" and stressed on the second syllable, may be either a female marquis or the wife or widow of a marquis or a gem, or coincidentally a combination of the last and one of the others.

MARSHAL

Note the spelling: only one *l*.

MARSUPIAL

Kangaroos and koalas and other weird animals whose females carry their young in a pouch are *marsupials*, from Greek *marsypion*, diminutive of *marsypos*, purse.

MARTIAL, *see* **CASUAL**

MARTINET
The English ridiculed the rigid disciplinarianism of Jean Martinet, inspector general of infantry under Louis XIV, and gave his name to any officer who was a stickler for military regulations and efficiency, especially in drilling. Incidentally and, one hopes, accidentally, Martinet was killed in battle by his own artillery while leading an infantry attack.

MARTINI
That which enables one to see the world in crepuscular color at the end of a colorless workday.

MASOCHIST / SADIST
One who derives sexual pleasure from being physically abused, either by another or by oneself, is a *masochist*, from Leopold von Sacher-Masoch, Austrian novelist, who described the perversion. One who derives sexual pleasure from inflicting physical abuse on another is a *sadist*, from Donatien de Sade, French playwright and author, who delighted in the perversion.

MASON-DIXON LINE
The boundary between Pennsylvania and Maryland, surveyed by Charles Mason and Jeremiah Dixon before the Revolution and considered the demarcation line between free and slave states, or North and South, before the Civil War.

MASSIVE
Strictly, except in medicine, *massive* denotes solidity rather than size.

MASTECTOMY, *see* **–TOMY**

MASTERFUL / MASTERLY
A *masterful* person is imperious, domineering, strong-willed, one who behaves like a bad master towards a slave. A *masterly* person is skillful, expert, practiced, one who behaves like a good master towards a pupil. In one sentence, Fowler gives a good example of the distinction: "The presentation in each case was masterly (perhaps in a few rare instances a trifle too masterful) and always the playing was crystal clear."

MASTHEAD

A boxed body of copy, sometimes appearing on the editorial page, sometimes on an early inside page, giving the publishing details of a newspaper. Do not confuse with *flag* (see EAR).

MATERIEL

Note the spelling of this originally French term for equipment, especially military, as distinguished from PERSONNEL. Stress the last syllable.

MAUDLIN, *see* MAGDALEN(E)

MAVERICK

Whatever about the disputed details of the origin of *maverick* as a term for a dissenter or party bolter, the fact is that Samuel A. Maverick (1803–70), a San Antonio, Texas, banker, was its eponym. There are several versions of how this came about. The most likely may be a version published by the *Wall Street Journal* in July 1977 in a letter from W. A. Seidel Sr. of Knippa, Texas, a friend of a grandson of Maverick.

Maverick leased an island in the Nueces River as pasture for a herd of cattle his bank had acquired, said Seidel, but the cattle, unattended, waded into riverbank pastures. When cattlemen found unbranded calves near the river, they would say, "That must be one of Sam Maverick's calves" or "There's another Maverick." Said Seidel: "An animal correctly called a maverick is simply an unbranded animal."

Hence an unbranded political or philosophical animal, one who pursues an independent course with no party or group affiliation, is a *maverick*.

MAVOURNEEN

A beautiful Irish term of endearment, from *mo* + *muirnin*, my darling.

MAXIMIZE

The word gained spurious currency during the Nixon years from his phrase "maximizing the incumbency," meaning in straight English "staying in office as long as I can." See –IZE.

MAY, *see* CAN / MAY; MIGHT

MAYDAY

The international radiotelephonic distress signal *mayday* is phonetic French for (*venez*) *m'aider*, (come) help me. See SOS.

ME

Because forms of the verb *to be* take the same case after the verb as before it, "It is I" (or "It's I") is strictly correct. The American Heritage usage experts vote 78 percent for "It is I" in formal writing. In speech, however, 60 percent of the experts accept "It is me" (or "It's me") because this usage "is felt by many persons to be much more natural in speech." But what's less natural about "It is I"? The question is the nature of the case, which in this case is nominative after *is*, not the objective case *me*. The vote here is for *I*, whether in writing or in speech.

MEAN, *see* AVERAGE

MEANDER

The Maeander River in Phrygia, now the Menderes in western Turkey, twisted and turned in seemingly aimless, listless fashion on its course to the sea, whence our English *meander*. Ovid wrote: "The limpid Maeander sports in the Phrygian fields; it flows backwards and forwards in its varying course and, meeting itself, beholds its waters that are to follow, until it fatigues its wandering current, now pointing to its source, and now to the open sea." In "Kubla Khan," Coleridge describes the Sacred River "five miles meandering with a mazy motion."

Moore says the sound-sequence of its syllables seems to fit the meaning of *meander:* "There is an inevitable slight pause after the first syllable which is suggestive of a lazy progress; and the latter part of the word is reminiscent of *wander*, perhaps."

MEANINGFUL, *see* DIALOGUE

MEASURABLE

Note the spelling: no *e* between *r* and *a*.

MECCA

A careless correspondent wrote: "Jerusalem was a mecca for tourists this Easter."

MEDAL OF HONOR

Though the medal is awarded in the name of the Congress, *Congressional* is not part of its title.

MEDIA

Bred by Madison Avenue and spread by Spiro Agnew, *media* is a bastard omnium-gatherum term for newspapers, news services, magazines, radio, television and other parts of what used to be called, simply, the press. Though radio and television don't use printing presses, their reporters and news editors and news announcers don't object to being generically described as the press. Along with journalists from newspapers and news services and magazines, radio and television journalists attend press conferences, carry press passes, consult press secretaries, receive press releases, sit in press boxes, belong to press clubs and press councils and are wooed by press agents.

Press should be preserved as the generic term for journalists. But if you use *media*, be sure to remember that the word is plural: "The media are," not "The media is," let alone "My media ain't showed up yet," as a newspaper subscriber complained by phone to the editor.

MEDIAN, *see* AVERAGE

MEDIEVAL
The more common spelling has no diphthong (ae).

MEDIOCRE
The word fittingly derives from Latin *mediocris*, in a middle state, from *medius* + *ocris*, halfway up a stony mountain.

MEDITERRANEAN
In "Lepanto," Chesterton called the Mediterranean "the inmost sea of all the earth." The word comes from Latin *medius* + *terra*, in the middle of the land.

MEGA-
A combining form meaning great, large, mighty and, in certain technical terms, a million, from Greek *megas*, great. Thus: *megalith*, a huge stone; *megaphone*, a device for large sound; *megaphonia*, the habit of talking too loudly; *megascopic*, large enough to be seen by the naked eye; *megacycle*, a million cycles (radio); *megaton*, explosive force equal to a million tons of TNT; and, yes, *megabuck*, a million dollars.

MEGALO-
Like *mega-*, *megalo-* is a combining form meaning great, large, but it also connotes exaggeration or abnormality, as in: *megalocardia*, abnormal enlargement of the heart; *megalocephaly*, abnormal enlargement of the head; *megalomania*, psychopathological delusion of grandeur; *megalopolis*, a very large complex of cities and their surrounds.

MEHITABEL, *see* ARCHY AND MEHITABEL

MEIOSIS
The opposite of **HYPERBOLE**, *meiosis* is rhetorical understatement, from Greek *meion*, smaller, less. It is similar to **LITOTES** but it does not require a negative for an affirmative. Calling Al Geiberger's PGA record 59 "a respectable round of golf" is *meiosis*, as is a description of a sumptuous Thanksgiving dinner as "a pretty decent snack."

MELANCHOLY
From Greek *melas + chole*, black bile, hence gloom, sadness, depression. Other words from the same adjectival root are: *Melanesia*, so called from the dark complexion of its natives; *melanoid*, blackish; *melanoma*, a malignant tumor of dark pigmentation; *melanosis*, abnormally dark pigmentation of tissue; *melanous*, swarthy.

A melancholy baby, however, is blue, and a melancholy collie, though originally black, is usually brownish.

MELBA TOAST
Dame Nellie Melba (1861–1931), Australian soprano, liked her toast very thin and crisp, whence *Melba toast*, and her ice cream laced with peach brandy, whence *Peach Melba*. Melba herself got her stage name from Melbourne, where she was born. Her real name was Helen Porter Mitchell Armstrong. She retired from the stage so many times that she gave another phrase to the language: "to pull a Melba," to come out of retirement.

MELD
In the sense of "merge, unite, combine, blend," *meld* is itself a blend of *melt* and *weld*.

MELLIFLUENT
A honey of a word, from Latin *mel*, honey, and *fluere*, to flow, hence flowing smoothly, sweet-sounding. Also *mellifluous*.

MEMENTO
After the national anthem, the stadium announcer intones: "Don't forget to pick up your team momentos at the concession stands." The word is *memento*, imperative of the Latin verb for *remember*, hence a souvenir (French, to come to mind, to remember), a keepsake, a reminder of the past. Its more common plural is *mementos*.

MEND FENCES
A political term for "showing one's face to the folks back home" or, as the English say, "nursing one's constituency." Mencken records that Sen. John Sherman of Ohio made a visit home in 1879, "ostensibly to look after his farm but actually to see to his political interests." He told reporters he had made the trip "only to repair my fences." *Repair* has become *mend* in political jargon.

MENU
From Latin *minutus*, small, the French *menu* for the details of a bill of fare has become English. See also NOTRE DAME.

MESMERIZED
To be entranced by someone or something, whether literally or figuratively, is to be *mesmerized*, from Franz Anton Mesmer (1734–1815), Viennese physician, who professed to be able to cure disease by animal magnetism, hypnotism, mesmerism.

MESSAGE
Not a verb.

METABOLISM, *see* BALLISTICS

METAMORPHOSIS
Change of form, alteration of appearance or character, from Greek *meta*, beyond, and *morphe*, form. Stress the antepenult, not the penult.

METAPHOR
When you call life "an empty dream" or "a pathless wood," you are engaging in *metaphor*, a figure of speech in which essentially unlike objects are implicitly compared or identified, from Greek *meta* + *pherein*, to carry beyond, to transfer. (For explicit comparison or identification, see SIMILE.) All metaphor is poetry, and just as there is good and bad poetry, there is good and bad metaphor (see MIXED METAPHOR). Worn metaphor becomes cliché. For detailed advice about the handling of metaphor, "this indispensable but ticklish instrument," see Fowler.

METATHESIS, *see* SPOONERISM

METEMPSYCHOSIS
The transmigration of souls, from Greek *meta* + *empsychoun*, to animate beyond. The primary stress is on the penult; the more common secondary stress is on the second syllable, not the first.

METEOROLOGY
The word has six syllables but is often mispronounced as if there were no *o* in *meteor*, from Greek *meteoros*, high in the air.

METHOD / METHODOLOGY
The terms shouldn't be confused. A *method* is a way of doing something (see ODOMETER). *Methodology* is the systematic study or science of methods. *Methodology* is often used by practitioners of scientism (see COMMUNICOLOGESE) when *method* is meant.

METONYMY
A figure of speech in which an attribute or associated term is substituted for the actual name of someone or something, from Greek *meta* + *onoma*, beyond the name, such as "Capitol Hill" or "the Hill" for Congress, "Wall Street" for American finance, "Watergate" for obstruction of justice, "wheels" for ground transportation, "the needle" for drug addiction. Beware of mixed metonymy, as in "The White House is at odds with Brezhnev"; change *Brezhnev* to *the Kremlin*.

METRIC SYSTEM
American cliché addicts will have to learn a whole new language when the metric system becomes standard in the United States. Item:
—A miss is as good as 1.61 kilometers.
—I beat him within 2.54 centimeters of his life.
—Give him 2.54 centimeters and he'll take 1.61 kilometers.
—It hit me like 907 kilograms of bricks.
   But at least one old twister will be easier on the tongue:
—Peter Piper picked 8.81 liters of pickled peppers.

METRONOME, *see* –NOMY

METROPOLIS
The word does not derive from Greek *metron*, measure, as so many English *metro-* words do, but from *meter*, mother. Hence a *metropolis* is strictly a mother city (*polis*) of a state or colony. By extension, a *metropolis* is any large city. And the metro editor of a metropolitan newspaper is the city editor, not the editor of the family section.

   Other words from the Greek for *mother* are: *metronymic*, the adjective for a name derived from the name of one's mother or other female ancestor; *metritis*, inflammation of the uterus (*metra*, from *meter*); *metrorrhagia*, abnormal hemorrhage of the uterus.

MICRO–
A combining form for small (Greek *mikros*), as in *microbe, microbiology, microcephalic, microcosm, microeconomics, microfiche, microfilm, Micronesia, microphone, microphysics, microscope, microwave.*

MIDDLE AGES, *see* DARK AGES

MIDEAST / MIDWEST
Either *Mideast* or *Middle East*, but no hyphens. Similarly, *Midwest* or *Middle West*.

MIDNIGHT
An hour after 11 p.m. Monday is midnight Monday, not Tuesday. Midnight refers to the ending day, not the beginning one.

MIDRIFF
Anglo-Saxon for the middle of your *hrif*, belly.

MIF
Short for "milk in first," *Mif* is the term applied by English snobs to cads who prefer to put milk in a cup before adding tea. U (upper-class) English people are expected to show their breeding by putting the tea in first. By this caste system, few Americans are Mifs: most put in the tea, albeit in a barbaric bag, even before they add water, let alone milk. See also U / NON-U.

MIGHT
Grammatically, *might* is the past tense of *may*, but both may be used for both the present and the future. Some lexicographers see a nuance between *may* and *might* in the context of probability. They contend that *may* indicates a greater degree of probability than *might*. For them, "I may go" indicates a stronger likelihood of going than "I might go." If such distinction exists in common language, the distinction is even thinner than nuance. *Might*, however, does have a meaning beyond its grammatical use as the past tense of *may:* in "You might remember who's paying for all this," *might* carries a tone of rebuke.

MIGRAINE
A migraine headache is usually confined to one side of the head, from Greek *hemi* + *kranion*, half the skull.

MILITARESE, *see* PENTAGONESE

MILITATE / MITIGATE
The words are sometimes confused. *Militate* means to have an effect or influence on, to operate as a force for or against, as in "His parole record militated in his favor" or "His lack of polish militated against his advancement." *Mitigate* means to soften, to assuage, to make more endurable, as in "Her reputation for compassion mitigated the vehemence of her criticism."

MILL
From Latin *mille*, thousand, a *mill* is a thousandth part of a dollar, or a tenth of a cent. When a governing body imposes, for example, a three-mill levy on property owners for some tax purpose, a property owner pays three-tenths of a cent on every taxable dollar of his official property appraisal, or $3 for every $1,000.

MILLENNIUM, *see* CHILIASM

MILLIARD, *see* BILLION

MILQUETOAST
The insipidness of toast soaked in milk, a dish for the digestively delicate, inspired cartoonist H. T. Webster to use Milquetoast as the surname for the chief character, Caspar Milquetoast, in his comic strip "The Timid Soul." The sobriquet *milquetoast* is now standard American for somebody wishy-washy, which adjective itself is almost onomatopoeic for tidbits of toast swishing and squishing in milk.

MILTONIC
We know we owe many commonly used English phrases to Shakespeare and the Bible. Not so well known is that John Milton is the source of many other such phrases, some of which have become clichés. Indeed, *Miltonic* (or *Miltonian*) is used to describe literary style that is sublime, majestic, imaginative. Here are a dozen examples of phrases we owe to Milton:
—A heaven on earth.
—All hell broke loose.
—All is not lost.
—Fallen on evil days.
—Food of the mind.

—Fresh woods and pastures new.
—Tears such as angels weep.
—Temper justice with mercy.
—The busy hum of men.
—The cricket on the hearth.
—The light fantastic toe.
—Where more is meant than meets the ear.

MINERALOGY
Not *minerology*.

MINIMIZE
Just as the superlative *minimum* means the smallest possible amount or degree, to *minimize* is to reduce to the smallest possible amount or degree. It does not mean "lessen" or "diminish" or "belittle." One minimizes one's chance of an accident by taking every possible precaution. One lessens one's chance of injury in an accident by buckling one's seat belt. And because *minimize* is an absolute, it should not be modified by an adverb of quantity, such as *greatly* or *vastly* or *somewhat*. See also MAJOR.

MINUSCULE
Please note the spelling. More often than not, one sees *minis-*, instead of *minus-*. From the Latin root *minus*, less, *minuscule* means "rather small." The stress is more commonly on the first syllable, not the second. See -CULE.

MIRV
Acronym for <u>m</u>ultiple <u>i</u>ndependently targetable <u>r</u>e-entry <u>v</u>ehicle, a *MIRV* is an intercontinental ballistic missile with several warheads, each of which can be directed to a different target.

MISANTHROPE
One who hates or distrusts mankind, from Greek *misein*, to hate, and *anthropos*, man. *Mankind* refers to all humans, not just male humans. Though there are *miso-* words in English to denote hatred of women, children, marriage, the clergy, God, the Greeks, the French, change, strangers, war, tyranny, mathematics, wisdom, reason, tobacco smoke and dogs, there is no *miso-* word for one who hates men. Such a lack seems to flout equal rights. How about *misandroist?*

Along with *misanthrope*, the most common *miso-* forms are: *misogynist*, one who hates women (*gyne*, woman); *misogamist*, one who hates marriage (*gamos*, marriage); and *misoneist*, one who hates change (*neos*, new).

MISCHIEVOUS
Note the spelling. Because the word is often mispronounced *mischievious*, as if there were an *i* immediately before -*ous*, *mischievous* is often misspelled.

MISLED
If you tend to say to yourself "mizzled" when you read the past tense or past participle of *mislead*, be not chagrined. Apart from its slang meaning of "slink away, get lost quietly" and its dialectal meaning of "rain mistily, drizzle," *mizzle* once had the meaning of "confuse, muddle, mystify, misinform." So if you're mizzled by *misled*, you're merely obsolete.

MISSILE
Note the spelling. It's not *missle*, which one so often sees. And the projectile isn't spelled *missal*, which is a book used at Mass.

MISSPELLING
Perhaps there is no misspelling quite so disconcerting as *mispelling*.

MISTRAL
Words don't always signify what they sound. *Mistral* sounds smooth, warm, misty, but it signifies a violent, cold, dry wind that blows from the north toward Mediterranean France.

MITIGATE, *see* MILITATE / MITIGATE

MIX
Though a legitimate noun, especially in a culinary context, *mix* seems to be replacing *mixture* in bureaucratic and academic jargon, as in "The bill contains a viable mix of inflationary controls and spending incentives" or "The program offers an exciting mix of relevant problem-solving and nontraditional input."

MIXED METAPHOR
A *metaphor* whose succession of implicit comparisons or identifications creates incongruous ideas is called *mixed*. Examples: "When John Dean blew the whistle on Richard Nixon, he drummed up a whole new can of worms on Watergate"; "Carter threw his hat in the ring and took the

Republican elephant by the horns"; "Kansas' slaughter of Nebraska last night was icing on the championship cake as the Jayhawks rubbed salt into the Cornhuskers' second-place wounds."

Striving to flavor their prose with poetic condiments, unseasoned writers salt their language with mixed metaphors and pepper their readers with incongruous images that don't cut the mustard.

MNEMONIC
A memory aid, from Greek *mnemon*, mindful. Note the spelling. Mnemonics come in many forms, from acronyms to pithy phrases to ribald ditties, to help one remember something by association, from car license numbers to the chronological list of U.S. presidents to the husbands of Elizabeth Taylor. A mnemonic, however, is of not much use unless it itself can be remembered. For daylight-saving time, is it "Spring forward, fall back" or "Fall forward, spring back"? Forget it. For a mnemonic that works, see STALACTITE / STALAGMITE.

MOB
Short for Latin *mobile vulgus*, the movable (excitable) common people, the fickle throng.

MOCCASIN
Note the spelling: double *c*, single *s*.

MODE, *see* AVERAGE

MOGUL
Journalese for a person of great wealth or power, as in "Hollywood mogul" or "network mogul."

MOLECULE, *see* –CULE

MOMENTARILY
When used with the future tense, *momentarily* is ambiguous. It means both "for a moment" and "in a moment." "I'll be there momentarily" means both "I'll be there for only a short while" and "I'll be there very soon." Avoid ambiguity; avoid *momentarily*, unless the context is otherwise clear. With the present or past tense, *momentarily* clearly means "for a moment, for only a short while."

MOMENTUM, *see* WENT

MONOLOGOPHOBIA
Synonym for SYNONYMOMANIA.

MOOD
Grammatically, mood is the manner in which a verb is used. English has four moods: indicative, imperative, infinitive, subjunctive.

The only mood that causes trouble for writers is the subjunctive. However, despite the reams that have been written about the subjunctive, for practical purposes all a writer needs to know about the subjunctive is that it should be used to express a condition contrary to fact.

Writers almost automatically, and often unconsciously, use the subjunctive when they express necessity ("It is important that he appear"), wish or prayer ("Hallowed be thy name"), contingency ("He should study lest he flunk"), the report of a command ("He ordered that she be released").

But writers stumble over whether to use *was* or *were* with the first and third person singular when condition is expressed. Follow this principle: If the condition is contrary to fact, use *were*. Thus: "If I were you, I would go" (I am not you); "If he were here, he would kill you" (he is not here). But: "If I was rude, I'm sorry" (I don't know whether I was rude; it may or may not be a fact that I was); "If he was late, it wasn't his fault" (you don't know whether he was late; it's not a condition contrary to fact).

MOOT
As an adjective, *moot*, from Anglo-Saxon *mot*, a meeting or assembly, means arguable, debatable, unresolved. It is mistakenly used to signify that something is beyond argument, that there is no point in arguing the question, except in the technical legal sense that something moot is something previously decided.

MORATORIUM
The word denotes delay, not death. *Moratorium* derives from Latin *morari*, to delay, not *mors*, death. To declare a moratorium on something is to authorize a delay or suspension of action, not a permanent ban.

MORE HONORED IN THE BREACH
Some critics seem to know more about an author's intentions and symbolism than the author himself. Shakespeare would be amazed at some

of the interpretations of some of his lines. When Hamlet tells Horatio that Claudius' drunken revelry is a custom "more honour'd in the breach than the observance," he is saying that sometimes it is more honorable to break an old-established custom than to observe it. Hamlet is not saying that the custom is more frequently broken than observed, which is the interpretation erroneously given the phrase by the unwitting, as can be seen from their context. See also MANNER BORN.

MORE IMPORTANTLY

The American Heritage experts are evenly split on the admissibility of *more importantly* in this kind of construction: "He set a record for most points in a championship game; more importantly, his team won the championship." Those who accept *more importantly* say it is idiomatic. It certainly isn't grammatical. In the example, the adverb *importantly* has nothing suitable to modify. Make it *more important*. The writer is saying that the championship was more important (adjective) than the record. Spelled out, the construction would be "what is more important, his team won the championship," wherein the adjective *important* qualifies *what*.

MORE IN SORROW

More Hamlet. Add "than in anger" and you have another cliché from a once fresh descriptive phrase. "What, look'd he frowningly?" Hamlet asks about the visage of his father's ghost. Horatio responds: "A countenance more in sorrow than in anger." The phrase is now used to describe the gamut of human behavior from a father's castigation of his child to a president's acceptance of an aide's resignation. Its nobility has been lost.

MORE PREFERABLE

Redundant. That which is *preferable* has already the connotation of *more*.

MORE THAN / OVER

In the sense of collective quantity, some authorities allow *over* instead of *more than*, as in "He earned over $30,000 last year" or "He weighed over 200 pounds." With countables, however, *more than* is better usage than *over*, as in "More than 10,000 people attended" or "The tornado destroyed more than 200 buildings." See also UNDER.

MORE THAN ONE, *see* ALL BUT ONE

MORGANATIC

Once upon a time, a nobleman customarily gave his wife a token gift the morning after their wedding. It was called "the morning gift." If, however, his wife was not of the nobility, that was her only dower; neither she nor their children acquired his rank or shared in his estate. A marriage between a man or woman of noble birth and a mate of lower rank is called *morganatic*, from Old High German *morgengeba*, morning gift, through Medieval Latin *matrimonium ad morganaticum*, marriage for (nothing but) the morning gift.

MORMON

Note the capitalization and hyphenation of *Latter-day* in the official title of the Mormon Church: Church of Jesus Christ of Latter-day Saints. Strictly, the term *Mormon* should not be applied to the other churches that resulted from the factional disputes after the death of Joseph Smith, founder of the Mormon Church. And note the spelling of the largest of these: Reorganized Church of Jesus Christ of Latter Day Saints.

MORNING GLORY

A vine whose flowers close late in the day, a *morning glory* is also a race-horse that is speedy in the morning workout but slow in the afternoon race, like an athlete who leaves his form on the practice field or driving range.

MORON

From Greek *moros*, dull, sluggish, foolish. See OXYMORON.

MORPHEUS

In the CLICHÉ entry, the cliché expert wanted to "fall into the arms of Morpheus." He should have known that Morpheus' father, Hypnos, not Morpheus, was the god of sleep. Only if the sleeper is dreaming is he "in the arms of Morpheus," the god of dreams and their shaper (Greek *morphe*, form, shape).

MOST

As an abbreviation for *almost*, *most* is deemed unacceptable in writing by 92 percent of the American Heritage usage panelists; in speech, it is deemed unacceptable by 53 percent. Why not write and say *almost?*

MOTHER-IN-LAW

Plural mothers-in-law. For mother-outlaw, see DAUGHTER-IN-LAW.

MOTHER'S DAY
Note the apostrophe and its position.

MPG / MPH
AP abbreviates "miles per gallon" and "miles per hour" without periods, *mpg* and *mph*.

MUCHLY
A barbarous adverbial affectation for *much*. Adverbs don't have to end in *-ly*. See also OVERLY and THUSLY.

MUGWUMP
From Algonquian *mugquomp*, big chief, great man, *mugwump* came into popular use during the 1884 presidential campaign as a term of opprobrium for Republicans who, according to the followers of the party candidate, James G. Blaine, were too high and mighty to support him and bolted the party to vote for Grover Cleveland. *Mugwump* has since come to signify any political independent, a political fence sitter with his mug on one side and his wump on the other.

MULTITUDINOUS, *see* INCARNADINE

MUMMY
The origin of this term for an embalmed body has nothing to do with *mother*. *Mummy* is from Persian *mum*, wax.

MUMPSIMUS
A young priest once corrected an old priest for saying *mumpsimus* instead of *sumpsimus* ("we have received") in the first prayer after Communion in the Latin Mass. "Son," said the old priest, "I've been saying *mumpsimus* for thirty years and I'm not going to change my old *mumpsimus* for your new *sumpsimus*."

Though rarely heard these days, *mumpsimus* has been in the language for more than four hundred years. It means: (1) an error, usually caused by ignorance, long embedded in language or in life; (2) obstinate adherence to the error after correction; and (3) a person who insists on perpetuating the error.

Mumpsimus, says Jacobs, is "a much needed word to describe an unlovely trait in human nature which, because of the force of habit or the sin of pride, resents the intimation that the first impression we form stands in need of revision." Jacobs regrets that *mumpsimus* is no longer in common use. Amen.

MURPHY'S LAWS
There are three:
1. Nothing is as easy as it looks.
2. Everything will take longer than you think it will.
3. If anything can go wrong, it will.

Nobody is sure who Murphy was. Morris reports this suggestion from a correspondent: "One day a teacher named Murphy wanted to demonstrate the laws of probability to his math class. He had thirty of his students spread peanut butter on slices of bread, then toss the bread into the air to see if half would fall on the dry side and half on the buttered side. As it turned out, twenty-nine of the slices landed peanut-butter side on the floor, while the thirtieth stuck to the ceiling."

Another of Morris' correspondents, unsure about Murphy's beginning, was sure about his end: "Murphy took a stroll along a country road one evening, being careful to walk on the left side of the road to face approaching traffic. He was struck and killed by an English driver who had just arrived in this country."

MUSCLE
When you "make a muscle," your arm ripples like a scurrying mouse. *Muscle* comes from Latin *musculus*, diminutive of *mus*, mouse, as does *mussel*, the shellfish, from its mouselike shape.

MUSICAL SCALE, *see* GAMUT

MUTUAL
If Jack is a friend of Jim and Joe, and Jim is a friend of Joe, then all three are mutual friends. If Jack is a friend of Jim and Joe, but Jim is not a friend of Joe, then Jim and Joe have a common friend in Jack.

The distinction is thin and hardly being preserved by usage. The point is that *mutual* strictly applies to something that two persons represent to each other or that more than two persons represent to one another. Dickens' *Our Mutual Friend* belies this, but the looser meaning of *mutual* was then common. Certainly, Dickens' title has not helped the strict interpretation of *mutual*.

Also, if two or more persons share an interest, they have a *common* interest, not a *mutual* interest; the interest is not a member of the group

Note, too, the redundancy of *mutual* with words such as *cooperation*, *collaboration*, *teamwork*.

MYRMIDON
The original Myrmidons were members of a warrior tribe who fought loyally with Achilles in the Trojan War. A modern *myrmidon* is one who blindly executes his leader's orders, possibly because in childhood he was taught to do what his myrmidon told him.

MYSELF
Overused, especially in speech, by the timid who need a case study of the difference between *I* and *me*. Says Red Smith, sports columnist and American Heritage usage panelist, *myself* is "the refuge of idiots taught early that *me* is a dirty word." See **PRONOUN**.

NAIVE
The feminine of the French adjective *naïf*, ingenuous, unaffected, is spelled *naive* in English, without the dieresis. The masculine *naif* is sometimes seen but it is somewhat affected.

NAME OF THE GAME
A cliché, as in "Money is the name of the game." Worse: "Babbitt is my name and real estate is my game."

NAMEPLATE, *see* EAR

NAPKIN
An American *napkin* is a British serviette. A British *napkin* is an American diaper.

NARCOLEPSY, *see* –LEPSY

NARY
Usually followed by *a* or *an*, *nary* sounds phony and studiedly quaint except on provincial lips.

NATION, *see* COUNTRY / NATION

NAUSEATED / NAUSEOUS
Just as one is poisoned by something poisonous, one is nauseated by something nauseous. One feels *nauseated*, not *nauseous*. The origin is Greek *naus*, ship, whence *nausia*, seasickness (English spelling *nausea*). See also AD NAUSEAM.

NAVEL
The orange is navel, because of the umbilical notch on its apex, not *naval*. A navel surgeon is the ultimate in specialized medicine.

N.B.
Abbreviation for Latin *nota bene*, note well.

NEARLY, *see* **ALMOST / NEARLY**

NEAR-RECORD
One can't set a near-record, any more than one can score a near-victory. One may nearly set a record or nearly score a victory. The time was near the record. The losing margin was small.

NEAT
Tot talk applies *neat* to almost everything, from acid to zippers, and is causing the word to lose its pristine meanings. See COOL and GAY.

NECESSARY, *see* **ESSENTIAL / NECESSARY**

NECRO–
A combining form for "death" or "the dead," from Greek *nekros*, corpse, as in: *necrology*, a list of the dead; *necromancy*, forecasting through supposed communication with the dead (*manteia*, divination)—formerly spelled *nigromancy*, whence black magic; *necrophilia*, abnormal attraction to dead bodies; *necrophobia*, morbid fear of death or horror of dead bodies; *necropolis*, a cemetery, especially a large one; *necropsy*, a post-mortem examination, autopsy (*opsis*, sight); *necrosis*, death of tissue.

NEE
The feminine past participle of French *naître*, to be born, *née* is used in English, usually without the acute accent, when a married woman's maiden name is added, as in "Mrs. Mary McCue, nee Barden." But not "Mrs. Mary McCue, nee Mary Barden"; she was born with her family name, not her given name.

NEEDLESS TO SAY
So why say it?

NEEDS NO INTRODUCTION
But you can bet he'll get a long one.

NEITHER, *see* **EITHER**

NEMESIS
Strictly, the word means an avenger or the act of vengeance, from Nemesis, the goddess of retributive justice. Loosely, however, *nemesis* has

come to mean enemy or traditional conqueror, especially in sportsese and usually preceded by *old*. Worse, it is sometimes applied to a thing or an event, such as a downfall, as in "Waterloo was Napoleon's nemesis."

NEPOTISM
The hiring or patronage, by reason of relationship rather than talent, of family members or close friends or good ol' boys, with an invitation to dine at the public trough or dig into the pork barrel. From Latin *nepos*, nephew.

NERVE-RACKING
If one's nerves are stretched almost to breaking point, the experience is *nerve-racking*, not *nerve-wracking*. To *rack* is to torture, to stretch upon a rack or wheel. To *wrack* is to wreck, to cause the ruin of. Authoritative dictionaries, however, allow *nerve-wracking* as a variant of *nerve-racking*.

NETWORK
Lexicographers sometimes have to resort to long words to define a short one. Samuel Johnson defined *network* as "anything reticulated or decussated, at equal distances, with interstices between the intersections," which maybe explains why we sometimes get ticked off at the TV networks and occasionally cuss them, especially for their too frequent commercial interstices.

NEW INNOVATION, *see* INNOVATION

NEW RECORD
In "He set a new record," *new* and *record* are redundant. The setting of a record is the setting of something new. He set a record. He broke a record.

NEWS JUDGMENT
The instinct that comes with widsom and experience and helps an editor decide how to choose and organize and play a story, news judgment is an instinct bred of things remembered and things half-forgotten. It can't be learned in courses such as Wisdom I, Maturity I, or Judgment I. Everything that an editor has learned, no matter how seemingly trivial, everything that he has experienced, everything that he is, all combine to develop news judgment, an editor's most important trait.

NEWSSTAND
Note the spelling: double *s*.

NEWT, *see* **ADDER**

NICKEL
Note the spelling. Not *nickle*, as in *pickle*. Your ma gave you a nickel to buy a pickle.

NICKNAME, *see* **ADDER**

NINETEEN AND EIGHTY
A provincialism for the year 1980. Drop *and* when you use words for the number of a year unless you include *hundred*.

9W, *see* **SAD HUMOR**

NITE
The word, said a writer in the 1930s, "connotes speakeasies, gin, cheapness and vulgarity," whereas *night* "suggests quiet, rest and beauty." Whatever, *nite* is an abomination.

NOBLESSE OBLIGE
This French phrase has long been standard in English and loosely translates to "Rank has its responsibility."

NO DOUBT, *see* **DOUBTLESSLY / UNDOUBTEDLY**

NOM DE PLUME
Straight French for pen name. So why not say *pen name?*

-NOMY
Many English words derive from Greek *nomos*, law. For example:
  —*anomie*, no law, lawlessness, societal collapse for want of law enforcement, alienation from society of an individual or group.
  —*astronomy*, the laws of the stars, the study of the universe beyond the earth.
  —*autonomy*, self-government, self-determination, independence.
  —*Deuteronomy*, the second statement of the law; see DEUTERO-.

—*metronome*, an instrument that marks time at exact intervals, especially in music, thus ruling the performer.

—*taxonomy*, the laws or principles of classification or arrangement (*taxis*).

NONCHALANT
From French *nonchaloir*, to be unconcerned, from the negative of Latin *calere*, to be warm; hence cool, standoffish, casually but carefully sophisticated.

NONE
Singular or plural? Grammarians disagree. According to 28 percent of the American Heritage experts, *none* must always take a singular verb. According to 68 percent (none of the remaining 4 percent has or have been heard from), *none* may take a singular verb or a plural verb, depending on the context.

Perhaps the best course is to treat *none* as singular when *no one* or *not one* can be substituted for *none*, as in "None of them is a genius" or "None of these stories has been verified." Also, even when *no one* or *not one* cannot be substituted, *none* must be singular when followed by a noun totally singular in context, as in "None of the furniture was secondhand."

When, however, the following noun is plural and can hardly be construed as having a singular form in the context, treat *none* as plural, as in "None of the clothes were secondhand." Sometimes, too, when rewriting would be strained, the context calls for plural number, as in "None were more miserable after the play failed than the now jobless actors."

NONRESTRICTIVE, *see* THAT / WHICH

NON SEQUITUR
When a writer tries to weave biographical material into a story, he sometimes weaves irrelevantly, joins unjoinables and commits a non sequitur (Latin, "it does not follow"). For example:

"A graduate of the University of Kentucky, he traveled extensively in the Far East." There is no relationship.

"A native of Brownsville, Texas, he devoted most of his life to mountaineering." If *mountaineering* were *U.S.-Mexican problems*, the construction would make sense.

"The spelling bee was won by Claudia Rowe, whose parents taught her to scuba dive when she was only two years old." Read *read* for *scuba dive*.

"The accident occurred when he pulled away from the side of the road, glanced at his mother-in-law in the back seat and headed over the embankment." No comment. See **BORN IN WAUKEGAN**.

NOR
Use *nor* only to correlate with *neither* or to introduce a negative clause connected to a previous negative clause, as in "He has never learned a foreign language, nor will he make the effort to learn one" (note the inversion of the subject and verb after *nor* by the insertion of the subject between the auxiliary and the verb). *Nor* is the equivalent of *and not*. See also **EITHER**.

NO RESPECTER OF PERSONS
A divine cliché for one who treats everybody alike, from Acts, wherein Peter says God is "not a respecter of persons."

NORMALCY
Fowler calls *normalcy* a "spurious hybrid" for *normality*. Its coinage is mistakenly attributed to Warren Harding, who said in a 1920 campaign speech that what this country needed was "not nostrums, but normalcy." Harding no more invented *normalcy* than did Woodrow Wilson's vice president, Thomas R. Marshall, invent the 5-cent cigar, or Herbert Hoover the chicken in the pot. *Normalcy* was coined long before Harding, but his opponents gave it popular currency as political capital. Its use is disapproved by 59 percent of the American Heritage experts as a needless alternative to *normality*.

NO SINECURE
A sinecure was an ecclesiastical benefice that paid a lot for little or no work (Latin *sine cura*, without care of souls). *No sinecure* is now a cliché for a demanding assignment.

NO SOONER, *see* HARDLY

NOSTALGIA
The pain of longing to return home, from Greek *nostos*, a return home, and *algos*, pain, hence homesickness, a yearning for times or things past or absent. Ulysses had it bad, said Homer.

NOSTRUM

A secret medicine, usually quack, or a pet scheme, usually social (Latin *nostrum*, neuter singular of *noster*, our, our own, hence invented by us and known to us only). *Nostrum* is not interchangeable with *panacea* (see PAN-).

NO SUBJECT

Like the story it is supposed to summarize, a news headline should be in sentence form. It should have a subject and a verb. A story under a no-subject head is like a restaurant check: to get thè bad news, as A. J. Liebling said in *The Press*, you have to read from the bottom up. "Throws Girl in River" is a famous example. Who threw her in?

No-subject heads are sometimes called verb heads because they begin with a verb. As column measure has widened and horizontal makeup become more popular, head counts have loosened and verb heads are fewer. Some large metropolitan newspapers, however, still use them abundantly: "Plans Trip to Europe," "Tells HEW to Mind Own Business," "Kills Three in Bank Heist."

One large metropolitan paper uses a quaint no-subject device as a head for stories of promotion or advancement, such as this Associated Press story out of Vatican City: "Pope Paul VI has named Arturo Tabera Araoz, archbishop of Pamplona, Spain, to head the Vatican Congregation of Rites, the Vatican announced yesterday."

The head said: "Up at Vatican."

Who's up? What's up? Who's on first?

NOTED, *see* LOADED VERB

NOT ONLY

The "not only . . . but also" construction should follow the principles of PARALLELISM. *Not only* should appear before the same part of speech as *but also*. For example:

(NOUN): "To reach the finals, Wade had to beat not only King but also Navratilova."

(VERB): "He not only learned but also put into practice what he learned."

(ADJECTIVE): "He was not only listless but also undernourished."

(PREPOSITION): "A good editor is concerned not only with style but also with content."

(CONJUNCTION): "He got angry not only when his students cut class but also when they came unprepared."

Note, however, that the "not only . . . but also" construction should be reserved for contexts of emphasis or delayed effect. Sometimes *and* suffices. If emphasis or delayed effect had not been sought in the examples, *and* would have sufficed.

NOTRE DAME
Though no authority on language, Emily Post, "the unchallenged arbiter of elegance in the United States," as Mencken called her, decreed almost a half-century ago that French words that had "already been Americanized" should be turned into "plain English." Thus French *menu* becomes English *men-you*, and the *t* is sounded in *valet*. "Certainly," she said, "it is in much better taste to call our American college *Noter Dayme* than to pronounce it as French, and yet we would (and should) say *Notrr Damme* when we mean the cathedral in Paris."

NOT TOO, *see* TOO

NOUN
From Latin *nomen*, name, a noun is the name of anything: animate or inanimate object, place, act, quality, idea. Nouns are usually classified into common (*person, animal, tree, refrigerator, town, song, beauty, thought*) and proper (*Alice, Seattle Slew, Judas, Frigidaire, London, Marseillaise, La Gioconda, Aristotelianism*). Nouns are further classified into concrete (*tree, refrigerator*) and abstract (*beauty, thought*). A collective noun denotes a group of beings or things of the same kind (*class, team, family, club, congregation*); see AGREEMENT OF SUBJECT AND PREDICATE for the use of collective nouns with verbs.

Many nouns may also be used as adjectives, especially when no suitable adjective exists: *car insurance, university education, television set.* News headlines have spread this practice. But one should be careful not to pile up a heap of nouns as adjectives: "the Los Angeles area air pollution prevention pilot program."

Note, however, that the use of a noun as an adjective is sometimes necessary even when the noun has an adjectival form: an education meeting is not necessarily educational; and a sports editor may not be sporting, or even sporty or sportive.

For the use of nouns as verbs, see VERBING NOUNS.

NOUN-HYPHEN-PARTICIPLE
Ugly is the word for this adjectival monstrosity: "a science-oriented student," "a virus-caused disease," "a community-sponsored project," "an

environment-related problem." And sloppy is the word for the wallower in this mess. Whoever perpetuates this jargon has declared war on the prepositional phrase. Why not "a student interested in science," "a disease caused by a virus," "a project sponsored by the community," "a problem related to the environment"?

Our language is English, not German. As Bernstein said in *Winners & Sinners*, "The German language has a peculiar way of agglutinating heaps of words into a sticky adjectival mass so that what you occasionally get is something like 'die überdieganzeverrücktecockeyedweltgespreadet hipchen movement.'"

Avoid the contrived combination of noun-hyphen-participle. See also ORIENTED.

NOUNING VERBS, *see* VERBING NOUNS

NO VERB

The missing link in the historical evolution of the American news headline is a verb. The old captions and titles were mere labels. They had no verb. What makes a news head a news head is a verb.

Who on reading the head "Glow on Mideast" in a prestigious American daily would know what the story was about, except possibly that it was the announcement of a second Bethlehem? The story concerned the optimism of a politician on his return from talks in the Mideast. In the same paper, what does "On with Bombs" tell the reader? He might want to add, "Let joy be unconfined," but the story concerned a renewal of the Christian crusades in Northern Ireland. And in the spirit of "Up at Vatican" (see NO SUBJECT) the paper ran the head "McGillycuddy to Helm," which meant that a Mr. McGillycuddy had climbed to the top of a corporate ladder, but the head sounded as if he had been chosen to man a tiller in the AMERICA'S CUP.

The present tense of the verb *to be* may usually be omitted in a headline because its presence is implied or understood: for example, in the active voice, "City Manager Unhappy with Council"; or in the passive voice, "City Manager Fired." On account of ambiguity, however, *is* or *are* sometimes should not be omitted: for example, "Rebels Say Hostages Well." *Well* is a versatile word. It can be noun, verb, adjective, adverb. One can imagine those rebels resonantly articulating *hostages*. Similarly, the omission of *is* or *are* can lead to this kind of ambiguity: "Egypt Maintains / Terrorists Killed." Were the terrorists the murderers or the victims?

NOVICE, *see* AMATEUR / NOVICE

NUCLEAR
From Latin *nux* (genitive *nucis*), nut, kernel. President Eisenhower had trouble pronouncing *nuclear*. Others still do. It's *new-klee-ar*, not *new-cue-lar*. Stress the first syllable.

NUMBER, *see* AGREEMENT OF SUBJECT AND PREDICATE; A NUMBER

NUNC DIMITTIS
The Latin title of the song of Simeon ("Now thou dost dismiss"), from its first words. Long promised that he would not die until he had seen "the Christ of the Lord," old Simeon held the infant Christ in his arms and sang with joy his "Nunc Dimittis." The words, lowercase, have become an English phrase for permission to depart, usually after a long and satisfying career.

NYMPHOLEPSY, *see* –LEPSY

NYMPHOMANIA
From Greek *nymphe*, a bride, *nymphomania* is abnormal and uncontrollable sexual desire in women. Its male equivalent is *satyriasis*, from *satyr*.

O / OH
When you cry, "O Alice, I love you," you are formally addressing your beloved and formally proclaiming that you love her. When you cry, "Oh, Alice, I love you," you are merely exclaiming that you love her. Note that *O* is not immediately followed by any punctuation mark, whereas *Oh* (or *oh*) is. *O* is always capitalized, whereas *oh* is capitalized only when it is the first word of a sentence.

OBESE
Except in medical usage, *obese* is often a euphemism for *fat*. The word derives from Latin *ob* + *edere*, to eat away, devour.

OBIT
Newspaper abbreviation for obituary, from Latin *obiit*, he went away, he died.

OBITER DICTUM
An incidental, non-binding opinion uttered by a judge, or any incidental remark (Latin for "said in passing").

OBJET D'ART
Drive around the United States and you'll see makeshift signs proclaiming "Objects d'Art" and "Objects d'Arts" and even "Objects Darts," often near wayside "Souvenier" stands. French *objet d'art*, an article of artistic worth, has become English and is so spelled in English. Its plural is *objets d'art*.

OBLIGATE / OBLIGE
Except in its legal sense of binding, why use *obligate?* What does it say that *oblige* doesn't. More than fifty years ago, George Bernard Shaw was quoted in the London *Times* as saying: "When President Wilson came to this country he gave us a shock by using the word *obligate* instead of *oblige*. It showed that a man could become President in spite of that, and we asked ourselves if a man could become King of England if

he used the word *obligate*. We said at once that it could not be done." A man can become president of the United States in spite of a lot of quirks, linguistic and other, but Americans are not obliged, thank God, to adopt his style of speech.

OBOE
Italian, from French *hautbois* (whence derives its English pronunciation), high wood, a wind whose critics say nobody blows good.

OBSTETRICS
Latin *obstetrix*, a midwife, from *ob* + *stare*, to stand before.

OBVIOUS, *see* APPARENT

OCARINA
Diminutive of Italian *oca*, goose, so called because the instrument, the "sweet potato," is shaped like the head of a goose.

OCCASION
Note the spelling: only one *s*.

OCCURRED
Note the spelling: double *r*; also in *occurrence*. See also ALLOTTED.

OCULIST, *see* OPHTHALMOLOGIST / OPTICIAN / OPTOMETRIST

ODDLY ENOUGH
Why *enough?* And why signal the coming oddity?

ODOMETER
From Greek *hodos*, way, road, journey, and *metron*, measure, an *odometer* is an instrument for measuring distance traveled. Other words from *hodos* are: *anode*, a way up (from the positive pole into the electrolyte) (*ana*, up); *cathode*, a way down (opposite of *anode*) (*kata*, down); *episode*, on the way (*epi*, on, besides); *exodus*, a way out (*ex*, out); *method*, a way after, a way of doing something (*meta*, after); *period*, a way round, a going round, an ending (*peri*, round, about); *synod*, a way together, a meeting (*syn*, with).

ODOR, *see* AROMA

OF COURSE

Sometimes the phrase helps the flow of a sentence and sometimes it helps emphasis, but one should avoid *of course* when it implies the intellectual pride of informing a reader that he should know that the writer knows that what is being said is well known, of course.

OFFENSE, *see* DEFENSE

OFF OF

A barbarism. One doesn't fall off of a horse. Drop the *of*.

OH, *see* O / OH

OK

The origin is vigorously disputed. Read Mencken on the subject if you want to know more than you need to know about how *OK* entered the language. It is certainly embedded in the language and no amount of fossilizing will uproot it. AP drops the periods in all forms of *OK* (*OK'd*, *OK'ing*, *OK's*) and rejects *okay* and its forms.

OLDER, *see* ELDER / OLDER

OLDSTER

Though they accept *youngster* as acceptable, some authorities reject *oldster* as depreciatory. Some prefer *senior citizen* because they think it has a touch of dignity; others think it is a stuffy euphemism.

OLIGARCHY

Government in which power lies with only a few or a small faction, from Greek *oligos*, few, little, and *archein*, to be first, to rule.

OMNIUM-GATHERUM

Dog Latin for a strange mixture of many things, from *omnium* (genitive plural of *omnis*, all) and *gather*.

OMPHALOPSYCHITES

Mencken's word for those who dream of bringing American English into line with English English. *Omphalos* is Greek for *navel*, whence also *omphaloskeptic*, one who dreams up bright ideas while gazing at (*skepsis*, a looking at) his navel.

ON
The preposition is usually dropped before a day or date, as in "The final show will be performed Monday" or "Registration will start Aug. 23." To avoid ambiguity, however, use *on* between proper nouns, as in "He married Mary on Monday" (she wasn't Mary Monday).

ONE ANOTHER, *see* EACH OTHER / ONE ANOTHER

ONE OF THE MEN WHO, *see* ANTECEDENT

ONGOING
Why not *continuing*? *Ongoing* is a faddish word, especially with *dialogue*. Newman says, "It is impossible to calculate how many academic and government careers have been preserved and furthered by the devising of *ongoing*, or the amount of foundation money shaken loose." U.S. presidents, he says, love what they consider an ongoing dialogue because it enables them to "communicate with the people," but at the end of a presidential press conference the ongoing dialogue "ceases on to go," and in President Johnson's administration "a dialogue never onwent; a monologue onwent."

ONLY
Generally, the modifier *only* should be as close as possible to the word, phrase or clause modified, preferably in front of it. "He had only two drinks," not "He only had two drinks"; "She stayed only an hour," not "She only stayed an hour"; "He has eggs for breakfast only on vacation," not "He only has eggs for breakfast on vacation" (but he may have only eggs for breakfast or he may have eggs only for breakfast). If you have nothing else to do, take the sentence "Only John and his wife eat lunch in the middle of the day" and move *only* to different positions to get different meanings.

Sometimes, however, idiom calls for a departure from this general principle. For example, "It can only be considered foolish" is smoother, less strained, than "It can be considered only foolish"; similarly, "I can only say that I think you're acting foolishly" is more natural than "I can say only that I think you're acting foolishly."

Songwriters may do as they please. "I have eyes only for you" wouldn't sound quite the same as "I only have eyes for you" and would only foul up the meter.

ONOMATOPOEIA

The formation of words that sound like their meaning, from Greek *onoma*, name, and *poiein*, to make, hence to make a name, such as *burp*, *buzz*, *cuckoo*, *fizz*, *whippoorwill*. Rhetorically, *onomatopoeia* is a device for conveying sense through sound, as suggested by Alexander Pope in his *Essay on Criticism:* "The sound must seem an echo to the sense." In unartistic hands, sustained onomatopoeia becomes banal, boring. The adjective is either *onomatopoeic* or *onomatopoetic*.

OP ED

In newspaper lingo, the *op ed* page is the page opposite the editorial page. It contains opinion columns (ideally of differing stance), letters to the editor, political and social cartoons. Again ideally, the op ed page, like the editorial page, should have no ads, but such virtuous detachment is not so common as it should be.

OPHTHALMOLOGIST / OPTICIAN / OPTOMETRIST

An *ophthalmologist* (Greek *ophthalmos*, eye) or oculist (Latin *oculus*, eye) is a doctor of medicine who specializes in diseases of the eye. An *optician* (Greek *optos*, visible) makes eye glasses from an ophthalmologist's or optometrist's prescription or sells optical goods. An *optometrist* (*optos*) tests eyes and prescribes lenses.

OPINE

A somewhat stilted synonym for "to hold or state an opinion, to think, to suppose."

OPISTHOGNATHOUS

One who has receding jaws is opisthognathous, from Greek *opisthen*, behind, and *gnathos*, jaw. The opposite is *prognathous*, having projecting jaws. Jaws just right are *orthognathous*. Incidentally, if you write on both sides of a sheet of paper, you're practicing both economy and opisthography.

OPSIMATH

One who learns late in life is an *opsimath*, from Greek *opse*, late, and *manthanein*, to learn. His education is opsimathy.

OPTICIAN, *see* OPHTHALMOLOGIST / OPTICIAN / OPTOMETRIST

OPTIMISTIC / OPTIMUM
Note the spelling of *optimistic*. It's not *optomistic*, which one often sees. The root has nothing to do with eyes. The word comes from Latin *optimus*, the best. And an optimum number is not the most, but the best, the most favorable under the circumstances.

OPTOMETRIST, *see* OPHTHALMOLOGIST / OPTICIAN / OPTOMETRIST

ORAL / VERBAL
Strictly, what is spoken is either oral or verbal. What is written is verbal, not oral. *Verbal* comes from Latin *verbum*, word, and *oral* comes from *os* (genitive *oris*), mouth. However, something agreed to in conversation, not on paper, is best described as an oral agreement; and something agreed to on paper is best described as a written agreement.

ORCHESTRA
The word comes from Greek *orcheisthai*, to dance, and originally referred to the semicircle on which the chorus of dancers performed in front of the stage in the ancient Greek theaters.

ORCHESTRATE
The word has gone beyond the composition or arrangement of music and has become a faddish word for the composition or arrangement of almost anything. A lobbyist orchestrates a scenario for a legislative group (he exerts or peddles influence, he manipulates). A coach orchestrates his game plan (he tells his players what he wants them to do). "Before long," says Nickles, "a gifted mechanic may orchestrate an engine instead of giving it a tune-up."

ORCHID
When a beau gives his belle an orchid for the junior prom, his ultimate intentions may or may not be honorable but you can bet neither knows the etymology of the flower: Greek *orchis*, testicle (from the shape of the plant's tuber). See also AVOCADO.

ORDINANCE / ORDNANCE
Both words come from Latin *ordo*, order, law, regulation, custom, but *ordnance* is a military term for weaponry, originally "the ordering of supplies."

ORGY
Soft *g*. See also AGAPE.

ORIENTED
Most American institutions of higher learning set aside an "orientation" period for new students, presumably to point them toward the east. Why not *occidentation* (west) or *meridionalization* (south) or *septentrionalization* (north), all equally ugly words? Or why not *adaptation* or *adjustment* or *introduction* or *settle-down* or *settle-in* or simply *welcome?*

After the orientation period, the student is expected to be campus-oriented and education-oriented and study-oriented in general, then specifically science-oriented or humanities-oriented or engineering-oriented or communications-oriented or human-development-and-family-life-oriented or Oriental-studies-oriented or whatever-oriented. No one any more, it seems, studies something or likes something or works at something or is interested in something or wants to be something. He is something-oriented. See also NOUN-HYPHEN-PARTICIPLE.

ORTHO-
Among the dozens of English words from Greek *orthos*, straight, right, correct, proper, are these: *orthodontist*, one who straightens teeth (*odon*, tooth); *orthodoxy*, right opinion (*doxa*)—orthodoxy is your doxy—heterodoxy is someone else's; *orthoepy*, the study of correct pronunciation (*epos*, word); *orthography*, the study of correct spelling (*graphein*, to write); *orthopedist*, a bone surgeon, one who prevents or corrects deformities, originally of children (*pais*, genitive *paidos*, child).

OSTRACIZE
To banish or exclude from social intercourse, from Greek *ostrakon*, tile, shell, piece of pottery on which Athenians wrote the names of those they voted to banish from the state for undemocratic behavior. See also COVENTRY.

OTHER THREE / THREE OTHERS
Five persons are present. Two are Italian and the three others French. Along comes another Italian. Now three are Italian and the other three

French. You cannot have "other three" (or any other number) unless you previously have "a three" (or the same number).

OUGHT / SHOULD
Whatever distinction used to exist between *ought* and *should* has been lost in American usage. Because *ought* is the old past tense of *owe*, some authorities thought *ought* should be used in the context of debt or obligation. But so ought *should*.

OUIJA
Trademark for the flimflam board, from the French and German words for *yes*. Pronounced either *wee-ja* or *wee-jee*.

OUT, *see* WANT IN

OUTSTANDING
Even fifty years ago, the word was overworked. "*Outstanding*," said Mencken, "began its career among the pedagogues, and they still overwork it cruelly, but it is now also used by politicians, the rev. clergy, newspaper editorial writers, and other such virtuosi of bad writing."

OVATION / TRIUMPH
An *ovation* is rarely seen or heard today unless preceded by *standing*, which is seen and heard too often, for every feat from dunking a basketball to being introduced at a meeting. From Latin *ovare*, to rejoice, exult, an ovation was granted a Roman consul for a victory less important than that for which a *triumph* was granted. For a triumph, a general entered Rome and was driven to the Capitol in a car drawn by white horses; for a little old ovation, sitting or standing, he either rode a horse or walked.

OVER, *see* MORE THAN / OVER

OVERALL
A 1943 dispatch from Washington had this to say about *overall*: "Of all Washington words, *over-all* [now usually spelled without hyphen] is the most habit-forming. Talk long enough to enough government officials, and you'll find yourself telling the little woman that she overcooked the Brussels sprouts, but that the *over-all* impact of the dinner was not bad."

The "impact" of *overall* is still with us and it's bad, monotonously bad. In such phrases as "the overall amount," "the overall returns," "his overall attitude," "the effect, overall," *overall* seeks to drive out more appropriate words such as *total*, *complete*, *general*, (*on the*) *whole*. Other victims of *overall* are *aggregate*, *average*, *comprehensive*, *inclusive*, *net*, *overriding*, *supreme*.

Overall should be restricted to the physical ("the overall measurements of the house, including attic, balconies and garage"). As Nickles says, "Should all the *overalls* in use today wind up in Mrs. Murphy's chowder, only her reputation as a cook would suffer."

OVERCROWDING
News headlines are supposed to be attractive. Overcrowding is slummy. Slums are repulsive.

A line in a head gets overcrowded when a copy editor tries to squeeze too many letters into it and does not give them breathing space. He should grant each group of letters a little space between one another for family privacy. Good fences make good neighbors. Some editors there are that do not love a wall.

When a headline writer forces a compositor to use tight spaces to set an overcrowded head, the result can be something like this: "Man Should Work for Common Goo" or "Billy Graham Revival / To Attract Large Crow."

OVERLY
Though 60 percent of its usage panelists accept *overly*, the American Heritage points out that the sense of *overly* is "expressed more concisely, and just as properly," by the hundreds of adjectives and adverbs formed with *over-*, such as *overabundant*, *overactive*, *overattentively*, *overcarefully*. Users of *overly*, says Barzun, "seek a fancied correctness," as if all adverbs had to end in *-ly*. See also MUCHLY and THUSLY.

OXYMORON
From Greek *oxys*, sharp, and *moros*, dull, foolish, an *oxymoron* is a rhetorical device that combines seeming contradictories in one word or phrase, such as *bittersweet*, *chiaroscuro*, *sophomore*, *cruel kindness*, *happy fault*, *sweet misery* (of life, at last I've found thee).

P

PACE
The ablative case of Latin *pax*, peace, *pace* (pronounced either *pay-say* or *pah-chay;* stress the first syllable) means "with all due respect to" and is used to introduce a contrary opinion, as in "'Pace Your Holiness, but I still say it moves,' declared Galileo."

PACHYDERM
A large, thick-skinned, hoofed animal, such as the elephant or hippopotamus, or rhinoceros, and by extension a thick-skinned, insensitive person, from Greek *pachys*, thick, and *derma*, skin.

PACT
An all-purpose word, beloved of headline writers, for *accord, agreement, bargain, compact, contract, deal, treaty, truce*. See also HEADLINESE and INK.

PAIR
The word takes a singular verb in a context of oneness, as in "A pair of scissors is a handy tool," and a plural verb in a context of individual separateness, as in "A pair of skunks have invaded our basement." The use of *pair* after a plural numeral, as in "three pair of trousers," smacks of the archaic. Make it *three pairs*. And don't say "a pair of twins" unless you're speaking of two sets.

PAJAMAS
Plural, except with *pair*. Thus: "These pajamas don't fit me, but that pair does." The British spelling is *pyjamas*. The derivation is Persian *pai*, leg, and *jamah*, garment.

PALINDROME
From Greek *palin*, again, and *dramein*, to run, a *palindrome* is a word, phrase, verse, sentence or paragraph that is the same when read forward or backward. Famous examples are Napoleon's lament, "Able was I ere I saw Elba," and Theodore Roosevelt's dream, "A man, a plan, a

canal, Panama." Thurber coined "He goddam mad dog, eh?" Espy gives many examples, among them "Sex at noon taxes," which Michael Gartner, editor of the *Des Moines Register*, stretched to "'Naomi, sex at noon taxes,' I moan." A palindromologist should drive a Toyota. And whatever happened to Lon Nol and U Nu? See MADAM, I'M ADAM.

PALL MALL / PELL-MELL

A fashionable London street on which a version of croquet, pallamaglio (Italian *palla*, ball, and *maglio*, mallet), was played three hundred years ago. The English pronounce *Pall Mall* as if it were *pell-mell*, London and the Lord know why. The adverb *pell-mell*, meaning helter-skelter, in disorderly haste, is not related to *Pall Mall;* it derives from French *pêle-mêle*, a reduplication from *mesler*, to mix.

PAN–

The neuter of the Greek word for *all*, *pan* is the stem of scores of English words, including combinations with the names of countries, such as *Pan-American*, *Pan-Germanic*, *Panhellenic*, *Pan-Pacific*. Here are a dozen common *pan-* words:

—*panacea*, all-healing (*akeisthai*, to heal), a cure-all; note that a panacea is a remedy for all ills ("To Grandma, castor oil was a panacea for all our aches and pains"), not just one; thus a cure for the glanders isn't a panacea; but if some panjandrum comes up with a cure for all our social ills, it will be a panacea, and also a miracle.

—*pancreas*, literally "all flesh (*kreas*)."

—*pandemic*, belonging to all the people (*demos*), universal, widespread, such as a disease spread over a wide area affecting many people.

—*pandemonium*, literally "all demons (*daimon*)," hence a state of mass uproar in which "all hell breaks loose," coined by Milton in *Paradise Lost* as the capital of hell.

—*Pandora's box*, a box filled with gifts (*doron*), but the gifts were curses heaped on humanity by Zeus, who sent Pandora, the first mortal woman, to earth with the box as a punishment because Prometheus had stolen from heaven the gift of fire; Pandora opened the box, out flew the world's evils, and everybody knows the troubles we've seen.

—*panegyric*, literally "an assembly (*agora*) of all," hence a formal public eulogy, often at a funeral.

—*panjandrum*, a mock title for a know-it-all, pompous official, coined by Samuel Foote, eighteenth-century English playwright, in a passage he wrote for Charles Macklin, an Irish actor who boasted he could repeat anything after reading it once. Foote stumped Macklin with "So she went into the garden to cut a cabbage leaf to make an apple pie; and at the same time a great she-bear, coming up the street, popped his head into the shop. 'What! no soap?' So he died, and she very imprudently married the barber; and there were present Picninnies, and the Jobillilies, and the Garyulies, and the Grand Panjandrum himself, with the little round button at top, and they all fell to playing the game of catch-as-catch-can, till the gunpowder ran out at the heel of the boots."

—*panoply*, literally "all armor (*hopla*)," hence any magnificent covering or array.

—*panorama*, a view (*horama*, sight) of a wide area.

—*pantheism*, the doctrine that everything in nature is God (*theos*).

—*pantheon*, a temple dedicated to all gods, a building dedicated to a nation's heroes.

—*pantomime*, all-imitating (*mimos*, mime).

PANDER
From Pandarus, a Trojan warrior represented by Chaucer and Shakespeare, among others, as the procurer of Cressida for Troilus.

PANGRAM
A phrase or sentence that contains all twenty-six letters of the alphabet and makes sense. Easy to write if some letters are repeated. Espy fudges with this thirty-one-letter effort: "The five boxing wizards jump quickly." If you want to try for twenty-six, good luck.

PANIC
A terrifying word, from Pan, the demigod of flocks and fields and forests, with the torso of a man and the legs, ears and horns of a goat. Pan aroused groundless fear in spooky places, labyrinthine woods, unhallowed hollows. Any weird sound or eerie sigh or bumping thing in the night was ascribed to Pan. He caused panic.

PANSY
As Moore says, "It was the French, of course, who first had the charming idea of naming that contemplative-looking flower after 'a thought,'" *pensée*, whence *pansy*. And it was the British who first had the idea of calling an effeminate boy a *pansy*.

PARABLE, *see* BALLISTICS

PARADOX
From Greek *para*, beside, contrary to, and *doxa*, opinion, a *paradox* is a seemingly contradictory statement that may be profoundly true: "Christmas celebrates the birth of the homeless and should be celebrated in every home"; "Men cannot agree about nothing any more than they can disagree about nothing"; "Freethinkers are occasionally thoughtful, though never free." These three paradoxes are from *The Thing*, by Chesterton, master of this rhetorical device.

PARAGRAPH
A new paragraph provides a break in thought and a break in monotony, a break greater than the break between sentences. In newspaper writing, the tendency is toward short paragraphs because of type size, column width and page length.

PARALLEL
Note the spelling: double *l*, single *l*.

PARALLELISM
In sentence construction, like should be joined to like. A grammatical element—clause, phrase, part of speech—should correspond with a similar element, not one of a different kind. Not "He loved her because she was beautiful and because of her vivacity"; make it "because she was beautiful and vivacious" or "because of her beauty and vivacity." Not "He was sleepy after work and after he had eaten dinner"; make it "after work and after dinner" or "after he had finished work and after he had eaten dinner." Not "He was a man of compassion and courageous"; make it "of compassion and of courage" or "compassionate and courageous." Not "She was not only interested in ideas but words"; make it "interested not only in ideas but (also) in words." Not "Herzog said he would either start Splittorff or Leonard"; make it "start either Splittorff or Leonard." See also ANACOLUTHON.

PARAMETER
This mathematical term for an arbitrary quantity has become a faddish word, in the plural, for boundaries or limits, by mistaken association with *perimeter*.

PARAMNESIA, *see* DÉJÀ VU

PARAPHERNALIA
Note the spelling. There's an *r* before the *n*. *Paraphernalia* is from Greek *para* + *pherne*, beyond the dowry, hence personal belongings, accessories, odds and ends of property. Note the pronunciation: the third syllable is *pher*, not *phra*.

PARDON, *see* EXCUSE / PARDON

PARENTHESIS
An explanatory word, phrase or sentence, or incidental comment, contained within the punctuation marks ( ) is in parentheses, the plural of *parenthesis*, from Greek *para* + *tithenai*, to put in beside, to insert. Because they distract a reader from flow and unity of thought, they should not be overused. See also BRACKETS.

PARENTHETICALITIS
A pestilent bug infects some writers and editors with parentheticalitis, inflammation of the parenthesis, an irritating disease, particularly within quotes. Here are examples from the sports pages of a respectable metropolitan newspaper:
—"When they (the school) gave Ted (Owens) a vote of confidence they (alumni) wanted a change in recruiting," the source said. "They wanted to be more wide open (in recruiting)."
—On whether he has suggested to Ali that he should retire, Joe Louis said: "No. I'd never do that. He has some good people around him (for that advice). Besides, I don't see the same fighters coming around (as when Louis made his abortive comeback). We had five former world champions fighting then. I don't see no (Rocky) Marciano now."
—"I spent two, three years out there before I said hello to Arnie (Palmer)," said Colbert, who joined the tour in 1966. "They come out now and they don't give a darn. That's why Tommy (Watson) and Ben (Crenshaw) are good for the game. They have respect (tradition) for the game."

Most of those parentheses are unnecessary. The information they give either is obvious or could have been paraphrased before or after the quote. Parentheses are often a sign of jerky writing. They bug the reader, especially when quotes are infested with them.

The sports editor of the paper from which the examples were taken agreed with the criticism. "Parentheses, like a bluff in poker, should be used sparingly," he said.

PARENTHETICAL SPEECH, *see* **SEQUENCE OF TENSES**

PARISH, *see* **DIOCESE**

PARISHIONER
Note the spelling. Not *parishoner*, as is often seen. There's an *i* immediately after the *h*.

PARKINSON'S LAW
Promulgated by C. Northcote Parkinson, British author and historian, in 1957, Parkinson's Law states: "Work expands so as to fill the time available for its completion" and "subordinates multiply at a fixed rate regardless of the amount of work produced."

PARLAY
Both verb and noun, from Italian *paroli*, dice. To *parlay* a bet is to take a winning bet and its stake and bet all the money on a subsequent race or event. Thus an original bet of $1 on a winning horse at odds of 4–1 becomes a bet of $5 on another horse, which, if it wins at odds of, say, 5–1, produces $30, a gain of $29 on the original stake. To compute the odds of a parlay, add the addition and multiplication of the odds on the two horses: $(4 + 5) + (4 \times 5) = 29$.

PARONOMASIA
The rhetorical term for punning or playing with words, from Greek *para* + *onomazein*, to name besides, to form a word by slight change.

PARSING
A dying art in American education, *parsing* is the description of the words of a sentence by their parts of speech and grammatical elements such as person, number, gender, case, degree, tense, mood, voice, special classification. A revival of parsing would help the survival of literacy.

PARTIALLY / PARTLY
Fowler says *partly* is to *wholly* as *partially* is to *completely*. *Partly* has the sense, usually physical, of "a part of the whole," whereas *partially* has the sense of "to a limited degree." Thus: "The lawn is partly zoysia" or "The basement is partly underground." And: "He was partially drugged" or "He was partially responsible for the accident." When in doubt, use *partly*. But remember that *partially* has the additional connotation of prejudice, as the opposite of *impartially*.

PARTICIPLE
See ABLATIVE ABSOLUTE, DANGLING PARTICIPLE and FUSED PARTICIPLE. And don't overdo the practice of beginning a sentence with a participle as a means of backing into a story.

PARTING SHOT
Because of similar sound, *parting shot* is a corruption of *Parthian shot*, a tactic of Parthian cavalry whereby they shot their arrows and immediately wheeled out of enemy range. A *parting shot* has come to mean the last word or exit line.

PARTS OF A VERB
The principal parts of a verb are the present infinitive, past tense and past participle: *walk, walked, walked; go, went, gone.*

PARTS OF SPEECH
Grammarians disagree on the number of the parts of speech. Some say nine, some eight, some seven. The seven parts on which all agree are *noun, pronoun, adjective, verb, adverb, preposition, conjunction.* Some add *article,* which is classified by others as adjective. Some add *interjection,* which is classified by others as adverb. Whatever their classification, the parts of speech are the musical notes of literary composition and should be mastered and manipulated by writers and speakers.

PARTY
Except in legal terminology and telephonic lingo, *party* should not be seriously used for *person.*

PASS AWAY / PASS ON
As Barzun says, "He passed on, did he? What did he pass on of?" See DIE.

PASSIVE, *see* ACTIVE VOICE / PASSIVE VOICE

PASS THE BUCK, *see* BUCK

PAST / PAST PERFECT, *see* SEQUENCE OF TENSES

PASTIME
Though it derives from *pass + time,* it is spelled *pastime,* not *passtime* or *pasttime,* as sometimes seen.

PATENT

The *a* is long in the sense of *patent* as obvious or not hidden and in the botanical sense of spreading open. Otherwise the *a* is short, as in *Patent Office*, *patent medicine*, *patent leather*, *letters patent*.

PATHETIC FALLACY

A poetic device whereby human traits are attributed to inanimate objects, from Greek *pathos*, passion, suffering, emotion. Fowler gives this example of pathetic fallacy: "Sphinxlike, siren-sweet, sly, benign, impassive, vindictive, callously indifferent the sea may seem to a consciousness addicted to pathetic fallacies."

PATHOS, *see* BATHOS

PAVILION

Note the spelling: only one *l*. Incidentally, *pavilion* comes from Latin *papilio*, butterfly, hence a tent or pavilion (from the resemblance to a butterfly's enfolding wings). For a less poetic derivation, see BUTTERFLY.

PAY

The past tense is *paid* except in the nautical *pay out*, to let out a line or cable, the past tense of which is *payed*.

PEACH MELBA, *see* MELBA TOAST

PEARLS BEFORE SWINE

In the Sermon on the Mount, Christ advised: "Do not give to dogs what is holy, neither cast your pearls before swine, or they will trample them under their feet and turn and tear you." The phrase "casting pearls before swine" has become a cliché, sometimes used by newspaper writers who overestimate the value of their gems and underestimate the intelligence of their readers.

PECKER

The word illustrates the perils of crossing the Atlantic. In Britain, *pecker* means courage, spirits, as in "Keep your pecker up" or the Defendant's apostrophe in Gilbert & Sullivan's *Trial by Jury*, "Be firm, be firm, my pecker." See also KNOCK UP.

PECULIAR
No mere synonym of *odd*, out of the ordinary, *peculiar* also connotes a quality that belongs solely to a particular individual or group, as in "Coody's habit of hitching the left leg of his pants before stroking a putt is peculiar to him" or "Haggis is a dish peculiar to the Scots." The derivation is Latin *peculium*, private property.

PEDAGOGUE / PEDANT
The first pedagogue was the slave who accompanied the young sons of a Greek family everywhere, including to school, from *pais* (genitive *paidos*), boy, and *agagos*, leading. *Pedagogue* became generic for teacher and specific for a dogmatic teacher. Similarly, *pedant*, from the same root, was generic for schoolmaster and became specific for a rigorous but impractical teacher, a doctrinaire, especially one who flaunts his learning.

PEDIGREE
A crane's foot, French *pied de grue*, resembles the three-pronged mark formerly used in a genealogical chart.

PEEPING TOM
Tom was the tailor who is said to have peeped at Lady Godiva, hairdresser, as she rode through Coventry on a horse and a bet with her husband (see SYLLEPSIS). One version of the legend says that Tom was struck blind, another that he was slain by the locals, some of whom must also have been cheating, because all were supposed to be behind drawn blinds, and Godiva's eyes were probably downcast. Somebody must have squealed on Tom. Anyhow, Tom lives on as the eponym for voyeurs.

PEER
From Latin *par*, equal, *peer* strictly means equal: judgment by one's peers is judgment by one's equals. Probably from association with the British peerage, however, *peer* is sometimes misused in the United States to mean "superior," as in "He has no peer, certainly no equal, as a craftsman."

PELL-MELL, *see* PALL MALL / PELL-MELL

PENINSULA
A long strip of land projecting into water and almost surrounded by it, a peninsula is almost an island, from Latin *paene*, almost, and *insula*, an island. Almost no man is a peninsula.

PENNY ANTE, *see* **ANTE**

PENTAGONESE
The jargon of the military, *Pentagonese is* GOBBLEDYGOOK at its bloodiest.

Composed by the Pentagon, Hamlet's soliloquy would have begun: "To exacerbate, or not to exacerbate—that is the dichotomy."

Says the commandant of the Marine Corps: "It has been decisioned that some form of unit rotation may be a desirable objective. . . . Recent CMC decisions have alleviated the major inhibitors allowing a fresh approach and revaluation of alternative methods of unit replacement." (You may experiment with unit rotation.)

Says a deputy assistant secretary of defense: "After careful evaluation of your proposal, it is the opinion of this office that it should not be implemented. As this project is transitional, it does not appear as candidate for separate program element status. To provide program element visibility for this project could establish a precedent for other types of Defense-supported programs, which would further proliferate the structure without providing comparable advantages." (Your proposal is rejected. If carried out, it might lead to other unnecessary programs.)

Says a congressman: "At issue is a budding military program that six months ago in the first blush of prototype flying looked merely huge but now looms as the fighter plane plum of the century." About this gibberish, columnist George Will remarked: "Ah, swing low, looming plum, over the fruited plains."

See also BUREAUCRATESE.

PENULT, *see* **ANTEPENULT**

PEOPLE / PERSONS
Use *persons* for a small or exact (note *or*) number, otherwise *people.* Thus: "Fifteen persons attended the meeting"; "There were 329 persons polled." And: "The show attracted 2,000 people"; "About 100 people showed up."

But how small is small? AP says *persons* "usually is used" for "a relatively small number of people who can be counted." Well, how small is relatively small? And relative to what? Probably a good guide for this distinction is to consider a number below 50 to be small.

PEOPLE'S
A Communist doublethink catchword, *People's* is applied to a nation (People's Democracy, People's Republic) or organization (People's Co-

alition, People's Front) whose members are free to do as their dictators tell them or else.

PER
A and *for* are English; *per* Latin. Try to restrict *per* to technical terms, such as *per capita* and *per diem*. *Per se* easily translates to *of itself*, just as *per annum* translates to *a year*. Above all, don't mix English and Latin, as in *per year*.

PERCENT
One word, according to AP.

PERCENTAGE POINTS
If the unemployment rate is 5 percent in May and 7 percent in June, the increase is 2 percentage points, not 2 percent. The increase in the rate is 40 percent.

PERFECT, *see* SEQUENCE OF TENSES

PERFECT INFINITIVE
Form the perfect infinitive of a verb by adding *to* and *have* to the past participle: *to have seen*. But don't combine the conditional perfect (*would have liked*) with the perfect infinitive. Don't say, "I would have liked to have seen her," because the perfect infinitive must refer to a time previous to that of the main verb. Make it either "I would like to have seen her" (conditional present and perfect infinitive) or "I would have liked to see her" (conditional perfect and present infinitive).

PERIGEE, *see* APOGEE

PERIOD
The British call the punctuation mark period (.) at the end of a sentence a "full stop." And that's what it is. Like a STOP sign on a road, a period, except in abbreviations, requires a full stop, a halt, as Nurnberg points out, not a mere SLOW DOWN, the punctuation sign for which is a comma. A period is included in the question mark (?) and the exclamation point (!) and is therefore not used immediately after these punctuation marks. For the misuse of a comma for a period, see RUN-ON SENTENCE.

PERIPATETIC
Aristotle walked up and down (Greek *peripatein*, to walk about) the Lyceum while he taught, wherefore his philosophy and methods of teach-

ing were called Peripatetic, and his followers belonged to the Peripatetic School.

PERISH
From Latin *per + ire*, to go away, to pass away, as in "Publish or perish," a cruel fact of academic life, denied by some administrators but practiced by their article-counting myrmidons.

PERMISSIVE
If God had intended a permissive society, He would have given us the Ten Suggestions.

PER SE, *see* PER

PERSEVERANCE
Note the spelling: *perseverance*, not *perserverance* or *perserverence* or even *perseverence*. From Latin *per + severus*, very serious, very strict.

PERSONAL
Unless you are contrasting personal friendship with some other kind of friendship, such as collegiate or commercial or political, don't use *personal* with *friend*. The phrase is usually redundant.

    Personal is also misused for *private*, particularly in contrast with *public*. The opposite of *public life* is *private life*, not personal life. The normally gentle Barzun waxes almost angry on this point: "The notion that anybody's life could be other than personal verges on madness."

PERSONALITY
The movies immortalized mere mortals with the Star System. Came then television and the celebrity ethos of the "TV personality," a name bestowed almost indiscriminately on anchorpersons, game show exhibitionists, happy-talk newspersons, talk show deities, whirling dervishes masquerading as singers and musicians, and sundry other trained seals. Why *personality*? Why not actor or announcer or performer or reporter? See also SUPERSTAR.

PERSONALIZE
Ugh! See -IZE.

PERSONALLY
Unless the contrast is one of surprise or abnormality, the use of *personally* with a personal pronoun is redundant. With *I*, the use of *personally* is also embarrassingly defensive, as if the writer or speaker needed to apologize for his opinion or to stress that it was merely his opinion. *I* is enough to make it personal. Get rid of *personally* from "I personally think" and similar expressions. If, however, someone does something he would normally delegate, the use of *personally* is valid, as in "The senator personally responded to the student's request for information about life in Washington."

PERSONNEL
The number of *personnel* (note the spelling: double *n*, single *l*) is either singular or plural. As a unit, singular: "Personnel in government offices is growing in accordance with Parkinson's Law." As a collection of persons, plural: "All factory personnel are to assemble at 3 p.m. today." When in doubt, treat *personnel* as plural. As a military term, *personnel* is distinguished from *materiel*.

PERSONS, *see* PEOPLE / PERSONS

PERSPIRE, *see* –SPIRE

PETARD
Hamlet said it was "sport to have the engineer hoist with his own petard," and people ever since have been using *hoist with his own petard* as a cliché for "caught in his own trap" or "blown up by his own bomb." Let its users be aware, however, of the derivation of *petard:* French from *péter*, to break wind, from *pet*, a fart.

PETER PRINCIPLE
Named after Laurence J. Peter, co-author of *The Peter Principle: Why Things Always Go Wrong*, the Peter Principle states: "In a hierarchy, every employee tends to rise to his level of incompetence." The employee then stays where he is or is removed by "Percussive Sublimation" (kicked upstairs) or "Lateral Arabesque" (transferred to a better furnished office in Siberia).

PETRIFIED, *see* AFRAID

PHARAOH
Commonly misspelled *Pharoah*.

PHENOMENAL
Originally a philosophical term meaning known through the senses rather than through the mind, *phenomenal* has come to mean extraordinary or prodigious. Such a shift, says Fowler, "was a sin against the English language, but the consequences seem now to be irremediable." The plural of *phenomenon* is *phenomena*.

PHIL–
Many English words derive from Greek *philos*, loving. Here are a dozen:
—*Anglophile*, one who admires things English.
—*bibliophile*, one who loves or collects books.
—*hemophilia*, a tendency to profuse bleeding (*haima*, blood), even from slight wounds.
—*Philadelphia*, the city of brotherly love (*adelphos*, brother).
—*philander*, to flirt (*aner*, genitive *andros*, man).
—*philanthropy*, love of mankind.
—*philately*, stamp collecting (*ateleia*, exemption from tax).
—*philharmonic*, loving harmony or music.
—*philodendron*, an ornamental plant, often tenderly cared for as a house plant (*dendron*, tree).
—*philology*, study and love of words.
—*philosophy*, pursuit and love of wisdom.
—*philter*, a love potion or charm.

PHILIPPIC
A speech or declamation of bitter invective, from the oratory of Demosthenes in denunciation of King Philip of Macedon.

PHILIPPINE, *see* FILIPINO / PHILIPPINE

PHILISTINE
The inhabitants of ancient Philistia were considered piratically barbaric, wherefore *Philistine* (sometimes lowercase) has come to be applied to boors unappreciative of the finer things in life.

–PHOBIA
Many English words derive from Greek *phobos*, fear. Here are a dozen:
—*acrophobia*, fear of heights (*akros*, highest, extreme).

—*agoraphobia*, fear of being in, or crossing, open spaces (*agora*, market place or open space).

—*ailurophobia*, fear of cats (*ailouros*); an ailurophobe is certain that cats sense the fear and slink toward their victim to stalk and harass and provoke terror; ailurophilic hosts should be considerate of ailurophobic guests.

—*Anglophobia*, aversion to things English.

—*astraphobia*, fear of thunderstorms (*astrape*, lightning); golfers should be astraphobes.

—*chionophobia*, fear of snow (*chion*).

—*claustrophobia*, fear of being in enclosed places (Latin *claustrum*, a confined place).

—*hydrophobia*, fear of water (*hydor*), rabies, a disease in which convulsions occur from attempts to swallow water.

—*ochlophobia*, fear of crowds, mobs (*ochlos*).

—*phobia*, fear and hatred, not mere fetish or obsession.

—*triskaidekaphobia*, superstitious fear of the number 13 (*triskaideka*).

—*xenophobia*, fear of strangers or foreigners (*xenos*, stranger).

PHOSPHORUS
Note that the spelling of the element is *phosphorus*, not *phosphorous*, which is its adjective.

PHRASE
Grammatically, a *phrase* is a group of two or more related words that don't form a clause.

PICA
Type that is 12 points deep, about one-sixth of an inch. Also a unit of measure of the width of a column. The width in which the type of this book is set is 26 picas.

PICARESQUE
Crooks with any knowledge of etymology should have recognized that the fencing operation set up in 1978 in a Kansas City warehouse bearing the business name of "A. Picaro & Associates" was a phony. The name was chosen by some philologist in the police department as a cover for a "sting" operation. *Picaresque*, from Spanish *picaro*, rogue, vagabond, means roguish, thieving, rascally. Do not confuse with *picturesque*.

PICKLE, *see* NICKEL

PICNIC, *see* **ARC**

PIDGIN
The *pidgin* of Pidgin English is a Chinese corruption of *business*.

PIECEMEAL, *see* **SONIC WRITING**

PIGEON
Note the spelling: no *d*.

PINCH HITTER
Strictly, a *pinch hitter* is expected to do a better job than the person he substitutes for. Loosely, a *pinch hitter* is any substitute.

PING-PONG
When used as a trademark for table tennis equipment, *Ping-Pong* is uppercase and hyphenated. When used as a synonym for table tennis, *pingpong* is the spelling.

PITILACKER
A word coined in 1926 for "one cruel to animals," *pitilacker* didn't catch on. Perhaps it should be revived these days. It fills a need, especially for environmentalists.

PLACEBO
Straight Latin for "I shall please," a *placebo* is an innocuous substance given as a medicine to a patient merely to humor him. See also GAZEBO.

PLAN AHEAD
The best way.

PLATITUDE
A dull, trite utterance that falls flat, from Greek *platys*, broad, flat.

PLAYWRIGHT / PLAYWRITING
Note the spellings. A playwright is engaged in playwriting.

PLEAD
Though *pled* as the past tense and past participle of *plead* has long been accepted in American usage, AP brands it "colloquial" and proscribes it.

PLURALITY, *see* MAJORITY

PLURALS

Except for singular-plural inconsistency (see AGREEMENT OF SUBJECT AND PREDICATE), the most common mistake with plurals occurs in the formation of plurals of proper nouns ending in *s*. This kind of mistake shouldn't occur, because such plurals are formed according to the general principle that *es* is added to form the plural of a singular word ending in *s*. Thus: Andrews, Andrewses; Chalmers, Chalmerses; Dykes, Dykeses; Jones, Joneses. No apostrophe is used unless the plural is possessive (see POSSESSIVES).

Authorities disagree on the plural forms of foreign nouns that have become English. When in doubt, use the English plural by adding *s* or *es*. Thus: apex, apexes; bureau, bureaus; dogma, dogmas; formula, formulas; genus, genuses.

But, despite the iconoclasts, don't add *s* or *es* to foreign words that are already plural. If the iconoclasts had their way, we would be encouraged to say: "Alumnis of various stratas have accepted honorarias and insignias and issued to the medias their dictas as addendas to the datas of the curriculas as stimulis to the phenomenas of the bacterias that have infected the vertebraes of language." Holy erratas!

For a long list of foreign nouns and their foreign and English plurals, see Opdycke; and follow his advice not to use foreign plurals "simply for the sake of showing off your vocabulary."

In compounds, make the modified word plural: attorneys general, major generals, sergeants major, courts-martial.

PLUS

The word is not a literary synonym for *and*. *Plus* is arithmetical and should be saved for arithmetical contexts. Furthermore (not *plus*), *plus* is a preposition, not a conjunction, wherefore "John plus his wife are going" is incorrect; change *are* to *is* (see AS WELL AS). Also (not *plus*), in an arithmetical context, "Two plus two is four," not *are*, because *two* is treated as a singular numerical unit and *plus* is a preposition. *Plus the fact that* is a sloppy circumlocution for *also*, *besides*, *furthermore*, *moreover*.

PLUS FOURS

This golf garb, now rarely worn in the United States, derives its name from the extra four inches of cloth needed for the baggy effect below the knees.

PLUTOCRACY, *see* **–CRACY**

PODIUM, *see* **LECTERN / PODIUM**

POETIC LICENSE
Issued only to true poets and other artists, not to hacks.

POINT
A vertical measure of type. There are 72 points in an inch. The textual matter of this book is set in 10-point type.

POINT OUT, *see* **LOADED VERB**

POLEMIC
From Greek *polemos*, war, hence an aggressive argument.

POLES APART, *see* **SONIC WRITING**

POLIO
Short for *poliomyelitis*, from Greek *polios*, gray, and *myelos*, marrow; inflammation of the gray matter of the spinal cord; also called infantile paralysis.

POLITE, *see* **COURTEOUS / POLITE**

POLITICS, *see* **–ICS**

POLY–
The language abounds in *poly-* words (Greek *polys*, much, many). Here are a dozen:
 —*polyandry*, the practice of having more than one male mate at a time (*aner*—genitive *andros*—man).
 —*polygamy*, marriage to more than one person at a time (*gamos*, marriage); see **-GAMY**.
 —*polyglot*, speaking or writing many languages, many-tongued (*glotta*, tongue).
 —*polygon*, a figure with many sides (*gonia*, angle); also a dead parrot.
 —*polygraph*, a copying machine, an instrument that records various body pulsations simultaneously, a lie detector (*graphein*, to write).
 —*polygyny*, the practice of having more than one female mate at a time (*gyne*, woman); see **GYN-**.

—*Polynesia*, a scattered group of many islands in Oceania (*nesos*, island).

—*polyp*, a zoological species with an oral opening surrounded by tentacles, a projecting growth of mucous membrane (French *polype*, octopus, from Greek *polypous*, many-footed).

—*polyphony*, multiplicity of sound, musical harmony (*phone*, sound).

—*polysyllabic*, many-syllabled, having more than three syllables (*syllabe*, a taking together of letters); see -LEPSY.

—*polysyndeton*, a rhetorical term for a close succession of conjunctions, as in "Eat and drink and carouse and be sorry tomorrow" (*syndetos*, bound together, conjunction); see ASYNDETON.

—*polyunsaturated*, a chemical term for compounds, such as fats, having many unsaturated bonds (Latin *satur*, full of food, sated).

POMPON
The brute culture of American sports, particularly football, would be less colorful without pompon girls, those young women who wave those feathers and their anatomy to beef up the bloody gladiators and whoop up the bloodthirsty throng. But spell their name correctly. It's *pompon*, one word, not hyphenated, and only one *pom*, unlike *pom-pom*, a cannon.

PONS ASINORUM
Straight Latin for "bridge of asses," *pons asinorum* is the nickname for Euclid's theorem that the angles at the base of an isosceles triangle are equal. The theorem was considered hard for beginners to understand, and *pons asinorum* has come to mean any problem tough for beginners.

POOH-BAH
A character in Gilbert & Sullivan's *Mikado*, Pooh-Bah was the Lord High Everything Else. The name is now given to a pompous person who holds many piddling positions and, as the Irish say, tries to fart higher than his ass.

PORE
When you study hard, you pore over books, not *pour*.

PORNOGRAPHY
Now that the disease has become a plague, the etymology of *pornography* ought to be known by its peddlers: Greek *porne*, harlot, from *pernemi*, I sell, and *graphein*, to write.

PORT / STARBOARD

When you face from stern to bow, the left side of a ship is port and the right is starboard. *Port* may come from *harbor*, but this is uncertain. The *l* of *larboard* (possibly from Middle English *ladeborde*, the loading side), the older term for *port*, made "left" easier to remember, but its resemblance to *starboard* probably caused *larboard* to be replaced by *port*. As Morris says, "In the teeth of a howling gale, it can be very important to have commands interpreted correctly." *Starboard*, the right side, comes from Anglo-Saxon *steorbord*, the steer side or rudder side, because ancient ships were steered from the right side with a paddle. See also POSH.

PORTMANTEAU WORDS, *see* CENTAUR WORDS

PORTUGUESE

Note the spelling: *u* before and after *g*.

POSH

Though most authorities deny the origin, this adjective for expensive sophistication is said by some to be an acronym for "port out, starboard home," a reference to the cabins chosen by the smart set on the shady side of ships steaming between England and India in the days of the raj.

POSITIVE

In *The Devil's Dictionary*, Ambrose Bierce defined *positive* as "mistaken at the top of one's voice."

POSSE

Short for *posse comitatus*, Medieval Latin for "the power of a county," hence a band of citizens summoned to help preserve peace.

POSSESS

For mere ownership, *possess* is a stilted word for *have* or *own*. In some contexts, however, *possess* is the right word, as in "Talent is what a man possesses; genius is what possesses a man."

POSSESSIVE ANTECEDENT

In "Humphrey's compassion set him apart from politics," the antecedent of *him* is *Humphrey's*, which is a noun in the possessive case. Some grammarians teach that a pronoun should not have a nounal antecedent in the possessive case. According to this principle, the sentence should read, "His compassion set Humphrey apart from politics."

Opdycke calls the principle "a good grammatical rule," but one that is "little respected by writers and authors—if, indeed, known." Barzun says, "There can be no logical link between a proper noun in the possessive case and a personal pronoun." Bernstein, in *Miss Thistlebottom's Hobgoblins*, says the principle is valid only when it "functions to preclude ambiguity."

Ambiguity arises in a sentence such as "Humphrey's son said he had great compassion for the underdog," in which the grammatical antecedent of *he* is *son*, but the inferential antecedent is *Humphrey's*. Say, "Humphrey's son said Humphrey had great compassion for the underdog," and avoid both the ambiguity and the issue.

POSSESSIVES
Widespread confusion has resulted from the contrary rules laid down by grammarians on the formation of the possessives of nouns. Despite the risk of oversimplification, try these two principles to help reduce the confusion:

1. Form the possessive of a noun not ending in *s* by adding *'s*. This includes nouns ending in *x* or *z*. Thus: *a woman's rights, women's rights, a fox's tail, Rodriguez's score*.

2. Form the possessive of a noun ending in *s* by adding only an apostrophe. Thus: *a witness' rights, witnesses' rights, John Jones' house, the Joneses' house*.

These principles do not include: the "frozen possessive" found in the official name of some institutions or organizations—*Teachers College, Teamsters Union;* and joint ownership—*John and Mary's house*. See **DOUBLE POSSESSIVE.**

POSSIBLE, *see* FEASIBLE / POSSIBLE

POST HOC; ERGO PROPTER HOC
Straight Latin for "after this; therefore because of this." This is the fallacy in logic of assuming that what happened before was the cause of what happened after. That a man had an accident after leaving a saloon doesn't necessarily mean that his visit to the saloon caused the accident.

POSTHUMOUS
Though *posthumous* means "after death," it does not derive from Latin *humus*, earth, soil, but from *postumus*, last. A posthumous child is one

born after the death of the father; a posthumous book is one published after the death of the author; posthumous disregard will be the fate of most of us (read Frost's "Provide, Provide").

POST-MORTEM
Note the hyphen. See AUTOPSY.

POSTPRANDIAL
After a meal (Latin *prandium*, repast), especially dinner, as in "post-prandial speeches."

POSTSCRIPT
Latin *postscriptum*, written after, abbreviated to P.S. A postscript to a postscript is a P.P.S.

POTPOURRI
Literally, "rotten pot" (French), but meaning any miscellaneous collection.

POURBOIRE
Literally, "for drinking" (French), meaning money for drinking, a tip.

PR
Short for "public relations." A PR man is defined by the Dictionary of Proper Names as "a publicity man who is paid to project, with some degree of verisimilitude, a favorable image of his client (a person, firm, political party, foreign government etc.) through the appropriate media (press, TV etc.) and to the extent necessary (and often far beyond it)."

PRACTICABLE / PRACTICAL
What can be done or used is *practicable*, though the details may not have been worked out yet. What has been successfully done or used is *practical*. Thus: "Your plan to build a better mousetrap is practicable but you'll need an HEW grant" and "Eating less is a practical way to lose weight." *Practicable* applies only to things; *practical* applies both to things and to persons ("His work on the house shows that he is a practical man"). The same principles apply to *impracticable* and *impractical*. See also FEASIBLE / POSSIBLE.

PRECARIOUS
From Latin *prex* (genitive *precis*), prayer, *precarious* means uncertain or insecure, as if depending on prayer. It is not a synonym for *dangerous*

unless both uncertainty and insecurity are present. Verbs from the same root are *deprecate*, *imprecate*, *pray*.

PRECEDE
Note the spelling. In journalistic jargon, the noun *precede* is an editorial note of explanation that introduces a story and usually is set in boldface type or in parentheses. The verb stresses the second syllable, the noun the first.

PRECEDENCE / PRECEDENT
The more common pronunciation of *precedence* stresses the second syllable. *Precedent* stresses the first syllable. In each word the *e* of *pre* is short.

PRECIPITATE / PRECIPITOUS
Though both adjectives derive from the same root (Latin *praeceps*, headlong), *precipitate* means excessively hasty and refers to actions, whereas *precipitous* means extremely steep and refers to physical objects. A decision may be precipitate. A cliff may be precipitous. The bishop who counseled against "precipitous marriage" either was ignorant of the distinction or was jumping to the conclusion that rash decisions lead to rocky adventure.

PRECOCIOUS
From Latin *prae* + *coquere*, to cook beforehand, to ripen early, hence applied to exceptionally early development, especially mental.

PREDICATE
Strictly, the verb *to predicate* means to affirm one thing of another, as in "In defense of his client, the lawyer predicated man's inhumanity to man." This, too, is the grammatical sense of the noun *predicate*, which comprises the verb and other grammatical elements that are affirmed of the subject.

Loosely, *to predicate* means to found, to base upon, as in "The lawyer predicated his defense on the compassion of the jury." Webster says this meaning is "not in good use." But 62 percent of the American Heritage usage experts say it is acceptable.

PREDOMINANT / PREDOMINATE
The adjective is *predominant*. *Predominate* is a verb, not an adjective. Thus: "He predominated throughout the match. His serve was the pre-

dominant feature of his game." The adverb is *predominantly*, not *predominately*.

PREFACE, *see* INEFFABLE

PREFER
You prefer something *to* something else, not *than*. You prefer tea to coffee. But a problem arises when the preference is between infinitives: you don't say, "We prefer to study to to play." Make it "We prefer studying to playing" or "We would rather study than play."

PREFERABLE
Stress the first syllable. And note the spelling: *preferable*, not *preferrable*.

PREMIÈRE
As a verb, *première* is rightly rejected by 86 percent of the American Heritage panel. Barzun says the antonym of *to première* must be *to derrière*.

PRE-OWNED
A car company's deceptive euphemism for *used* or *secondhand*. Another is *semi-new*.

PREPOSITION
A preposition is a word that relates a noun or a pronoun to some other word. The noun or pronoun is called the object of the preposition. In "The report of the meeting was written by me," the object of the preposition *of* is *meeting*, the object of the preposition *by* is *me*, *of* relates *meeting* to *report*, and *by* relates *me* to *written*.

Because a pronoun governed by a preposition is the object of the preposition, the pronoun is in the objective case. Yet one often hears and sees the barbaric "between you and I" instead of "between you and me," or, worse, "to she and I" instead of "to her and me."

PREPOSITIONAL VERB
Sometimes a preposition is so tied to a verb that together they form a *prepositional verb* rather than a verb and a preposition. In "Chief Justice Burger swore in the new Cabinet," Burger was administering oaths, not uttering them. *To swear in* is a prepositional verb. In the example, *Cabinet* is the object of the verb, not of the preposition *in*.

PREPOSITION AT END
Some mossbacked pedagogue once decided that because *preposition* came from *prae + ponere* (Latin), to place before, a preposition must be placed before its object and certainly never at the end of a sentence. So generations of pupils were taught that constructions such as "What did you write about?" and "The teacher gave him a problem to work on" were incorrect and had to be changed to "About what did you write?" and "The teacher gave him a problem on which to work." Such tergiversation is to be laughed at. Let euphony be your guide. *With* is sometimes a good word to end a sentence with.

PRESAGE
The noun stresses the first syllable, the verb the second. In the noun, the second syllable has the sound of *idge;* in the verb, the second syllable has the sound of *age*.

PRESCRIBE / PROSCRIBE
To *prescribe* is positive: to require, to lay down as a directive. To *proscribe* is negative: to prohibit, to condemn.

PRESENT, *see* SEQUENCE OF TENSES

PRESENTED WITH, *see* FALSE PASSIVE

PRESENTLY
Because *presently* means both *now* and *soon*, why not say *now* when you mean *now*, and *soon* when you mean *soon?*

PRESENT WRITER
The use of "the present writer" is third-person false modesty for the first person. So is "this reporter."

PRESS, *see* MEDIA

PRESTIGE
French, "illusion brought on by magic," from Latin *praestringere*, to bind up, to blind, *prestige* has indeed changed meaning. The status now derives from praiseworthy performance or powerful position rather than from prestidigitation (from the same root as *prestige*, by way of French *preste*, nimble, and Latin *digitus*, finger, hence sleight of hand, legerdemain, a juggler's tricks).

PRESUME, *see* **ASSUME / PRESUME**

PRESUMPTUOUS
Note the spelling: *uous*, not *ious*.

PREVENT
Football coaches would contort this verb into an adjective, as in "a prevent defense," the pronunciation of which they similarly contort by stressing the first syllable of each word. See **DEFENSE**.

PREVIOUSLY
Up to then, up to that time. See **HITHERTO**.

PRIAPISM
Erection of the penis as a persistent pathological condition, from Priapus, god of procreation and the personification of the erect phallus.

PRIMA FACIE, *see* **A POSTERIORI / A PRIORI**

PRIMARY TENSES, *see* **SEQUENCE OF TENSES**

PRINCIPAL / PRINCIPLE
The spellings are often confused. *Principal* is both adjective and noun. *Principle* is a noun. As an adjective, *principal* means chief, leading, main, most important; as a noun, it means chief figure, leader, person in charge and, financially, the capital sum on which interest is paid. A *principle* is a fundamental law or truth, a standard, a rule of action.

PRINCIPAL PARTS, *see* **PARTS OF A VERB**

PRIORITIZE
Ugh! See **-IZE** and **VALUE**.

PRIOR TO, *see* **AFTER**

PRIVILEGE
Note the spelling: *privi*, not *prive*; *lege*, not *ledge*. *Privilege* comes from Latin *priva* + *lex* (genitive *legis*), private law, a law affecting an individual.

PROBABILITY SEMINAR
An academic euphemism used as a domestic excuse for a poker game.

PROBE
Whether noun or verb, *probe* is ugly headlinese. For a short noun, try *hearing, inquiry, study*. For a short verb, try *delve, inquire, plumb, scan, sift, sound, study*. *Probe* in headlines produces such monstrosities as "Hospital Abortions Probed" and "Sheriff Orders / Internal Probe / Of Jim White." Almost sixty years ago, an American newspaper editor wrote: "I am morally certain that *probes* would not be so important a part of the activities of our government if the headline writers had not discovered that word. People generally do not become excited about a thing called an *investigation*, an *inquiry*, a *hearing*, or whatever other name such an interrogatory affair might be called by. But a probe is an interesting thing." See HEADLINESE.

PROBLEM, *see* BALLISTICS

PROCRASTINATE
From Latin *cras*, tomorrow.

PROCRUSTEAN
A gigantic brigand of ancient Greece, Procrustes (Greek for "The Stretcher") used to place his victims on a bed, stretch the short ones and amputate the tall ones to make everyone fit the bed. A *procrustean* idea or system is one designed to force preconceived uniformity by violent or arbitrary methods.

PROCTOLOGIST / PROCTOR
Though academic disciplinary supervisors may be a pain in the anatomy to cheats and rowdies, *proctor*, the word for this kind of overseer, derives from Latin *procurare*, to take care of, not Greek *proktos*, anus, whence *proctologist*, a specialist in diseases of the anus and rectum.

PROFANITY, *see* FANATIC

PROFFER
Note the spelling: double *f*.

PROGNATHOUS, *see* OPISTHOGNATHOUS

PROLEPSIS, *see* –LEPSY

PROLLY
What many Americans say when they mean *probably*.

PROLOGUE, *see* EPILOGUE / PROLOGUE

PROMETHEAN
Prometheus ("The Forethinker") was the Titan hero among whose many accomplishments were said to be the creation of man from mud and the stealing of fire from heaven for man. Thus *promethean* has come to mean daringly original, life-giving.

PRONEQUARK
Does a sentence such as "Would you please shut up" require a question mark? Some say yes, some no. To resolve the question, Bernstein invented the pronequark, a prone question mark (ᵔ.), for what he called a "noninterrogatory question." If you think this weird, would you please refer to the entry for INTERROBANG ᵔ.

PRONOUN
A pronoun is a word used instead of a noun or another pronoun. These are the main classes of pronoun:

PERSONAL: *I, you, he, she, it, we, they* and their objective and possessive forms.

RELATIVE: *who, whom, whose, that, which, what* (that which), which relate to a noun or another pronoun and act as relative conjunctions; see CLAUSE; CONJUNCTION; THAT / WHICH.

DEMONSTRATIVE: *this, that, these, those,* which point out someone or something; sometimes called demonstrative adjectives.

INTERROGATIVE: *who, which, what,* which ask a question.

REFLEXIVE: *myself, yourself, himself, herself, oneself, itself, ourselves, yourselves, themselves,* which turn back the action to the subject, as in "I hate myself" or "John loves himself," or which emphasize or intensify, as in "I myself did it" or "John cooked it himself"; *hisself, ourself, theirself, theirselves, themself* are barbarisms.

INDEFINITE: *all, another, any* (and its compounds), *both, each, either, every* (and its compounds), *few, many, much, neither, none, other, own, several, some* (and its compounds), *such* and many others; indefinite pronouns are so called because they refer to something indeterminately without specifying identity.

For a detailed discussion of pronouns, see Opdycke.

PRONOUN AGREEMENT, *see* ANTECEDENT

PRONUNCIATION

If you pride yourself on your pronunciation, try this passage, which, according to Espy, is given to prospective radio announcers at WQXR, owned by the *New York Times*, to be read aloud:

"The old man with the flaccid face and dour expression grimaced when asked if he were conversant with zoology, mineralogy, or the culinary arts. 'Not to be secretive,' he said, 'I may tell you that I'd given precedence to the study of genealogy. But, since my father's demise, it has been my vagary to remain incognito because of an inexplicable, lamentable, and irreparable family schism. It resulted from a heinous crime, committed at our domicile by an impious scoundrel. To err is human . . . but this affair was so grievous that only my inherent acumen and consummate tact saved me.'"

PROPAGANDA

Note the spelling: not *pog*.

PROPHECY / PROPHESY

The noun is *prophecy* (the last syllable pronounced as in *sea*), the verb *prophesy* (the last syllable pronounced as in *sigh*). There is no such word as *prophesize*.

PROPORTIONS

Though 65 percent of the American Heritage panelists consider *proportions* acceptable in such phrases as "condominiums of huge proportions," "floods of huge proportions," "taxation of huge proportions," *dimensions* or *extent* or *size* seems more appropriate, according to the context. *Proportion* strictly refers to the relationship of part to whole. *Epidemic proportions* is a cliché.

PROSCRIBE, *see* PRESCRIBE / PROSCRIBE

PROTAGONIST

The protagonist is the leading actor in a performance, the leading character in a book or the one who has the leading role in some endeavor. There is no such person as *a* protagonist. The word is wrongly used to mean any prominent character or proponent of some cause. Its derivation is Greek *protos*, first, and *agonistes*, actor, from *agon*, a gathering or contest, from *agein*, to lead.

Right: "Laurence Olivier was the protagonist in the 1948 movie version of *Hamlet*"; "Stalin was the protagonist at the Yalta Conference." Wrong: "Vivien Leigh was one of the protagonists in *Gone With the Wind*"; "Jane Fonda was a protagonist in the antiwar demonstrations."

Those who would cry that all this was fine for the Greeks but the word is now English and has changed in meaning should hearken to Fowler. The Greek scholar, Fowler admits, cannot expect to "be allowed to forbid us a word that we find useful," but he then asks rhetorically, "Is it useful? Or is it merely a pretentious blundering substitute for words that are useful?"

Instead of using *protagonist* as a pretentious blundering substitute, use it for the chief character and try some of these useful words for the wrong meanings given to *protagonist: advocate, champion, combatant, defender, partisan, proponent, supporter.*

Note that the *pro* in *protagonist* is not the prefix *for* but part of *protos*, first; so don't use *protagonist* as an antonym for *antagonist* (*anti* + *agon*, against in the contest), opponent, adversary.

PROTEAN
Proteus was a wily old Greek sea god who assumed different shapes to elude capture. A *protean* person is a versatile character who can vary his attitudes and policies at will.

PRO TEM
Short for Latin *pro tempore*, for the time being, temporarily, as in "Because of the mayor's illness, Jones was appointed mayor pro tem."

PROTEST
The more common pronunciation of the verb stresses the second syllable. The noun stresses the first syllable. Note the spelling of *protester: er*, not *or*.

PROVEN
As the past participle of *to prove*, *proven* is not acceptable to 73 percent of the American Heritage panelists. The preferred form is *proved.* But *proven* is standard usage as an adjective ("proven ability") and as a technical term ("The charge was not proven"). See also EXCEPTION PROVES RULE.

PROVERBIAL
If you want to use a cliché, go ahead and use it, but don't insert *proverbial* to soften the blow, as in "He hit the proverbial hay" or "He slept like the proverbial log." See CLICHÉ.

PROVOST
As an academic or ecclesiastical term, *provost* is pronounced as spelled. As a military term, it is pronounced *provo*, as in Utah.

PRURIENT
This word for the excessively lustful comes from Latin *prurire*, to itch.

PSEPHOLOGIST
A pollster, a gatherer of public opinion, an election forecaster, from Greek *psephos*, a pebble, used by the Greeks in voting.

PSEUDO
Greek *pseudos*, false, whence *pseudonym*, a fictitious name, a pen name, and words coined by the addition of *pseudo* to connote sham or fakery, such as *pseudointellectual, pseudoscientific*. Note the spelling: not *psuedo*, as is often seen.

PSYCHO-
Many English words derive from Greek *psyche*, breath, life, soul, spirit, mind. Here are a dozen:

—*psyche* (two syllables), the soul, mental life; the verb *to psych* (one syllable, no *e*) means to fake someone into making a wrong move, as in cards, business, politics and other sports.

—*psychedelic*, hallucinatory, seemingly visible but actually distorted; though the effect of psychedelic drugs is destructive, the root is Greek *delos*, clear, visible, not Latin *delere*, to destroy.

—*psychiatry*, the study and treatment of mental disorders (*iatreia*, the art of healing).

—*psychic*, pertaining to the mind, extrasensory, unexplained by physical causes; as a noun, someone seemingly responsive to nonphysical forces, a medium.

—*psycho*, slang for someone behaving as if out of his mind.

—*psychoanalysis*, Freudian investigation of mental processes by encouragement of mental self-revelation (*ana + lyein*, to loosen up).

—*psychokinesis*, mind controlling matter (*kinein*, to move).

—*psychology*, the study of mental processes and behavior.

—*psychopath*, one severely suffering from mental disorder, especially antisocial (*pathos*, suffering, disease).

—*psychosis*, severe mental derangement, accompanied by withdrawal from reality (*-osis*, suffix for state or condition, especially abnormal).

—*psychosomatic*, pertaining to a bodily disorder induced by mental disorder (*soma*, body).

—*psychotherapy*, mental treatment of illness (*therapeuein*, to take care of).

PSYCHOLOGICAL MOMENT

The phrase came into the language as a misinterpretation of German *Moment*, momentum, not moment. Used by a German newspaper in 1870 to refer to the "mental effect" or "psychic factor" involved in the bombardment of Paris, *psychological moment* was misinterpreted to mean "the critical moment" or "in the nick of time" and has become a cliché.

PTOMAINE

From Greek *ptoma*, dead body. Note the spelling.

PUBLICIST

The word was originally a term of dignity for a specialist in public law or a journalist specializing in public policy, but *publicist* has deteriorated into a euphemism for a flack or press agent.

PUBLICLY

Note the spelling: *ly*, not *ally*.

PUBLIC RELATIONS, *see* PR

PUBLIC TEAT

An old Americanism, *public teat* could stand revival as a vivid term for the breastwork of the welfare state.

PUKKA

An Anglo-Indian word for genuine, first-class, as in "pukka sahib" or "His behavior was hardly pukka" (similar to the slang meaning of *kosher*), *pukka* comes from Hindustani *pakka*, cooked, ripe, solid.

PULITZER
Pronounce it "pull it sir."

PUMPERNICKEL
Like *clam chowder soup*, *pumpernickel bread* is redundant. Made from coarsely ground rye, pumpernickel is difficult for some persons to digest, which accounts for its name, from early New High German *Pumpern*, a fart, and *Nickel*, devil.

PUN
Before you publish a pun, try it out on some intelligent person who has a sense of humor. It may not be as funny as you think. One's man fish is another man's poisson or, as George S. Kaufman said, "One man's Mede is another man's Persian." See SAD HUMOR.

PUNCTUATION
See separate entries for the various punctuation marks.

PURCHASE, *see* BUY

PURGE / SPLURGE
Because the brain tends to be more active but less critical at night than in the morning, O'London advised writers "to splurge in the night hours and in the morning to purge."

PURPORT
Because the verb *purport* already has the passive connotation of "supposed to be" or "represented to be," it should not be used in the passive voice. Say, "The signature purports to be Hancock's but it is a forgery," but not "The signature is purported to be . . ."

Fowler gives a second "idiomatic limitation" that the subject of *purport* should be a thing, not a person, unless the person is "viewed as a phenomenon of which the nature is indicated by speech, actions, etc.," but the distinction is perhaps too fine.

The more common pronunciation of the verb stresses the second syllable; the more common pronunciation of the noun (meaning intended meaning, import, broad understanding) stresses the first syllable.

PURPOSE / RESULT
Don't confuse *purpose* and *result*. In "Trevino missed the putt to lose the tournament," change *to lose* to *and lost*. The *result* of the missed

putt was the loss of the tournament. If his *purpose* had been to lose the tournament, Trevino would have been drummed out of the PGA for life.

PURSUE
Note the spelling: *pur*, not *per*.

PUSILLANIMOUS
From Latin *pusillus*, very little, and *animus*, the mind, *pusillanimous* means small-minded, weak-willed, chicken-hearted, gutless.

PYRO–
Many English words derive from Greek *pyr*, fire. For example: *pyre*, a pile of combustible material, usually wood, for burning a corpse; *Pyrex*, a trademark for a species of heat-resistant glass; *pyromaniac*, a firebug; *pyrophobia*, irrational fear of fire; *pyrophoric*, fire-bearing, spontaneously igniting; *pyrotechnics*, fireworks.

PYRRHIC VICTORY
One gained at too great a cost, from Pyrrhus, king of Epirus, whose victory over the Romans in 279 B.C. at Asculum led him to remark that one more victory like that and "Pyrrhus is undone."

Q.E.D.

Short for Latin *quod erat demonstrandum*, which was to be demonstrated (proved). Written at the end of the solution of a geometric or other problem.

QUADRIVIUM, *see* LIBERAL ARTS

QUALITY

The shibboleth "quality education" raises the legitimate question: "What kind of quality?" We already have enough education of lousy quality and mediocre quality. As a graffito in a classroom of a journalism school of high quality says, "Quality is not an adjective."

QUANTUM JUMP

A technical term in physics, *quantum jump* has leaped into bureaucratic jargon to mean any sudden change in knowledge. See also BREAKTHROUGH.

QUARANTINE

From Italian *quaranta*, forty, because the period of enforced isolation was commonly forty days.

QUASI

Straight Latin for "as if," hence almost, seeming, to some degree, as if it were, as in *quasi-judicial*, *quasi-scientific*, *a quasi argument*, *a quasi union*.

QUESTION MARK

The punctuation mark (?) is used after a direct question: Will you be at work tomorrow? It is not used after an indirect question: He asked whether she would be at work tomorrow.

The question mark is placed inside quotation marks if the quote is a question: "Will you be at work tomorrow?" he asked. But it is placed outside quotation marks if the quote is not a question: Why did you say to me, "I don't trust you"?

Because a question mark already contains a period, don't repeat the period. Authorities differ on the use of a comma after a question mark, as in: When he asked her, "Will you marry me?," she didn't know what to say. The more common practice is to drop the comma.

Try to resist the temptation to put a question mark in parentheses as a way to convey cute sarcasm, as in: Brezhnev promised (?) to abide by the treaty.

See INTERROBANG and PRONEQUARK.

QUESTIONNAIRE
Many boondoggles would be thwarted if everybody who received a questionnaire headed *questionaire* would shred it.

QUIDDITY
From Latin *quid*, what, the *quiddity* of a thing is its whatness, its essence, what makes it what it is.

QUIDNUNC
Straight Latin for "what now?" A *quidnunc* is a gossip, a busybody.

QUID PRO QUO
Straight Latin for "something for something."

QUINTESSENCE
From Latin *quinta essentia*, the fifth essence. Pythagoras added ether, the stuff of heavenly bodies, to the four essences of fire, air, water and earth. Today the *quintessence* of something is its exemplar, its consummate or most typical embodiment, as in "Gene Kelly's dancing is the quintessence of grace" or "Idi Amin is the quintessential bastard."

QUIP
As a verb, *quip* has become journalese, especially sportsese. If hack sports writers are to be believed, coaches and athletes don't tell jokes or say funny things. They quip. And in case the reader can't see the humor, the hack will add the attribution "he quipped." When was the last time you heard a reasonably intelligent person say "he quipped"?

QUISLING, *see* EPONYM

QUIZ
As a noun on campus, *quiz* is acceptable for *examination* or *test*. As a verb, it is headlinese for *ask*, *doubt*, *inquire*, *query*, *seek*.

QUORUM / QUOTA

If the language butchers ever discover that *quorum* is masculine (the masculine genitive plural of Latin *qui*, who), there will be a new word for the minimum number of persons required to be present for the valid transaction of business. Then what will they do with *quota*, feminine of Latin *quotus*, of what number, how many?

QUOTATION MARKS

The British call quotation marks (") and (') inverted commas. The double quotation mark introduces and ends quoted material; the single quotation mark introduces and ends quoted material within quoted material. Thus: He said, "I didn't say, 'I don't like your mother'; I said, 'I don't want your mother to live with us.'" Note that the semicolon is placed outside the quotation mark, and the period inside. Similarly, colons are placed outside, and commas inside. For the position of the question mark, see QUESTION MARK.

Don't use quotation marks apologetically, as if to say, "I don't like this phrase, so I'll put it in quotation marks to show you I don't like it." For example: He "copped out" on the witness stand. If *copped out* is too slangy for you, choose another phrase. Similarly, don't use quotation marks sarcastically, as: The "gentlemen" sat while ladies stood. Rephrase the idea. Don't resort to typographical gimmicks to point up your moods.

QUOTE

Though 85 percent of the American Heritage usage panelists consider the noun *quote*, for *quotation*, unacceptable in writing, its use as such is standard in the publishing business.

QUOTE HANDLING

The two most important things to remember about quote handling are:

1. Don't use more than one attribution ("he said") for the same quote.

2. When you break up a quote into paragraphs, don't unquote any paragraph except the last.

Consider this example:

He said, "If I had to name the chief causes of the nation's current economic ills, I would list excessive government spending, irresponsible demands by organized labor and lack of confidence in the current administration. Add to these the social ills of crime and illiteracy, brought on by the disintegration of the family, the decline of religious belief and the no-fault standards of public education. What we need are leaders with a sense of public responsibility and citizens with a sense of personal responsibility."

There are several other ways to handle this quote. Here are some:

"If I had to name the chief causes . . . current administration," he said. "Add to these . . . personal responsibility."

He said, "If I had to name the chief causes . . . current administration.

"Add to these . . . personal responsibility."

"If I had to name the chief causes of the nation's current economic ills," he said, "I would list . . . current administration.

"Add to these . . . personal responsibility."

Another important thing to remember is that when you introduce a different speaker the attribution should come at the beginning. Otherwise the reader may assume that the same person is still speaking. Thus:

"I call on organized labor to hold down wage demands," President Carter said.

AFL-CIO President Lane Kirkland said, "I maintain that wage demands will decrease if prices are held in check."

RABBI, *see* **JEWISH SYNAGOGUE**

RACCOON
The more common spelling has a double *c*.

RACK, *see* **NERVE-RACKING**

RADAR
Acronym for <u>ra</u>dio <u>d</u>etecting <u>a</u>nd <u>r</u>anging.

RAISE / REAR
The old distinction between raising animals and rearing children has all but disappeared. Animals are raised and children are either reared or raised or drug up.

RAISE / RISE
As verbs, *raise* is transitive, *rise* intransitive. The landlord raises the rent when maintenance costs rise. As nouns, *rise* is more common than *raise*, which is mostly restricted to an increase in pay, as in "A large raise accompanied his sudden rise to executive office."

–RAMA
The suffix *-rama* is an abbreviation of Greek *horama*, sight, view, as in *panorama*, a view of a wide area, and other legitimate words, such as *cinerama*, wide screen movie projection, and *cyclorama*, a large composite picture encircling a viewer.

But, as Morsberger says, *-rama* has "spread like a mindless fungus until it has become simply advertising jargon," as in such monstrosities as *bowlerama, foodorama, healthorama, horrorama, launderama, slenderama, stripperama, tacorama, wrestlerama*. Morsberger gives the ghoulish example of *death-a-rama* for a "Discount Funeral Parlor" and the sacrilegious example of *Christorama* for a store that sells religious items. See also **–THON**.

RANDOM SAMPLE, *see* AT RANDOM

RAP

To connote opposition, *rap* is headlinese. To connote conversation, *rap* is a faddish word whose vogue, thank heaven, is fading. Like other juvenilia, *to rap*, for *to talk*, ill fits the mouth of an educated person, no matter how he tries to sound like one of the mob.

The expressions "I don't give a rap," "I don't care a rap," "It's not worth a rap" come from the worthlessness of a rap, a counterfeit halfpenny circulating in Ireland in the eighteenth century, worth about half a farthing.

RAREBIT, *see* WELSH RABBIT / RAREBIT

RAREFY

Note the spelling: *e*, not *i*.

RATHER THAN

Because *than* is a conjunction, grammar dictates that the grammatical forms joined by *than* should be of the same kind, as in "He decided on driving rather than flying" and "He decided to drive rather than fly." But what about "He drove rather than flew"? *Flew?* Or "He drives rather than flies"? *Flies?* Here idiom transcends grammar and one is justified in saying: "He drove (drives) rather than fly." As Fowler says, "It is well, on the one hand, not to fly in the face of grammar, but rather to eschew what is manifestly indefensible; and, on the other hand, not to give up what one feels is idiomatic in favour of an alternative that is more obviously defensible."

RATIO

The relationship of part to part.

REACTION

A *reaction* is a response to some stimulus. It is automatic, impulsive. *Reaction* is not a synonym for *opinion*, which is reflective, considered, weighed. If one asks, "What was your reaction to the president's speech?" you should give some knee-jerk response such as "I blew my top." If one asks for your *opinion*, you should give some reasoned reply. *Reaction* is thoughtlessly overworked. Choose the appropriate word for the context: *attitude, conclusion, conviction, feeling, impression, judgment, opinion, reply, response, thought, view.*

READ WHERE
The construction "I read (or *saw*) in (or *by*) the papers where . . ." is a barbarism. Change *where* to *that*.

REAL / REALLY
The adjective is *real*, the adverb *really*. See ADJECTIVE / ADVERB.

REAR, *see* RAISE / REAR

REASON IS BECAUSE
The grammatical reason for the error in "The reason he failed is because he didn't study" is that *the reason is* calls for a nounal clause: "The reason he failed is that he didn't study." The adverbial conjunction *because* is correct in "He failed because he didn't study."

A simpler reason is that *because* means "for the reason that" and therefore one would be saying, "The reason he failed is for the reason that . . . ," which is as redundant as saying "The because is because."

REASON WHY
The phrase seems as redundant as *the reason is because*, but there are constructions in which *reason why* is idiomatically justified. After "non-scientific study and inexhaustive thought," Bernstein concludes in *Miss Thistlebottom's Hobgoblins* that *reason why* is necessary when: (1) something comes between *reason* and *why*, as in "I see no reason, sound or unsound, why he is tired"; and (2) a negative comes before *reason*, as in "No reason why he is tired can be found."

REBUT / REFUTE
In reporting, *rebut* and *refute* are LOADED VERBS. They carry the sense of successful argument, disproof, and therefore imply editorial judgment.

RECEIVE
Note the spelling: *e* before *i*. Some may think an apology should be required for an entry on the spelling of so common a word. The apology, in the strict sense of the word, is the long, disheartening experience of seeing *recieve*.

RECOGNIZE
Some public speakers, who should know better, need to be informed that *recognize* has a *g* and that the *g* is sounded.

RECOIL, *see* **CULOTTES**

RECORD, *see* **NEW RECORD**

RED-LETTER
Feast days are often marked in red on church calendars, whence a *red-letter* day is a specially happy day to be remembered.

REDUNDANT
From Latin *redundare*, to overflow, to rise back in waves (*unda*, a wave), hence using more words than are needed to convey an idea.

REFER
See ALLUDE / REFER. As a noun, *refer* is a newspaper term for a reference, often in an EAR, to a story on another page of the paper.

REFLEXIVE, *see* **PRONOUN**

REFUTE, *see* **REBUT / REFUTE**

REGALIA
Plural.

REHEARSAL
Note the spelling: not *rehersal*, as the word is pronounced. From Latin *hirpex*, a harrow, a *rehearsal* is literally a harrowing again, hence a repetition for practice. *Hearse* comes from the same root, a reference to the spiked framework of the candelabrum over the coffin at a funeral in church, and then by extension the vehicle in which a coffin is carried.

REIGN / REIN
Note the different spellings, as in "Henry VIII gave free rein to his appetites during his reign."

REITERATE, *see* **ITERATE**

RELATE
The American Heritage says *relate* in the sense of "interact with others in a meaningful or coherent fashion" is jargon, as in "She relates well to her peers." She gets along with them.

RELATIVE PRONOUN, *see* PRONOUN

RELEVANT
To what? Don't leave *relevant* dangling without a prepositional phrase. Yes: "My college courses were not professionally relevant to my eventual career." No: "My college courses were not relevant."

About *irrelevant*, Strunk astutely observes: "A student who finds society out of joint, or himself out of joint, takes refuge in the word *irrelevant*, using it as a general term of disapprobation. He damns history and wipes out the past with a single stroke. There is a kind of arrogance in labeling everythiing that has taken place in the world as 'irrelevant.' What the student means, of course, is that he finds the story of the past curiously unrelated to the spectacle of the present. This is his privilege, as well as his hard luck. But the relationship should be stated, not left to the imagination."

And if you're hooked on *relevant*, spell it right. The word isn't *revelant*.

REMAINDER, *see* BALANCE

REMINISCENCE
Note the spelling.

RENEGE
Literally, from Medieval Latin *renegare*, to *renege* is to deny strongly, hence its use in cards for the dastardly act of not following suit. Hence also *renegade*.

REPEAT, *see* ITERATE

REPEL / REPULSE
Both verbs connote driving back, successful resistance, rejection, but *repel* also connotes aversion, disgust. Bernstein gives this good example of the distinction: "She repulsed the suitor because he repelled her."

REPLICA / REPRODUCTION
Strictly, a *replica* is a *reproduction* by the original artist. Loosely, a *replica* is any *reproduction*. According to the context, why not choose the most appropriate word for a work of art reproduced by a different artist, such as *copy, duplicate, facsimile, imitation, miniature, reproduction?*

REPLICATE

The verb is not an automatic synonym for *repeat*. As well as its meaning of "fold over" or "bend back" (from Latin *re + plicare*, to fold back), *replicate* has the scientific meaning of "conduct a study using the same methods as a previous study."

RESIDE

Don't use *reside* as a synonym for *live*. Restrict *reside* to dwelling in some official or historic mansion: "When in Sacramento, Governor Reagan resided in the governor's mansion, but Governor Brown lives in a bachelor apartment"; "President Truman resided at Blair House while the White House was being repaired." See MAKES HIS HOME.

RESPECTIVELY

The word is often unnecessary, as in "Dallas and Pittsburgh eliminated Los Angeles and Houston, respectively, from the Super Bowl" or "Commencement dates for 1980 and 1981 have been changed to May 19 and 25, respectively." Drop *respectively* or rephrase if you think a sensible reader will be confused.

RESTAURATEUR

Note the spelling: *restaurateur* is commonly misspelled with an *n*, as in *restaurant*. Both words derive from French *restaurer*, to restore, but *restaurant* is the participial form, wherefore the *n*.

RESTRICTIVE, *see* THAT / WHICH

RESULT

The phrase *as the result of* is often misused for *as a result of*, as in "Thousands were left homeless today as the result of tornadoes that swept through the Midwest." Homelessness was only one of the many results of the tornadoes. See PURPOSE / RESULT.

REVEAL, *see* DISCLOSE / REVEAL

REVENGE, *see* AVENGE / REVENGE

REVEREND

Because *Reverend* is an honorific adjective, not a noun, a clergyman should never be called "a reverend" or addressed as "Reverend," as in

"Hi, Reverend." Also, *the* should precede *Reverend*, usually abbreviated to *Rev.* in writing: the Rev. John Smith. Note, too, that *Rev.* should never be used immediately before a surname. Either a first name or a title should come between. Thus: the Rev. John Smith or the Rev. Mr. (or Fr. or Dr.) Smith. The same principles apply to other honorifics, such as *Honorable* (*Hon.*).

RHETORIC
One of the seven classical liberal arts, *rhetoric* comes from Greek *rhetor*, orator, and refers mainly to the art of clear, persuasive language, whether in speech or in writing. *Rhetoric* has been debased by some as a synonym for *bombast, braggadocio, exaggeration, fustian, ranting, rodomontade*, as in "That's just a bunch of rhetoric." The pristine meaning of the word should be preserved. There are plenty of other words for foolish talk.

RHETORICAL QUESTION
Posed for effect without expectation of a spoken answer, a *rhetorical question* is really a statement in question form. A rhetorical question assumes that only one true answer is possible and that the reader or listener will silently provide it. Thus, "Have you ever heard anything more ridiculous in your whole life?" calls for the tacit agreement of "Hell, no, never."

RH FACTOR
This substance present in red blood cells gets its name from the rhesus monkey, in which it was first detected.

RHINOCEROS
From Greek *rhis* (genitive *rhinos*), nose, and *keras*, horn. Other *rhin-* words pertaining to the nose are: *rhinal*, nasal; *rhinitis*, inflammation of the nose; *rhinology*, medical study of the nose; *rhinoplasty*, plastic surgery of the nose; *rhinoscope*, an instrument for examination of the nose.

RHUBARB
To simulate crowd noise offstage, a few extras backstage merely have to intone sonorously the word *rhubarb*. As Partridge attests, this gimmick is an ancient tradition on the London stage. From it derives the use of *rhubarb* for a ruckus, especially in baseball. In *Rhubarb*, H. Allen Smith described a *rhubarb* as "a noisy altercation, a broil, a violent emotional upheaval brought on by an epical dispute—such as whether one

grown man had touched another on the body with a ball the size of a smallish orange."

RHYTHM
Note the spelling.

RIGHT ON
An overworked exclamation of agreement or encouragement, once popular in the rent-a-protest street talk of the don't-trust-anyone-over-thirty prodigies, but now dying as fast as the gamins of the 1960s senesce into over-thirty decrepitude.

RIGHT WING, *see* LEFT WING

R.I.P.
Only coincidentally does *R.I.P.* stand for "rest in peace." The abbreviation comes from Latin *requiescat in pace*, may he (she) rest in peace.

RISE, *see* RAISE / RISE

ROBBERY, *see* BURGLARY / ROBBERY / THEFT

ROBOT
The word comes from Czech *robota*, slave labor, drudgery, and was made popular in the early 1920s by Czech dramatist Karel Čapek's play *R.U.R.* (Rossum's Universal Robots). The play is set in a degenerate society dependent upon soulless mechanical men, robots, who eventually revolt against their masters and destroy them.

ROB ROY
A drink made from Scotch whisky, sweet vermouth and bitters, named after Robert (Rob Roy) MacGregor, the legendary Scottish Robin Hood, a man tough enough to handle so potent a potion. See also ALEXANDER.

ROBUST
From Latin *robur*, oak, strength, whence also *corroborate* and *rambunctious*. The more common pronunciation of *robust* stresses the last syllable.

ROCK 'N' ROLL
Note the spelling of this breed of jungle music: apostrophe before and after the *n*.

RODEO
In rodeo country, the pronunciation that stresses the first syllable of *rodeo* (second syllable pronounced as in *dee*) has all but supplanted the Spanish pronunciation, which stresses the second syllable (pronounced as in *day*).

ROMAN A CLEF
Literally, French for "a novel with a key," hence a novel whose characters or events are real persons or actual events in disguise.

ROMANCE LANGUAGES
Languages that developed from the Roman tongue, the principal among which are French, Italian, Portuguese, Romanian, Spanish.

ROMANIA
AP requires the spelling *Romania*, rather than *Roumania* or *Rumania*.

ROSEMARY
The derivation of the word for this shrub, whose leaves are used as a cooking herb, has nothing to do with *rose* or with *Mary*. The word comes from Latin *ros*, dew, and *marinus*, marine, hence sea dew. But the English twisting of the Latin to form the pleasant association of *rose* and *Mary* out of the similarly pleasant *sea dew* doesn't bother Moore, who says: "Who cares? We made a name for the homely herb that aptly matches it, that has endearing associations, and that is most perfectly suited to our tongue."

ROSTRUM
Latin for the beak of a bird, from *rodere*, to gnaw, to nibble at, *rostrum* was the name given to a Roman ship's prow, shaped like a giant curved beak. Because the Roman Forum was decorated with the prows of captured enemy ships, its speakers' platform became known as the rostrum. See also LECTERN / PODIUM.

ROUNDBALLER
Sportsese for a basketball player, as if a basketball were the only round ball used in sports.

ROUTE
The more common pronunciation of *route* is *root*, not *rout*. See also
EN ROUTE.

R.S.V.P.
Abbreviation for French *répondez s'il vous plaît*, please reply.

RUBE, *see* HICK

RUMMAGE
This term for a sale of odds and ends comes from the French word for
the cargo in a ship's hold. *Rummage* sale and *rummage* around, according to Shipley, came from "the confusion in which cargo lay on the
wharf."

RUN-ON SENTENCE
A false sentence in which a comma is used instead of a period is a run-on
sentence, sometimes called a *comma splice*, such as "She missed class,
afterwards she apologized." Perhaps the most common form of the error
occurs with adverbs mistakenly used as conjunctions, such as *however*,
as in "She missed class, however she apologized afterwards." Make it:
"She missed class. However, she apologized afterwards."

RUSTLE
In the sense of cattle stealing or foraging, *rustle* is a blend word from *rush*
and *hustle*.

RUTHLESS
Having no ruth, no compassion. The noun *ruth*, from Anglo-Saxon
rewen, to rue, is now obsolete.

S

SACRED COW
In newspapers and magazines, *sacred cows* are topics untouchable by members of any caste lower than editor or publisher. Sacred cows sometimes take the form of words unmentionable or ideas conveyable only in words ordained by a Brahmin.

SACRILEGIOUS
Because *sacrilegious* pertains to religion, it is often misspelled *sacreligious*. The derivation of *sacrilegious* is Latin *sacer*, sacred, and *legere*, to gather, pick up, steal. The derivation of *religion* is Latin *re + ligare*, to bind back, hence the bond between human and divine.

SADDER BUT WISER
The phrase is a cliché unless peculiarly pertinent to the context, as it was to the context of the desire of Professor Harold Hill, Meredith Willson's music man, for "a sadder but wiser girl." The phrase *sadder and wiser* comes from Coleridge's "The Rime of the Ancient Mariner" in reference to the wedding guest, "A sadder and a wiser man, he rose the morrow morn."

SAD HUMOR
Humor is in the wit of the beholder. It may be happy or sad. You be the judge. Behold:
- *Acupuncture*. Needlepoint.
- *Allidile*. A cross between an alligator and a crocodile.
- *Barque*. The sound made by an old sea dog.
- *Bison*. A plice where an Ostrylian washes his fice.
- *Blunch*. A drink between breakfast and lunch.
- *Crocogator*. A cross between a crocodile and an alligator.
- *Footnotitis*. A disease endemic in beginning graduate students and pseudoscientists, painful to their readers.
- *Futilitarian*. One who thinks all human endeavor useless.
- *Gladly*. Pet name for all cross-eyed bears, from the old Sunday School hymn "Gladly the Cross I'd Bear."

—*Happy Medium.* A drunken poltergeist.

—*Infracaninophile.* One who loves to root for the underdog.

—*Logarithm.* Didgeridoo music.

—*Mandate.* A gay evening.

—*Mishmash.* A drunk who doesn't wake up for church.

—*9W.* What Wagner replied when asked whether he spelled his name with a *V*.

—*Ovicephalic.* An egghead.

—*Propound.* A brothel.

—*Scabbard.* A nonunion poet.

—*Tenacity.* Wimbledon.

—*Universal Joint.* Any bar frequented by automobile mechanics.

—*Withholding Tax.* Anti-trust legislation.

SADIST, *see* MASOCHIST / SADIST

SAHARA DESERT
Because *Sahara* comes from Arabic *sahra*, desert, *Sahara Desert* is redundant. Make it *Sahara* or *the Sahara*. Similarly, *Sierra mountains* is redundant because a *sierra* is a ridge of mountains. Make it *the Sierras*.

SAID, *see* SYNONYMOMANIA

ST. JAMES('S)
Three things should be noted about St. James:

1. Two of the apostles were named James: James the Greater, son of Zebedee and brother of John; and James the Less, son of Alpheus.

2. James the Less wrote an Epistle but he didn't translate the Bible. The Authorized Version is the King James Bible, published by command of King James I, not the St. James Bible, as is occasionally heard.

3. The formal name of the British royal court, to which ambassadors to the United Kingdom are officially accredited, is "the Court of St. James's." Note the *'s*.

SALACIOUS
From Latin *salax* (genitive *salacis*), fond of leaping, lustful, from *salire*, to leap, jump, from which root come many other English words, such as *assail, desultory, exult, insult, result, salient, sally, sauté* (tossed in a pan and frequently turned over), *somersault*.

SALAD DAYS
In Shakespeare's *Antony and Cleopatra*, Cleopatra says that her love for Caesar was in "my salad days, when I was green in judgment, cold in blood" and that it paled before her passion for Antony, "the demi-Atlas of this earth." Says Evans: "As a term for youth, especially naive and inexperienced youth, green and fresh, *salad days* is now wilted."

SALARY
From Latin *salarium*, money for salt, whence the phrase "worth his salt."

SALISBURY STEAK
Named after an English dietitian, the dish retains the English pronunciation of his name: two syllables, not four, *Sawlz-bree*.

SALT OF THE EARTH
In the Sermon on the Mount, Christ called his disciples "the salt of the earth," but the phrase has become a cliché, having long since lost its savor.

SANDMAN
The genie who closes children's eyes for sleep by sprinkling a little sand in them got his name from *sandblind*, partially blind, which, according to Shipley, derives not from *sand* but from Anglo-Saxon *sam-*, half.

SANDWICH
Meat or other filling between slices of bread is an ancient repast, but *sandwich* didn't enter the language till the eighteenth century. The Fourth Earl of Sandwich, First Lord of the Admiralty during the American Revolution (the Sandwich Islands, now Hawaii, were named after him), so loved cards that he wouldn't quit to eat. He therefore ordered that chunks of meat between bread slices be served to him at the gaming table. Hence *sandwich*, which now ranges in size from thin cucumber to Dagwood.

SARCASM, *see* IRONICALLY

SARDONIC
When you grin sardonically, sneeringly, your mouth twists as if you had eaten something distasteful, such as *herba Sardonia*, a Sardinian poisonous herb, the eating of which convulsed the face in a death throe, wherefore *sardonic*.

SATELLITE
Note the spelling.

SATYRIASIS, *see* NYMPHOMANIA

SAUNTER
Shipley suggests that *saunter* comes from French *Sainte Terre*, the Holy Land, because of the unhurried pace of pilgrims strolling there. See also CANTER.

SAUTÉ, *see* SALACIOUS

SAVINGS
As a noun, *savings* is plural, as in "His savings are enough for him to retire on." *Savings* should therefore not be preceded by *a*, as in "Quitting smoking meant a savings of $30 a month for her." Make it *saving*.

SAVOYARD
A native of Savoy is a *Savoyard*, but the word more commonly refers to a Gilbert & Sullivan buff, most of their operas having been first staged at the Savoy Theatre, London.

SAWBUCK
The legs of a sawhorse were originally shaped like an X, which is the Roman numeral for 10, which is why a $10 bill is called a *sawbuck*.

SAXOPHONE
Note the spelling: *saxo*, not *saxa*. The *saxophone*, often abbreviated to *sax*, got its name from its inventor, Adolphe (christened Antoine) Sax, a nineteenth-century Belgian craftsman of musical instruments.

SCAN
Aside from its electronic connotation, the verb *scan* has contradictory meanings: (1) to examine thoroughly, as in the metrical analysis of verse; and (2) to look over hastily, as in the fast reading of a publication. The second meaning is now the more common: when one leafs through a book, one scans it.

SCATOLOGY
The study of filth, or obsession with it, from Greek *skor* (genitive *skatos*), dung.

SCENE
Nickles calls *scene* a "bedraggled word," rendered limp by such over-worked and unnecessary phrases as *making the scene, the drug scene, the Hollywood scene, the literary scene.*

SCHOLAR
The word derives from Greek *scholazein*, to have leisure, which must be the world's craziest etymology.

SCIENTISM, *see* COMMUNICOLOGESE

SCOFFLAW
Mencken records that *scofflaw*, a term for a habitual lawbreaker, was coined in 1924 by the winners of a contest promoted by a prohibitionist for the best word to apply to "the lawless drinker to stab awake his conscience."

SCONE
See BISCUIT. (No, not the horse.)

SCOTCH
When the wounded Scarus told Antony in Shakespeare's *Antony and Cleopatra*, "I have yet room for six scotches more," he was boasting of his capacity to stand six more clouts, not six more shots. According to the AP, *Scotch* is uppercase with *whisky* but lowercase in "I'll have a scotch."

A native of Scotland is a Scot or a Scotsman or a Scotswoman. The people are the Scots. The adjective is *Scottish*, except in certain combinations such as *Scotch broth, Scotch egg, Scotch terrier* and the trademark *Scotch tape*.

SCOT-FREE
The *scot* in *scot-free* does not refer to the apocryphal parsimony of the Scots, but to the Anglo-Saxon word for *tax*.

SCRAM
Short for *scramble.*

SCREAMING SENSATIONALISM
Though sensational headlines scream usually in the gutter press, some otherwise respectable newspapers will tend to be unduly sensational

when they let their urge for a daily front-page banner overcome their judgment of whether the news in the lead story deserves banner treatment.

Some papers still insist on an across-the-page head of an inch or more on the front page, often in solid uppercase, no matter what the news is. Everything from a presidential assassination to the county fair gets the same kind of banner treatment. Thus readers, seeing a screamer every day, lose either their news perspective or their faith in the paper's news judgment. Editors shouldn't lock themselves into a daily makeup formula that shuts out news judgment.

Screaming sensationalism has subsided in the American press over the years as the social responsibility of the press has risen. Other reasons for the silencing have been the increase in home delivery of newspapers and the decrease in newsstand sales. Also, because of the rise of monopoly and the fall of competition, papers publish fewer editions these days. The economic urge for street sales breeds bastard banners, newsworthy only for the emotionally undernourished fan clubs of intellectually under-privileged gossip columnists.

If a story isn't sensational, its head shouldn't be. If a story doesn't scream, its head shouldn't.

"Why scream at a man in the quiet of his living room?" asked a member of the American Society of Newspaper Editors in a survey of headline habits.

A minority report in the survey disagreed: "Headlines should not be subjected to reform. Only a few newspapers are supposed to be decorous in their attire. The rest should go their rowdy way, with small stories often blowing off big headlines and black type jarring lazy minds. Most Americans like newspapers that act like people, with disordered liveliness and the human touch. An outspoken and loud headline helps preserve the freedom of the press."

If this is so, some newspapers are doing a bang-up job of preserving the freedom of the press.

SCREW

The American vulgarism has a different meaning in Britain, where it is slang for *pay*, *wages*. Aghast was the young American advised by an English friend to quit his job as a cab driver and join the armed forces "because you'll get a better screw in the army." See also KNOCK UP and PECKER.

SCROD, *see* BOSTON ACCENT

SCRUPLES
From Latin *scrupulus*, a small sharp stone, hence a nagging attention to minutiae; also, a state of conscience characterized by the conviction that innocent acts are sinful.

SCUBA
Acronym for <u>s</u>elf-<u>c</u>ontained <u>u</u>nderwater <u>b</u>reathing <u>a</u>pparatus.

SCULPT, *see* BACK FORMATION

SCUTTLEBUTT
The water cooler in a school or office or factory is a gathering place for mongers of gossip, rumor, scuttlebutt. The keg of drinking water in old ships was called the *scuttlebutt*, from *scuttle*, hatch, and *butt*, cask.

SEALING WAX, *see* SONIC WRITING

SEAMY
Long before Madison Avenue invented the term *body odor* to make people feel insecure, body odor was a normal concomitant of the human condition because everybody smelled more or less the same. Especially skunky was the inside of their garments, the side with the rough seams, wherefore the expression *the seamy side of life* for the less presentable, the rough, the sordid.

SECEDE, *see* ACCEDE

SECONDARY TENSES, *see* SEQUENCE OF TENSES

SECRETIVE
In speech, distinguish between the two meanings of *secretive* by stressing the first syllable for the reference to silence, reticence, and the second syllable for the reference to the process of secretion.

SEED MONEY
Bureaucratese for the down payment on what may grow up to be a breakthrough or just another boondoggle.

SEEM
A copulative verb. See ADJECTIVE / ADVERB and CAN'T SEEM TO.

SEEMING, *see* APPARENT

SEERSUCKER
That jacket or dress you break out in the summer gets its name from Persian *shirushakar*, literally "milk and sugar," a reference to the stripes and crinkles.

SEE WHERE, *see* READ WHERE

SEIZE
Note the spelling: *e* before *i*.

SELENOLOGY
A romantic-sounding word, *selenology*, from Greek *selene*, the moon, is the astronomical study of the moon.

SELF-CONFESSED
Redundant.

SELF-DESTRUCT
Nickles calls this graceless neologism "a barbaric mad-scientistic back formation created needlessly, because the gracious good English of *to destroy itself* would have served."

SELL LIKE HOT CAKES, *see* HOT CAKES

SEMESTER
Originally a period of six months, from Latin *sex*, six, and *mensis*, month, a *semester* is now an academic period of about four months of instruction.

SEMICOLON
The punctuation mark semicolon (;) provides a greater break between clauses or ideas than a comma, but a lesser break than a period. As was noted in COLON, the semicolon is used much less today than formerly, especially in newspapers. Because newspapers prefer short sentences to long and because the modern tendency in newspapers is to regard a sentence as a group of words between periods, the use of semicolons is regarded as cheating on sentence length. When in doubt, use a period.

Semicolons are needed, however, to separate the parts of a series that contains a comma within each part, as in "The search committee comprises these members: William Hogan, associate executive vice chancellor; David Kraft, dean of the School of Engineering; Ambrose Saricks, professor of history; Jerry Sass, graduate student in journalism; and Elizabeth Schultz, professor of English." Note the semicolon before the *and* in the final item of the series.

SEMIMONTHLY, *see* BIMONTHLY / SEMIMONTHLY

SEMINAR
A *seminar* is a small group of students and a professor who sow seeds of knowledge, from Latin *semen* (genitive *seminis*), seed. In Shakespeare's *Antony and Cleopatra*, Cleopatra calls the eunuch Mardian "unseminar'd."

SEMIWEEKLY, *see* BIWEEKLY / SEMIWEEKLY

SENATE
Literally, an assembly of old men, from Latin *senex*, old.

SENIOR CITIZEN, *see* OLDSTER

SENSATIONAL, *see* AFRAID

SENSATIONALISM, *see* SCREAMING SENSATIONALISM

SENTENCE
A sentence is a grammatical unit that conveys a complete thought and contains a subject and a predicate, either or both of which may be unstated but understood. Sentences are principally classified as simple, compound, complex, compound-complex, complex-complex. Thus:

A simple sentence consists of one independent clause: "He knows almost nothing."

A compound sentence consists of two or more independent clauses connected by a coordinating conjunction: "He knows almost nothing and he doesn't want to study" and "He knows almost nothing and he doesn't want to study but he may change."

A complex sentence consists of an independent clause and one or more dependent clauses: "He knows almost nothing because he refuses to study" and "Because he refuses to study, he doesn't know what he should."

A compound-complex sentence consists of two or more independent clauses and one or more dependent clauses: "He knows that he should study but he doesn't want to" and "He knows that he should study but he doesn't think that he has a chance of passing."

A complex-complex sentence consists of an independent clause and a dependent clause that is subordinate to another dependent clause: "He got mad when I told him that he should study."

SEPARATE
Note the spelling: *par*, not *per*.

SEQUENCE OF TENSES
Reporters use three speeches:

DIRECT SPEECH: "I am weary," he said, "but I will go."

PARENTHETICAL SPEECH: He is weary, he said, but he will go.

REPORTED SPEECH: He said (that) he was weary but (that) he would go. (See THAT.)

DIRECT SPEECH. Direct speech is quoted speech. The words are exactly those of the speaker.

The attribution in direct speech may come at the beginning or in the middle or at the end. Thus:

He said, "I am weary but I will go."

"I am weary," he said, "but I will go."

"I am weary but I will go," he said.

Because the *said* verb in direct speech has no grammatical effect on the quoted words and because the words are exactly those of the speaker, neither the tenses of verbs nor the persons of pronouns are changed. Tense and person are those used by the speaker.

PARENTHETICAL SPEECH. In parenthetical speech, the words are not necessarily those of the speaker. The ideas are. The speaker's words may be paraphrased, but his meaning may not be changed.

The attribution in parenthetical speech may come in the middle or at the end. It may not come at the beginning. Thus:

Yes: He is weary, he said, but he will go.

Yes: He is weary but he will go, he said.

No: He said, he is weary but he will go.

Because the *said* verb in parenthetical speech is merely parenthetical and therefore has no grammatical effect on the sentence, the tenses of the other verbs are not changed. They are those of the speaker.

The persons of pronouns, however, are changed because American reporting style is in the third person except in quotes. Therefore, first person must be changed to third person, and second person to third person. Thus:

—*Direct:* "I am weary," he said, "but I will go."

—*Parenthetical:* He is weary, he said, but he will go.

—*Direct:* "You are inconsiderate," Alice told John, "but you will mature."

—*Parenthetical:* John is inconsiderate, Alice said, but he will mature.

REPORTED SPEECH. In reported speech, the *said* verb is the governing verb and therefore controls the tenses of the subordinate verbs.

In reported speech, when the *said* verb is in the past tense, the primary tenses of subordinate verbs must be changed to secondary tenses. These are the primary tenses and their corresponding secondary tenses:

Primary		*Secondary*	
Present	I go	Past	I went
Perfect	I have gone	Past Perfect	I had gone
Future	I will go	Conditional	I would go
Future Perfect	I will have gone	Conditional Perfect	I would have gone

Accordingly, present is changed to past, perfect to past perfect, future to conditional, and future perfect to conditional perfect. Thus:

—*Direct:* "Though I am old," he said, "I am energetic."

—*Reported:* He said that though he was old he was energetic.

—*Direct:* "I have aged," he said, "but I have not lost my energy."

—*Reported:* He said (that) he had aged but (that) he had not lost his energy.

—*Direct:* "I will go," he said, "but I will be late."

—*Reported:* He said (that) he would go but (that) he would be late.

—*Direct:* "I will have lost my patience by then," he said.

—*Reported:* He said (that) he would have lost his patience by then.

As in parenthetical speech, the persons of pronouns in reported speech are changed from first to third, and from second to third.

In reported speech, the attribution must come at the beginning.

The sequence of tenses makes sense. Notice how we talk:

Jack: I'm leaving town today but I'll be back tomorrow.

Jim: What did Jack say?

Joe: Jack said (that) he was leaving town today but (that) he would be back tomorrow.

Some authorities allow an exception to the sequence of tenses when what is said is something that is perpetually true. Thus: He said a triangle has (not *had*) three sides.

For other aspects of the sequence of tenses, see ACCORDING TO and the next-to-last paragraph of COMMA.

SERENDIPITY
When Horace Walpole, eighteenth-century author, read the fairy tale *The Three Princes of Serendip*, he was impressed by the heroes, who "were always making discoveries, by accidents and sagacity, of things they were not in quest of." He was also struck by the lack of an English word to describe this happy knack and so he coined the sweet-sounding *serendipity*. Serendip is an old name for Ceylon, the new name for which is Sri Lanka.

SERIOUS CRISIS
Most crises are.

SERIOUSLY, HOWEVER, *see* GUEST SPEAKER

SERVE / SERVICE
The verbs are not automatically interchangeable. *To service* something is to perform some task of maintenance, repair, supply, installation, inspection. *Service* is usually limited to mechanical things, as in "service the car, the furnace, the garbage Disposall." But a bus company *serves*, not *services*, a city; and a university newspaper *serves*, not *services*, a campus.

SERVED AS
Journalese for *was*, as in "Floyd Arbuthnot served as president of the Chamber of Commerce for five years." Was he or wasn't he? And what did he serve? Restrict *served as* to temporary positions, as in "After Smith's death in office, Jones served as chairman of the board until its members could be convened for an election." The same principle applies to the other tenses of *serve as*.

SESQUIPEDALIAN
Long words like *sesquipedalian*, and those who love to use them, are sesquipedalian, from Latin *sesqui*, one-half more, one and a half, and *pes* (genitive *pedis*), a foot, hence words a foot and a half long. Another

sesquipedalian word is *sesquicentennial*, a century and a half old, the 150th anniversary.

SET
This is probably the most overworked verb in headlines. Newspapers have to announce many events, and *set* becomes a handy short-count headline word. Its use, however, dulls, especially when several heads on the same page are announcing that some person or some group is "set" to do something. Most of the time, the word can simply be omitted. "Lions Set to Meet Friday" can become "Lions to Meet Friday." For other meanings, try *agree, aim, fix, map, plan, plot.*

SEVENTH HEAVEN
The phrase, now a cliché, comes from the belief of some religions that because the seventh ring of stars is the farthest from the earth it is God's dwelling.

SEW / SOW
Use *sew* for stitching and *sow* for seeding.

SEWAGE / SEWERAGE
Sewage is what goes through the *sewerage* system.

SHAGGY DOG STORY
For the origin of *shaggy dog story*, see the 407-word explanation by Morris, itself a shaggy dog story.

SHAKE
The past tense, not the past participle, of *shake* is *shook*. The past participle is *shaken*. Her death shook him. He has been shaken, not *shook*, by her death.

SHAKESPEAREAN
Knowingly or unknowingly, writers and speakers of English quote Shakespeare more than they quote any other author. Here are a score of common Shakespearean phrases, many of which, alas, have become clichés:
—A foregone conclusion.
—A man more sinned against than sinning.
—A ministering angel.
—Brevity is the soul of wit.

—Every inch a king.
—I have been in such a pickle.
—I'll not budge an inch.
—In my mind's eye.
—It's Greek to me.
—More in sorrow than in anger.
—One who loved not wisely but too well.
—Pride, pomp, and circumstance of glorious war.
—The better part of valour is discretion.
—The course of true love never did run smooth.
—The game is up.
—The milk of human kindness.
—The primrose path.
—There is something in the wind.
—Though this be madness, yet there is method in it.
—Thus conscience doth make cowards of us all.

SHALL / WILL

Except in Britain, the distinction between *shall* and *will* is moribund. In the United States, *will* is by far the more common future auxiliary. The old rule was that for simple futurity *shall* was to be used with the first person and *will* with the second and third persons and that for emphatic futurity *will* was to be used with the first person and *shall* with the second and third persons.

The resulting confusion is illustrated by this old example: "I shall drown; nobody will save me" is a desperate cry for help, whereas 'I will drown; nobody shall save me" is the cry of a desperate suicide.

SHAMBLES

Though some authorities would restrict *shambles* to its original meaning of a butcher's bench (Latin *scamnum*, bench) or a slaughterhouse, and thus by extension to any scene of carnage, the word has broadened to mean any scene of complete disorder or ruin. As such, *shambles* is acceptable to 85 percent of the American Heritage usage panel, as in "The painter is here, and the apartment is a shambles."

SHAMMY, *see* CHAMOIS / CHAMMY / SHAMMY

SHANDY

Short for *shandygaff*, a *shandy* is a sacrilegious mixture of beer with a soft drink such as ginger ale, ginger beer or lemonade.

SHANKS
The *shanks* is a disease dreaded by golfers. Shot from the shank of a club, a ball that is supposed to sail straight veers almost 90 degrees to the right. After one shanked shot, a golfer experiences the next-shoe syndrome.

SHERIFF
Note the spelling: single *r*, double *f*. See SHRIEVALTY.

SHERRY
From Jerez in Andalusia.

SHIBBOLETH
The Book of Judges thus describes the shrewdness of the Gileadites and the plight of the Ephraimites who attempted to cross the Jordan after the Gileadites had seized its fords: "When any of the fugitives of Ephraim said, 'Let me go over,' the men of Gilead said unto him, 'Art thou an Ephraimite? If he said, 'Nay,' then said they unto him, 'Say now "Shibboleth"'; and he said, 'Sibboleth,' for he could not frame to pronounce it right. Then they laid hold on him and slew him at the fords of the Jordan." This tricky password led to the massacre of "forty and two thousand" Ephraimites.

    Shibboleth, Hebrew for "ear of corn" or "stream in flood," survives in English both as an identifying characteristic of a group and as a pet phrase, slogan, rallying cry or password.

SHILLELAGH
Named after the village of Shillelagh in County Wicklow, Ireland, noted for its oaks and blackthorns, a *shillelagh* is a cudgel or a walking stick.

SHILLY-SHALLY
This term for hesitancy or dawdling comes from a duplication of "Shall I?"

SHIMMY
When your sister Kate danced in the 1920s, her chemise shook, whence *shimmy* for any vibrating or wobbling.

SHINE
The normal past tense and past participle of *shine* are *shone*, pronounced as in *own* in the United States and as in *con* in Britain. In the sense of

"to cause to shine," *shined* is more common, as in "He shined his shoes every morning" and "She has shined her car for the parade."

SHIRTTAIL
In newspaper jargon, a *shirttail* is additional material related to a more important story and separated from it by a dash or some other typographical gimmick.

SHIVAREE
The American version of the French and British *charivari* is *shivaree*. *Charivari* derives from Greek *karebaria*, heavy head, headache, a fitting result of any felicitously uproarious serenade outside a bridal suite. A more dignified serenade is an *epithalamium* (Greek *epi* + *thalamos*, at the bridal chamber).

SHORT SHRIFT
When you give someone *short shrift*, you pay him little attention or give him little time. The phrase, now a cliché, derives from the brief time given a condemned man for sacramental confession (Anglo-Saxon *scrifan*, to shrive, to absolve a penitent) in the days when there was little time between judgment and execution.

SHOULD
As the conditional tense of *shall*, *should* is rarely heard in the United States but is common in Britain. The common American form is *would* (see SEQUENCE OF TENSES). In the United States, *should* connotes obligation (see OUGHT / SHOULD).

SHRIEVALTY
Unlike *mayoralty*, *shrievalty* is rarely used. It's a handy word for the office or jurisdiction or term of office of a sheriff.

SHRINK
The past tense of *shrink* is either *shrank* or *shrunk*, more commonly *shrank*. The past participle is either *shrunk* or *shrunken*. As a noun, *shrink* is a DYSPHEMISM for a psychiatrist.

SHUFFLE OFF THIS MORTAL COIL
Hamlet soliloquized about the dreams that might come in the sleep of death "when we have shuffled off this mortal coil." A punishment to

fit the crime of using this cliché, says Evans, "would be to require the user to explain exactly what it means." "The habitual offender," he says, "should be compelled to read all of the explanations of its meanings offered by the various commentators."

SIC
The appropriate use of *sic* (Latin, thus) is in textual criticism or in a context in which absolute exactness is required. Don't use *sic* to point up someone else's error or your own cuteness, as in "He said he was going to lay (*sic*) down for a while" or "He moved slowly but surly (*sic*)."

SIC TRANSIT
The phrase doesn't refer to the sorry state of public transportation but, elliptically, to the Latin *sic transit gloria mundi*, thus passes away the glory of the world. An epitaph for a legendary movie star might read "Sic Transit Gloria Swanson."

SIDEBAR
A newspaper term for a story related to another story.

SIDEBURNS
By semantic switch, these side whiskers got their name from Ambrose E. Burnside, a muttonchop-bewhiskered Union general in the Civil War.

SIDE OF THE ANGELS
In the late nineteenth-century dispute over evolution, Disraeli said he was "on the side of the angels" rather than the apes. The phrase now signifies that someone is on our side, the right side, in a dispute.

SIEGE
Note the spelling.

SIERRA MOUNTAINS, *see* SAHARA DESERT

SIGNPOST WRITING, *see* ABOVE-MENTIONED

SILHOUETTE
Madame de Pompadour (whose real name, incidentally, translates into the not so glamorous Jean Fish) wiled Louis XV into appointing the parsimonious Étienne de Silhouette finance minister when France was

going bankrupt during the Seven Years War. Silhouette's petty reforms caused his name to become identified with anything plain and cheap (*à la Silhouette*), whence its use for the drawings of the less costly art form of shadowgraphy or profile drawing.

SILLY SEASON

The term was once applied to the dog days of the holiday month of August, when nothing of much importance was happening and newspapers would blow up any old foolish story into screaming headlines. As the Dictionary of Proper Names observes, "The years 1914 and 1939 have rather dented this tradition." Then the year 1945 really dented it, and Richard Nixon cracked it in 1974.

Politically, in modern times, the silly season starts shortly after a presidential inauguration, when the press starts an almost four-year speculation about who the candidates will be in the next presidential election.

SIMILE

A simile is a rhetorical device for the explicit comparison or identification of essentially unlike objects, usually with *like* or *as*, such as "The man ran like a dromedary with the staggers" or "His movements were as slow as a wet week."

Clichés with *like* or *as* abound and, as Nickles says, should be "dropped like a bad habit." Nickles lists fifty *like* clichés from "go through someone like a dose of salts" to "look like the wrath of God" and sixty-five *as* clichés from "as nutty as a fruitcake" to "as Irish as Paddy's pig." See also CLICHÉ and METAPHOR.

SIMON-PURE

Genuine, the real thing. In the eighteenth-century comedy *A Bold Strike for a Wife*, Simon Pure is a character who is impersonated by a rival but who eventually establishes his real identity.

SIMONY

Financial trafficking in the sacred. In Acts, Simon Magus (Simon the magician or sorcerer) tried to bribe Peter and John into selling him spiritual powers.

SIMPLE REASON

Don't use *simple reason* to imply the intellectual pride of informing readers or listeners that they should know that you know that the reason is simple. Often, too, *simple reason* may cover the truth that the reason is really not so simple. And *for the simple reason that* is prolix for *because*.

SIMPLISTIC
A faddish word for *simplified* or *oversimplified*.

SIMULCAST
A blend word from *simultaneous* and *broadcast*, a *simulcast* is a program that is simultaneously broadcast over both radio and television or over both AM and FM radio.

SINCERE
The source of *sincere* is not Latin *sine cera*, without wax, as some have ingeniously suggested, possibly because an unsealed letter has nothing to hide. The derivation is pure Latin *sincerus*, pure, clean, straightforward.

SINECURE, *see* NO SINECURE

SINE DIE
Straight Latin for "without a day," hence adjourned to no specified date, indefinitely.

SINE QUA NON
Straight Latin for "without which not," hence an essential condition, a necessity.

SING
The past tense of *sing* is either *sang* or *sung*, more commonly *sang*. The past participle is *sung*.

SINISTER
When they sought signs from the heavens, Roman augurs faced south, whereas Greek augurs faced north. Auspicious omens were supposed to come from the east, which was the Roman left and the Greek right. The Latin word *sinister*, left, originally meant good, lucky. But Roman authors were Hellenophiles and *sinister* came to mean evil, unlucky.

SINK
The past tense of *sink* is either *sank* or *sunk*, more commonly *sank*. The past participle is *sunk*.

SINUOUS / SINUS, *see* INSINUATE

SIR
An old form of address by youth for older men, now replaced by *Hi.*

SI SAPIS, SIS APIS
A Latin pun with a message: "If you are wise, be (like) the bee." From honey and wax, enjoy sweetness and light. The wise Sophocles was known as The Bee because of the sweetness of his diction.

SISYPHEAN
A *Sisyphean* job is an endless, thankless task that requires much toil but produces no reward. Sisyphus was the evil king of Corinth whose everlasting punishment in Hades was to push up a mountain a huge stone that always rolled down to the bottom just before it reached the top.

SITUATED, *see* LOCATE

SITUATION
When *situation* is tacked onto another noun as an unnecessary abstraction, it becomes what Nickles calls a "first-class drone word, posturing in sentences but lacking the power to invigorate them." Here are a dozen examples:
  —a panic situation (a panic).
  —children in a play situation (at play).
  —creates a no-win situation (you can't win).
  —creates a profit situation (you can make money).
  —in a crisis situation (in a crisis).
  —in an emergency situation (in an emergency).
  —in a pressure situation (under pressure).
  —in a stress situation (under stress).
  —in the classroom situation (in class).
  —in the home situation (at home).
  —is in a punting situation (has to punt).
  —the unemployment situation (unemployment).

SKELETONIZE, *see* CABLESE

SKID ROAD / SKID ROW
If you're talking about Seattle, say *skid road*, because the term originated there as the name for the road made of greased logs over which lumber-

men skidded timber to the mills. Elsewhere, say *skid row* for a section of town in which derelicts, people on the skids, congregate.

SLANG
Language cannot be permanently pigeonholed into standard and nonstandard. *Slang* is generally defined as nonstandard vocabulary but, as was noted in COLLOQUIALISM, last year's slang may be this year's colloquialism and next year's common language. The test is time.

Mencken calls slang "a kind of linguistic exuberance," related to standard vocabulary "a great deal as dancing relates itself to music." Everyone, "including even the metaphysician in his study and the eremite in his cell," he says, uses slang. Chesterton said, "All slang is metaphor, and all metaphor is poetry." Moore calls slang "a prodigal use of language; its bright bubbles effervesce out of man's invention, they take our fancy with their shimmer and sheen, but they are unstable, and very soon the changeable winds of fashion blow them away."

Not all slang, however, is blown away. Study the more than 1,500 pages of Partridge to learn the history of thousands of formerly slang words and phrases that are now respectable English.

SLATED
The word is ambiguous. *Slated* may mean: scheduled, registered for an appointment or consideration; or reprimanded, criticized slashingly. In its meaning of "scheduled," *slated* is overworked, especially in headlines.

SLAVE
The word came into English from Medieval Latin *Sclavus*, a Slav, because the Slavs were continually forced into slavery by the marauding German tribes. The slave drivers have changed in modern history.

SLOGAN
From Gaelic *sluagh*, army, host, and *gairm*, shout, outcry, a *slogan* is a battle cry, a rallying cry, a catch phrase, an advertiser's device for gaining attention. The noun *slew*, in the sense of "a whole slew of people," comes from *sluagh*.

SLOUGH
The word has several meanings and pronunciations. For a quagmire or swamp, *slough* is pronounced either *slew* or as in *cow*, more commonly *slew*. For a state of dejection or despair, as in the Slough of Despond in

Pilgrim's Progress, the preferred pronunciation is as in *cow*. For dead tissue, *slough* is pronounced *sluff*.

SLOW / SLOWLY, *see* ADJECTIVE / ADVERB

SLUG
So that every item of newspaper copy may be separately identified as it passes through the several stages of the production process, each item has its own distinguishing word or words written at the top. This identification is called a *slug*, which derives from the hot-metal process of casting slugs of type.

SMART MONEY
The phrase originally referred to the compensation awarded soldiers who had received smarting injuries. *Smart money* now refers to the investments or other bets of people who get information from the horse's mouth.

SMELL, *see* AROMA

SMELL A RAT
This cliché has lost its bouquet.

SMITHSONIAN INSTITUTION
Institution, not *Institute*.

SMOG, *see* CENTAUR WORDS

SMOOCH
This is not a coinage of the Jazz Age, but a variant of the old English word *smouch*. Evans reminds us that in 1583 Philip Stubbes, in *Anatomy of Abuses*, inveighed against dancing around the Maypole because it was the occasion of "clipping . . . culling . . . kissing . . . smouching and slabbering of one another . . . filthy groping and unclean handling."

SMORGASBORD
The Swedes gave us *smorgasbord*, literally bread-and-butter table. Hence *Swedish smorgasbord* is redundant.

SNACK, *see* BITESIZE SNACKS

SNAFU
Originally, British army slang for $\underline{s}$ituation $\underline{n}$ormal $\underline{a}$ll $\underline{f}$ucked $\underline{u}$p.

SNEEZE
The English *sneeze* is onomatopoeic, but not as onomatopoetic as the Choctaw word for *sneeze*, *ha-bish-ko*, stressed on the second syllable.

SO, *see* **AS . . . AS / SO . . . AS**

SO-CALLED
Hyphenate the adjective when it precedes a noun. And don't put the noun in quotes.

SOCCER
Short for "association" football.

SOCRATIC METHOD
In a pose of ignorance, Socrates used to lure his students into a display of supposed knowledge by carefully framing a series of questions the answers to which would force the students step by step to the conclusion Socrates had reached before the class began. This is known as the *Socratic method.*

The pretense of ignorance in the method is known as Socratic irony, practiced by Socrates in arguments with his intellectual enemies, whom he drove to distraction and who eventually drove him to drink.

SODA
From Medieval Latin *sodanum*, headache remedy, from *soda*, headache, from Arabic *suda*, splitting headache.

SOL
Old Sol (Latin, sun) is what the synonymomaniac calls the sun after he has once used *sun*.

SOLDER
The *l* is dropped in American pronunciation but retained in British.

SOLECISM
Aghast that Greek colonists didn't talk Greek real good like a good Greek should, Athenian purists looked down on the corrupt dialect

spoken by the inhabitants of the Greek colony of Soloi in Cilicia (now part of Turkey) and called their language *soloikismos*, whence the English *solecism* for a grammatical error. Don't confuse with SOLIPSISM.

SOL-FA SYLLABLES, *see* GAMUT

SOLID STATE STEREO
Redundant. See STEREO-.

SOLILOQUY
From Latin *solus*, alone, and *loqui*, to speak. Note the spelling.

SOLIPSISM
From Latin *solus*, alone, and *ipse*, self, *solipsism* is the theory that the self is the only reality or the only thing knowable. By extension, a solipsist is a self-centered person and his thoughts and deeds are solipsistic. Don't confuse with SOLECISM.

SOLON
From Solon, the ancient Greek lawmaker, *solon* is headlinese for *lawmaker, legislator, congressman, representative, assemblyman, councilman, commissioner*, all long words for a headline. The plural *solons* is an especially handy headline word for a group of legislators with different titles. One may sneer at *solon*, but nobody has yet come up with a better short synonym.

SOLSTICE, *see* ARMISTICE

SOMBER / SOMBRERO, *see* ADUMBRATE

SOME, *see* ABOUT

SOMEBODY / SOMEONE, *see* ANYBODY / ANYONE

SOMEDAY / SOMETIME
For indefinite future, both *someday* and *sometime* may be spelled as one word, as in "Someday my prince will come" and "Come up and see me sometime." The two-word spellings, however, are preferred when the reference is to some more specific time, as in "Check your calendar and choose some day when you don't expect to be unusually busy" and "Arrange the meeting for some time that will suit you."

SOME OF MY BEST FRIENDS
The phrase is often heard in deprecation of the suspicion of bigotry, as in "Some of my best friends are Jews." One thinks of the lament of the rabbi of a fashionable New York synagogue, many of whose members had become Quakers: "Some of my best Jews are Friends."

SOME PLACE
Either two words or *somewhere*.

SOME WAY
Either two words or *somehow*.

SOMNAMBULATE
From Latin *somnus*, sleep, and *ambulare*, to walk, hence to walk in one's sleep. Other *somnus* words are *insomnia* (sleeplessness), *somnifacient* (sleep-producing, hypnotic) and *somnolence* (drowsiness).

SONAR
Acronym for <u>so</u>und <u>na</u>vigation <u>r</u>anging.

SONIC WRITING
In a love affair with words, eyes must be focused and ears must be tuned. Words must be clearly photographed and faithfully recorded. When the ear neglects the eye, however, sonic writing may develop. Here are a dozen examples of sonic writing (and see MALAPROPISM):
—His son's balling woke him up.
—He bubbles over with bon ami.
—It was a bonified deal.
—Fix it with ceiling wax.
—She strained her vocal chords.
—He lacks esprit decor.
—Don't take her for granite.
—She escaped by a hare's breath.
—He's a loser for all intensive purposes.
—They furnished their home peacemeal.
—He and she are polls apart.
—He preferred suffering to youth in Asia.

SON-IN-LAW, *see* DAUGHTER-IN-LAW

SON-OF-A-GUN

This may have become a euphemism for an epithet but it was originally a reference to boys born at sea in the days when women were allowed to travel with their husbands in naval vessels.

SOONER, *see* HARDLY

SOPHOMORE

A wise fool, from Greek *sophos*, wise, and *moros*, dull, foolish. *Sophomore* often is strangely mispronounced *southmore*. See also OXYMORON.

SOS

The letters of the international radiotelegraphic distress signal are not an abbreviation of "Save Our Ship" or "Save Our Souls" or anything else. They were arbitrarily chosen because they are easily transmissible and distinguishable in code: three dits, three dahs, three dits. See also MAYDAY.

SOUTHPAW

In the days before sportscasters could announce, "The rest of the action is under the lights," baseball parks were built so that batters faced east and thus were not troubled by the afternoon sun. Pitchers therefore faced west, and a left-handed pitcher thus threw with his south paw. *Southpaw* was coined by Finley Peter Dunne (Mr. Dooley) in the 1880s. Baseball players, Mencken observes, "believe that all left-handed pitchers are more or less balmy, just as musicians believe the same of oboe-players."

SOUVENIR

Note the spelling. See also MEMENTO and OBJET D'ART.

SOW, *see* SEW / SOW

SPAY

When her ovaries are excised, a female animal is spayed, not *spaded*, though *spay* comes from Greek *spathe*, broad blade, whence also *spade* and *spatula*.

SPEAR SIDE, *see* DISTAFF

SPECIOUS
Though *specious* comes from Latin *speciosus*, beautiful, handsome, good-looking, it now means superficially or deceptively attractive or fallaciously plausible.

SPELLING
Several attempts have been made over the years to simplify English spelling, but none has caught on. Even the mighty *Chicago Tribune* abandoned the cause. Whatever the advantages of spelling reform, they have been greatly exaggerated by its advocates, many of whom, as Mencken notes, have been "notably over-earnest and under-humorous men."

Correct spelling is aided by a photographic memory and some familiarity with etymology, especially Latin and Greek. Misspelling is a not innocuous disease against which writers should inoculate themselves with a potion of Latin and Greek roots and regular checkups at Dr. Webster's, the best resort for a spell.

SPHYGMOMANOMETER
Note the spelling of this word for an instrument that measures blood pressure, from Greek *sphygmos*, pulse, *manos*, thin, and *metron*, measure.

SPIRAL
A *spiral*, from Latin *spira*, a coil, can move in any direction, not necessarily up. Loosely, however, *spiral* has come to connote upward movement and as such is accepted by 78 percent of the American Heritage usage panel.

-SPIRE
Latin *spirare*, to breathe, is the root of many English words connoting breathing, such as:
- —*aspirate*, to pronounce with a breathing, to sound the letter *h*.
- —*aspire*, to breathe to, to strive toward, to desire eagerly.
- —*conspire*, to breathe together, to plot.
- —*expire*, to breathe out, to breathe for the last time.
- —*inspire*, to breathe in, to stimulate.
- —*perspire*, to breathe out, to sweat.
- —*respire*, to breathe again, to breathe in and out, to breathe easily again after help from a respirator.

—*suspire*, to breathe from below (whence also *cesspool*), to sigh.
—*transpire*, to breathe across, to leak out.
And all the words from *spirit*, breath of life.

SPIT

The past tense and past participle of *spit* are *spat* or *spit*, more commonly *spat*.

SPIT AND IMAGE

Originally, probably *spirit and image*. Certainly not *spittin' image*.

SPLIT HEADS

Some newspapers uphold the norm that each line of a head should be a "complete thought" or at least an integral grammatical structure. The violation of this norm is called a split head.

Some newspapers don't like to split the first line of a head from the second but don't mind splitting the second from the third. Some don't like any split at all. Others just don't care, splitting heads whenever they want to, refusing to split hairs.

Bernstein, in *Headlines and Deadlines*, gives this rationale for unsplit heads: "The eye in reading successive lines is compelled to pause ever so briefly and shift focus at the end of each line. If the content of what is read has a corresponding resting place, no matter how slight, at the end of the line, quick and comfortable reading is facilitated. It is on this principle that the avoidance of split heads is based. The copy editor strives to achieve a clean break at the end of each line. If each does not express a complete thought, it at least stands on its own grammatical feet."

To avoid split heads:
—Don't separate a preposition from its object: "Ship Sinks in / Hudson River."
—Don't separate an adjective from the noun it qualifies, if the noun comes after the adjective: "Sadat Sees New / Hope for Peace." Because nouns are sometimes used as adjectives in headlines, this is a split head: "FBI Solves Murder / Mystery in Alaska." But a head is not split if the adjective comes after the noun: "Youth Holds Police / Captive for 8 Hours."
—Don't separate an adverb from the verb it modifies, if the verb comes after the adverb: "Ford Often / Slices Shots." But a head is not split if the adverb comes after the verb: "Ford Slices / Shots Often."

—Don't separate a conjunction from the clause it introduces: "Bonn Agrees But / Moscow Refuses."
—Don't separate the parts of a compound verb: "Carter Will / Visit Moscow."
—Don't separate the parts of a prepositional verb: "Burger Swears / In New Cabinet."

SPLIT INFINITIVE

Fowler says that the English-speaking world may be divided into: "(1) those who neither know nor care what a split infinitive is; (2) those who do not know, but care very much; (3) those who know and condemn; (4) those who know and approve; and (5) those who know and distinguish." He then expatiates on the split infinitive for about 1,800 words.

Splitting an infinitive means inserting one or more words between the *to* and the verb, as in "to thoroughly appreciate" or "to at least appreciate."

Banning the split infinitive is ridiculous. The so-called rule has no foundation in grammar, logic, rhetoric or common sense. The ghost of the split infinitive should have been exorcised long ago. Go ahead and split if you want to. Let euphony be your guide. Never to split is to seriously stifle.

Splitting an infinitive should not be confused with splitting the parts of a compound verb, as in "I have often walked down this street before." Those who would ban splitting a compound verb are even more antediluvian than the antisplitinfinitive troglodytes.

SPLURGE, *see* PURGE / SPLURGE

SPLUTTER, *see* CENTAUR WORDS

SPONSOR
Note the spelling: *or*, not *er*.

SPOONERISM
William A. Spooner, an Oxford clergyman (1844–1930), was helplessly addicted to metathesis, the transposition of the letters, sounds or syllables of a word, from Greek *metatithenai*, to place differently. He was so addicted that metathesis is now far better known as *Spoonerism.* Here are some examples attributed to Spooner:
—Aren't you occupewing the wrong pie?

—It is kisstomary to cuss the bride.

—Let not your prayer be a half-warmed fish.

—The Lord is a shoving leopard.

—We pray for Victoria, our queer old dean.

—Were you sewn into this sheet?

—We will now sing "When Kinkering Congs Their Titles Take."

—You hissed my mystery lecture.

Famous examples from radio are Harry Von Zell's introduction of the president of the United States, "Mr. Hoobert Heever," and Lowell Thomas' reference to Sir Stafford Cripps, British cabinet minister, as "Sir Stifford Crapps."

Perhaps this is the topper: "She's too titty to be a preacher."

SPORTSESE

As Hohenberg says, "The sports pages have produced some of the best writing in American journalism; also, some of the worst."

Some of the best has come from great sportswriters of an older generation, such as this dozen: Heywood Broun, Finley Peter Dunne, Paul Gallico, Ernest Hemingway, John Kieran, Ring Lardner, A. J. Liebling, Henry McLemore, Westbrook Pegler, Quentin Reynolds, Grantland Rice, Damon Runyon. And here are a modern dozen: Roger Angell, Jimmy Breslin, Arthur Daley, Ron Fimrite, Jerome Holtzman, Dan Jenkins, Pat Jordan, Jack Murphy, Jim Murray, George Plimpton, Red Smith, Herbert Warren Wind.

Unfortunately, there have been and are more bad sportswriters than good. The good write in literate English. The bad write in sportsese, a sample of which is this all-purpose interview:

"How do you figure your chances for the upcoming season?" the scribe asked the mentor.

"We'll play every game one at a time," the coach opined. "We'll come to play and we'll be representative. We'll have a lot to say about who wins the conference."

"How does this year's team stack up with last year's squad?" he was queried.

"Well, yunno, what I mean is, like, last year we didn't play up to our potential," the pilot riposted. "But if we could have scored more, we would have won more."

"Do you have any promising rookies?" this reporter questioned.

"We have this transfer who was a frosh phenom in juco last year," he averred. "He's a coachable kid with lotsa desire. He'll give you 110 percent effort."

Asked if this year would be a building year, the sideline general explained, "This year will be, like, a building year."

"And how do you rate your foes?" this writer interrogated.

"They pull on their pants one leg at a time same as us," the grizzled veteran quipped.

"Our kids have character," he continued.

"They're rarin' to go," he added.

"They're real dedicated," he concluded.

Enough. But see also AS; PURPOSE / RESULT; SYNONYMOMANIA.

SPRING
The past tense of *spring* is either *sprang* or *sprung*, more commonly *sprang*. The past participle is *sprung*.

SQUAWK, *see* CENTAUR WORDS

SQUINTING MODIFIER
An adverb between two verbs squints at each and may cause ambiguity, as in "A writer who thinks carefully chooses the right words." Make it either "A writer who carefully thinks chooses the right words" or "A writer who thinks chooses the right words carefully."

SQUIRREL
From Greek *skia*, shadow, and *oura*, tail, a squirrel makes shade with its tail.

STAID
Frost's advice that we should "choose something like a star to stay our minds on and be staid" is more than a pun. *Staid* is the archaic past participle of *stay*.

STALACTITE / STALAGMITE
Both words come from Greek *stallassein*, to drip, but a stalactite hangs and a stalagmite rises. A MNEMONIC for the distinction is that the one hanging has to hold on tight.

STALEMATE
From chess, a *stalemate* is an absolute deadlock. It cannot be broken. It is final. *Stalemate* is incorrectly used to describe any temporary lack of action or advantage. See also GAMBIT.

STANCH / STAUNCH
The verb is more commonly spelled *stanch* and the adjective *staunch*.

STANDING OVATION, *see* OVATION

STARBOARD, *see* PORT / STARBOARD

START, *see* BEGIN / COMMENCE / START

STATES
For U.S. states, newspapers use the abbreviations of AP instead of those of the confusing U.S. Postal Service. Eight states are not abbreviated: Alaska, Hawaii, Idaho, Iowa, Maine, Ohio, Texas, Utah.

STATIONARY / STATIONERY
Standing still is *stationary*. Writing material is *stationery*. The words have the same origin, however. Stationers were tradesmen licensed to set up permanent stalls outside churches and thus were stationary, unlike the transient hawkers. Because the clergy composed much of the literate population, stationers specialized in selling writing material and books and were stationed in the right places for this business.

STATISTICS
Statistics is a difficult science. Statistics indicate his superiority. See -ICS.

STATUS QUO
Straight Latin for "state in which," hence an existing condition, the present state of affairs, *status quo* has become a cliché.

STAUNCH, *see* STANCH / STAUNCH

STEATOPYGIAN, *see* CALLIPYGIAN / STEATOPYGIAN

STENOGRAPHY
From Greek *stenos*, narrow, and *graphein*, to write, stenography is the art of writing in shorthand.

STENTORIAN

A herald in the *Iliad*, Stentor had a powerful voice. Homer described it as "a voice of bronze, as loud as the cry of fifty men." *Stentorian*, extremely loud-voiced, comes from Stentor, whose name came from Greek *stenein*, to groan, moan. Stentor eventually met his match in a shouting match with Hermes, herald of the gods, and died as he heard the voice of doom.

STEREO-

The Greek word *stereos*, solid, helps form many English words, among which are technical terms with the meaning of "three-dimensional," such as *stereochemistry*, *stereography*, *stereoscopy*, *stereovision*. "Solid" words from *stereos* are: *cholesterol*, originally found in gallstones; *stereotype*, cast from a mold (see CLICHÉ); and *stereo* itself, short for stereophonic sound. Ads for "solid state stereo" are etymologically redundant.

STERNUTATION / STERTOROUSNESS

Sneezing and snoring.

STET

Straight Latin for "let it stand," *stet* is an instruction to a printer to retain a word or words marked for correction or omission. See also CQ.

STINK

The past tense of *stink* is either *stank* or *stunk*, more commonly *stank*. The past participle is *stunk*.

STOGY

This type of cigar is spelled either *stogy* or *stogie* or *stogey*. The plural of *stogy* and *stogie* is *stogies;* the plural of *stogey* is *stogeys*. The word comes from the Conestoga valley in Lancaster County, Pennsylvania, where Conestoga wagons were first built. Many of the pioneers traveling west in these wagons rolled their own tobacco into crude cigars, which came to be known as stogies.

STOMACH

A euphemism, says Mencken, for "the whole region from the nipple to the pelvic arch." See ABDOMEN; BELLY; and the last sentence of –TOMY.

STOOL PIGEON

This term for a spy or an informer comes from the practice of tying decoy pigeons to a stool.

STORY

Latin *historia*, historical narrative, history, story, is the source of *story* in both its English meanings: a tale and a horizontal section of a building. In medieval times, the different levels of some buildings were decorated with pictures or legends, usually on the windows.

STRAFE

"Gott strafe England" (God punish England) was a German slogan in 1914, whence the English *strafe*, bombard, rake with machine-gun fire.

STRAIT JACKET / STRAIT-LACED

Note the spellings. *Strait* comes from Latin *stringere*, past participle *strictum*, to draw tight.

STRANGLED TO DEATH

Redundant.

STRATAGEM / STRATEGY

Note the spellings.

STRATA

Not *stratas*. *Strata* is already plural (singular *stratum*). See PLURALS.

STRENGTH, *see* LENGTH / STRENGTH

STRESS, *see* LOADED VERB

STRINE

The Australian language. See AORTA.

STRINGER

A newspaper term for a writer who is not a member of the regular staff. A *stringer* is paid on the basis of the amount of his copy that is published, measured in the old days by a piece of string notched at one-inch intervals. A stringer keeps his clips in a stringbook, which is also a term for the scrapbook kept by a regular staff member.

STRONG VERBS
Most English verbs form their past tense and past participle by the addition of *ed* or *d*, as in *look, looked, looked* or *gaze, gazed, gazed*. These verbs are called *regular* or *weak*.

Verbs whose past tense and past participle are formed by internal change, as in *begin, began, begun* and *swear, swore, sworn*, are called *irregular* or *strong*. English has about 200 strong verbs.

STUDENT BODY
A gross anatomical collective for *students*. We have *citizenry*. Why not *studentry?*

STUPENDOUS, *see* AFRAID

SUAVE, *see* ASSUAGE

SUBEDITOR
The British term for a copy editor.

SUBHEAD
A newspaper term for a minor heading inserted to break up the gray effect of a long story.

SUBJUNCTIVE, *see* MOOD

SUBPOENA
Straight Latin for "under penalty," *sub poena* are the first words of a writ commanding a witness to appear and testify. The term is spelled as one word in English, both as noun and as verb.

SUCCESSIVE, *see* CONSECUTIVE / SUCCESSIVE

SUCCUMB, *see* DIE

SUDDEN DEATH
Some squeamish broadcasters prefer *sudden victory* to *sudden death* as a term for extra competition in a tied sports event, but *sudden death* seems more appropriate to brute culture. Partridge traces *sudden death* to 1834 in the gambling context of letting everything ride on one roll of the dice, one turn of a card, one flip of a coin. Winning or losing may

not be as important as playing like a good sport, but paying one's gambling debts is even more important in the face of sudden death.

SUICIDE
The word is used for both the act itself and the person who has committed the act.

SUITE
Though the American Heritage allows the pronunciation *soot* (as in *boot*) for a suite of furniture, the more common pronunciation is *sweet*. See also CHAISE LONGUE.

SUMMON / SUMMONS
The verb is *summon*, the noun *summons*. The plural of the noun is *summonses*.

SUPER, *see* AFRAID

SUPERCILIOUS
From Latin *super + cilium*, over the eyelid, hence the eyebrow, *supercilious* means haughty, scornful, descriptive of the impression one conveys by raising one's eyebrows at something or somebody one disdains.

SUPERSEDE
Note the spelling: *sede*, not *cede*. See ACCEDE.

SUPERSTAR
The movies created stars. Television has created superstars, in sports and other forms of entertainment. Almost all players and performers are now stars. Those who rise above the mediocre or get more lucrative contracts are superstars. The word gained popularity with the show *Jesus Christ Superstar*, the title of which was at least less tasteless than "Jesus Christ Top Banana."

SUPREME COURT, *see* JUDGE / JURIST / JUSTICE

SURGEON, *see* CHIRO-

SURPRISE
Note the spelling: not *suprise*.

SURROUND
Because *surround* means to encircle, to enclose on all sides, phrases such as *completely surrounded* and *surrounded on all sides* are redundant and *partly surrounded* or *surrounded on three sides* are contradictory.

SUSPENSIVE HYPHEN
A hyphen is needed after *two* in the construction "a two or three-hour delay." The hyphen is called *suspensive* because *two-* is suspended without a nounal adjective until *three-hour* appears. Similarly, *pro* needs a hyphen in "pro and anti-government forces." If you want to avoid the device, recast the phrase by repeating the nounal adjective: "pro-government and anti-government forces."

SUSPICION
Good noun, lousy verb.

SUSTAIN
A slight majority of the American Heritage usage panelists accept the use of *sustain* for *suffer* or *receive*, as in "He sustained multiple injuries," and *sustain* for *suffer* or *incur*, as in "He sustained financial losses." Perhaps *sustain* is better restricted to the sense of supporting or prolonging existence, as in "Food sustains life" or "His determination to survive was sustained by thoughts of his family."

SWASTIKA
The perversion of a symbol is exemplified in the history of the swastika, which originally was a religious symbol of well-being, from Sanskrit *svastika*, a sign of good luck, and today is an irreligious symbol of evil.

SWING
The past tense and past participle of *swing* are *swung*. The archaic past tense *swang* is in a class with *slud*.

SWITCHED VOICES
In the sentence "Food is taken without paying for it," the passive voice of *is taken* switches to the active voice of *paying*. This produces a dangle *(see* DANGLING PARTICIPLE*)* because *food* is not the subject of *paying;* the food isn't paying. Making both verbs passive, however, produces the awkward "Food is taken without its being paid for." Unclutter the sentence by using the active voice for both verbs: "People take food with-

out paying for it" or "People take food but they don't pay for it." See
ACTIVE VOICE / PASSIVE VOICE.

SWORD OF DAMOCLES
Impending disaster or the constant threat of danger is signified by this
phrase, by now a cliché. Cicero records that Damocles, a sycophantic
courtier of Dionysius the Elder, tyrant of Syracuse, was invited by Dionysius to a sumptuous banquet at which Damocles' seat was directly under
a sword hanging from a single hair. This party favor left Damocles un-
envious of royalty and hungry.

SYLLABLE, *see* -LEPSY

SYLLEPSIS
Under **-LEPSY**, *syllepsis* (Greek *syn* + *lepsis*, a taking together) is described as a taking together of words governed by a single word used in
a different sense for each of the words governed. In the example "He
failed his final exams and his parents," *failed*, the sylleptic word, has the
different senses of academic and filial failure. Under **PEEPING TOM**, in
the sentence "She rode through Coventry on a horse and a bet with her
husband," *on*, the sylleptic word, has the different senses of physical posture and causality. Don't overdo syllepsis, especially this banal type:
"Three innings and six homers later, the pitcher was yanked." See also
ZEUGMA.

SYLLOGISM, *see* SYN-

SYMBIOSIS, *see* SYN-

SYMBOL, *see* BALLISTICS

SYMPATHY, *see* EMPATHY / SYMPATHY

SYN-
The Greek prefix *syn*, together, helps form hundreds of English words.
Before the letters, *b*, *m* and *p*, *syn* becomes *sym*, and before *l*, *syl*. Among
syn- words discussed elsewhere are *asymmetry*, *asyndeton*, *syllable*, *syllepsis*, *symbol*, *sympathy*, *syndrome*, *synecdoche*, *synod*, *synthesis*.
Here are a dozen other common *syn-* words:
  —*syllogism*, a reckoning all together, a reasoning (*logizesthai*, to
    reckon, reason).

—*symbiosis*, a living together (*bios*, life).

—*symphony*, a sounding together (*phone*, sound), consonance, harmony.

—*symposium*, originally a drinking together (*posis*, drink), now a conference or collection.

—*symptom*, a falling together (*piptein*, to fall), a sign or indication of something.

—*synagogue*, a bringing together (*agein*, to lead), an assembly or meeting place for Jewish worship.

—*synchronism*, a timing together (*chronos*, time), concurrence, chronological arrangement.

—*syncopation*, a cutting up together (*koptein*, to strike, cut off), shift of musical beat, ragtime.

—*syndicate*, originally a judging together (*dike*, judgment), now any association for business.

—*synonym*, a naming together (*onoma*, name), a word similar in meaning to another word.

—*synopsis*, a viewing together (*opsis*, view), a general view, condensation, abstract.

—*syntax*, an arranging together (*tassein*, to put in order), the grammatical arrangement of words in a sentence.

SYNDROME, *see* DROMEDARY

SYNECDOCHE

From Greek *syn* + *ekdechesthai*, to take from, to receive jointly, *synecdoche* is a figure of speech in which a part is used for the whole, such as *bread-and-butter* for *food*, or the whole is used for a part, such as *the press* for *a newspaper*.

SYNONYMOMANIA

The coinage is Bernstein's for the affliction of a writer who suffers from "a compulsion to call a spade successively *a garden implement* and *an earth-turning tool*." A synonym for *synonymomania* is *monologophobia*, another Bernstein coinage, the affliction of a writer who "would rather walk naked in front of Saks Fifth Avenue than be caught using the same word more than once in three lines."

A synonym should be used to convey a nuance, a shade of difference in meaning. A synonym should not be used merely to avoid repetition.

The disease of synonymomania afflicts all hack writers, especially the breed of sportswriters for whom *home run* successively becomes *homer, circuit blast, circuit clout, circuit smash, four-bagger, four-ply blow, roundtripper* and for whom *pitcher* successively becomes *hurler, twirler, moundsman, fireman, fireballer, flame thrower.*

The most virulent outbreak of synonymomania occurs among writers feverishly trying to avoid repeating *said,* for which there are several hundred synonyms. In one recently published newspaper interview of about 3,000 words, there were these forty-four synonyms for *said,* almost all of them unrelated to the context of what was being said: *added, admitted, advised, affirmed, agreed, announced, answered, argued, asserted, attested, avowed, bubbled, charged, claimed, commented, conceded, concluded, confessed, continued, declared, disclosed, elaborated, emphasized, explained, giggled, grinned, indicated, laughed, maintained, noted, observed, opined, pointed out, put it, queried, quipped, reasoned, related, remarked, reported, replied, revealed, smiled, stressed.*

Said is a good word. If the context calls for a synonym, use a synonym. But don't strain to avoid repeating *said.* One of the marks of smooth reporting is the repetition of *said* so unobtrusively that the reader is hardly aware of the word.

See also ADDED; LOADED VERB; and SPORTSESE.

SYNTHESIS, *see* ANALYSIS / SYNTHESIS

TABLE

In the United States, to *table* a motion is to postpone or shelve it. The term has a contrary meaning in Britain, where to *table* a motion is to put it on the agenda. Editors of foreign copy should be aware of the difference.

TABLE D'HÔTE

Straight French for "the host's table," *table d'hôte* refers to a restaurant meal that has a fixed price, as opposed to *à la carte*, French "by the menu," a menu on which each item has a separate price.

TABLOID

Usually abbreviated to *tab*, a *tabloid* is a newspaper whose print format is about 16 inches deep by 10 inches wide, about half the area of a standard newspaper page. In the more bawdy days of American journalism, tabs became equated with sensationalism, but today this isn't necessarily so. *Tabloid* comes from the trademarks for drugs and chemicals compressed into tablets.

TABOO

From Tongan *tabu*, sacred, prohibited, *taboo* is sometimes spelled *tabu*.

TABULA RASA

Straight Latin for "erased tablet," hence the clean slate of the mind before it receives impressions of some subject; also cynically applied to a student who seems to learn nothing.

TACHOMETER

From Greek *tachos*, speed, and *metron*, measure, a *tachometer* is an instrument for measuring speed, as opposed to an ODOMETER, an instrument for measuring distance traveled. Popularly, each instrument is called a *speedometer*.

TACTICS
Tactics is a science taught in service academies. His tactics appall his colleagues. See -ICS.

TAKE
In newspaper terminology, a *take* is a page of copy.

TALENT
One who has talent and doesn't use it is like unto the unprofitable servant who buried his talents and was condemned by Christ to be cast forth into the darkness, "where there will be the weeping, and the gnashing of teeth."

The ancient *talent* was a sum of money, from Greek *talanton*, a balance, a thing weighed, the value of the thing weighed. Because the talents in Christ's parable were given to each servant "according to his particular ability," medieval theologians gave *talent* the figurative meaning of "natural ability," which meaning, along with that of acquired ability, *talent* has today. It is still very much a marketable commodity and a bugbear of egalitarian extremists.

TALESMAN / TALISMAN
A *talesman* is a juror summoned under a writ of *tales de circumstantibus* (Latin, "such of the bystanders") when there aren't enough regularly summoned jurors. A *talisman* is a charm of superstitiously supposed magical powers, from Greek *telos*, fulfillment, initiation, incantation.

TALLY
An election *tally* derives from Latin *talea*, a stick, on which notches were cut to keep score.

TANDEM
Time became space in the evolution of Latin *tandem* from the temporal meaning of "at last, at length," to the spatial meaning of "one behind another," as on the bicycle built for two, upon whose seat Daisy would look sweet.

TANGERINE
She dressed in clothes from Macy's mezzanine and was toasted in every bar across the Argentine and had eyes of night and lips as bright as flame, the color of the fruit she was named after, which was named after the place where it first grew, Tangier.

TANTALIZE
Tantalus (Greek, "The Sufferer"), a nasty Lydian king, was punished by being forced to stand in a lake in Hades under a bough of fruit and in water up to his chin. The fruit or water receded whenever Tantalus tried to eat or drink. Thus, to be tantalized is to be tormented or teased by the sight of something desired but unattainable. Of the same origin is *tantalus*, a locked stand in which spirit decanters are displayed.

TAPINOSIS
A reverse form of anthropomorphism (see ANTHROPO-), *tapinosis* (Greek *tapeinos*, mean, base) is the derogatory use of inanimate terms for humans, such as this ennead: *battle-ax, blockhead, dope, ham, heel, scab, screwball, scum, stiff.*

TASK FORCE
A faddish metaphor taken over from the military for a temporary investigatory committee, academic, political, sociological or other kinds.

TAWDRY
The word is a shortening of *St. Audrey*, at the annual fair in whose honor in the Isle of Ely cheap finery and knickknacks and neckpieces known as "St Audrey's laces" were sold, whence *tawdry* for anything gaudy and cheap. Audrey died of a throat tumor, which she believed was divine punishment for her youthful pleasure in wearing necklaces.

TAXIDERMY
From Greek *taxis*, arrangement, and *derma*, skin, taxidermy is the process of preparing, stuffing and mounting animal skins in lifelike form. Other words from *taxis* are *ataxia* (lack of coordination), *syntax* (see SYN-), *tactics*, *taxonomy* (see -NOMY). The *tax* in *taxicab* originally came from Medieval Latin *taxare*, to charge.

TEEN-AGER
AP hyphenates the noun *teen-ager* and the adjective *teen-age* and frowns on the use of *teen-aged*, whether hyphenated or not.

TEETOTALER
The *tee* of *teetotaler* is a duplication of the first *t* of *total* to emphasize the total totality of total abstinence from booze.

TELE-
From Greek *tele*, at a distance, far off, come many English words, among them *telecast, telecommunication, telegenic, telegram, telegraph, telemetry, telepathy, telephone, telephoto, teleprinter, Teleprompter, Teleran* (Television radar air navigation), *telescope, Teletype, television, Telstar.*

TEMBLOR
From Spanish *temblar*, to shake, *temblor* is seen more often in headlines than in copy and is headlinese for *earthquake*. As such, it is unnecessary, *quake* and *tremor* being shorter. *Temblor* is more common in California papers, but even Californians don't meet in the street and ask one another, "Felt any good temblors lately?" See also HEADLINESE.

TEMPEST IN A TEAPOT
Cicero didn't drink tea. Wine was his cup of tea. The attempt to trace the cliché *tempest in a teapot* to Cicero's "Excitabat fluctus in simpulo" is anachronistic. The translation of Cicero's sentence is "He stirred up waves in a wine ladle," to which Cicero added "ut dicitur" ("as the saying goes"), which indicates that the phrase was a cliché even in Cicero's time.

TENDINITIS
Note the spelling: no *o*. From Latin *tendere*, to stretch; New Latin adjective *tendinosus*.

10 DOWNING STREET
METONYMY for the executive leadership of the British government, 10 Downing Street is the address of the prime minister's official residence.

TENNIS
The game probably originated in the Middle East and its name probably originated from Arabic *tanaz*, to leap, bound. *Racket*, which spelling is now more common than *racquet*, comes from Arabic *raqat*, a piece of cloth wound around the palm of the hand.

TENNIS, ANYONE?
Partridge traces the phrase to the British social comedies of at least the 1920s as a catch phrase to open a conversation or a ploy to start a flirtation. "Tennis, anyone?" was also a ploy used on Broadway: a playwright would bring on a romantic juvenile, racket under arm, who would clear

the stage, except for the leading man and lady, by announcing, "Tennis, anyone?"

TENSE, *see* SEQUENCE OF TENSES

TENTERHOOKS
From Latin *tendere*, to stretch, a tenter is a frame on which newly woven cloth is stretched and fastened by hooked nails so that it will dry without shrinking or wrinkling. To be *on tenterhooks*, now a cliché, is to be under strain or tension or anxiety stretched almost to the breaking point.

TENURE
Academically, *tenure*, from Latin *tenere*, to hold, hence the right to hold onto a professorial appointment, is both a blessing and a curse: a blessing for those who need on-the-job security and academic freedom; a curse for those who would oust the drones who equate tenure with on-the-job retirement and academic torpor. See also WHITE ELEPHANT.

TERMITE, *see* ATTRITION

TERRIBLE / TERRIFIC, *see* AFRAID

TEST
Just as metal was examined in earthen vessels (Latin *testa*), so students being examined are earthen vessels whose mettle is being tested.

THAN
Be careful with case after the comparative conjunction *than*. In "John likes Alice more than I," the pronoun after *than* is in the nominative case because the meaning is that John likes Alice more than I like Alice. In "John likes Alice more than me," the pronoun after *than* is in the objective case because the meaning is that John likes Alice more than he likes me.

Ambiguity may arise when the word after *than* is a noun. "Alice likes me more than Mary" may mean either that Alice likes me more than Mary likes me or that Alice likes me more than she likes Mary. To avoid the ambiguity, spell out the sentence or rephrase it.

For other aspects of THAN, see DIFFERENT; NO SOONER; and RATHER THAN.

THANATOPSIS
The title of a poem by William Cullen Bryant, *thanatopsis* comes from Greek *thanatos*, death, and *opsis*, view, hence a view of death, a meditation on death. From the same Greek word for *death* come *euthanasia* (see EU-) and *thanatophobia*, fear of death. Aimée Thanatogenos was the junior cosmetician in Evelyn Waugh's satire of American death rites, *The Loved One.*

THANKS
As an expression of gratitude or acknowledgment of a favor, *thanks* is perfectly polite. It is elliptical, but so is *thank you.* The full sentence *I thank you* is somewhat formal in everyday speech.

   Thanks a lot and *thanks very much* and *thanks a million* are often automatically uttered without thought to the degree of thanks intended. *Thanks much* is an affectation. *Thanks muchly* is a barbarism (see MUCHLY).

   "You're welcome," the standard American response to *thanks,* is rarely heard in Britain, where the equivalent is "Don't mention it" or "Not at all" or "That's all right" or "Quite all right." The British pronunciation of *thank you* is often *kyuh* and, as H. Allen Smith says in *Smith's London Journal,* "the British response to 'Kyuh' is 'Kyuh,' the second 'Kyuh' being uttered in a higher tone than the first, and I assume it could go on forever."

THAT
The nounal conjunction *that* may usually be omitted before a nounal clause, such as "He said he was going." In this simple kind of construction, *that* is unnecessary, but it may be used. Let euphony be your guide. If you think the rhythm of a sentence calls for *that,* use *that.* If you don't, don't. But see AND THAT.

   Sometimes, however, *that* is necessary. Take the sentence "Anderson said when the engine quit they lost altitude rapidly." Anderson didn't say this when the engine quit; he said it later. Make it "Anderson said that when the engine quit they lost altitude rapidly." The principle is that when an adverbial clause of time immediately follows a *said* verb, and the clause is part of what was said, *that* must be inserted between *said* and the adverbial conjunction of time.

   Similarly, does the sentence "Anderson said Monday the plane was in good shape" mean that Anderson made the statement Monday or that he said the plane was in good shape Monday? To avoid ambiguity, insert *that* after *Monday* if he made the statement Monday ("Anderson said Monday that the plane was in good shape"); and insert *that* before *Monday* if he said the plane was in good shape Monday ("Anderson said that Monday the plane was in good shape").

Also, *that* must be inserted between a transitive *said* verb and a noun immediately following. In the sentence "In his U.N. speech, Carter warned the Soviet Union, which had promised not to interfere in the internal affairs of African nations, might soon control most of the African continent," Carter wasn't warning the Soviet Union; he was warning *that* the Soviet Union might soon control Africa. To avoid ambiguity, insert *that* after *warned*.

Follow this general principle: Don't use the nounal conjunction *that* unless you think it helps rhythm or sense; but when in doubt, use it.

For a discussion of the relative pronoun *that*, see THAT / WHICH and THAT / WHICH / WHO.

THAT / WHICH

In the sentence "The FCC has banned obscenity which is not artistic," the use of *which* changes the intended meaning. As it stands, the sentence means that the FCC has banned all obscene shows because obscenity is not artistic. But the intended meaning is that the FCC has banned only nonartistic obscene shows. Change *which* to *that* because the relative pronoun *that* is restrictive, defining, and the relative pronoun *which* is nonrestrictive, describing.

Words convey ideas. The words *that* and *which* convey different ideas.

If you are told to go to the third house *that* has green drapes, you may pass many houses before you reach the one you are looking for, the third green-draped house. If you are told to go to the third house *which* has green drapes, you will pass only two houses before you reach the one you are looking for, the third house, which, by the way, has green drapes.

If you can end the sentence immediately before the relative pronoun and not change the meaning, the relative pronoun you are looking for is *which*. If you can't, it's *that*. For instance, if your guide had simply said, "Go to the third house," he would not have changed the meaning of the sentence that added "which has green drapes," because he added this merely to give you incidental description in case you lost count.

Another test is to put a comma before the relative pronoun. If you can, the word you are looking for is *which*. If you can't, it's *that*.

An exception to the *that* / *which* general principle is the use of the relative *which* after the demonstrative *that*, *this*, *those*, *these*, as in "Give me only that which (better *what*) I seek" or "Give me only those books which I asked for."

THAT / WHICH / WHO

Whereas the relative pronoun *that* may refer to persons, animals or things, the relative pronoun *which* refers only to animals and things, and the relative pronoun *who* refers only to persons.

For the choice between *that* and *who* for persons, Fowler suggests *who* for a particular person or persons, as in "The man (men) who came to dinner came on time," and *that* for a generic person or type, as in "A man (anyone) that is invited for dinner should come on time."

See also WHO / WHOM.

THEATER / THEATRE

In the United States, the British spelling of words such as *centre* and *metre* and *saltpetre* has long since given way to *center* and *meter* and *saltpeter*. So, too, *theater*. But some American theater owners use *theatre* in the name of their building. The word should be spelled as it appears in the official name. Also, some publications prefer *theatre* in generic reference to the performing arts, as in "the Broadway theatre" or "American theatre" or "love of the theatre," but the more common form is *theater*.

THEFT, *see* BURGLARY / ROBBERY / THEFT

THENCE, *see* HENCE / THENCE / WHENCE

THE NUMBER, *see* A NUMBER

THEO–

Many English words derive from Greek *theos*, god, including given names such as *Dorothy*, *Theodore*, *Timothy*. Here are a dozen words from this root:

  —*apotheosis*, deification or glorified ideal (accent more commonly on the penult).
  —*atheism*, disbelief in the existence of God, godlessness; see AGNOSTIC.
  —*enthusiasm*, originally ecstasy, divine inspiration, religious ardor; now zeal, excitement.

—*pantheism*, see PAN-.

—*pantheon*, see PAN-.

—*polytheism*, belief in many gods.

—*theism*, belief in the existence of God as the creator and ruler of the world and the source of supernatural revelation, as opposed to *deism*, belief in the existence of God as creator, but not ruler or revealer.

—*theocentric*, considering God as the heart of everything, accepting divine sovereignty.

—*theocracy*, rule by the clergy or their representatives.

—*theology*, study of religion.

—*theomorphism*, attribution of divine qualities to man.

—*theosophy*, belief in the attainment of knowledge of God by mystical intuition or occult revelation.

THERETOFORE, *see* HITHERTO

THERMO-

Among the many English words from Greek *thermos*, heat, are *diathermy* (treatment by heat), *thermal*, *thermodynamics*, *thermometer*, *thermonuclear*, *thermos* (formerly a trademark for a vacuum bottle or flask, but now in the public domain and therefore spelled with lowercase *t*), *thermostat*.

THESE KIND / THOSE KIND, *see* KIND OF A

THINCLADS

Sportsese for the runners, jumpers and throwers of track and field.

THINK, *see* BELIEVE / FEEL / THINK

THIS REPORTER, *see* PRESENT WRITER; SPORTSESE

THITHERTO, *see* HITHERTO

-THON

The legitimate MARATHON has bred many bastard American words because of the fallacy that the *thon* of *marathon* refers to endurance or long duration. Hence the ugly *danceathon, jogathon, phoneathon, rockathon, runathon, saleathon, skateathon, talkathon, telethon, trampolinathon, walkathon.* Nickles says that the next *-thon,* "as X-rated movies become better than ever," may be *sexathon.*

THOROUGHLY ENJOYED
Mindlessly, *thoroughly* too often accompanies *enjoyed.* Whatever happened to simple enjoyment?

THOUGH
As a conjunction of concession, *though* is a shortened form of *although.* As an adverb, *though,* as in "He didn't go, though," is common in speech but has not gained widespread respectability in writing. To 61 percent of the American Heritage usage panel, *though* as an adverb is acceptable in "informal contexts and dialogue," but unacceptable in "more formal written usage." Use *however* or *nevertheless.*

But poetic license legitimizes *though* in "Whose woods these are I think I know; the irons are Arnold Palmer's, though." See also AS IF / AS THOUGH.

THREE-LETTER MAN
Phenom university athletes should note that the original three-letter man was a thief (Latin *fur*). Plautus, oldtime Roman comic playwright, called a *fur* a *homo trium literarum.*

THRESHOLD
Note the spelling: only one *h* in the middle, unlike *withhold.*

THRUST
As pseudotechnical diction for "purpose" or "main point," *thrust* has become a faddish noun or, as Strunk says, "a showy noun, suggestive of power, hinting of sex," and "the darling of executives, politicos, and speech-writers." The bureaucrat who wants you to "communicate the thrust of your input" really wants you to tell him the main points of your information. Save *thrust* for swordplay and physical contexts. To rid the nation of the fad, Newman calls for an "Anti-Thrust Act."

THUD
Why are all thuds "dull" or "sickening" or both?

THUSLY
A barbarous version of *thus. Thus* is already an adverb. See also MUCHLY and OVERLY.

TILL / UNTIL
Either *till* or *until*, but not *'til*.

TILT
As a noun, *tilt* is journalese for *contest*, *game*, *match*.

TIME ELEMENT
Because past tense pinpoints time, a *time element* is needed the first time a verb in the past tense occurs in a straight news story. In the lead "The City Council rejected a motion to reduce property taxes," a time element is lacking. When did the council reject the motion? In the lead "John Jones, a local plumber, died after injuries received in a two-car accident," the reader isn't told when Jones died and when the accident occurred. See TODAY / TOMORROW / YESTERDAY.

TIMESTYLE
Brain child of joke-making, china-dog-collecting, cordovan-shoe-wearing Briton Hadden more than of *Time*-co-founding, beetle-browed, baggy-britched Henry Luce was Timestyle. Wrote Wolcott Gibbs in a *New Yorker* profile of Luce: "Backward ran sentences until reeled the mind. Where it will all end, knows God!" Ended has inversion since Godwent Luce.

TIP OF THE ICEBERG, *see* ICEBERG

TITLED, *see* ENTITLED / TITLED

TMESIS, *see* –TOMY

TO BOOT
Something *to boot* is something extra, profitable, advantageous, helpful. See BOOTLESS.

TODAY / TOMORROW / YESTERDAY
AP uses *today* in stories whose events happened or will happen on the day of publication. In stories whose events happened yesterday or will happen tomorrow, AP uses the day of the week. If the time element is in a quote, however, don't change it.

The usual order is time, day, place, as in "10 a.m. Tuesday in 108 Flint Hall."

TOGETHER, *see* **JOIN TOGETHER**

TOM, DICK AND HARRY

As a symbol for *everyone*, "Tom, Dick and Harry" has become a cliché. Perhaps we should change to "Jimmy, Jody and Ham" or "Duane, Floyd and Delbert." And in fairness to women, maybe "Bella, Betty and Midge."

-TOMY

Many English words come from Greek *temnein*, to cut. Here are a dozen:

—*anatomy*, cutting up, dissection.

—*appendectomy*, cutting out the vermiform (wormlike, from Latin *vermis*, worm) appendix.

—*atom*, uncut, from the old theory that the atom was the smallest, indivisible particle of matter.

—*dichotomy*, cutting in two (Greek *dikha*), jargon of social scientists for division or choice, as if Hamlet had said, "To be, or not to be—that is the dichotomy."

—*entomology*, study of insects (Latin *insecare*, to cut into, for Greek *entemnein*), because their bodies appear cut into, divided.

—*epitome*, a cutting to the essence of something, an abstract, a representative part (Greek *epi*, upon; hence to cut upon the surface, to cut short).

—*hysterectomy*, cutting out the womb (Greek *hystera*).

—*lobotomy*, cutting into a lobe of the brain.

—*mastectomy*, cutting off a breast (Greek *mastos*).

—*tmesis*, a cutting of a word or phrase for the insertion of another word, such as *inde-bloody-pendent*, *self-de-bloody-fense*, *House of Bloody Commons*.

—*tome*, a section of a work cut off, bound into a separate volume.

—*vasectomy*, cutting off a part of the vas deferens (see VAST DIFFERENCE), the spermatic duct.

Temnein, to cut, is not, however, the root of *colostomy*, which, like *stomach*, comes from Greek *stoma*, mouth.

TONIC SOL-FA, *see* GAMUT

TOO

When a reviewer writes, "I cannot recommend this book too highly," does he mean that he gives the book his highest recommendation, or that he doesn't think very much of it? The *too* is ambiguous. Incidentally, don't cook spaghetti too long. See also IT ALL BEGAN.

TOPO-, *see* **UTOPIA**

TOPSY
In Harriet Beecher Stowe's *Uncle Tom's Cabin*, Topsy's exact words were: "I 'spect I grow'd." In *Watch Your Language*, Bernstein growls: "No 'just,' no 'jes,' no 'growin',' no nuffin'. Anyway, Topsy, Queen of the Clichés, should drop dead."

TORNADO
The more common plural is *tornadoes*. The derivation is Spanish *tronar*, to thunder, from Latin *tonare*.

TORPEDO
Plural *torpedoes*. In shape and shock, the projectile resembles the electric ray fish known as the torpedo (Latin for stiffness, numbness, from *torpere*, to be stiff), whence the name for the projectile. From the same root comes *torpor*.

TORTUOUS / TORTUROUS
Though both words come from the same root, Latin *torquere*, to twist, they have different meanings. *Tortuous* means twisting, winding, as on a road full of bends and curves, and has the figurative sense of crooked, devious, deceitful, not straightforward. *Torturous* means torturing, causing severe physical or mental pain.

TOTAL, *see* **A NUMBER**

TOTO, *see* **DOROTHY**

TOWARD / TOWARDS
Most authorities consider *toward* American and *towards* British. But a case can be made for *towards* in American usage when the following word begins with a vowel sound. There is sibilant smoothness in "towards evening."

TOWHEADED
Watch this adjective for blond or flaxen hair (Anglo-Saxon *towe*, flax). Hydra-headed typesetting gremlins delight in transposing the word to *twoheaded*, which seems to bother parents of towheads.

TRADEMARK

Capitalize the first letter of a term that has been officially registered as a trademark unless the term has lost its legal protection and has passed into the public domain. These former trademarks are now in the public domain and are lowercase: *aspirin, cellophane, corn flakes, cube steak, dry ice, escalator, kerosene, lanolin, linoleum, milk of magnesia, mimeograph, nylon, raisin bran, shredded wheat, thermos, trampoline, yo-yo, zipper.*

TRANSISTOR, *see* CENTAUR WORDS

TRANSITIVE, *see* INTRANSITIVE / TRANSITIVE

TRANSPIRE

Information that *transpires* leaks out (see -SPIRE), emerges from secrecy, comes to light gradually, becomes known by degrees. *Transpire* has a narrower connotation than *happen*. As a synonym for *happen*, *come to pass*, *occur*, the word is rejected by 62 percent of the American Heritage usage panel.

TRAVAIL / TRAVEL

Though both words come from the same root, Old French *travailler*, to work hard, they have different meanings. *Travail* means strenuous exertion. *Travel* means moving from place to place, journeying, touring. Come to think of it, in these days of clogged highways and cattle-car cramping in airplanes, *travel* and *travail* are about the same.

TREMENDOUS, *see* AFRAID

TRENDY

A faddish word to describe the latest fad or its faddists, *trendy* has the life expectancy of a fad.

TRIAL BALLOON

A project or promotion that a politician or a press agent inflates and floats in the press to test whether public opinion will sail along with it or shoot it down. If shot down, a trial balloon becomes a lead balloon.

TRIBULATION, *see* ATTRITION

TRIO
Don't use *trio* as a synonym for *three persons* unless they have some organizational bond or close association. Three suspects arrested in a bank robbery are a trio. Three persons killed in weekend accidents are not a trio.

TRITE, *see* CLICHÉ

TRIUMPH, *see* OVATION / TRIUMPH

TRIVIA
Whenever people gather on street corners or public squares or at crossroads to while away time or whittle at it, they usually talk trivia, which are etymologically appropriate to such a setting. *Trivia* comes from Latin *trivium*, a place where three roads meet, a public square. Note that *trivia* is plural: "One man's trivia are another man's truisms."

TRIVIUM, *see* LIBERAL ARTS

TROGLODYTE
From Greek *trogle*, a cave, *troglodyte*, cave dweller, is an expressive term for somebody who looks or smells or acts as if he had just crept from some putrefacient pit.

TROPHY, *see* ATROPHY

TRY AND, *see* BE SURE AND SEE

TSITSER
An uninvited kibitzer who hovers in the background, tongue in teeth, and goes "Ts! Ts! Ts!"

TUMMY, *see* BELLY

TU QUOQUE
Straight Latin for "you, too," *tu quoque* is an esoteric refinement for "So's your old man" or "Same to you, fella."

TURNED UP MISSING
How's that again?

TUTOYER
To address familiarly, to thee-and-thou, from French *tu*, thou. Pronounced *too-twa-yay*.

TUXEDO
Often shortened to *tux*, the formal evening jacket got its name and its popularity from Tuxedo Park, a ritzy community about forty miles north of New York City, when a local aristocrat rebelled against tails and started the fashion of wearing a short dinner jacket. More conservative gentlemen, however, prefer *dinner jacket*.

TWELVE, *see* ELEVEN

TWELVE DAYS OF CHRISTMAS, *see* EPIPHANY

TWIG
The verb comes from Irish *tuigim*, I understand.

TWILIGHT, *see* CREPUSCULAR

TYCOON
Originally Chinese for "great prince," later a Japanese title applied to the shogun, *tycoon* was made popular in the 1920s in the United States by *Time* as a term for a business magnate.

TYPE
As a noun, *type*, in the sense of *kind* or *sort*, must be followed by *of* before another noun. Thus: "this type of house," "a new type of house"; not "this type house," "a new-type house." See also KIND OF A.

TYPO
Short for "typographical error," *typo*, like charity, covers a multitude of sins for those who commit SOLECISMS and try to pass them off as typos.

U / NON-U

Short for "upper-class" and "non–upper-class," these abbreviations refer to a snobbish British system of classification of people by their speech, based on what the Dictionary of Proper Names calls "upper-class shibboleths." See also MIF.

UGLY SCAR

In a news story, don't say, "He has an ugly scar on his face." Drop *ugly*. Ugliness is in the eye of the beholder. Don't force the reader to subscribe to your sensitivities.

UKASE

Journalese for any kind of edict. Save *ukase* for a Russian edict. Try *act, command, decree, edict, law, order, rule, writ*.

UKULELE

Note the spelling. Most of the time *ukulele* appears as *ukelele*. The word is Hawaiian for *flea*, from *uku*, insect, and *lele*, to jump, a reference to the fingers flitting across the strings. See also ACCORDION.

ULT, *see* ANTEPENULT

ULTERIOR MOTIVE

Rarely does one hear *ulterior* without *motive*, and the phrase usually has a derogatory connotation. *Ulterior*, the comparative of Latin *ulter*, beyond, hence farther, more remote, has taken on the meaning of "beyond what is shown," hence hidden, secret, undisclosed, all of which are suitable adjectives to qualify an unstated motive. An undisclosed motive is not necessarily deceitful.

UMBRAGE

From Latin *umbra*, shade, shadow, *umbrage* is most often seen in the phrase, *take umbrage*, which Evans calls "a fine phrase, suggesting one shadowed in offended pride, retreating into the darkness of proud indignation, withdrawing into dark clouds of wrath whence will come the lightning of rebuke and retribution and a thunderclap of scorn."

UMPIRE, *see* ADDER

U.N.
AP spells out *United Nations* as a noun and abbreviates it to *U.N.* (with periods) as an adjective. In a quote, preserve the form used by the speaker.

UNALIENABLE
All men, says the Declaration of Independence, "are endowed by their Creator with certain unalienable Rights." The word now is almost always rendered *inalienable*.

UNAWARE / UNAWARES
The adjective is *unaware*, the adverb *unawares*, as in "She was unaware of my arrival" and "My arrival caught her unawares."

UNBELIEVABLE, *see* AFRAID; INCREDIBLE

UNCTUOUS
Oily, greasy, slimy, soft-soaping, 'umble like Uriah Heep, *unctuous* comes from Latin *ungere*, to anoint. Note the spelling; not *unctious*.

UNDATED STORY
In newspaper terminology, an *undated story* is a nonlocal story that has no dateline. An undated story may be a roundup of a certain category of news, such as business, politics, sports, weather, or may emanate from many places and cannot be conveniently assigned to one specific dateline. Such a story, however, will appear under a byline, either a general byline, such as "By The Associated Press," or a byline with the writer's name and identification.

UNDER
In the sense of collective quantity, some authorities allow *under* instead of *less than*, as in "He earned under $10,000 last year" or "He weighed under 120 pounds." With countables, however, *fewer than* is better usage than *under*, as in "Fewer than twenty persons attended." See also FEWER / LESS and MORE THAN / OVER.

UNDERACHIEVER, *see* DISADVANTAGED

UNDER WAY
Two words.

UNDOUBTEDLY, *see* **DOUBTLESSLY / UNDOUBTEDLY**

UNDUE EXCLAMATION

Telegraphed punches either land weakly or miss completely. Likewise flat and unprofitable are punchlines and puns and assorted funnies that are signaled by typographical devices such as bold face, italics, underlining, capital letters, quotation marks, exclamation points. The true wit doesn't point up his humor. He underplays it. When he shrieks, he isn't funny.

A sense of humor is the ability to see through things. Intelligent readers like to find their own way through stories without obvious guideposts of kindergarten condescension. If a story cannot speak for itself without unduly exclamatory gimmicks, it needs to be reworded.

An editor who needs exclamation points except for genuine exclamations is a master of the obvious. He should learn to save his ecstatic jubilation for the few events in life that call for WHOOPEE!!!!

UNDUE FAMILIARITY

Noblesse oblige, even in a republican democracy or a democratic republic. American newspapers need not be scared that Britain will revoke the peace treaty of 1783 if they show a little respect for public officials who deserve it. The White House won't become Buckingham Palace, or the Senate the House of Lords, if the press quits using nicknames and affectionate diminutives for the nation's leaders.

Undue familiarity, however, does not always breed contempt. The press' undue familiarity toward those who breed contempt does not breed it. The undue familiarity bifurcates, breeds more undue familiarity, which adolesces into bemused tolerance instead of benighted contempt. "Uncle Joe" Stalin got to be so familiar that he fathered a family of peace-loving nations. The press familiarly called one of his brethren "Mr. K," a title and a diminutive that implied respect and affection for a benevolent brigand beloved by freedom-loving captives everywhere.

In headlines, the editor has to make a judgment. One criterion is whether the subject deserves familiarity. Another is whether the subject would consider the diminutive unduly familiar, provided his public life gives him the right to consideration.

Ike, for example, liked *Ike*. It helped put him in the White House twice. Its neat 2½-count must have earned him the vote of every copy editor in the country.

The practice of using initials for presidents and other prominent persons, such as FDR, JFK, RFK, LBJ, HHH, is now widespread. 'Twas not ever thus. American history was not always recorded in headline initialese. Imagine our forefathers waking up to their breakfast newspaper with headlines such as these suggested by copy editors of the Utica *Observer-Dispatch:* "GW Delivers Farewell Address"; "To Victor / Go Spoils, / AJ Boasts"; "USG Vows / He'll Fight / All Summer"; "Drop Arms, / Get Farms, / REL Advises"; "AL Makes / Short Talk / At G-Burg."

UNEASY TRUCE
Is there some other kind? If there were, nobody would know about it, because an easy truce isn't news. Reporters, says Newman, "go to the Middle East because it is a tinderbox filled with fertile soil . . . in which an uneasy truce may grow."

UNGOTHROUGHSOME
English is a bastard language, bred by miscegenation with almost all other languages. Occasionally, writers have bewailed the loss of what they consider her purity as if purity, says Moore, were "a quality as desirable in language as it is supposed to be in daughters." One fifteenth-century Latinophobe plumped for *ungothroughsome* to replace *impenetrable*, but his message doesn't seem to have gonethroughed the years.

UNICAMERAL, *see* BICAMERAL

UNINTERESTED, *see* DISINTERESTED / UNINTERESTED

UNIQUE
Because *unique* is an absolute, it does not admit of degrees. A thing cannot be *more unique* or *most unique* or *rather unique* or *very unique*. However, *unique* may be modified by adverbs that do not imply degree, such as *almost, perhaps, truly*. To appease those who think that *unique* derives from Latin *unus equus*, one horse, instead of *unicus*, alone in its kind, this example does double duty: "Podunk is a unique town."

UNITED KINGDOM, *see* BRITAIN

UNITED NATIONS, *see* **U.N.**

UNITED STATES, *see* **U.S.**

UNIVERSITY
In the United States, one goes to college, but to the university; in Britain, one goes to university.

UNKEMPT
The original meaning of *unkempt* was "uncombed," from Anglo-Saxon *kemb*, comb, but the word has extended to other messes.

UNKNOWN
Crime stories sometimes report that the victim was unknown. Surely he hadn't gone through life unknown by anyone. Somebody must have known the poor guy. Make it *unidentified*.

UNLESS AND UNTIL, *see* **IF AND WHEN**

UNMORAL, *see* **AMORAL / IMMORAL / UNMORAL**

UNNECESSARY TIME
In the headline "Ten Hurt Yesterday," *yesterday* is unnecessary. Readers ought to be able to assume that their morning papers are reporting the news of yesterday, and their evening papers the news of today or last night. Immediate past time is therefore superfluous and space-eating.

Moreover, adverbial phrases of past time become anachronistically incongruous when they modify verbs in the present tense, as in "19 Americans / Die Last Week / In War Zone."

When a day of the week is used with a verb in the present tense, a reader naturally assumes that the day is future. The result is incongruous in heads such as "Bing Crosby / Dies Friday."

Some papers use *today* with a verb in the present tense in heads for stories of death. The result is like an announcement of doom, an appointment in Samarra, especially if the person is identified only by occupation. Professors curl into a tight ball and want to roll into a corner and hide till after midnight whenever a newspaper serves notice of motion such as "PROFESSOR DIES TODAY."

But the prize must go to "Early Morning Rainfall / Due Again Here Tonight."

UNPRECEDENTED

Facile enthusiasm sometimes prompts youth to believe that something they have never before experienced has never before happened. The wheel is reinvented daily. In their search for additions to the *Guinness Book of World Records*, young reporters sometimes reach for words like *unprecedented* without running a reasonable check on possible precedents. Watch *unprecedented*. Use it cautiously.

In *Miss Thistlebottom's Hobgoblins*, Bernstein says: "If the mayor of Limping Horse, Wyoming, stands on his head for fifteen minutes to boom a charity campaign, some devotee of the gee-whiz school of journalism is sure to tag it *unprecedented*, only to have a newspaper reader write in the next day, saying in effect, 'Pshaw, when I was a kid in Czechoslovakia the mayor of Krakup did that.'"

UNTIL, *see* TILL / UNTIL

UNTOLD WEALTH

On an April day, *untold wealth* may be unreported income, but *untold* in the phrase means uncounted, from Anglo-Saxon *tellan*, to count, as in *teller* for a bank clerk or a vote counter and phrases such as *all told, a telling blow, every shot tells*.

UNVARNISHED

Furniture excepted, *unvarnished* usually precedes *truth* and is preceded by *plain* to form a phrase that, in Nickles' words, "protests too tritely and too much, as if truth unadorned were dirty or nasty to look at."

UNWIELDY

Not *unwieldly*.

UPCOMING

Why not simply *coming* or *forthcoming* or *approaching*, all of which refer to the future? The redundant *upcoming*, which probably originated in cablese, is unacceptable to 71 percent of the American Heritage usage panel. See also ONGOING.

UPDATE

Television is nouning this verb.

UPI, *see* AP / UPI

UP OVER, *see* **DOWN UNDER**

UPPERCASE
One word in AP. See *Lowercase*.

UPTIGHT
Originally death-house slang, then street language of the 1960s, *uptight* needs to pass the test of time to see whether it will lose its gutter connotation and gain respectability as a synonym for *tense, nervous*. The odds are against it.

UP TILL
Why *up?*

UP-TO-DATE
Two hyphens, whether before a noun or as a predicate.

U.S.
AP spells out *United States* as a noun and abbreviates it to *U.S.* (with periods) as an adjective. In a quote, preserve the form used by the speaker. *U.S.A.* is less frequently used; *the U.S. of A.* should never be. *These United States* should be left to speakers at the national political conventions.

USED TO, *see* **DIDN'T USED TO**

UTILIZE
Use can usually be used instead of *utilize*, but *utilize* has the specific sense of "make useful, turn to profitable use," especially when nothing more useful is available. But see **-IZE**.

UTOPIA
Thomas More derived the name of his book and the name of his land of perfection, *Utopia*, from Greek *ou* + *topos*, not a place, nowhere. More than three centuries later, Samuel Butler's utopia was set in Erewhon, *nowhere* spelled backwards—almost. Other words from the same root are *topic, topography, topology, toponymy.*

V-1 / V-2

Abbreviations for German *Vergeltungswaffe eins* and *zwei*, retaliation weapons one and two, the missiles Germany used against Britain late in World War II. The principal designer of the V-2 was Wernher von Braun, subject of a filmed autobiography, *We Aim at the Stars*, to which, according to Morris, critic Alistair Cooke added "and usually hit London."

VACCINATE

Note the spelling: double *c*. From Latin *vacca*, a cow, *vaccine* gets its name from the virus of cowpox used in its preparation.

VALET, *see* NOTRE DAME

VALUE

The *value* in *value judgment* is redundant in most contexts. *Values* is steadily replacing *morals*, but *priorities* is steadily catching *values*.

VANILLA

A species of the Vanilla orchid has seed pods from which *vanilla* is prepared. The word comes from Spanish *vainilla*, dimunitive of *vaina*, pod, sheath, from Latin *vagina*. See ORCHID.

VANISH INTO THIN AIR

The cliché should be brought up-to-date by the substitution of *thick* for *thin*.

VARIETY, *see* A NUMBER

VARIOUS AND SUNDRY

A redundant cliché.

VASECTOMY, *see* –TOMY

VAST DIFFERENCE
Why are differences of every magnitude from tiny to gigantic usually called *vast?* The phrase is a cliché, and a seedy pun in Newman's "Having a man around the house does make a vas deferens."

VEEP
The first vice president of the United States to be called *the Veep* was Alben W. Barkley, veep (1949–53) under Harry Truman. Any vice president of anything is now a veep. See also VICE.

VEGETATE
Though *vegetable* comes from Latin *vegetare*, to be active, one who vegetates is passive.

VENGEANCE, *see* AVENGE / REVENGE

VENIREMAN
A person summoned for jury duty by a writ of *venire facias*, Latin for "make come," is a venireman, a member of the venire, the panel from which the jury will be chosen.

VENI, VIDI, VICI
Caesar wrote snappy leads. See ASYNDETON.

VENTRILOQUIST
A gutsy entertainer, a *ventriloquist* is one whose voice seems to come from elsewhere than his mouth, from Latin *venter*, belly, and *loqui*, to speak.

VERB
The verb, the most important part of speech, is discussed in many entries. See, especially, ACTIVE VOICE / PASSIVE VOICE; ADJECTIVE / ADVERB; AGREEMENT OF SUBJECT AND PREDICATE; DANGLING PARTICIPLE; FINITE VERB; PARTS OF A VERB; SEQUENCE OF TENSES. Also see ABLATIVE ABSOLUTE; AUXILIARY VERB; CLAUSE; FUSED PARTICIPLE; INTRANSITIVE / TRANSITIVE; MOOD; SPLIT INFINITIVE; STRONG VERBS; SWITCHED VOICES.

VERBAL, *see* ORAL / VERBAL

VERB HEAD, *see* NO SUBJECT

VERBING NOUNS

Verbs and nouns crossbreed as language evolves. Some verbs become nouns, and many nouns become verbs. Nouns such as *fool, sleep, verse, walk, handout, hangover, hideaway, kickback, pushover* began as verbs or verb compounds. Hundreds of verbs began as nouns, such as the old *bridle, harness, saddle, hail, rain, snow, thunder* and the more recent *alibi, blueprint, highlight, intern, intrigue, mastermind, needle, package, pancake, pressure, recess, referee, solo, thumb, vacation.*

The noun is the dominant parent. Nouns can adulterate the cross-breeding process and produce such grotesqueries as "She *authored* a book," "We plan to *car* Europe this summer," "When he plays golf, he prefers to *cart*," "The reviewer *critiqued* the book," "Ford will *debut* its new models," "He *gifted* me a watch," "She *guested* on the show," "He *inked* his contract," "They *parented* a child," "He *signatured* the check."

Let nouns be nouns, and verbs verbs, unless crossbreed coinage is needed to convey an idea for which no appropriate word already exists. See AUDITION; CHAIR; and CONTACT.

VERMOUTH

From German *Wermut*, wormwood, which may be why more than a few drops of the stuff spoil a perfect drink.

VERNACULAR

From Latin *verna*, a slave born in his master's house, *vernacular* originally meant "domestic, native," whence the vernacular is the pattern of speech of a particular community or profession.

VERNAL, *see* EQUINOX

VERY

Authorities have argued for generations about the use of *very* before a past participle. Perhaps one can resolve the argument by applying this test: Has the past participle become a true adjective? If so, *very* properly modifies it, as in "He was very disappointed."

Some past participles, however, are more verb than adjective and require a different modifier because *very* doesn't modify a verb. (We don't say, "I very dislike you.") With such past participles, use *much*, as in "He was much disliked," or *very much*, in which usage *very* modifies the adverb *much* and not the verb.

Don't overuse *very*. Don't exaggerate. Shaw quotes a teacher who told his students "never to say or write *very* unless they meant *damn* or *damned*, and then to delete the profanity." Use *very* very sparingly.

VETERAN
From Latin *vetus* (genitive *veteris*), old. AP omits the apostrophe in *Veterans Administration* and *Veterans Day*.

VETERINARIAN
Six syllables, not five. One often hears the word pronounced without *-er* or without the first *i*. *Veterinarian* comes from Latin *veterinarius*, the adjective applied to a farm animal old enough to be put to work.

VIA
Strictly, *via*, the ablative of the Latin word for road or journey, means "by way of," as in "from Denver to Seattle via Boise." Loosely, *via* is used to mean "through the medium of," as in "from Denver to Seattle via bus," which usage Fowler calls a vulgarism (make it *by*), or "by means of," as in "order via discipline" (make it *through*).

VIABLE
This knee-jerk word is Newman's choice as "the one word that expresses the spirit of the age," an age in which "not only has eloquence departed, but simple, direct speech as well, though pomposity and banality have not." *Viable* today seems automatically tacked onto words such as *alternative, arrangement, concept, idea, notion, plan, project, proposal, scheme, situation*. Newman says, "Automatic recall should be visited on anyone on the public payroll who says *viable*."

VIATICUM
Originally, this Latin word meant traveling money, provisions for a journey, whence its ecclesiastical use for the sacrament of the Eucharist given to the dying.

VICE
AP drops the hyphen in combinations of *vice* with titles such as *admiral, chairman, chancellor, consul, president, principal* and spells them as two words. The hyphen is retained, however, in other forms of these words, such as *vice-presidential, vice-presidency, vice-chancellorship, vice-consulate*.

VICIOUS CIRCLE
Except as a term in logic to describe the ring-around-the-rosy fallacy of using premise and conclusion to prove each other, *vicious circle* is a cliché. In logic, *vicious* means flawed, defective. In the cliché, *vicious* is meaningless, and the phrase, in Nickles' words, is a "merry-go-round banality."

VIETNAM
AP spells *Vietnam* as one word, but *Viet Cong* as two words.

VIGORISH
The percentage of a payoff retained by American bookmakers is called the *vigorish*. Mencken spells it *viggerish* and quotes a source who traces the term to *vicarage*, a reference to tithing in some ecclesiastical benefices.

VILIFY / VILLAIN
Note the spellings: single *l* in *vilify*, double *l* in *villain*. *Vilify* comes from Latin *vilis*, vile, cheap. *Villain* comes from Latin *villa*, a farm, a country house, whence *villain* became an urban term of contempt for the rural and later acquired the meaning of scoundrel.

VINEGAR
Sour wine, from Old French *vinaigre* (*vin*, wine; *aigre*, sour), from Latin *vinum* and *acer*, sharp, biting. Thus a vinegary person is bitter, sour, crabby.

VIRGIN BIRTH
The term for the birth of Christ is ignorantly confused with the IMMACU-LATE CONCEPTION.

VIRGIN QUEEN
A name for Elizabeth I, who, says the Dictionary of Proper Names, "at any rate, never married." No royalist, a saintly old Irish priest once said of Elizabeth in a sermon, "They call her the Virgin Queen. Wirra, she was no more a virgin than I am."

VIRGULE
The typographical mark for a slash (/), from the diminutive of Latin *virga*, a rod.

VIS-A-VIS
Overworked bureaucratese (a seeming contradiction), *vis-à-vis* is French for "face-to-face." Use the English *about, against, compared to, as opposed to*, depending on the context. See **ABOUT**.

VISIT
In the intransitive sense of *chat* or *converse*, as in "We visited awhile" or "He visited with me," *visit* and *visit with* are provincialisms.

VITA, *see* CURRICULUM VITAE

VIZ.
Short for Latin *videlicet*, namely. Instead of the Latin tag, why not use *namely?*

VOCAL CORDS, *see* CORD / CHORD; SONIC WRITING

VOCATION, *see* AVOCATION / VOCATION

VODKA
Etymologically, a diminutive of Russian *voda*, water. Bibologically, an intensifier.

VOICE, *see* ACTIVE VOICE / PASSIVE VOICE

VOLKSWAGEN
Note the spelling: *wagen*, not *wagon*. In a recent test of 23 students owning Volkswagens, 14 misspelled the name of their own car and 17 spelled *Beetle* as in *the Beatles*. That's the volks populi.

WAIVE

In the sense of "to dispense with, to relinquish claim to," the spelling is *waive*, as in "He waived the math requirement" or "She waived her rights to the property," not *wave*.

WALKOVER

When there is only one starter in a horse race, the horse must go over the course at any old pace, even walking. The formality is called a *walkover*, a term also used for any contest easily won.

WALLYDRAG

A Scottish term for a feeble or slovenly creature or the youngest of a brood. See CATCHWORD.

WALTER MITTY

A character created by James Thurber, Walter Mitty has become an eponym for an ordinary person who daydreams of extraordinary accomplishments such as winning the Masters, starring at the Met, conquering Mars, rescuing hordes from disaster, or merely being George Plimpton.

WANT FOR YOU TO, *see* FOR YOU TO

WANT IN

Elliptic phrases such as "He wants in" and "He wants out" are what Nickles calls "village idioms" and should be left to bumpkins.

WAS A FORMER

Redundant, as in "She was a former student of mine." Either drop *former* or change *was* to *is*.

WATERSHED

A ridge that divides drainage systems is a *watershed*. Figuratively, a *watershed* is an extremely important or dividing event or period, as in

"The Vietnam War was a watershed in the history of American foreign policy" and "Watergate was a watershed in the relations between the press and the presidency."

WATS LINE
Acronym for Wide Area Telephone Service line, a service for which one pays a flat charge for all calls within a certain area instead of paying for each call.

WAX
In the sense of "polish" or "rub," the verb *wax* takes an adverb, as in "She waxed her car vigorously." In the sense of "grow" or "pass from one state to another," *wax* is a copulative verb and therefore takes an adjective, as in "She waxed eloquent" (see ADJECTIVE / ADVERB).

Newman quotes a *New York Times* story in which an actress, Patricia Elliott, "was waxing ecstatically about the new set." Newman comments: "The *Times* thereby created a picture of Miss Elliott happily shining the furniture on the theater stage, presumably after an agreement between Actors Equity and the Stagehands Union."

WAY
The apostrophe has been dropped in the contraction of *away*, as in "His actions were way out of line." In this usage, *way* has gained respectability, but *ways* has a long way to go as a substitute for *way* in such phrases as "a long way to go."

WE
As monarchs of their patients, some nurses uses the royal plural, as in "We're going to have our enema now," the hearing of which sickens the patient more than his disease and tempts him to reply, "OK, nurse, you go and have yours and I'll settle for a gin and tonic." Leave the royal plural to editorial writers and other royalty.

WEAKER SEX
Porcine sexism.

WEAK VERBS, *see* STRONG VERBS

WEAK VOICE, *see* ACTIVE VOICE / PASSIVE VOICE

WEASEL WORDS

Weasels suck eggs. They suck out the meat and leave the shell superficially intact. Weasel wordsmiths suck the meaning from words and leave but a wraith behind. In *Words in Sheep's Clothing*, Mario Pei defines *weasel words* as "any word of which the semantics are deliberately changed or obscured to achieve a specific purpose, or that is used in a given context for the sole purpose of impressing and bamboozling the reader or hearer." They are words to which one can respond emotionally without thought.

Theodore Roosevelt made the term *weasel words* popular when he chastised President Woodrow Wilson in 1916 for Wilson's advocacy of "universal voluntary training." Roosevelt said: "You can have universal training or you can have voluntary training, but when you use *voluntary* to qualify *universal*, you are using a weasel word; it has sucked all the meaning out of *universal*. The two words flatly contradict each other."

For a witty but ruthless excoriation of hidebound weasel words in advertising, anthropology, art, bureaucracy, civil rights, cybernetics, economics, education, foreign affairs, journalism, labor, law, linguistics, literature, military science, movies, music, patriotism, politics, propaganda, psychology, race, science, sex and sociology, see Pei.

WEATHER

It was Mark Twain's brother-in-law, Charles Dudley Warner, not Twain, who first wrote, "Everybody talks about the weather, but nobody does anything about it" (editorial in the *Hartford Courant*, Aug. 24, 1897). From too much exposure, the sentence has become weather-beaten.

WEAVE

In the sense of fashioning textiles or baskets or plots, the more common past tense of *weave* is *wove*, and the past participle *woven*, as in "He wove baskets for college credit" and "He has woven a good yarn." In the sense of steering a course or swaying, the past tense and past participle are *weaved*, as in "The ambulance (has) weaved its way through heavy traffic" or "He (has) drunkenly weaved his way home."

WEIRD

Note the spelling: *e* before *i*.

WELKIN

Clown tells Viola in Shakespeare's *Twelfth Night*, "Who you are and what you would are out of my welkin: I might say element; but the word is overworn." Long overworn is the phrase *make the welkin ring*. Its careless users equate *welkin* with some kind of bell, whereas it refers to the sky, from Anglo-Saxon *wolcen*, a cloud, which meaning doesn't ring a bell with the bromidic.

WELL
The word is both adjective and adverb and thus sometimes causes confusion. In "I am well," *well* is an adjective. In "He swims well," *well* is an adverb. But in "He feels well," *well* is either adjective or adverb, depending on the sense: if the reference is to his health, *well* is an adjective because *feels* in this context is a copulative verb; if the reference is to his sense of touch, *well* is an adverb. See ADJECTIVE / ADVERB.

In combination with an adjective, the adverb *well* and the adjective are hyphenated when used before a noun, as in "a well-known man," but the words are separated when used as a predicate, as in "He is well known."

WELL-NIGH
Cliché for *almost*, *nearly*.

WELSH RABBIT / RAREBIT
Just as Yorkshire pudding isn't pudding, and mountain oysters aren't oysters, and horseradish isn't made from horses, so Welsh rabbit isn't rabbit. *Welsh rabbit* is melted and seasoned cheese poured on toast or crackers. The name started as a lowbrow joke, but the highbrows changed *rabbit* to the genteel *rarebit*.

WENT
Shockingly, *went* is schlockingly used as the past participle of *go*, as in this sentence by the sports editor of a metropolitan daily, "If they had made that bucket, they might have went into halftime with momentum." He should have went to school. And, ah, momentum, that mystic force that moves lily-livered louts to fight like gutsy gladiators and snatch a win for the Gipper from the jaws of defeat.

WHENCE, *see* HENCE / THENCE / WHENCE

WHEREABOUTS
Singular, as in "His whereabouts is a mystery." Plural only in the sense of different whereabouts, as in "The children scattered when they left home, and their whereabouts are unknown."

WHERE'S IT AT?

Understood in *where* is the notion of *at* or *in* or *to*, wherefore *where's it at?* is redundant. It is also sloppy. Figuratively, one who doesn't know "where it's at" doesn't know the score, doesn't know what's going on.

WHETHER, *see* IF / WHETHER

WHETHER OR NOT

Because *whether* means "that-or-that-not," *or not* is usually superfluous after *whether*, as in "I don't know whether or not I'll go" and "I don't know whether I'll go or not." Strike *or not* in each sentence.

Sometimes, however, *or not* is needed to stress the alternative, as in "I'll love you whether or not you leave me." To decide whether *or not* is needed, substitute *if* for *whether*. If the substitution changes the meaning, *or not* is needed. "I'll love you if you leave me" is decidedly different from "I'll love you whether or not you leave me."

WHICH, *see* THAT / WHICH; THAT / WHICH / WHO

WHICH DOCTOR

One who charmingly restores editorial health to copy that abuses the distinction between *that* and *which*, which are often confused.

WHILE

Strictly, *while* is a conjunction of duration, simultaneity, as in "While I was reading the papers, you were watching television." The two things were happening at the same time.

Loosely, *while* has taken on the sense of *although* and has become a conjunction of concession, as in "While I disagree with you, I respect your opinion." In this loose sense, *while* can be ambiguous, as in "While the highway was built three miles away, the city has grown out to it over the years" and "While Edgar Bergen's first dummy, built in 1922, cost $27, the latest version set him back $2,000."

While is also loosely used as a substitute for *but*, as in "He likes coffee while she prefers tea." Better *but*. Similarly, *while* is used for *and*, as in "He is from Los Angeles while she is from San Francisco." Make it *and*.

The American Heritage experts score 68 percent for *while* as *although*, 59 percent for *while* as *but* and 37 percent for *while* as *and*.

WHILST

Most authorities label *whilst* "chiefly British." Some call it affected. But *whilst* slides smoothly into words beginning with a vowel sound. Not all elegance is affectation. See also TOWARD / TOWARDS.

WHISKEY / WHISKY

The old style was *whiskey* for U.S. liquor and *whisky* for imported. But AP now says *whiskey* for all, unless *Scotch* and *whisky* are used together. *Whiskeys* is the plural of *whiskey*, and *whiskies* is the plural of *whisky*. The word comes from Irish *uisce beathadh*, water of life, a convivial derivation whatever the spelling.

WHITE ELEPHANT

In Siam, white elephants were so rare that at birth they became the property of the king and were not allowed to be put to work or killed. If the king disliked someone, he would give him a white elephant and laugh like Yul Brynner while the new owner went broke catering to the elephantine appetite of an unemployed pet. Such a puzzlement perplexes the owner of any expensive, unproductive, unsalable property that costs a fortune to maintain. He owns a white elephant. See also TENURE.

WHITE FEATHER

This term for cowardice probably comes from cockfighting. A crossbred cock with a white feather in its tail was considered a loser.

WHO / WHOM

The objective case of *who* is *whom*. The usage is tricky, however, when the pronoun looks as if it should be objective but isn't. This, for example, is wrong: "He knows a girl whom he thinks will go." *Whom* should be *who*, the subject of *will go*, not the object of *thinks*.

When in doubt, substitute a personal pronoun for the relative pronoun. You wouldn't say, "He thinks her will go."

This, too, is wrong: "Give it to whomever wants it." *Whomever* should be *whoever*, the subject of *wants*, not the object of *to*. The object of *to* is the whole clause, "whoever wants it." The principle is that pronouns agree with their antecedents in person, number and gender but take their case from the clause in which they stand. See also ANTECEDENT and THAT / WHICH / WHO.

WHO HE?

The story began: "A man was killed this morning in a two-car wreck on I-70 five miles west of town.

"John Jones, 39, of Lincoln, Neb., was driving a late-model station wagon east when it jumped the median and crashed head-on into a westbound car, police said."

Was Jones the victim? If so, say so. Identify Jones as the man who was killed. Begin the second paragraph, "The victim, John Jones, . . ." Don't force a reader to ask himself, "Who he?" Don't force him to decide whether Jones is the man referred to in the first paragraph. Don't put an obstacle in the path of the reader's comprehension. The obstacle, as Bernstein says in *Watch Your Language*, is not insuperable but it is "a low hurdle that interrupts his stride." Competition for a reader's time is keen these days. Don't slow him down.

WHOSE

Don't confuse *whose*, the possessive relative pronoun, with *who's*, the contraction of *who is* or *who has*.

WICOPY / WIDGEON, *see* CATCHWORD

WIDOW / WIDOWER

For obituaries, AP says a man "is survived by his wife," not *widow*, and a woman "is survived by her husband," not *widower*. For identification in stories that are not obituaries, use *widow* and *widower*, but not the redundant "widow (widower) of the late. . . ."

WIELD

Note the spelling. See also UNWIELDY.

WILL, *see* SHALL / WILL

WILLOW

A sad word, probably from its association with *weeping* or the song of the tomtit.

WIMBLEDON

Note the *d*. Many American announcers substitute *t* for *d*.

WIN HANDS DOWN

When a jockey, sure of winning, loosens his grip on the reins and drops his hands, he wins *hands down*, whence the cliché. But he still has to win. Willie Shoemaker lost hands down when he dropped them on Gallant Man in the 1957 Kentucky Derby and finished second by a nose because he mistook the 1/16th pole for the winning post.

–WISE

"Sleepwise, I haven't been obeying orders doctorwise. Healthwise, this affects my work energywise and my profits saleswise. Marriagewise, I'm in trouble doghousewise. None of this is good for me wisewise."

And none of this is good for English languagewise. The preposterous paragraph illustrates the abomination of indiscriminately adding *wise*, in the sense of "concerning" or "as regards," to any old noun to form an adverb.

The suffix *-wise* has two legitimate uses: (1) to signify "in the manner of," as in *clockwise*, *lengthwise*, *likewise*, *otherwise*, in the sense of *ways;* and (2) to signify "knowing about" or "wise in the subject of," as in "a ring-wise boxer," "a stage-wise performer," "a weather-wise strategist," "a worldlywise clergyman."

Concerning the indiscriminate use of *-wise*, Strunk says: "There is not a noun in the language to which *-wise* cannot be added if the spirit moves one to add it. The sober writer will abstain from the use of this wild additive."

WITH

With a participle, *with* is at best clumsy and at worst meaningless.

In "A plan for a proposed Pan-African peacekeeping force seems to be winning qualified moral support and perhaps logistic backing from Western allies, with even Saudi Arabia and India willing to pitch in with weaponry," the writer couldn't bring himself to put a period after *allies* and write a new sentence with a finite verb: "Even Saudi Arabia and India are willing to . . ."

In "With the president leading the way, Democratic Party officials spread out from Washington yesterday on a barnstorming tour to replenish party coffers," *with* is wasted in the absolute construction. Also, the sentence would have been strengthened by the use of a finite verb instead of the participle: "The president led the way yesterday when . . ."

In general, try to avoid *with* with a participial phrase. See also
ABLATIVE ABSOLUTE and FINITE VERB.

WITHHOLD
Note the spelling: double *h*.

WONDERFUL, *see* AFRAID

WOODSHED
If you trace the tragedies of the human comedy to something ugly that
happened to you in childhood, you saw "something nasty in the wood-
shed," which Grandma saw in Stella Gibbons' brilliant *Cold Comfort
Farm*.

WORD REPEATED
A norm against repeating a word in a headline, except minor words such
as articles and prepositions, exists because repetition takes up space that
could be used for additional information. But when the avoidance of
repetition results in undue strain, repeating is better than reaching far
out for a weird synonym, as in "Student Runs Out of Money, / Sends
Home for Green Stuff" or "Village Short of Water / Gets Bottled Aqua
Pura" or, worse, "Crazy Chimpanzee Ape / About Bananas Swipes /
Elongated Yellow Fruit."

Observance of the norm, however, helps prevent obvious padding in
headlines, such as this example from *The Art of Editing*, by Floyd K.
Baskette and Jack Z. Sissors: "Wind-Lashed Blizzard / Lashes Plains
States." From the same source comes this example of valid repetition
when used for effect: "Thinkers Failures, / Professor Thinks."

WORLD SERIES
Each fall, in what scribes describe as "the annual fall classic," two baseball teams chosen from fourteen U.S. states and two Canadian prov-
inces decide the championship of the world, and the hell with the rest of it.

WORLDWIDE
No hyphen. The same spelling principle applies to other territorial combinations with *wide*.

WORTH HIS SALT, *see* SALARY

WOULD HAVE

After *if*, the conditional perfect auxiliary *would have* is incorrect because condition has already been expressed by *if* and the action is past. The correct form is the past perfect auxiliary *had:* "If you had been late, I would not have waited"; not "If you would have been late, I would not have waited."

Similarly, after *wish*, use *had* instead of *would have* because condition is implied by *wish* and the action is past: "I wish we had seen you"; not "I wish we would have seen you." See also **PERFECT INFINITIVE**.

WOULD OF

A barbarism probably caused by the slurred pronunciation of would've.

WOWSER

Originally Australian, *wowser* describes one who doesn't enjoy life and doesn't want anyone else to. The origin of *wowser*, like the mind of a wowser, is obscure.

WRACK, *see* NERVE-RACKING

WRONG TENSE

News headlines use the present tense for news immediately past. It is the historic present and it gives a vivid sense of immediacy. It is also usually shorter than the past tense.

There are three exceptions: (1) future stories; (2) obituaries; and (3) old stories that newly become news.

The headline of a future story should obviously be in the future tense, but copy editors sometimes get confused on this point. When the president announces he will veto a bill, the head "Carter Vetoes Tax Bill" is in the wrong tense and should be "Carter to Veto Tax Bill."

On a page of obituaries, the verb *dies* is often omitted in heads because the page is obviously a page of news of deaths, and *dies* would appear in every head on the page. Sometimes, however, a verb in the past tense is used to describe the dead person's former occupation or achievements, as in "John Jones; / Was Banker" or "John Leary; / Won Pulitzer."

When old stories become news, a headline verb may be in the past tense but the attributing verb will still be in the present tense, as in "FDR Philandered, / Historian Declares."

This head was certainly in the wrong tense: "Man Slain at Wichita / Lives at Vinton, Iowa."

WROUGHT

The story said, "Tornadoes wrought havoc in the Midwest yesterday." They didn't. They wreaked havoc. *Wrought* is the past tense and past participle of *work*.

XENOPHOBIA, *see* **-PHOBIA**

XEROX
The Xerox Corporation doesn't want *Xerox* used as a verb, but its use as such has gone probably too far to stop. Moreover, *Xerox* is used as a verb for photocopying processes other than Xerox. As a trademark, however, *Xerox* should be uppercase, both as noun and as verb. The word comes from Greek *xeros*, dry, whence also *elixir*, from its form as dry powder.

XMAS
Though 88 percent of the American Heritage usage panelists consider *Xmas*, for *Christmas*, unacceptable "in general usage on a formal level" and some people consider it blatantly commercial, disrespectful and even sacrilegious, *Xmas* is neither a modern commercial invention nor a term of disrespect for Christ. *Xmas* has been in print for more than four hundred years and *X* goes back to early Christian times as a religious symbol (Greek *chi*) for Christ.

    Xmas is a handy word for headlines and is a lot more Christian than another four-letter word, *Yule*, originally a heathen feast.

XYLOPHONE
Note the spelling: *x*, not *z*. From Greek *xylon*, wood, and *phone*, sound.

YAHOO

In Swift's *Gulliver's Travels*, the Yahoos were the unspeakable human brutes held in subjection by their unpronounceable equine masters, the Houyhnhnms. As a modern term for a lout, *yahoo* is lowercase.

YARBOROUGH, *see* CHICANE

YE

Proprietors who would have their establishments smack of what they feel is olde Englishe refinement give them names such as Ye Olde Englishe Trucke Stoppe or Ye Olde Englishe Clippe Jointe. That's their privilege. But note that the *ye* in such names is not the old English *you* but an old corruption of *the* and is pronounced *the*.

YELLOW JOURNALISM

The color of journalism at its worst derived from a comic strip printed in yellow, "The Yellow Kid," in the ultrasensational *New York World* of the 1890s. Some ultrasensitive activists now consider the term racist, but yellow journalism knows no ethnic bounds.

YEN

In its sense of yearning or intense desire, *yen* is Chinese for smoke, opium, addiction.

YIELD

Note the spelling.

YORICK, *see* ALAS

YOUNGSTER, *see* OLDSTER

YOUR BASIC, *see* COMMON OR GARDEN

YULE, *see* XMAS

YUNNO

"You know," usually uttered "yunno," punctuates modern speech with maddening staccato. The listener wants to scream, "No, I don't know." There is perhaps a high inverse correlation between the amount a person knows and the number of times he says "you know." See KNEE-JERK WORDS.

Z

ZEBEDEE
A standard question on intelligence tests is: "Who was the father of the sons of Zebedee?" For the answer, see ST. JAMES('s).

ZERO
"Zero population growth" is a contradiction. The only growing zeros these days are in government spending.

ZEUGMA
The word is Greek for a yoke, a joining. A rhetorical figure, *zeugma* is a faulty version of SYLLEPSIS. In *zeugma*, one word is joined with two or more other words, with only one of which it makes sense, as in "Police arrested the escaped prisoners and the stolen car" or "All he ate for lunch was a ham sandwich, a cup of coffee and two cigarettes."

ZOOM
When airplanes zoom, they fly upward suddenly and rapidly. *Zooming up* is redundant. *Zooming down* is impossible. But *zoom* is also used for continuous humming sound, for rapid motion with that sound and for rapid photographic maneuvering.

ZZZ
The party's over.